THE CHILDREN ARE ACTING LIKE ASSHOLES

BY

MARIE AARON

First paperback edition June 2021

Cover illustration by Gina Zupo Moats
Cover design by ebooklaunch.com

ISBN 978-1-7371134-0-9 (paperback)
ISBN 978-1-7371134-1-6 (ebook)

Published by Marie Aaron
www.marieaaron.com

To "Jessica"

Thanks for the material

PROLOGUE

When I see the diamond coming at me, I throw up my arms like I'm blocking a punch.

"No!" I bark.

James flinches but persists. "Don't do this now! *Please* don't do this now," I say.

He drops to one knee awkwardly and holds the ring out toward me.

"Please, can we do this later?" I ask in shrill tones. I avert my eyes, as if not looking at the ring will make it disappear.

"I'm doing it now." His voice holds a spark of anger and dimly I register a corresponding spark of desire within me. *Goddammit.* Why do I always find it sexy when he's angry?

"Marry me, Marie," he says, and now I'm angry, too. He didn't ask, "Will you?" It's a statement, not a question; it doesn't require an answer.

"James, please," I sputter. "Not . . . not like . . . Can we do this over? Can we do it *later?* This is not—"

"It is what it is," he says baldly.

Well, shit. In all my thirty-eight years of anticipating this moment, never did I envision it would bomb so badly. I sit in my hard-backed chair, staring at him. He's knee-down on the

1

concrete next to a garbage can, his arm outstretched toward me. A splotch of bird crap decorates the pavement beside him.

We aren't even in a pretty spot. We're behind San Francisco's Ferry Building, crammed into the only square of shade we could find because it's eighty-five degrees outside and I am foolishly dressed head to toe in black. I'd wanted to look chic for my birthday, and then I just wanted to avoid getting sweaty. I realize suddenly why James was trying to steer me toward the picturesque bench in the sun, but I wasn't having it.

James' arm wilts a little and his determined expression flickers. I see that underneath he is anxious. I see the deep well of feeling for me in his eyes and I am torn by indecision. I've been basically begging this man to marry me for years. And now he is on his knee in front of me and I cannot say yes.

"James, I . . . " I steal a glance at the ring. It's a princess-cut solitaire, a sizable diamond in an ornate setting. Surprisingly, anger flares within me again. I've always told James that I want a simple ring. *Wasn't he listening?*

Suddenly a woman's head is between us. "Would you like me to take a picture?" she asks with a smile. *Jesus, where did she come from?* Her face is inches from mine and I didn't even see her approach.

James growls at her, "No!" The lady beats a hasty retreat. It would be funny if the moment weren't so tense.

I take a deep breath. "James, sweetheart. Get off your knee, please. Sit beside me." Slowly he lifts himself into the adjacent chair. I give him a hug, bury my face in his shoulder. "I love you," I say.

"I love you, too," he says. "Marry me."

Again, a statement. Where's the "Will you?"

We sit for a time, holding hands, eyes locked together. We sit for so long that another well-meaning passerby offers to take our picture. This time I wave him away. James seems to be out of words. I feel like crying.

"It must be time to catch the ferry," I finally say. "It's been half an hour. Shall we go?"

"Can I put the ring on you?" he asks me in a small voice.

I shake my head. "Put the ring away."

PART I

THE SWEET OBLIVIOUS

1

In The Beginning

In the beginning I thought he was kind of a dick.

Those were the exact words I used in my head, which surprised me because I didn't talk like that very often. Not back then, anyway.

We were at some church function; I don't remember what it was. He'd offered me a lift home and I'd gladly accepted to avoid taking the train.

"Why are you going out to the East Bay?" I asked, knowing he lived down south.

"I have to pick up my kids in Emeryville," he said. "It's the halfway point between my house and my ex-wife's." He made a wry face.

I nodded politely and said, "Oh." I didn't really care about his kids or his ex-wife, but I lived near Emeryville, so it worked out well for me.

James de Graaf was a bass in our church choir and I was a soprano. Although I'd known him for a few years, I couldn't say I knew him well. We stood on opposite ends of the risers and had never spoken much. He seemed to be a quiet guy.

I was a choir soloist and therefore pretty visible at church. I'd heard rumors that James was interested in me, which made me a little uncomfortable around him. Of course, I didn't consider this until I was stuck in his car, a hostage to the traffic jam near the Bay Bridge.

What should have been a twenty-minute drive stretched into an hour as we inched painfully along. Having exhausted the small talk early, James launched into a series of unflattering tales about his ex-wife. He was newly divorced, I learned, and brimming with fresh bitterness. He made his ex sound like an awful bitch.

I found the conversation off-putting. I didn't care much for trash talk and I barely knew this guy—what made him think that I wanted to hear about his ex-wife? After a few vague *mm-hmms*, I tuned out and began to stare desperately out the window. Was there an accident out there? Could I get out and walk back to the train?

Maybe James registered my discomfort because he abruptly changed the subject. "Did you see what Ruby was wearing today?" he asked.

Inwardly, I winced. I knew what he meant, but it seemed tacky to say it. Ruby sang in the choir with us. She favored short, tight clothes that bordered on inappropriate for church. Of course, our church bordered on inappropriate in many ways, but even so, her boobs were pushing the boundaries.

"I just don't know why anybody would want to dress like that," James said. He cast me a sidelong glance and I understood: he was trying to tell me that he didn't go for scantily clad women. It was meant to be a compliment to me.

And that's when I thought: *This guy is kind of a dick.* I tugged at my turtleneck and willed traffic to move faster.

James knew I had a boyfriend and he'd always been respectful, but the rumors persisted that he liked me. I never took them seriously. I'd been with Malcolm for years and we were definitely going to get married . . . one of these days. Besides, James had kids, and I can't emphasize enough how disinterested I was in *that* scene. I liked kids and I definitely wanted some—just not somebody else's.

They were cute enough, his girls. I think they may have been ages five and seven at the time. Throughout the ride James kept referring to them as "my little angels", which I found extremely irritating. It's okay to *think* your kids are angels, but you can't go around saying it, or people will want to punch you in the face.

Finally, we reached my street and the endless ride was over.

"I'm late to meet my kids," James remarked as he pulled up in front of my house. "I'm sure my ex will be furious. She'll probably make a scene in front of the girls."

I decided then that his ex was probably a nice lady who was being grossly misrepresented. At that moment, I was all for female solidarity.

"I'm sorry if I made you late," I said. He would have been late anyway, but it seemed like the right thing to say.

"Don't be sorry. I enjoyed your company." He smiled at me and I paused, gripping the door handle. He had a very nice smile.

But I'd already made up my mind about him.

"Thanks for the ride," I said perfunctorily and got out of the car. He gave me a short wave as he drove off, and I decided to avoid him for the next couple of years.

* * *

And avoid him I did. In fact, I don't really remember another encounter with him until several years down the line. Oh, I'd see him at choir practice and at church on Sundays, but we didn't interact much. Although we shared common friends, I never had a reason to talk to him.

Sometimes the choir would be invited to perform at outside events. Our church was well known in San Francisco, and we often sang for local politicians, corporate functions, and the occasional national anthem. Usually we would sing and disperse, but sometimes there was a party, and we'd be treated like guests. These were always the best functions because they offered food and an open bar. It's amazing how fast a church choir can decimate an hors d'oeuvres station.

We'd cluster in groups at these gigs, hanging out and consuming the free booze. It took me a while to realize that James was often in my circle, and I never found it odd when he'd hand me a glass of wine because the wine was usually free. When my glass was empty, he'd get me another.

The cumulative effect of the alcohol must have swayed my feelings toward him over the years because after a while, I found that I enjoyed his company. Although we were always surrounded by other friends, I laughed more when he was nearby. He was funny, I realized, and interesting. He didn't seem like the same person whom I'd so disliked a few years previously.

He also didn't talk as much about his ex-wife, which helped.

Now and again one of our friends, thinking to confide, would share with me the old rumor that he liked me. I still didn't take it seriously.

By then I'd ended my eight-year relationship with Malcolm and jumped into a terrible rebound with a guy named Patrick. Pat was our sound technician at church. He had a lousy temper and we were a bad match, but I was hanging in there, desperate to prove that I hadn't steered my life off course.

I was having a glass of wine with James at one of these events when Pat appeared at my elbow and threatened to leave without me. He stormed through the crowd, making for the front door, and I swore under my breath. Pat was my ride home.

"I'm sorry, I have to go," I said abruptly, plonking my wine glass onto the table and grabbing my purse. James looked startled and I couldn't blame him; it was a rude goodbye.

"Thank you for the wine," I called over my shoulder, and his expression seemed to shift, the surprise in his eyes giving way to something else. He smiled at me.

On the drive home, Pat made a nasty crack. "Sorry to tear you away from your new *boyfriend.*" Pat was moody and jealous, and I often had to convince him that I wasn't flirting with other men.

"Marie, that guy likes you," he accused me.

I bit back a sigh. Throughout the drive home, I tried to persuade Pat that I had nothing but friendly feelings for James. And I believed what I was saying.

But both men recognized what I had not: I was starting to like James, too.

Then one Sunday morning during church, I was standing onstage with the choir, singing to the congregation. I hadn't realized that James wasn't on the risers with the rest of us, but as I looked up into the balcony I saw him slip in late and take a seat. He was with a tall blonde woman and two small children. Squinting, I saw that the kids were not his; they were too young. I guessed that he must be in a relationship with this woman—and if her children were along, it must be serious.

I was seized by an odd disappointment. *Well,* I remember thinking, *I guess I missed that boat.*

But that's all I recall. Everything else about us is a blank until the week of the church drag show.

* * *

By now it's probably evident that our church is a bit . . . different.

Mercy Memorial is a San Francisco landmark, renowned throughout the Bay Area for its good works, its far-left politics, and its Sunday morning celebrations. Once a respectable and boring Methodist church, Mercy was turned upside down in the early sixties when the Reverend Lewis Early came to town.

He arrived from San Angelo, Texas, in an Afro and a dashiki. Among his first acts were to take down the crucifix and throw out all the staid hymnal books. He turned the pulpit into a stage, which he filled with gospel music and dynamic, relevant speakers.

Mercy's location on the edge of the Tenderloin put Lewis in close proximity to the neighborhood's residents, made up in large part of immigrant families, homeless, prostitutes, gays, hippies, and addicts. Instead of hiding inside his church, Lewis threw open the doors and invited them all inside. The small congregation of old white ladies mostly fled, and over time, a new community was born.

When I arrived some forty years later, Mercy had an eight-piece jazz band, a hundred-member gospel choir, a soup kitchen, medical clinic, various offshoot centers, and about eighty wellness programs. Everybody in the city knew about Mercy; it was a San Francisco institution.

I stumbled on it quite by accident, and the place just blew my mind. I hadn't been to church since I was a kid and I didn't remember it being so . . . *cool*.

I was drawn to the music. It was so vibrant that it almost seemed like a living thing—so very different from the timid hymns that had accompanied our Catholic services growing up. The gospel filled my chest, expanding into all the empty places that I hadn't known were empty. And the sermons caught my attention in a way that no church talk had ever done before.

"You are welcome here," was the first thing they said every Sunday. "Whatever color you are; whatever your sexual orientation, your political affiliation, or your legal status; no matter your religion, or if you're rich or poor; if you have forty years of sobriety or forty minutes—*you are welcome here.*" They said it every week.

I knew Mercy was a haven for many folks who'd been shunned by their home churches, and it sought to undo that damage with unconditional love. That wasn't my story, but I warmed to it anyway because it felt good. A place meant for everybody was a place where I wanted to be! I loved being part of the community, and soon I joined the choir. Mercy became the cornerstone of my week.

I had fancied myself open-minded, but my world view grew in leaps and bounds from the moment I walked through those doors. I met all kinds of people who were different from me: drag queens and transgender folks, old jazz cats with fascinating stories, people who'd lived on the streets, and others who lived in mansions. They were flamboyant and colorful, honest and raw. Each week they forced me to reconsider my notions of "normal" just by being themselves.

I changed a lot in those early years at Mercy. It softened me, I guess. As the reverend had done with his church, I threw open the doors of my heart and welcomed people in.

On the other side of the risers, James was changing, too. Which is why it took a few years for me to look across the room and see a man that I suddenly wanted to get to know.

* * *

Mercy's Pride Team was planning a drag show to raise money for San Francisco's Pride Weekend. The fundraiser, dubbed Divalicious, would pay for entry to the Pride Parade and for materials to build the float.

I wasn't planning to attend the drag show, but before choir rehearsal one night I was cornered by Angel, who was coercing people into buying tickets. "Are you coming to Divalicious, Marie?" he asked me. "You know I'm performing." He whipped open a decorative fan with a satisfying *thwap* and eyed me coquettishly from behind its folds.

After that I felt I had no choice, so I forked over my money and pocketed the ticket.

I was a little early for rehearsal, so I ducked into the green room, hoping for cake. With such a large Mercy staff, it seemed like there was always leftover birthday cake. No luck that day, but there were some cardboardy gingersnaps on the table. I leaned over them, considering.

"I don't recommend the cookies," said Russell, "unless you want to break a tooth."

"Thanks," I replied, but as Russell returned to his conversation with James, I filched one anyway. It takes a lot for me to turn my back on a cookie.

There were several other choir members in the room, and I waved hello to everyone, including James, who smiled at me. I sank onto the beat-up leather couch and nibbled at my cookie, experimentally.

And then, I swear to God, I didn't give James another thought . . . until one of his daughters (Annabelle? I wasn't sure of her name) climbed onto his lap and buried her face in his neck. She was too big to fit comfortably, like she'd outgrown his lap a while ago. Perhaps she wasn't feeling well.

James didn't pause his conversation but put an arm around Annabelle automatically and stroked her hair. She snuggled against him, content.

And something inside me *burst* open.

I dropped my cookie, shocked by this instant, intense reaction—shocked further still that it was seemingly in response to James' fatherly instincts. I'll say it again: I had *no interest* in men with kids. I wanted my own children, but I definitely did not want to inherit a . . . what, eight-year-old?

My stomach flipped over and I nearly groaned with recognition. Since junior high, that stomach flip has meant that I have serious feelings for a guy. Usually there's a warning, a crush that develops into something more, but this came out of nowhere. I was caught wrong-footed, utterly stunned. I stared at James in dismay.

"Are you boys coming to Divalicious?" Angel sauntered over to James and Russell and waved a ticket in their faces. "It's this Saturday night."

"I'll be there," said Russell. "There is an elevator, right?" He indicated the motorized scooter that he used to get around.

"Yes," Angel assured him. "How about you, James?"

"I don't think so," said James. "I've got my kids this weekend."'

"That's too bad," said Angel. "Marie just bought her ticket, didn't you, Miss Marie?" Everybody looked at me.

I don't think it was meant to be a gibe; Angel was just talking. But James immediately said, "Well, maybe I'll get a babysitter." In a flash, he produced a twenty-dollar bill, nearly unseating Annabelle in his haste to reach the wallet in his back pocket.

James looked at me and our eyes locked. My stomach did another crazy somersault when he smiled.

Oh shit, I thought.

2

DRAG SHOW

It was crappy timing for me to develop a crush. I had only just called it quits with Pat.

I should have done it months earlier, and I'd tried a few times, but it never seemed to stick. I recalled a Seinfeld episode that described the situation perfectly: "Breaking up is like knocking over a Coke machine. You can't do it in one push. You gotta rock it back and forth a few times, and *then* it goes over." That was my relationship with Pat.

My roommate, Mandy, had been there with me throughout all the long months that I'd tried to topple the machine. She was that great kind of friend who withheld comment when you pursued a mistake, but was there for you when the mistake kicked you out of his car and left you stranded on the curb. I tried to be the same for her.

By unspoken agreement, our house was a judgement-free zone. We supported one another in our poor relationship choices, knowing that we were better, smarter women somewhere on the inside . . . but not quite ready to *be* them.

At present, we were both newly single and spent a lot of time drinking wine on the couch. I came home from choir rehearsal to find Mandy doing just that, a bottle of cabernet on the table beside her. As I went to fetch a glass, I wondered if I should tell her about my newfound crush. But I was still shaken from the discovery and decided, for the time being, to keep it to myself.

Mandy heaved a big sigh as I reentered the room with my glass and a box of chocolate-covered caramels. Wine was always better with chocolate.

"Long day?" I asked her.

"Every day is long," she replied. She slid onto the floor and grabbed a foam roller, hoisting it under her hips. Mandy was petite and athletic. She biked to work most days, and I sometimes laughed when I saw her tiny bike shoes lined up next to my own size-tens. Her wavy blond hair fell over her face, her toned, prone body draped across the roller.

"I need a change," she said as she rolled back and forth. "I need to meet some new people."

This was true. The last time Mandy had endeavored to meet new people, she'd joined a mountain-biking group and had met Nick, a man with overdeveloped calves and underdeveloped emotions. Mandy fell for him hard, but when she told him she loved him, he'd responded with a brooding, "I'm not sure I know what love is." We'd gone through a lot of wine over Nick before Mandy set him free to disappoint another girl. Unfortunately, she didn't feel comfortable returning to the group and had lately been mountain biking alone.

"Ow," she groaned from the floor. "My muscles are so tight! Can you hand me my wine, please?"

"You know, if you really want a change, there's a job opening up at my company," I said, passing over her glass. "That writing position I was telling you about."

Mandy and I had worked together at New Trails, an adventure-travel company in Berkeley. She was still employed there, but I'd been laid off and had since moved to Roaming Expeditions, another travel company in San Francisco that had also hired a few of our friends.

"I don't know," said Mandy from the floor. "That seems like a big move." Mandy didn't make big decisions lightly.

"Come on, it would be so great! You, me, Naomi . . . Keegan's over there now, did I tell you?" I popped a chocolate into my mouth. "It really is a good place to work. And you don't have to worry about getting hit on." The owner of New Trails had a habit of pursuing his female employees.

"Ugh." Mandy made a face. "I guess it would be nice to work someplace where they didn't do that."

"Then you should apply!" I urged. "I actually *like* every single person I work with. I never wake up dreading going to the office anymore."

"Would I get to work with Ken?" she asked hopefully. Mandy thought Ken was a trip.

"Not directly, but you'd definitely get the flavor of him," I said.

"Hmm." She tipped back her wine. "I'll think about it."

* * *

I'd been at my job for about seven months and considered myself very lucky. I was on Roaming Expeditions'

Frontline team, which meant I was one of two receptionists who fielded calls, managed the mail, and did other standard administrative tasks. My colleagues were cool, my boss was genuinely delightful, and I left every day at five o'clock on the dot. It was a step down from my old position in the Marketing department at New Trails, but I didn't care—my days were peaceful and I had a steady paycheck.

My teammate on Frontline was Ken, who started at the company just three weeks after I did. Ken had a shaved head and a handlebar mustache, and he wore loud shirts and a porkpie hat. He was obsessed with the supernatural, loved a good haunted hotel, and subscribed to the *Bigfoot Times*. But the best part about Ken was the stuff that came out of his mouth. The things he said in earnest were unintentionally funny, and I kept a secret list of his best quotes—which I emailed, on occasion, to my friends. Mandy was a big fan.

"Hey, do you like my socks?" Ken asked me the next afternoon. He pulled up his pants leg to display one. They were blue with pink flamingos and they went up to his knees.

"I do."

"Guess how much they cost. It's the most money I've ever spent on socks."

"How much?" I asked.

"Twelve dollars. I had a hard time committing to this one. But then I started doing the math, and if I buy one new pair of socks each month, it works out to, like, forty-two cents per day." He admired the flamingos for a second, then shook his pants leg down. "Then my girlfriend said to me, 'Just get off the bus now and go get those socks.' So I did."

I hadn't met Ken's girlfriend yet. I wondered what kind of woman it took to date this man.

"Do you and Pia live together?" I asked.

"Naw," he said, "but she's hinting. We actually dated a long time ago, and this is Round Two."

"Do you think you'll get married?"

"Oh, I don't know," he said. "I'm not Italian, but my eyes are always Rome-n."

"Nice one." I rolled my eyes. "Hand me another stack of catalogs, would you?" Roaming Expeditions released a beautiful annual catalog and we kept hundreds of copies on hand to mail to prospective clients.

"What are you up to this weekend?" I asked as we stuffed and stamped envelopes. Ken always had good weekend plans.

"I might head up to Sacramento and do a little ghost hunting with my old friend Walrus. How about you?"

For once I had something that could compete. "I'm going to a drag show," I said.

Ken raised an eyebrow. "Coolio," he replied. "Asia SF?"

I shook my head at the mention of the well-known drag club. "Nah, it's a Mercy fundraiser, a church event. It's being held at some club on Market Street. A bunch of my friends are performing."

Ken dropped an armload of catalogs in the mail bin and remarked casually, "You know, you can always tell a woman who used to be a man because she cannot walk in heels."

I frowned. "That's not universally true. Come to church with me sometime and I'll introduce you to several men who wear heels more comfortably than I do."

"But here's the thing," Ken said. "It's only black guys and Asian guys. White men do not know how to walk in heels. They just don't get it. And they dress like Ross from 1982."

I was puzzled. "Ross from 1982?"

"Yeah, you know." He picked up the mail bin and backed out the door. "Ross Dress For Less, the bargain basement store."

* * *

Ken might be right, I thought as I surveyed the crowd in the club that Saturday night. Out of a dozen drag queens, only one was white and she did not look too confident in her shoes.

It was with some reluctance that I'd come to Divalicious. I wasn't ready for this. I'd spent the last few days consumed with thoughts of James and it was jarring—just last week I'd barely considered him and now I couldn't stop.

I blamed the kid.

There was something about that exchange in the choir room; I couldn't get it out of my head. When I saw James cradle Annabelle in his lap, his gentleness shook me.

He'd held her like an afterthought. By which I mean: he held her so naturally that it seemed to take no thought. I'd never noticed that about him before—but then, in the wake of my volatile relationship with Pat, I had new eyes for soft-spoken people who hadn't held my attention previously.

James' love was easy and evident. He moved me.

I was not ready to be moved. I'd just gotten out of a draining relationship. I wanted to have a series of affairs, emotionless flings with no strings attached. I'd discussed this with Mandy just days before.

"They should be International Men of Mystery," I'd declared. "Each with a different accent." (Mandy had had a fling with a British guy a while back and we'd both been enthralled by his accent.) I gestured with my nearly empty wine glass. "They will be as unique and beautiful as this box of assorted chocolates, and I will devour them with as much enjoyment and as little regard."

"I think you're drunk," she'd replied.

But now I was afraid I might be developing feelings, and that was not in my game plan. So I arrived at Divalicious an hour late on purpose, not entirely sure that I wanted to be there. I could hear the place from half a block away, and when I entered the club the volume of the music nearly blasted me back out onto the sidewalk. I took refuge in the corner to get my bearings and scanned the room.

It wasn't a very large club and the crowd was packed in like sardines. People were pressed against the little stage and along the catwalk, where the performers were strutting their stuff. I watched as Angel, Perry, and Sasha lip-synced to Destiny's Child. They were decked out in jewel-toned evening gowns, and a disco ball scattered light over them like confetti.

A few minutes later the queens took a bow and exited the stage. Raymond, dressed as an elderly church lady and playing emcee, stepped up to introduce the next act. I felt a plucking at my sleeve and turned to find my friend Henry grinning down at me. "Hey, girl." He gave me a big hug— and in the momentary quiet, whispered into my ear: "James is here."

I took a step back, unnerved. Was my attraction so evident? How could it be? I had only just discovered it myself!

I clocked James across the room and as I noticed him, he noticed me. He was trapped in conversation and I ducked out of his sight line, slipping over to the bar. I was not ready to talk to him. I bought myself a glass of wine so James wouldn't have an excuse to bring me one. Besides, I thought I might need the courage. Being suddenly single was a rather alarming feeling.

The music crashed on again and three women dressed as men took the stage and started dancing. Two of them were clearly women in drag, but the third struck such a masculine figure that it was hard to tell. She wore a thin beard that traced her jawline and was flat-chested in a man's tank top and open sports coat. I spotted my friend Renee and waved her over. "Do we know these women?" I yelled in her ear.

"I know two of them," she hollered back. "That's Chandra's friend Emilia, and the one who actually looks like a guy is Toni."

"She *really* looks like a guy," I shouted. "That facial hair is . . . very misleading!" I was used to seeing men in drag, but I'd never seen a woman dressed so convincingly as a man. Seven years at Mercy and I was still having my horizons widened.

James edged up beside us and nodded hello. It was too loud to talk, so we all just stood around watching the performance. After a few minutes Renee seemed to spot a friend and wandered away. I thought I caught her smirking at me as she left.

I was harboring a strange mix of feelings. It was exciting to be near James, and that was new. But I also felt belligerent. I didn't want to like this man, with his two kids and his pre-planned life. I was single for the first time in ages and I wanted to build my own life! I resented my friends for their subtle encouragement. I felt like everyone was steering me toward something that I wasn't sure I wanted.

But as I sipped my wine, our eyes met over the rim of my glass and my stomach swooped dangerously. There was no denying that James was having an effect on me.

Mercifully, someone turned down the volume on the music and we could finally hear each other. James had a funny laugh, like a seal barking. But his smile was kind and his eyes were interested. Other friends mingled in and out, but he and I stood by the pool table for an hour, drinking wine and talking about nothing in particular. I found again that I enjoyed his company and it flustered me. When he excused himself to go to the restroom, I escaped to the other side of the club. I found Henry talking with Christopher, another choir friend, and I attached myself to them, seeking protection.

James was undaunted and he sought me out again. "You guys make a nice picture," he said, indicating the three of us. "Let me take a photo." I put an arm around each of my friends and we smiled for the camera. My stomach swooped again when James leaned in to show me the picture.

The evening wore on and the crowd started getting unruly. One of the performers dropped to her hands and knees and started writhing on the dance floor.

"Who is that?" asked James.

"That is Sonia," said Angel, plopping down beside us in a sequined gown. He looked disdainfully in Sonia's direction. "Those boobs are new, and she is mighty proud of them, walking around backstage, chest out, like everybody's interested. I said, 'Honey, don't nobody want to see your business.'" Angel hollered at Sonia's retreating behind. "Cover your business, Sonia!" I giggled.

Angel pursed his lips and cooled himself vigorously with a red silk fan, setting the bangs of his wig to fluttering. "Honey, it's a church fundraiser, but not everybody around here goes to church, you know what I'm saying?

"You see, I am a lady," he continued. "I don't walk around with my business out, do I? No. I got class, just like you, Miss Marie."

Angel regarded me fondly for a moment, cupping a hand under my chin. "Isn't she pretty, James?" A brief flush crossed James' face, and I felt my own cheeks warming.

"I want to be just like you when I grow up, Miss Marie." With that, Angel blew me an air kiss and sauntered away.

The drag show ended and the club personnel began ushering us out. "But it's still early," I protested.

"Exactly. They want to turn the crowd over. They charge a cover after nine o'clock," Henry said.

I found I was reluctant to leave, so when he asked, "Who's hungry?" I piped up quickly, "I could eat."

"Me too," said James.

Five of us went to the Thai place across the street. I squeezed around the circular table between Henry and Christopher, and across from Raymond and James.

"Oohwee!" said Raymond. "I am glad to take off those heels." He had swapped out his church-lady costume for regular wear, but there were still smudges of makeup around his eyes.

"I would call that evening a success," said Henry. "It looked like y'all raised a ton of money."

"They were still counting it when we left," said Raymond. "That should be enough to pay for the Pride float."

I'd marched in the Pride Parade every year since I'd discovered Mercy, and it was great fun. Each year the church built a float and the congregation followed it down Market Street, blasting a recording of songs by the choir and dancing along. One year I'd convinced Mandy to come with me, and she and I hula-hooped the entire parade route. We were a big hit, but by the time we reached City Hall I was sure I'd ruptured my appendix.

"When is Pride?" asked James.

"Next month," said Christopher. "It's always near the end of June. Are you going to march in the parade?"

"I never have before," said James.

"Never?" The rest of us were surprised.

James shrugged. "I usually have my kids."

"You should bring them," Christopher suggested. "They can ride on the float."

James shook his head and laughed. "My ex would have a heart attack. She doesn't exactly support gay pride. I'd wind up back in court." He stole a glance at me. "I'll check my calendar though. Maybe I don't have them this year."

"How often do you have your kids?" I asked him.

"Most of the time. They live with me. They visit their mum every other weekend and half the summer."

Damn, I thought. That was a lot of the time.

When the check arrived I still wasn't ready for the evening to end. I thought we'd wind up at a nearby bar, but it turned out that James and I were the only drinkers in the group. Such is the hazard of hanging with a church crowd—half of our friends were in recovery from something.

As we stood up to leave, Henry saw that it was raining. "Who's going to drive Marie to the train?" he asked pointedly.

"It's not raining hard; I can walk," I said.

"I'll drive you," offered James, not missing a beat. Henry didn't trouble to hide his grin.

I hesitated for a moment. "Okay," I said softly. "Thanks."

The MUNI station was literally steps from the restaurant, but James was determined to drive me somewhere. "I'll take you to a closer station," he said. "I mean, a further one. I mean, I don't want you to have to ride on the train as long."

I got more soaked walking to his car than I would have if I'd just darted into the MUNI station, but I didn't care. The car windows fogged up when we climbed inside.

"Thanks for the lift," I said.

"I'd drive you all the way home, but I have to get back for the babysitter," James explained.

"Of course."

We drove past one train station, then another. Traffic was at a crawl because of the rain and it became clear that this excursion was an inconvenience for both of us, but James didn't seem to care. He was going to drive me all the way downtown.

As we pulled up to the last train station this side of the bay, James said casually, "Hey, give me your phone number and I'll text you that photo I took of you, Henry, and Christopher." He handed me his phone.

I bit back a smile. *Clever,* I thought. I typed my number into his phone and handed it back to him. "Here you go."

"Great." James turned to smile at me and suddenly I felt happy, excited. It was one hundred and eighty degrees from how I'd felt the last time I'd ridden in his car. *I like this guy,* I admitted to myself. I hoped he would call.

"Good night," I said as I got out of the car. James raised his hand and smiled at me again. I bounded down the stairs toward the train, feeling upbeat. Feeling like something new was on the horizon.

3

FIRST DATE

James didn't waste time. He texted me the next morning, sending me the photo, along with a message: "Last night was fun. But I was thinking it might be nice to get together without all our other friends."

I spent a while crafting the perfect response. Eventually I settled on: "That sounds nice."

He wrote back right away. "The thing is, between work and kids, I have a packed schedule. I'm free this Saturday, then busy for the next three weeks."

Hmm. He didn't dissemble. And he didn't leave much room for me to play coy. I decided to be straightforward, too. "I'm free on Saturday," I wrote.

"Great," he responded. "It's a date."

* * *

"I have a date tonight," I announced to my knitting group.

Their faces lit up. "You do?" demanded Alex. "Tell us!"

The knitting group hailed back to my early days in California. Seeking new friends, I'd responded to an online ad for a local Stitch and Bitch group. More than half the women dropped out after those first gatherings, but a core group of us had been meeting ever since. Over the years we'd been to each other's weddings, knit blankets for each other's children, and become close friends.

Nicole, Christine, and Karen had eventually moved away, and Janet had a new boyfriend who took up all her time. But I still got together regularly with Hailey, Alex, and Katia, and Mandy sometimes joined us, too. Truthfully, we didn't knit much anymore. The yarn was just a prop that we brought to our Eating and Drinking group.

This morning we were lounging in the sun at Lake Merritt, spread out on blankets with a bevy of snacks, our discarded knitting off to the side.

"So, who is this guy?" Hailey asked, spreading Brie on a cracker.

"His name is James," I said. "He sings in the choir with me."

"So, you've known him for a while?" Alex questioned.

"Yeah, a few years." I did a little mental math. "I think he and his kids started coming to Mercy a year or two after I did."

There was a pause. Alex cocked an eyebrow. "He has kids?" she asked pointedly. "That sounds serious."

Inwardly I bristled, but I could understand her concern. These women had seen me through the worst of my months with Pat. Like Mandy, they'd been nothing but supportive, but I knew they were relieved when I'd ended that relationship. Given how recently that was, I could understand their caution in expressing support for a new romance.

"It's not serious," I assured them. "I don't want that right now. It's just . . . it's been so long since somebody's kissed me without any trace of sadness, you know?"

That sounded dramatic, but it was true. I'd had two failed relationships in a row. Malcolm and I had spent our last year struggling and my entire rebound with Pat had been a battle. The break-up lasted longer than the relationship.

"I just want to have fun," I said. "I just want to go out to dinner and maybe make out a little bit, and have a good time. It feels awesome to be excited about something again."

Hailey smiled. "Where is he taking you?"

"We're supposed to meet in SoMa tonight. I hear there's a new pod of food trucks down there."

"Food trucks are suddenly the thing, aren't they?" she said.

It seemed they were popping up everywhere. A few months ago, I'd spotted a cupcake truck in my neighborhood—the first I'd ever seen—and it was like my dreams had come true. I'd walked in circles around the empty truck trying to peer through the windows and calling out, "Hello? Is this real?"

* * *

As it turned out, the food trucks weren't open. I was hot-footing it across town, running ten minutes late, when I got James' text. He suggested we meet at a bar a few blocks away.

I arrived at the corner flushed and out of breath, willing myself not to sweat. As I waited for the light to change, I caught sight of James outside the bar. He was standing, flamingo-style, with one foot propped against the building. His chin was tilted down and sunlight winked off the top of his head.

I stood there and looked at him, studying his appearance for perhaps the first time. James was tall and slender. He had a head of fine brown hair—minus a good-sized circle in the center. The bald spot didn't bother me; he was handsome enough to pull it off. He wore wire-rimmed glasses and a few days of stubble, which was surprisingly sexy.

As if he could feel my eyes on him, James looked up. He smiled at me across the street, and my stomach took a dangerous dive again. I had that weird cocktail of first date feelings.

"This is the only place open around here," he said, by way of greeting. Then, "Hi."

"Hi," I said. "This is fine."

He opened the door for me and we stepped inside the dark little bar. It was not a first date kind of place. The air smelled stale, the regulars had clearly been at it for hours, and the bar was sticky. But I was suddenly feeling shy and a drink seemed like the right idea.

We ordered a couple of beers and regarded each other timidly.

"So . . . how's your weekend going?" James asked. "What'd you do today?"

I nattered on nervously about my morning and we made small talk for a while. James revealed that he'd spent the day cajoling his kids into cleaning the house.

"Your girls are getting big," I remarked. "How old are they now?"

"Avery's ten and Annabelle is eight," he said.

"Wow," I remarked. "I remember when they were little things, running around the church during choir rehearsal."

"Yeah. They're getting older now. They're less sociable than they used to be. Well, Avery is. She usually just brings a book. But Annabelle's less inhibited; she still likes to run around and play." He smiled fondly.

"So . . . " I wanted some information, but I wasn't sure how to begin. "How long have you had your kids? I mean, how long have you been a single dad?"

James traced his finger through the rings of condensation on the bar, thinking. "Let's see. We moved here from Vancouver when Avery was three; Annabelle was just a year old. And within the year my wife started having an affair. Then she moved out. She left the kids with me, said she wanted to focus on her career. But instead, she moved in with that guy and bought a big house with my inheritance." He made a face.

"You're kidding," I said, shocked.

"Nope. My mum left me a fair amount of money when she died. I sunk it into real estate, but right before Jessica left—Jessica's my ex—I'd sold a house and temporarily put the money in our joint account. Stupid move. She withdrew it and bought a house of her own with that fucker." He caught a glimpse of my astonished face. "Sorry," he apologized.

"Don't be sorry!" I exclaimed.

"Still a little bitterness there." He gave a short laugh.

"Couldn't you get it back?" I was outraged for him.

"Not without suing," he said. "And she didn't have a Green Card, so there was a very real possibility that she'd be deported. And then my kids would've been without a mum." He said this simply and shrugged, taking a sip of his beer.

"But you've got citizenship?" I asked.

"I've got a Green Card, so I was safe. But if we'd divorced, she'd have been here illegally." He paused. "Of course, a few months later she got engaged to that asshole—which solved that problem. And then she took me to court for custody."

"You're kidding!" I said again.

"Nope. The kids had been living with me for nearly a year. We'd agreed that Jessica would have them every other weekend, but a lot of the time she didn't even bother. She was too busy with her new life. When she decided she was ready to be a mum again and told me she wanted the kids, I told her to go to hell. And we had a trial."

"And you won," I prompted.

"Kind of. I mean yeah, I did, in the end. Jessica's estranged from her family, which is too bad. They're nice people. Kinda weird, but nice. When they heard there was going to be a trial, the family sent her sister Jocelyn to come testify—on my behalf."

"No!" I was riveted.

"Yeah. Jocelyn testified that Jessica had told her that I was the better parent, and that Jess was planning to move to Washington, D.C., to focus on politics. She and Jessica haven't spoken since. I've always felt bad about that." He smirked. "Well, not that bad."

"And the judge awarded you custody?"

"No. The judge said we were both good parents who'd made errors. He awarded fifty-fifty custody and ordered that the kids attend school in between us. Jessica had just bought that big house up in Vacaville, and I'd moved down to San Carlos, about ninety minutes away. Alameda County is the halfway point. So I said, okay, I'll move up there and send the kids to school in Piedmont." Piedmont was an affluent suburb of Oakland, not far from where I lived. "But then Jessica said that didn't work for her. She wasn't interested in moving. So she agreed that I could have primary custody— if I would pay ten thousand dollars toward her legal bills."

"You're shitting me," I said.

"Nope."

"And what about the money she'd stolen from you?"

"That was part of the agreement, that I wouldn't contest it."

"That's nuts!" I exclaimed.

Again he shrugged. "All I cared about was keeping my kids. That's all that mattered to me."

I regarded him for a minute. Although he clearly didn't like his ex, he didn't seem to be dripping with bitterness anymore. In fact, I was much more aggrieved listening to this story than he was telling it. This was a different guy than the one who'd driven me home several years before.

"I'd be furious," I admitted to him. "How do you get over something like that?"

He laughed. "Don't get me wrong, I hate her guts." He said it easily, without fire. "But we had a terrible marriage and I'm glad to be free of her. We were married for thirteen years. I got married when I was eighteen years old," he explained, seeing the look on my face.

"Wow," I said.

"Yeah. Stupid move. But I was raised in the Dutch Christian Reformed religion, and that was a pretty normal thing to do. We'd slept together, so we had to get married.

My mum actually had to sign a permission slip to make it legal." I laughed at that.

"Ridiculous, right? And I probably never would have divorced her because divorce was not acceptable. So . . . I guess, if she hadn't cheated on me, I'd still be stuck in a miserable marriage. But instead I'm a single dad and I get to raise my two little angels my way."

There was that *angels* reference again. I tried not to wrinkle my nose.

"So, do the kids have a good relationship with their mom?" I asked.

Now James wrinkled his nose. "They idolize their mum," he said. "Unfortunately. She was the absent parent, and they've always been desperate for her attention."

I made a scandalized face.

"They don't know a lot of what happened between us, and the parts they do know, they've rewritten in their minds." James paused. "It's a lot for a kid to absorb. They can't admit that their mum has made some . . . questionable choices, so they rewrite history."

"What do you mean?"

"Well, like if you ask them how they wound up living with me, they'll say that mum couldn't move to Alameda County because she needed to be in Vacaville, near family."

"Wait, what? Is her family in Vacaville?"

"No, her family's in Canada. Her husband's family is in Vacaville."

The obvious kicked in a minute too late. "Aren't *her kids* her family?" I asked, angrily.

He huffed a dry laugh. "That's what I've asked. But the girls don't have an answer for that question. They just get upset, so we don't talk about it."

"So, they don't understand that she cheated on you and then left them?" I could feel myself getting seriously riled up.

James considered this. "I think Avery understands," he said. "She's older; she remembers more. She knows that her mum and Max started dating before we were divorced. But she tries hard to rationalize it. Mum must have had her reasons." He smiled ruefully. "And Jessica is very manipulative. She makes up reasons why she wasn't around. She's told them that Daddy kidnapped them, that the judge made a mistake . . . It's all bullshit, but the kids believe anything she says."

"*Why?*" This story was killing me.

"Well, it's a defense mechanism. I mean, it's hard for a kid to process. How do you understand, at age ten, that your mum made a choice not to raise you? It's not like she had an addiction, or couldn't support them financially, or had some other legitimate issue. She chose a big house on a golf course over her kids." Now I could hear the bitterness in his voice. My heart hurt for him.

"Annabelle's different," he went on. "She was only four when her mum got remarried. She doesn't have any memories before Max." He twisted up his face. "That asshole."

"What's he like?" I asked.

"I honestly couldn't tell you. I've had exactly two conversations with him in my life. Well, 'conversation' is probably the wrong word. Both times I just warned him to stop telling my kids to call him 'Max Daddy'. That fucker." James polished off his beer and set the bottle down decisively. "Shall we go? I wouldn't mind a change of scenery."

His tone suggested that he was ready for a change of subject, too. The bar was getting full and noisy now. We surrendered our seats and decided to find a place to eat.

Out on the street an awkwardness settled over us again. I was burning from his story and wanted to pepper him with more questions, but I sensed that James didn't want to talk about it anymore. We walked in silence to the Mission District, and I was starting to wonder if prolonging the date was a good idea. For the life of me, I couldn't think of anything else to talk about.

Although the Mission was bursting with restaurants, it was hard to find one that fit the bill. It was still fairly early on a Saturday night and most places were giving off an empty vibe. We finally settled on a Mexican spot that I'd never seen before. It didn't look that impressive, but we were both hungry and tired of walking.

In between bites of enchilada and tacos—which were surprisingly tasty—we tried to resuscitate the conversation.

"So, what brought you to Mercy?" I asked, curious.

"An ex-girlfriend, actually," he said. "The first woman I dated after my divorce. Her name was Mary Jo. We didn't go out that long, but when we broke up, she said, 'James, you should really go to Mercy.' So I went, and I brought my kids. And it made me really uncomfortable at first." He grinned. "All those people hugging and dancing and clapping? People don't do that where I come from. Raising your hands in church would get you sent to hell."

"I sense you're exaggerating," I said with a smile.

"I'm not, though. That was the kind of thing we were taught. Dutch people don't show emotion."

"I thought you were Canadian?" I said, confused.

"I'm Dutch Canadian. My parents came over from Holland."

Ah! An International Man of Mystery! "Do you speak Dutch?" I asked him.

"Stroopwafel," he said.

"What's that?"

"A Dutch wafer cookie. That's about all I can say."

Okay, that was mildly disappointing. But if I was going to learn only one word of a foreign language, I'd probably choose *cookie,* too.

James asked how long I'd been attending Mercy, and we calculated that he'd joined the choir about two years after I had. But we didn't remember meeting each other. That's often the way it went at Mercy; there were just too many people to remember meeting each one.

"Let's see . . . the summer you joined the choir was the summer I shaved my head," I recalled. "And I wore a bandanna everywhere for months."

James put down his fork and looked at me. "Wait— *you're* Bandana Girl?" he exclaimed.

"Um, yeah. I guess."

"Oh my God!" He was all excited. "I totally remember you! Except I didn't realize it was *you.* I just remember there was this girl who wore a bandana all the time. I always wondered why." James cracked up. "Even my kids called you Bandana Girl!"

"It wasn't my best look," I said with dignity.

"Why did you shave your head?"

Now I was embarrassed. "I thought I'd look like an elegant black queen," I mumbled.

"What?"

I sighed. "I thought if I shaved my head I'd look like an elegant black queen."

I'd had the idea that if I shaved my head, my hair would grow in all natural and kinky, like an Afro. But I am only half-black—and my hair, it seems, is all-white, at least until it becomes long enough to curl. It grew in perfectly straight and stuck out like porcupine quills until it was about an inch long. So I wore a bandana the whole summer. It was a challenging time.

Embarrassed, I explained this to James, who laughed that seal-bark laugh of his. I found myself giggling, too. "I guess it's funny," I said. "Growing up I always wanted straight hair, but I was never so happy to see my curls come back!"

"I love your curls," James blurted out. He flushed slightly. "You have beautiful hair."

Now I flushed. "Thank you."

"So, you're biracial?"

"Yes," I said. "A lot of people can't tell 'cause I'm so light-skinned. My younger brother's a little darker than I am and he's got kinkier hair. But my grandmother used to say that I could pass."

"Pass?"

"Pass for white," I explained.

James furrowed his brow a bit, and I could tell he found it an odd thing to say. But my grandmother could remember a time when passing for white was a good option to have. I, on the other hand, might have preferred to be a shade or two darker. Sometimes I felt very different from one half of my family.

"That's one of the reasons Mercy's so important to me," I said. "There are so many different colors of people. I've never seen such a multiethnic gospel choir before, have you?"

James shook his head.

"I remember once, years ago—this is when I was living in New York—I heard gospel music coming out of this basement church. It was the first time I'd ever heard it live. I got so excited that I dropped to my hands and knees on the sidewalk and tried to peer in through the windows, but I couldn't see anything. I wanted to go inside and sing with them, but I felt too . . . conspicuous, I guess." I gave a half-shrug. "It sounds silly now, and I'm sure they would've been welcoming, but still . . . " I'd had a keen sense that it wasn't my place. "And all these years later I found Mercy, and it was like . . . finding home."

James regarded me thoughtfully. The moment grew heavy between us and I suddenly felt like I'd shared too much. I looked down at my plate and busied myself with my taco.

But then James said, "Well, I couldn't tell what color you are. I'm color blind."

"Really?" I asked. "What does that mean, exactly? You see everything in shades of gray?"

"Well, no. I can see some bright colors, like yellow. But greens and blues and browns all look the same to me. I can tell a black person apart from a white person, but I can't always see the skin tones in between. And I have a hard time parking. I can never tell what color the curb is."

"So, what happens when you can't tell?"

"I get a ticket."

I laughed. "How did you even find out that you're color blind? Did you flunk coloring in kindergarten or something?"

"Yeah, I was coloring the sky green and the grass blue. But my older brother is color blind, too, so my parents were on the lookout for it with me. It's pretty common in boys; my sister doesn't have it."

"Wow," I said. "So, you have one brother and one sister?"

"Yup. Rachel's a year older than me and Adam's a year older than her."

"Are you guys close?" I asked.

"To Adam? No. Not at all." James took a sip of his drink. "He was a bully when we were growing up, and he's still kind of an asshole, sorry to say. We don't really keep in touch. But Rachel's a total sweetheart. She lives in Florida and I don't get to see her that much—although she did come visit with her kids recently. I brought her to church, which was cool."

The penny dropped. "She has two little blond kids?" I asked.

"Yeah, Mya and Sam."

I smiled to myself. "I think I saw them."

James pointed at me with his fork. "How about your family? Do you have more siblings? Or is it just the two of you?"

I nodded. "Yeah. Just me and Theo. He's three years younger."

"Are you close?"

I considered this. "We were super close growing up. Then we drifted apart when I went off to college. My folks split up around that time and Theo kind of turned away. He wasn't interested in keeping in touch." I toyed with the salt shaker, remembering. "But he's thirty now. He's finally growing up." I smiled. "Now sometimes he'll call me and we'll talk for an hour. The first time that happened, it was amazing. I thought to myself, 'This guy is so interesting! I feel like I could talk to him forever!'"

James smiled. "That's cool."

"Yeah. It's been really nice getting to know him again."

"It's been nice getting to know *you*," James said. I flushed once more.

We finished our meals and left the restaurant, ambling aimlessly down Valencia Street. The Mission was fully awake now, with music, lights, and people pouring out of its doorways onto the sidewalk. James paused in front of a lively looking bar. "Do you want to stop for one more drink?"

"Sure." I was having a good time again. We stepped inside and threaded our way through the crowd until we found an empty loveseat—the only seat available. My pulse sped up when James slid in beside me and handed me a beer. "Thanks," I said. It was unnerving, being so close to him that our bodies were touching.

We must have talked some more, but I don't remember what we said. I don't remember him leaning in either, but suddenly he was kissing me.

Perhaps it's strange, but I've never been moved by a first kiss. The first kiss, for me, is an analysis, a weird exercise where I put my face against a stranger's and tally my observations. James' lips were incredibly soft. I don't know why that surprised me, but it did. I felt the rasp of his stubble press against my chin, but it didn't scratch. His kiss was very gentle.

Realizing I had my eyes open, I shut them hastily—but not before I got an up-close look at his kissing face. I felt oddly guilty, like I was spying on him. He smelled good. My brain spun, trying to process all the sensory details and spit out a verdict: *Do we like? Yes or no?*

While the cogs were still turning, James did a foolish thing. He heaved a happy sigh, opened his eyes and smiled at me, then rested his head on my shoulder.

"Do you have any idea how good it feels to hold you?" he asked me, dreamily.

Alarm bells rang in my head. My brain seized, then blared: *ABORT! ABORT!*

I leaned severely backward and his head slipped off my shoulder.

"Hey," I said gracelessly. "I don't mean to be rude, but you're starting to freak me out." I tried to smile, but it was an awkward rictus with too much teeth.

James laughed. I think he was a little embarrassed.

"Sorry," he said, withdrawing an arm that had somehow slipped around me. "I just . . . I just like you. A lot." He smiled quickly and dropped his gaze, but I could sense him studying my reaction beneath lowered lids.

"Thank you," I said. "I like you, too. But . . . " I paused. *How to explain?* "But I am really not ready for a relationship. I just want you to understand that. I don't want to be anybody's girlfriend."

"Should I not have kissed you?" he asked me.

I thought about it.

"The kiss was nice," I decided. "But the next part was a bit too much." *There. That was clear.* James nodded like he understood.

But as we left the bar he took hold of my hand. Gently, I slid it out of his grasp.

"Too much," I said softly.

"Sorry." He smiled, but it didn't quite reach his eyes.

Ever the gentleman, James insisted on driving me home, even though it was far out of his way. It was after eleven when we reached my place, which is late when there's church in the morning.

I turned to him, feeling awkward. "I don't want to field any questions at Mercy tomorrow," I said. "Can we keep our business to ourselves for now?"

"Of course," he said, graciously.

"I had a really nice time," I told him, and I meant it.

"So did I," James said. "Thanks for coming out with me."

I waited for him to kiss me good night. Now that the experimental first kiss was out of the way, I was ready to try it again. James cut a handsome profile in the dim light from the dashboard. He had a strong, fine jawline and chiseled cheekbones. I could just make out the cleft in his chin beneath the hint of beard. My gaze traveled down his neck, to the open collar of his shirt and the hair on his chest beneath. Suddenly I was very, very interested in kissing him. My lips parted slightly, and I waited.

But James didn't try again. "Good night," he said.

Disappointment seized me. I fumbled for the door and opened it. James remained firmly strapped into his seat with the engine running. He was not going to walk me to the door. I'd done a good job of discouraging him.

"Good night," I said, and he left.

Well, shit.

4

SECOND DATE

I looked forward to seeing James at church the next morning. I smiled when I caught his eye across the room. But he took matters beyond discretion, all but ignoring me whenever we crossed paths.

"Good morning," I said when I passed him in the hallway. He gave me a brief nod and kept walking.

I frowned. Was he mad at me for not kissing him? If so, I could sort of understand. *I* was mad at me for not kissing him.

I kept looking his way while we were on the risers, but he avoided my gaze. Finally, feeling somewhat miffed, I sought him out between services.

"Boy, if I hadn't been there last night, I'd swear we'd never gone on a date," I muttered, a little irritation in my voice.

He looked surprised. "You asked to keep it between us."

True. Still.

"You're sure good at acting like nothing happened!" I said.

He gave a blithe shrug. "I'm a very good secret-keeper," he replied and walked away.

But as he left, he brushed against me, accidentally-on-purpose, and his hand swept the back of my leg.

My heart banged; my stomach swooped. My brain telegraphed: *Next time, kiss him, dumbass.*

* * *

But it was three weeks before I would have another chance. True to his word, James didn't have a break in his schedule for nearly a month. Between his kids and his business trips, there wasn't much time left for a social life. In fact, I only laid eyes on him once during that entire time, the Wednesday after our date, when he brought his kids to choir rehearsal.

The girls sat in the front row of the sanctuary, knitting. I watched them covertly, chewing over my new knowledge of their family. *I went on a date with your dad,* I thought to myself. *Weird.*

Rehearsal wound to a close and choir members lingered, gathering belongings and chatting with friends. Annabelle ran onstage to hasten her father's departure, but Avery stayed seated in the pew, regarding her work with a critical eye. I approached her and gestured toward her yarn. "What are you knitting?" I asked. It was the first time I could recall speaking to her directly and she seemed a little taken aback.

"A scarf," she said. "We're going skiing at Lake Tahoe this weekend."

"Skiing? But it's May."

"It's spring skiing," she explained. I was not a skier, so this was news to me.

"That's cool," I said. "Sounds like fun."

"Yeah. But I need to get my scarf done before we go." I saw that she had knitted exactly one row in the last two hours. She had some work to do.

"Do you knit a lot?" I asked.

"I'm actually just learning," she replied. "I asked Annabelle to show me because they taught her at school. I had more rows done, but I had to take them out because my stitches were uneven."

"I'll give you a tip," I said. "If you pull the yarn tight after the second stitch, your whole row will tighten up."

She looked at me with big blue eyes, a touch wary of my advice. Or maybe she was just confused as to why I was talking to her for the first time ever. For a split second, we studied each other. She was a pretty kid. She had straight brown hair that hung to her shoulders and bee-stung lips, the kind that would be sexy when she grew up. At age ten she was a little gangly, mostly arms and legs. She had James' height, I saw when she stood, but Annabelle was already gaining on her.

James staggered over to join us, pulled as he was by Annabelle, who had his arm in a tight lock. "Can we go home?" she asked him. James ignored her. He was looking at me.

"Hi," I said.

"Hi."

"Avery was showing me her knitting," I explained lamely. "She said you guys are going skiing this weekend, and she's making a scarf."

"Dad, let's go," Annabelle requested again. Annabelle had soft brown eyes like James. Her hair was the same shade as Avery's, tied up in a messy ponytail. She had no interest in me.

"Yeah. We're going to Tahoe this weekend, and then next weekend I have a business trip, so I won't be around for a while." I knew this already, but I understood he was reminding me.

"Will you be back in time to sing at the Moffat auction?" I asked.

"I should be," James said. He gave me a little smile. "Are you going to be there?" I smiled back and nodded. Avery regarded us curiously.

"I'm planning on it," I said. "I guess I'll see you there."

"Dad, can we *go?*" Annabelle asked insistently. "It's nine o'clock! I have to go to bed!"

"I'd better head out," James said to me, as Annabelle tugged him off balance. "Annie, stop! Yes, we're leaving. Grab your coat."

"I'm wearing my coat!" exclaimed Annabelle.

"I didn't bring one," Avery said. "It's warm out."

"Okay then, let's go. Say goodbye to Marie." The kids mumbled goodbyes to me as they herded James toward the stairs. Over their heads he flashed me a brief but brilliant smile.

Okay, three weeks. I could wait three weeks.

* * *

"Morning, Ken," I greeted him as he walked in the door. "How are you doing?"

Ken hung his hat and jacket on the coat rack. "Doing good, doing good," he said. "Not too shabby for a Monday."

He switched on his computer, sat down, and leaned back contentedly in his chair. "This morning on the bus, I purposely sat between two really big ladies, so I wouldn't get bumped around," he said. "It was so nice and warm in there, I just went to sleep."

I laughed and leaned back in my own chair. "What'd you do this weekend?" I asked.

"Oh, I took a quick trip down to San Luis Obispo to visit my dad. He was bottling up some pinot."

"Oh yeah? Is he a winemaker?"

"No, he's a soil scientist for the forest service. He just likes to get drunk cheap." Ken turned on the radio and a soft bossa nova tune filled the room.

I had to admit, our job was really easy. We didn't have much to do beyond answer the phones and sort the mail. In fact, the only reason there were two of us was because sometimes all the phone lines lit up at once.

But our days were usually pretty mellow, so we had a lot of time to chat. I also had a lot of time to banter with James, and we'd been texting frequently. Ken saw me glance at my phone.

"What about you?" he asked, with a hint of suggestion in his voice. "Did you do anything good this weekend?"

"No, just hung out with my roommate. Hey, she's interviewing for the Marketing position." Mandy had decided to try her luck at the job.

But Ken had sensed he was onto something. "How about next weekend?" he pressed. "Any plans?"

I paused. I wasn't ready to tell him about James. Luckily the phone rang, interrupting our conversation.

"Roaming Expeditions," answered Ken. "One moment please, I'll see if he's available." He put the caller on hold and dialed an extension. "Hey, Kirk. There's a woman named Carrie Topless on the phone for you. *Bom-chicka-wow-wow!*"

The phone call was enough to divert him. "Hey, I forgot to tell you the true highlight of my weekend," he said. "When I was with my dad on Saturday, I sneezed nine times in a row and almost fainted! I think if I'd sneezed ten times, I would've died!"

* * *

The next Friday night was the Moffat auction, an annual fundraiser for Mercy. Walter Moffat, wealthy business magnate and notable philanthropist, auctioned off a lunch with himself every year and gave the proceeds to the church. The bidding was due to close on Friday evening at seven o'clock, and the choir was singing at the event.

I was eager to get out of the house, not only to see James, but because Mandy's aunt Beth was visiting. This, too, was an annual event.

"I just saw her when I went home for Christmas," Mandy complained. Already edgy over her job interview, the impending visit had not improved her mood.

"That was five months ago," I pointed out.

"Still. We'll have nothing new to say to each other."

I'd met Beth the previous year and I knew it was true. Mandy's aunt wasn't much of a conversationalist. She insisted on visiting regularly, but she didn't want to go anywhere or do anything. This drove busy Mandy insane. She'd tried to take her aunt on all sorts of outings, but Beth didn't seem to recognize fun. Eventually Mandy resorted to her regular schedule and just let Beth follow her around like an intern. In fact, Beth planned to accompany Mandy on her job interview and sit in the hallway.

"Are you going to be around this weekend?" she asked me hopefully.

Uh-oh. "I have a Mercy gig on Friday night," I said. I hoped she wouldn't ask about Saturday, when I was scot-free.

She frowned. "Damn. I'm trying to figure out what to do on Friday. On Saturday I'm taking her to Muir Woods."

"Didn't you do that last year?"

"We've done that for the last two years."

"Oh. Does she really like it?"

"No. But it fills the day."

I changed the subject. "I'm going out with James again after the gig."

Mandy brightened. "Second date! Wow. What took so long?"

"His schedule is crazy," I said. "It seems like he's always on a business trip."

"What does he do?"

I stopped and thought. "Something with batteries?" I said slowly. I was horrible at remembering peoples' jobs. "He manages a branch of a battery company. I think." He seemed successful.

"Hmm. Where's he taking you?"

"I don't know. We're going to play it by ear. My biggest concern is sneaking out of the gig together without anybody following us."

"Hey, could we come?" she asked hopefully. "Not on your date, but to the other part?"

"Sorry, it's a closed event," I said apologetically.

"Eh. Just grasping at straws. Beth probably wouldn't want to go anyway." Mandy heaved a sigh. "I guess we'll rent a movie. Hey, if your date gets romantic, you might want to take it to his house. She'll be sleeping on the pullout couch."

"Thanks for the warning." Ours was technically a one-bedroom house, and I slept in the converted dining room. I could hear the living room activities loud and clear from behind my bedroom door. I could only imagine it worked the same way in reverse.

The Moffat gig was at San Francisco's Ferry Building. I'd never been on the upper level before and it was a cool venue, with balconies overlooking the marketplace below. To the choir's delight, it was one of those fancy gigs with free food and alcohol. We wolfed down as much as we could before singing.

Across the crowd, I spotted James. He gave me a little smile.

For the past three weeks, we'd been texting and emailing, our messages increasing in intensity. We were getting to know one another and flirting like crazy. It was great fun.

I knew, for instance, just how much he'd been looking forward to this evening. His kids had accused him of being distracted while they were skiing in Tahoe. Avery was particularly perceptive. "Why are you smiling so much?" she'd asked him.

And James knew that I wasn't interested in anything serious. "I fall too fast," I'd confessed during one late-night text session. "I'm a serial monogamist. I just want to take some time and date around." I'd even told him about my International Men of Mystery plan.

The funny thing was, James didn't appear interested in a casual fling. I thought most men would jump at the suggestion, but he claimed it wasn't his style. He had a complex set of rules for romance, I learned. These included: *Only date single mums* and *No sex until Date 10.* It was clear this guy had been hurt before.

So, I wasn't entirely sure where we were going with this second date, but since he'd already broken the single mums rule, it appeared these were not set in stone. In any case, neither of us seemed willing to call it off.

Now I watched him across the room. For a while we orbited one another, chatting with friends, on course to connect. When we wound up in the same group of people, he said to me casually, "Gelato?" and offered me a lick from his ice cream cone.

I raised my eyebrows, certain that someone would pick up on our intimacy. But nobody was paying any attention to us. I took a quick lick of icy chocolate. "It's good," I said. James' eyes were alight. He wore a gray corduroy jacket over a white button-down shirt. The shirt was open at the collar in an appealing sort of way. My gaze lingered on his neckline for a moment too long.

"Mercy Ensemble, on stage!" someone called.

There was no stage, per se, but we congregated at the front of the room. The choir sang three numbers, then paused for speeches by Reverend Lewis and his wife, Mae. Mae was Mercy's founding president and a great lover of speech giving, and when she took the mic, I heard a few people around me sigh. This meant we'd be standing for at least ten more minutes. I shifted a bit in my attractive, uncomfortable boots.

After the speeches, the Ensemble sang one more upbeat tune, then disbanded. A DJ replaced us on stage and the party kicked into high gear. Some folks began dancing. Others made a mad rush for the bar. I caught James' eye across the room.

He dipped his head in a discreet signal. Immediately I gathered up my purse. Dispensing with my usual round of goodbyes, I hurried down the steps and out onto the sidewalk. A minute later James was at my side.

"Oh, are you leaving, too?" I asked, all faux innocence.

"I am," he said. "I have a date."

"Really? Where are you going?"

"North Beach. And let's hurry up before somebody tries to tag along with us." He took my hand and led me away.

In North Beach, we settled on a little Italian place off Columbus Avenue, where we split a pizza and a bottle of wine. The night was warm and we sat side by side at an outdoor table, enjoying the neighborhood. James glanced at me appreciatively. "That's a really nice dress," he said.

I was sucked into a zebra-striped mini-dress with long sleeves and a deep V-neck. I'd paired it with black leggings and high-heeled black boots. I felt confident and sexy, and I was thrilled when James ran his gaze over me.

But when he said, "Are you up for walking?" I wilted a little bit. My sexy boots weren't exactly comfortable.

"What did you have in mind?" I asked.

"I know a very romantic spot," he said. "But it involves climbing a hill."

Well, that settled it. Comfort trumped sexy without a fight. "Let's do it," I said. "Just give me a second to change my shoes."

As a former New Yorker, I never went anywhere without shoes that I could walk in. James' face fell noticeably when I pulled a pair of flats out of my large purse. He looked as though he'd undressed me and discovered a bra stuffed with Kleenex.

"Were your boots uncomfortable?" he asked lamely.

"Yes," I said.

"Oh. You looked really nice in them."

I sighed. *Men.* I didn't see any of them walking around on stilts, trying to attract women. He was just going to have to deal with it. "Thank you," I said. I shoved the boots in my bag and gave him a measured look. "Shall we go?"

For a minute he stared sadly at my shoes. Then he raised his gaze to mine and grinned. "I'll race you."

We chased each other up the hill, laughing the whole way. "Are we going all the way up to Coit Tower?" I asked, panting.

"Not quite," he said. He led me along a path and we emerged after a while in a curious little neighborhood. The houses faced inward along a series of staircases that switchbacked above and below us, farther than I could see in either direction. Trees and shrubbery pressed in on us as we wandered slowly down the steps, marveling at the nearly full moon above. Occasionally a gap in the foliage offered views of the city sprawled out below.

"This is amazing," I said. "Where are we?"

But James ignored my question. He took me by the wrist and drew me to him. "I've been wanting to do this all night," he said, then leaned in to kiss me.

This time my whole body responded; electricity shot through my wrist where he held me, all the way up my arm and down my other side. I moved in and kissed him back urgently, scraping my lips against the rasp of his chin. He pressed up against me and the breath caught in my throat. I could feel his muscles beneath his clothes and his belt buckle poking anxiously against my knit dress.

When our kiss broke apart, James continued to hold me close. In an achingly beautiful gesture, he ran his hand over my hair, then down the length of my face. No one had ever done that to me before. It was the kind of thing that happens in the movies, but rarely in real life.

"You look beautiful," James said softly.

"Thank you," I breathed.

A rustling nearby announced people coming up the stairs. "Let's keep moving," I said.

But it was a long, slow descent. Every few minutes James stopped and pulled me into a clinch. By the time we reached the street below, my lips were swollen and raw. It was close to midnight.

"Should I take you home with me?" James asked, kissing the side of my face.

I pulled back a little. "What about your kids?"

He kissed the hollow beneath my ear. "Sleeping over with friends."

My insides were molten and I was dying to go home with him. But my feelings hadn't changed; I still didn't want to pursue anything serious. I told him so.

I could see emotions battling across his face as he made his decision. He took a deep breath and stepped back. I saw him adjust his pants slightly.

"Okay," he said. "I'd better take you home. To your own house."

But he seemed to change his mind when we were in the car. At every junction before the bridge he asked, "Are we sure?" until I was laughing.

"Are *you* sure?" I countered. "These are your rules."

He sighed heavily. "Yeah."

Fifteen minutes later he pulled up outside my house and parked the car. This time he stopped the engine and looked at me with longing.

"You can't come in," I said apologetically. "My roommate's aunt is asleep on our couch."

"Probably a good thing," he murmured as he stroked my hair. "Otherwise I'm pretty sure I'd break one of my rules."

"You know," I told him, leaning in, "some rules are meant to be broken."

"Not this one," he said, but even as he said it, he was kissing me.

James seemed to be in no hurry to drive away. The front seats of his car had a deep recline, we discovered, but the center console was a nuisance. I laughed as we tried awkwardly to navigate around it. It wasn't sexy.

"Hang on," James said, and after some fumbling, I wound up straddling him in the passenger seat. I looked down at him and the laughter died in my throat.

"Now *this* is sexy," he whispered, and pulled me down to him.

The car windows fogged up around us. For hours—truly, hours—we sat in that little car, kissing and talking and laughing. James' hand tried to edge up my dress, but he drew back in confusion when he didn't find skin.

"Leggings," I said. "Sorry."

"Leggings? What are leggings? How far up do they go?" he asked, his hand patting around inquisitively.

"All the way up. They're like tights without feet," I explained, and I saw the flash of recognition. He had little girls.

"Oh. I hate tights," he said, withdrawing his hand. "Now I hate them even more." I laughed.

James dropped back against the seat and regarded me. "You know what?"

"What?"

"This doesn't feel weird."

"Um, thanks?" I said.

"No, I mean . . . it's nice to laugh with you. Making out isn't always . . . *fun* like this. But I'm having fun with you." He smiled shyly at me.

I smiled back. "Thank you." I kissed him on the nose. "I'm having fun with you, too."

James' smile widened. "Also," he said, "you're really fucking hot." I threw my head back and laughed as he pressed me up against the dashboard. My hair traced ribbons across the steamed-up windshield as his lips found the cleft in my dress.

At four a.m. I finally crawled out of the car. My legs were so cramped that I nearly fell onto the pavement when I opened the door.

"Thank you for a lovely evening," James said, giving me one final kiss.

"I had a wonderful time," I said. My voice sounded loud in the early-morning air, and I dropped it to a whisper. "Get home safe."

I straightened my dress and dug into my purse for my keys. As quietly as I could I unlocked the front door, stepped inside, and closed it behind me. I could see the lump of someone's body passed out cold on the couch.

As I tiptoed across the living room, Mandy's groggy voice startled me.

"Was it good?" she mumbled.

I paused. "It was really, really great."

"Awesome," she replied. Then she conked back out.

5

THIRD DATE

"So, two more weeks until you see him again?" Mandy asked me the next morning.

I'd barely slept, having been awakened early by breakfast noises in the kitchen. Now Beth was in the shower and Mandy was curled over a bowl of cereal.

"Yeah," I said, pulling a mournful face. I yawned and reached for a teacup, switching on the burner beneath the kettle. "I swear, he's the busiest guy I've ever met. It's going to take us six weeks to accomplish three dates."

"Third date," Mandy mused. She raised an eyebrow at me. "Are you going to sleep with him?"

I laughed, feeling a little self-conscious, and shrugged. "I don't know. It's kind of up to him." I plopped down on a kitchen chair. "He's got all these rules for self-conduct that are kinda cramping my style." Mandy grinned. "I mean, here I am, trying to have loose morals for the first time in my life, and the first guy I like is having a morality complex."

"Just your luck," said Mandy.

"Isn't it?" I paused, thoughtful. "He's awfully nice though. I feel very . . . comfortable with him."

I hadn't slept with a lot of men in my life and the thought of adding someone new to that list, while titillating, was also scary. But James didn't scare me. I knew instinctively that he would treat me with care.

Our written conversations were getting more intense.

> Marie,
> Today was a great day. I took the girls to Chrissy Field to fly kites. It was totally gorgeous out and the kids were happy running around. And I found myself wishing you were there to share the moment with us. It kind of scared me to feel that after only two dates. For the last several years, I haven't let anyone I've dated meet my kids.
> I'm not sure what to make of that.

> James,
> On one hand, it would be nice to spend time with your kids. On the other hand, that sounds pretty serious. And we're not doing serious. Right?
> But since you brought it up, let me lay a heavy hypothetical on you: Would you even want more kids one day? Because eventually, I want to get married and have my own children. I don't get the sense that you're looking for that.
> So, we can step forward and have no expectations . . . Or you can decide that feelings are running too high to go any further right now.

But you should probably make that call before we have another date because you suck at keeping your hands to yourself.

Marie,

OK. Let's talk seriously for a minute.

You know some of my history. I spent fifteen years in a brutal relationship with an awful woman. She manipulated me to get the things she wanted and chased away people I cared about. And she will always be in my life now, which sucks. The worst part is watching her control my kids.

If I'd had a good marriage, I do think I would have wanted another child. I had a vasectomy after Annabelle was born because Jess demanded it. I remember the doctor asking me if everything was good at home and lying to him. I remember feeling like complete shit. I have thought about reversing the vasectomy, but at this stage in my life there's no point. All I can say is I regret doing it.

So, to answer your question—would I ever want to have another child? The answer is maybe. I didn't get to have a baby with a wife that I loved. That whole process should be amazing . . . and in my life, it wasn't.

But I love my children. They are the best. And the idea of bringing another child into this house is awesome.

So, I need to think about what to do next. If we go to bed together, how will I feel the next day? So far, I feel blissful with you, and I want to keep it that way.

James,
Well, maybe the sex will be crap and we can stop all this needless worrying.

Marie,
With the kind of chemistry we have? We both know it will be amazing.

I couldn't sleep that night.

* * *

We scheduled a third date for the following Friday. We didn't talk about what it meant. On Thursday evening, I tucked a few overnight articles into my purse.

But on Friday morning I woke up with a scratchy throat. Once vertical, I realized that my nose was also runny. *Damn.* I closed my eyes and willed myself not to be sick.

It was a busy day at work with lots of phone calls. Just as I hung up with one client, the phone rang again.

"Roaming Ek-shpeditions," answered Ken. After transferring the call, he complained, "I don't know what's wrong with me! All week long I've been having trouble with the word 'ex-pe-di-tions'. Ever since I made fun of Sean Connery last week, I can't say it right."

I sneezed.

"How are you feeling over there?" he asked, not-so-surreptitiously wheeling his chair further from mine. "You sound kind of sick."

"I'm good," I assured him.

"Really? 'Cause you've killed a box of Kleenex already."

"No, no, I'm great," I said. "I mean, I can't breathe through my nose, but I'm upbeat about it." I popped a lozenge into my mouth.

"Are you going to cancel your date?"

I had finally told Ken about James the previous week. "Aha!" he'd said. "My Spidey Senses were tingling."

Now I shook my head. "No, I don't want to cancel. It'll be weeks before we can get together again. James leaves for another business trip on Sunday night. Dude's busier than the President." I sneezed again twice, in quick succession.

Ken frowned. "You guys should go to a nice quiet movie. That way you can take a nap in the middle if you need to."

"Don't worry," I said. "I'm going to the pharmacy on my lunch break. I'll get all kinds of drugs. By five o'clock, I'll be in great shape."

"Pick me up some hand sanitizer," Ken requested from far across the room.

By quitting time, I was giddy with cough syrup and nerves. I had texted James to warn him of my potential contagion. He was undaunted—no doubt fueled as I was by two weeks' worth of sexually charged text messages.

We decided to take another shot at the food trucks, this time at Fort Mason. I met James there at five-thirty, arriving on foot just as he was getting out of his car. He wore jeans, a black pullover sweater, and a happy, nervous smile.

"Remember, I'm a little bit sick," I warned him as he approached. I tried to turn my face away from his hug.

"I don't care," said James, and he kissed me. I held the kiss as long as I could—until my nose threatened to drip on his sweater. Then I broke away, hoping he wouldn't notice.

It was a beautiful evening; the weather was mild and the sun would shine for several hours. James offered me his hand and I took it gladly. We strolled toward the food trucks in no particular hurry.

"I've been distracted all day," he told me. "I totally blanked out in a meeting because I was thinking about our date."

"Me too," I confessed. "I accidentally hung up on a client when I was trying to transfer her call. She was pretty annoyed when she called back." James laughed.

I gave him a gentle elbow in the ribs. "Hey, it's not funny. I've got a good job; I can't go screwing it up because I'm distracted by . . . thoughts of you."

He gave me an intense look. "Maybe we'd better have sex before we both lose our jobs."

My face reddened. I opened my mouth for a smart retort, but it turned into a cough. Suddenly I was doubled over, hacking furiously. James bent down beside me, alarmed.

"Are you okay?"

I nodded, drawing ragged breaths.

"I'm sorry," he said quickly. "I was just kidding. We don't have to do anything tonight. We can just chill out on the couch and watch a movie. I just want to spend time with you."

I got my coughing under control. "I don't want to make you sick."

"I won't get sick," James said confidently. "I have this special cough syrup from Canada. It tastes disgusting, but it works. I'll give you some."

"I've already had half a bottle of cough syrup today," I said, showing him the pharmacy in my purse. "I'm actually feeling kind of high."

James laughed. "Okay, well, maybe you should eat something."

The food trucks formed a circle in Fort Mason's parking lot. James and I strolled the perimeter, stopping to sample the various wares. The hands-down winner was a bright red truck featuring Coca-Cola-braised pork buns. "These are awesome," James said. I agreed, but refused a second helping. The night still had the potential to get romantic, if my nose would stop dripping.

"So, what shall we do now?" James asked, when we'd had our fill. "It's still early. Do you want to get a drink? Or should we head for my house?"

James' house was on the Peninsula, forty-five minutes from my own and in the complete opposite direction. We both knew I wasn't going over there to watch a casual movie. I was going to spend the night.

Nerves suddenly overtook me. "I don't have sexy pajamas," I blurted out. "I wear sweatpants. I packed sweatpants." *Oh God.*

He grinned. "I don't like sexy pajamas," he said. "My ex used to spend lots of money on sexy pajamas and then not have sex with me."

I smiled. "Then let's go to your place."

* * *

"I have to warn you," James said, as we pulled into his driveway, "my house is kind of bizarre."

"Bizarre? In what way?"

"You'll see. My landlord has some really . . . particular tastes."

As soon as we entered the house I saw that he wasn't kidding. The kitchen was painted in arresting shades of red and yellow. Colorful clay tablets depicting the Italian countryside dotted the walls. Closer inspection revealed that they were plastered directly *into* the walls.

"Yeah, they don't come off," commented James, as I pried at one experimentally with my finger.

The cabinets were painted with murals of San Francisco. I spotted Coit Tower, Fisherman's Wharf, and an unfinished Golden Gate Bridge. The bridge was merely sketched in, and a large pocket of unpainted white cabinet drew the eye.

"I think he ran out of money before he could get it finished," James said.

I was surprised. "You mean this was commissioned? I thought he must have done it himself." It was not the best artwork I'd ever seen.

"Oh yeah. Take a peek in my bedroom."

I poked my head into the room off the kitchen. Just like mine, James' bedroom had once been the dining room, but his had a sliding glass door that led onto a back deck. Another mural covered the wall, this one featuring karst islands rising from a body of water. I squinted at it. "Is that . . . Vietnam?" I asked. It sort of resembled the pictures I'd seen at work of Halong Bay.

"Is it?" said James. "I have no idea."

"It looks like it. But . . . well, it doesn't really fit with the rest of the theme." I surveyed the plastic grapevines that festooned the kitchen chandelier. Maybe there was no theme.

"Go check out the kids' bathroom," James instructed. "Down the hall." I followed his directions and stopped short.

"Holy shit," I called back over my shoulder. "What the hell is this?"

The kids' bathroom was painted dark blue. The ceiling and walls were covered in stucco to create a cratered moonscape, a bizarre 3D effect. It looked like an amateur movie set—or perhaps a climbing gym.

James came up behind me. "Are we supposed to be underwater or in outer space?" I asked him.

"I don't know," he said. "This room mystifies me."

"Do the kids like it?"

"No, the kids hate it. They think it's weird."

I wandered on, continuing my tour. "This is Avery's room," James said. Avery's room was pretty normal. It was also the only bedroom with a door, I noticed.

Annabelle's room seemed to be a converted den. One wall was dominated by bookcases. While there were a few children's books on the lower shelves, most seemed to be thick novels, and two entire shelves were dedicated to *National Geographic* magazines.

"Those are the landlord's," James explained. "He left a bunch of his stuff here and he comes by entirely too often to access it. His car's even in my garage." James shrugged. "But the rent's affordable and we're in a good school district, which is all I care about."

"Um, have you looked through these books?" I asked, scanning the shelves.

"No, why?"

"I don't think all of them are appropriate for your kid's room." I plucked a thin volume off the shelf. "'*The Sensuous*

Woman,'" I read the title aloud. "'The first how-to book for the female who yearns to be all woman.'"

"*What?*" James exclaimed, pulling it out of my hands. He flipped through it rapidly. "Oh shit."

"'Masturbation,'" I read over his shoulder. "'Hand Manipulation. How to Drive a Man to Ecstasy.' Wow, this is just the Table of Contents?"

"'Men's Fantasies, One Through Six,'" James read. "'Pleasing the Polygamist? *Party Sex—Swapping and Orgies?*'" He sounded stricken.

"Do you think Annabelle has seen this?" I asked, laughing. "I mean, these are important lessons for an eight-year-old girl."

He didn't respond, just flipped through the chapters.

"Wait, slow down! 'That Thing That Turns Him On You Think Is Sick.' Oh my God!"

At that, James snapped the book shut. "I'm getting rid of this," he said.

Back in the kitchen, James trashed the offending book and offered me a glass of wine.

"Thanks," I said, taking it. I glanced around his living room. Little girl things were strewn about: a hairbrush, a backpack, some plastic beaded jewelry. There were quite a few young adult books scattered on the chairs and coffee table.

"Are your kids big readers?" I asked.

"Not so much Annabelle, but Avery loves to read. She goes through a ton of books. Good thing *The Sensuous Woman* wasn't in her room." He shuddered.

We stood for a few minutes in companionable silence, sipping our wine. I was surprised by how comfortable I felt. I had wondered, without realizing it, what James' house was like. I'd observed him over the years, in little snippets, both with and without his kids. But I didn't know any other full-time single dads. It hadn't hit me, how . . . *immersive* it was, until I entered their home.

Because it was *their* home, I saw. It was not the house of a part-time dad, with a few kid toys stashed away for the weekends. This was a family's house. There were board games stacked under the coffee table and a plastic pony forgotten on the armchair. When I sat on the couch, it made a crinkling sound—a math worksheet, trapped beneath the cushions. James pulled it out and tossed it onto the table. "Sorry," he said with a smile. "I've been out of town. I didn't have much of a chance to clean up."

I wasn't bothered by the moderate clutter. In fact, I found it welcoming, even a little endearing. James' life was so different from mine, I had thought. He'd been married before; he traveled all the time for his big-deal job . . . he seemed so *adult*. Meanwhile, I was living with a roommate again at age thirty-three. But looking around James' living room—at the little-girl sock peeking out from beneath the couch and the *Harry Potter* books stacked haphazardly on the end table—I felt completely at ease. I felt like I understood this place.

"I like your house," I told him.

He smiled. "I like you," he said simply, and leaned in to kiss me.

We didn't pretend to watch a movie. We didn't finish our wine. We moved into his ridiculously painted bedroom and lay down together, patient, unhurried, entwined.

As he moved astride me, I may have gasped—something caught his attention and he froze, looking at me with concern. "Are you in pain?" he asked.

He didn't say, "Did I hurt you?" in that typical macho way that suggested that his Giant Manhood was certainly capable of it. He asked me, "Are you in pain?" For some reason, this choice of words struck me, laid me naked in a completely different way. I looked into his eyes and saw such kindness there. I had not known, until then, how desperately ready I was for kindness.

I smiled at him, and he opened his mouth wide in a soundless laugh. It was like his joy needed an escape route. James didn't wear his heart on his sleeve, I'd learned; he kept his emotions pretty close. But I saw that he was naked, too. He had laid himself bare in front of me, and as I'd known he would, he loved me with extreme care.

And then he loved me with extreme care five more times.

6

SECRET SUMMER

Thus began the best summer of my adult life. It was the summer of secret sex: an affair kept from our mutual friends—and of course, James' children. Since the kids spent every other week with their mother during the summer, James and I were able to spend considerably more time together, and we made excellent use of it.

Naturally, after our third date we both were sick. My cold reared up with a vengeance and took James down, too. But it couldn't dampen our romance. I met him at the airport as he returned from his business trip, and we spent another weekend in bed, swapping germs.

I was having a fantastic time. Secret rendezvous suited me to a tee. I awoke every morning upbeat and passed my days in great humor.

And I found that I appreciated my nights alone just as much as those spent with James. Despite all my big talk about staying single, it was against my habit to take things slow. I'd never really done it before, and I probably wouldn't have succeeded this time if James weren't so busy. Since I was only able to see him every other week, I had time to anticipate our dates—and that in itself was an unexpected thrill.

What's more, I used my time alone to great effect, enjoying my friends, my solitude, and just about everything that crossed my path. It was a downright golden time. I was unreasonably happy.

* * *

"Do you think we should hang out with the kids?" James asked me, his fingers twined through mine.

We were lying together in my bed, wasting away a Sunday afternoon. We'd had church, then brunch, then sex, and it had been a lovely day.

"Why, do you?" I asked. It wasn't the first time he'd brought it up.

Hanging out with the kids ran contrary to everything we'd agreed upon, but we kept flirting with the idea. In marathon texting sessions that ran late into the night, James would describe his kids and the daily ups and downs of their household. I became enthralled with the tiny sagas of Avery's pierced ears and Annabelle's new "frenemy", Shelby.

I was hyperaware of these children in a new way, and it didn't sit entirely easily with me. These kids didn't factor into my carefree summer—or my overall life—so why did I care that Shelby, that little punk, had not invited Annabelle to her birthday party?

The kids were becoming aware of me, too. A few weeks ago, I'd arrived at choir practice early and sat knitting. I admit that this was a calculated move on my part. As I'd suspected (as I'd hoped?), Annabelle saw what I was doing and weaved her way through the room to appear at my side. It was as if she were a cat, attracted to my yarn.

She leaned over the arm of my chair in that utterly unselfconscious way of children. At age eight, she was not yet enveloped in the bubble of her personal space. She ran a hand over my yarn. "What are you making?" she asked me.

I wasn't making a damn thing. I was laying a trap.

"A scarf," I lied.

"Oh. Who's it for?"

"It's for a friend."

Annabelle jabbered on for a while about all the colors of yarn she had, and I observed her. Although it was summer, she was wearing a red wool coat with black toggle buttons. The coat had clearly seen better days and it could no longer cover her growing arms, but she wore it everywhere and often kept it on indoors. She leaned her upper body across the cushioned arm of my chair, her little denim butt poking up in the air. I had a sudden urge to hug her to me, but kept my cool.

Across the room, I saw James watching us intently. My heart seemed to beat a little harder when I caught his gaze.

At the end of rehearsal both kids hugged me, unprompted. I was startled. James' kids weren't big huggers. In the effusive Mercy crowd, they stood apart, reserved. I caught a whiff of their clean hair as they threw their skinny arms around me and felt that throbbing in my chest again.

Maybe I was having a heart attack.

Later that night James texted:

> *Are you sitting down? I just put the kids to bed. As I gave her a hug, Avery said, "Out of all the girls at Mercy, if you ever get married again, you should marry Marie." Thank God the lights were off and she*

couldn't see my face! I asked her why and she said,
"Marie is just really nice."

Clearly there was an energy circulating between the four of us, and the kids had been on both of our minds.

Now I raised myself up on one elbow. The afternoon light shone through my yellow curtains, illuminating James in a beautiful way. I loved the hair on his chest. When I lay my face against it, it was silky and soft. Falling asleep against James' chest was a delight that I'd never expected. In fact, so many things about him were unexpectedly delightful.

He made me feel loved. Which was, I realized, a separate thing from being *in* love. I knew that if we parted ways tomorrow, I'd still feel that for the rest of my life. I looked at our fingers wrapped together and thought of our bodies wrapped together moments before.

I decided that, sometimes, sex is its own kind of love: beautiful and elemental and independent of the rest of it. I imagined telling my daughter one day that there are no rules to sex, but that she should be ready, be safe, and be loved.

I imagined telling James' daughters this.

And suddenly, I saw myself doing everything I'd said I wasn't going to do. The romantic inside me was skipping gaily toward new love. The silly bitch was twirling on a mountain top like Julie Andrews, envisioning a lovely life with a houseful of adoring stepchildren.

I looked at James reclining against the pillows in my bed and realized I needed to take a step back.

"You know," I said, "I haven't been on a date with anybody else all summer."

There was a brief silence as he studied me. I was slightly uncomfortable.

"I just think . . . before we involve the kids, I should probably do that. It might . . . clarify how I feel."

James nodded. "Okay." He sat up and pulled on his shirt. The lazy intimacy of the moment was gone.

"Hey," I said. I held his arm to prevent him from getting out of bed, but then I didn't know what to say. "It's just . . ." I hesitated, then decided to speak plainly.

"I really like you," I said. "And I'm afraid that it would be too easy to slip into a relationship with you, and your kids. But for all my talk of meeting new people, I haven't made any effort to do that. So, I need to measure this against something." I spread my hands, unconsciously miming a scale, seeking balance. "I need to make informed decisions. If you and I have something here, I want to go into it with my eyes open." I faltered, out of words.

James looked at me for a long moment and I couldn't read his expression. Finally, he said, "Then speed it up. Go online, make a profile. Go on some dates. Either it feels right or it doesn't." His voice was neutral but removed.

"You could do the same," I suggested.

"No. I get where you're coming from, but that doesn't feel right for me." He reached for his glasses on the nightstand and slid them on. "Honestly, I've had to close some doors to be open to you. But I trust you to talk to me if you think I could get hurt. And I trust that you'll put an end to us if we don't feel right or if something else does." He paused. "An innocent kiss wouldn't bug me. I'm sure you can figure out what would."

Then he kissed me, rather hard, on the lips.

* * *

So, I registered with *PairUp*, a free online dating service. I'd never tried online dating before, and it was kind of interesting to surf through the catalog of available men near me.

Some of them I ruled out immediately. Men with profile names like *Regener8Liver* and *yummymale* weren't what I was looking for. In fact, *yummymale* appeared to be looking for other yummy males. I wondered about the success ratio of this website.

It was fun at first. I could see how many men had viewed my profile, and it was exciting whenever somebody sent me a private message. Although nobody struck my fancy, I figured I had to start somewhere, so I made a date with Eddie, a very nice, very tall fellow from Kenya.

Eddie had won a visa lottery to come to the United States and study law. He had left his extensive family behind and come to America to make a better life. Eddie had twelve brothers and sisters, some of whom he barely knew because they were just little kids when he left for San Francisco. He had a fascinating background, a charming accent, and a sweet personality—he was a prime candidate for an International Man of Mystery.

And yet I spent our entire date thinking about James— who met me at my house later that evening for an enjoyable romp.

I wasn't too good at this "dating around" thing.

But I kept trying. Carl was an Oakland police officer. His profile didn't blow me away, but he was responsive, decent looking, and didn't make any grammatical mistakes in his correspondence. My standards had dropped significantly within a few short weeks.

We arranged to meet at a local restaurant on a Thursday evening. (My weekend was reserved for James.) At work that afternoon, Ken wanted details about the date. Second only to Mandy, he kept close tabs on my love life. "This is the copper, right?" he asked me.

"Yeah, he's OPD," I said. I felt kind of weird saying it; it sounded so official.

"Nice!" Ken's eyes lit up. "Think he'll take you on a ride-along?"

"Geez, I hope not."

"But that would be rad! Then you could go down to the precinct and help him put the squeeze on a coupla perps!"

I shook my head. "Sorry to disappoint you, but we're just going out to dinner. I'm supposed to meet him at a restaurant at six."

"Oh. Well, that sounds nice, too," said Ken politely.

It dawned on me that I'd forgotten the name of the restaurant. So, I quickly logged onto *PairUp* and scrolled through my messages to find the correspondence with Carl.

At first, I couldn't spot it. Then I realized he'd changed his profile picture, which made my eye skip right past his message. I squinted at the screen. What was this new picture? I clicked on the image to enlarge it.

"Oh no," I said.

"What?"

"Ken, come over here."

Ken came over to my desk and looked at my screen. "Are you looking at porn?" he asked, confused.

"No! That's my *date!*"

Carl's new profile image was a tight shot of his pelvis. The picture spanned from belly button to upper thigh. He wore tighty-whities and displayed a small bulge.

I looked at Ken in horror. "What do I do?"

He stroked his mustache in contemplation. "That's an interesting choice you've made," he said. "If I'd known you were into that, I could've introduced you to some guys."

"I'm *not* into that!" I said, appalled. "He changed his profile picture! Yesterday it was a nice, normal picture of his face!"

Ken regarded the screen again. "Do you think he's sending you a message?"

I gasped. "Oh shit! Do *you* think he's sending me a message?"

"Maybe."

"Oh no!" I wheeled away from my computer, shaking my head. "No, no, no!"

"This is a bold move," said Ken. "This is a man without fear."

"What do I do?" I asked again. "Our date starts in three hours! I can't cancel at the last minute, can I?" Above all things, I hated to be rude—especially to an officer of the law.

Ken just stroked his mustache.

I wrung my hands in dismay. "This is misrepresentation!" I complained. "I signed up for a nice, normal face picture. Now it's a blatant crotch shot!" I pointed at the evidence onscreen. "This man is a *police officer*, for God's sake!"

"Well he *is* arresting," Ken deadpanned.

I turned to him. "Help me," I said urgently. "What do I do?" Rational thought had fled me. I realized that I didn't remember what Carl's face looked like. How was I going to find him at the restaurant? I'd have to scan everybody's crotch.

"Marie," Ken said seriously, "don't go out with that dude."

Relief flooded through me and I heaved a huge sigh. "Thank you."

The phone rang, and Ken returned to his desk to answer it. "Roaming Expeditions . . . Who may I say is calling? Just one moment please." He put the caller on hold and dialed an extension. "Hey Kirk, Carrie Topless is calling again about her Bhutan trip. That gal should have her own show. *Ba-dum-bum!*"

He hung up, then said to me, "I am a little disappointed that you won't be dating a police officer. 'Cause I've got this pick-up line that would sound so much better coming from a cop; check it out: 'Are your parents drug dealers? 'Cause you're so dope!'"

* * *

The next guy to contact me came on strong.

> Hi Gorgeous,
>
> I am seeking a discreet, NSA FWB who can keep up with me intellectually and sexually. Believe you could—in spades. Would be great to meet in person, maybe over lunch, and take it from there. Interested? I know that I am.
> Magic Shaun

I decided I was done with online dating.

7

GETTING SERIOUS

The first time I hung out with James' kids, it was without any prior planning. We'd spent another beautiful Sunday afternoon lounging in my bed. Evening was approaching and it was nearly time for James to pick up the girls, but he lingered, unwilling to leave.

He threaded his fingers through my curls. "The kids start school again next week," he said, sounding wistful.

"Already? Man, the summer went by so fast!" I sighed.

"Yeah." He kissed the top of my head. "Our schedule's going to change again. They'll be back with me full time, and I'll be free only every other weekend. I'll have less time to spend with you."

I knew this was coming, but it was still a bummer. I gave him a little squeeze.

James leaned over and looked at the clock. "Shit, I've really gotta get going. I'm going to be late."

Reluctantly, I released him. He stood up and paused for a minute, gazing down at me. "Why don't you come with me to get the girls?"

I sat up. "Really?"

"Yeah. Come with me."

"But . . . what would we tell them? Why would I be with you?"

He thought. "We could say we were at a Mercy event and I'm bringing you home. And then we can spontaneously decide to go out for dinner."

This sounded flimsy to me. "But what if they ask more questions?"

"They won't."

"But what if they do?"

"Marie," he sounded a little exasperated. "I'm the grown-up. I don't have to answer their questions."

Oh. Right.

"Hurry up," he urged, pulling on his clothes. He'd spent the night at my place and now he was throwing belongings into his backpack. I jumped out of bed and into my jeans, but I couldn't find the shirt I'd been wearing—James had a habit of flinging my clothes across the room as he undressed me. I pulled on a fresh shirt and tried to tame my hair.

We met the girls in the back corner of the Home Depot parking lot, a convenient ten minutes from my house. The home improvement store was the court-appointed spot for the kid exchange. It was supposed to be neutral ground, but James had developed a fierce hatred for the place.

When we arrived, the kids were already there, waiting in the back of their mom's car. James pulled up on Jessica's passenger side, putting himself between us, but I caught a glimpse of her profile: she wore a ponytail and dark glasses. I saw her notice me, turning her head toward our car.

"Her manservant's not with her tonight," James observed. "That's unusual."

He was referring to her husband. Apparently, Max was the one who usually drove the kids back and forth. Sometimes Jessica came with him, often she didn't, but somehow she'd convinced him to be the children's primary chauffeur. Amazingly, during the school year, he'd even drive the three hours round trip to pick the kids up from school in San Carlos rather than wait for James to get off work and deliver them. This was all so Jessica could spend an extra hour with them on her Fridays. But she never made the trip herself.

The adults didn't acknowledge one another, not even with a wave or a nod. The kids just hopped from one car to the other. I'd been prepared for this, but it was still bizarre to witness.

Neither girl had a bag, nor anything to indicate that they'd been away for a week. James had told me about this, too.

"They have clothes at both houses," he explained. "But for years Jessica would send them back to my house on Sunday evening in the same exact clothes they were wearing on Friday afternoon, down to their underwear. They weren't allowed to carry a backpack or bring a stuffed animal back and forth, nothing. Mum's things stayed at Mum's house and Dad's things stayed at Dad's house."

I thought this sounded fucked up and I'd told him so.

"You think that's fucked up?" James had said. "The minute the girls arrive at Jessica's house, she makes them take a shower."

"Why?" I asked.

"She says it's because I have a cat. She's apparently allergic—although she was never allergic to cats when I knew her. But really, it's about control. They have to wash away Daddy's house before she'll give them a hug." I'd frowned at this disturbing story, but James spoke casually. It was how things were.

Now the girls let themselves into our car and regarded me curiously. James pulled away quickly, before Jessica could get a good look at me, I suspect.

"What are you doing here?" Annabelle asked me.

"Say hi to Marie," James prompted her.

"Hi. What are you doing here?" She seemed pleased by this unusual turn of events. Avery was quiet, regarding me in the rearview mirror. I gave her a little wave and she waved back.

"We had a Mercy event and I'm giving Marie a ride home. She lives nearby," James explained. I waited for the girls to launch into questioning, but they accepted this without comment.

"Although—are you hungry? I'm kinda hungry." James glanced at me and I nodded. "Are you girls hungry?"

Both kids said yes.

"Shall we go get some pizza?" asked James, smoothly choreographed.

"Yeah!" Annabelle said.

"Is Marie coming, too?" Avery asked. There was something in her voice that reminded me that she was not as young as her sister.

"If she wants. Marie, do you want to join us?" James gave me an encouraging smile.

"I'd love to join you," I said nervously.

Annabelle chatted nonstop throughout the meal, thrilled to have a new audience. She wore a little navy-blue sailor dress and frilly socks, in contrast to her sister's simple jeans and t-shirt. I was not prepared for her childish energy.

She rocked back and forth in her chair, repeatedly banging into the guy behind her. I helped her shift closer to the table and made our apologies. Every time she took a sip of water she set her glass near the table's edge, which set my nerves on edge. Tensed for a spill, I kept pushing her glass to safety. Within minutes I was exhausted.

Avery barely said a word all evening, but watched me carefully from behind lowered eyelids. I tried to engage her in conversation, but Annabelle monopolized my attention. Was this what it was like living with an eight-year-old? How did people do it?

"You don't have to entertain her every minute," James reassured me later on the phone. "It's okay to relax."

I was a bit wound up. "Do you think they bought our excuse?"

"Sure."

"But Avery was so quiet."

"She can be quiet around new people. She had a nice time though."

"She did?"

"Yes. But *I* had the nicest time." He paused. "It was good, being with you and my kids. I'm glad we did that." I said I was glad, too.

But two nights later I could've eaten my words. James called me after work. His voice had a hushed quality.

"Are you sitting down?" he asked in a low voice.

"What? I can barely hear you. Where are you?"

"I'm in my bathroom," he said. "I don't want my kids to hear me."

"What's going on?"

"The kids found out about us."

"What? What do you mean?"

"They found your shirt in the washing machine," he whispered.

"WHAT?"

"They found your shirt—"

"I heard you, but what the hell are you talking about? Why was my shirt in your washing machine?"

There was a rustling sound and James called out, "I'm in the bathroom!"

"James!"

He was whispering again. "I threw a load of wash in the machine, but I didn't turn it on. I guess you left one of your shirts here, and it got in there somehow. Then Avery decided to wash her sneakers and pulled everything out. She found your shirt and asked me whose it was."

"Wait, *what shirt?"* I asked desperately. "I never threw any of my clothes in your laundry!"

"A tank top?" James guessed in the manner of one who pays no attention to clothes.

"A purple tank top?" I demanded.

"I'm color blind," he reminded me. "It could've been purple."

I actually slapped myself on the forehead. "James, I didn't leave that at your house. You took it from *my* house! That's the shirt I was wearing on Sunday! I couldn't find it when we were getting dressed because you'd shoved it in your backpack!"

"Right, sorry. So, Avery came out waving your shirt, asking whose it was—"

"And did you tell her?"

"No! I didn't say anything at all. But I think I turned bright red . . . I'm a horrible liar, I'm sorry."

I was agitated. "So how did they know it was mine?"

He laughed. "Actually, this part's kind of funny. You know how Annie's not a big reader? Well, she's been working on the *Nancy Drew* series and really coming along. All of sudden it's like she enjoys reading and I've been really proud of her . . . "

Get to the point! I wanted to shout.

"So, she takes the shirt from Avery, sniffs it—for clues, I guess—and says, 'This smells like Marie.'"

"'This smells like Marie?'"

"Yeah. Like, how you smelled at dinner the other night."

Oh dear. Did I stink? I rarely wore perfume, so that couldn't be it. Then a horrible thought crossed my mind: *Did I smell like sex?* We had just climbed out of bed. *Oh God.*

I couldn't bear to voice this to James. I prayed she was smelling my citrus deodorant.

"Did you tell her it was mine?" Now my voice sounded small.

"I neither confirmed nor denied!" he said fervently. "But I think I blushed again."

"Oh, James!"

"I'm sorry."

I was mortified. I lay the phone down and covered my face with both hands. But then a thought occurred to me. I picked the phone back up.

"What happened next?" I asked him.

"Huh?"

"What did you do next?"

"I faked having to go to the bathroom so I could come in here and call you."

"You mean—you just *left* it like that?"

"Well, I wasn't sure what to do."

"Oh, *James!*"

"I'm sorry! I'm a horrible liar." There was another rustling and then he said, "I gotta go."

"No! Wait! What are you going to tell them?"

"I don't know. But if I stay in here much longer they're going to know something's up."

"Wait! We need a plan! Don't hang up!"

"I'll figure it out. I gotta go. I'll call you later." *Click.*

"James!!!"

* * *

James told the girls that we'd been hanging out at their house before a Mercy gig, and I'd changed into my concert attire, accidentally leaving my tank top behind. It was a dumb excuse, but it was all he could think of. I'm sure his delivery was most unconvincing, said with a slight stutter and crimson cheeks.

So I lay low for a while in hopes that the kids would forget about me. Of course, they didn't. Kids aren't stupid. I'm always amazed when adults try to slip one past them because kids see and hear everything. "Are you texting Marie?" Avery asked every time James looked at his phone.

But with school starting again, the girls were preoccupied. The shift in their schedule was significant. I reverted to seeing James only every other weekend, when his kids weren't around.

I found that I missed him. With less time together, we usually spent our kid-free weekends holed up at his place. I'd return to work on those Mondays in a dreamy state.

"You're humming again," Ken commented as I idly slapped labels on envelopes.

"Huh? Sorry," I said.

"Nice weekend?" he asked pointedly.

I hid a little smile. "Very nice, thank you." I stacked my envelopes in a neat pile and slid them aside. "Do you have any more labels?"

Ken frowned at his screen. "I've been trying to print some. Have you been getting that printer error that says, 'Turn printer off and back on again'?"

"Hmm." I tried to think. "I know the printer's been acting up today, but I haven't gotten the 'Turn me on' error."

There was a pause as we both digested what I'd said. I felt a blush creep into my cheeks.

Ken cocked an eyebrow at me. "Still thinking about your weekend, huh?"

As Ken went off to collect the mail, the phone rang and I answered it. I put the caller on hold and dialed Kirk.

"Hi Kirk. Carrie Topliff is on extension six hundred for you. Her name is not Carrie Topless, as Ken led us to believe."

* * *

Two weekends later, James and I lay in his bed, his arms wrapped around me. It was a warm evening and we had the sliding door open. I could see the city lights twinkling far beyond the back deck.

James said, "This is good, isn't it?"

"What's good?"

"You and me."

I stretched like a cat, smiling up at him. "It's very good." I meant it. "It's like . . . *movie* good. Like, somebody's about to *die* kind of good."

He hoisted himself up on one elbow and looked at me seriously.

"You okay?" I asked.

He didn't reply, just stared down at me for what felt like a long time.

"Hey," I said softly. "What's up?"

James looked like he was struggling for words. As I watched, beads of sweat broke out on his forehead. Suddenly I was alarmed.

"What? What is it?" I asked. He opened his mouth, and then closed it.

Oh God, I thought. *This is when he tells me something terrible.* My mind raced as I ran through the scenarios, wondering what words he might be choking on.

It took James several moments to speak. Sweat was actually dripping off his forehead. Finally, he said, "I . . . I wanted to say . . . "

"Yes?"

"I . . . want it to be you and me."

I just looked at him.

"I mean, I want it to *just* be you and me. I want us to be together, for real. Exclusive." His eyes searched my face. He looked petrified. He looked beautiful.

I took his hand. "Okay," I said softly.

"I love you," he ventured. Then he added hastily, "A little bit."

That made me laugh. I'd been trying—and failing—to pinpoint my own feelings, but that pretty much summed it up.

"I love you a little bit, too," I said, and kissed him.

We spent the night curled together, breathing in tandem.

* * *

When I arrived at work on Monday, Ken was just finishing a call. He put the phone down and greeted me with a quizzical look. "Do you know, that woman's name isn't Carrie Topless after all?"

8

FEELING LIKE FAMILY

James decided that there was no further point in hiding me from the kids.

"We're not fooling them," he said. "They know we're dating. We might as well come clean; at least we'd get to spend more time together."

We tested the waters with an afternoon at Jack London Square. There was a food truck festival, which seemed like just the thing to break the ice. When that went well, we grabbed some lunch one Sunday after church. Another week we took a long walk through Golden Gate Park. The kids were getting used to me and even seemed to like having me around.

And I was surprised by how much I was enjoying getting to know them. Avery was not the shy, quiet kid she appeared to be at first glance. When relaxed, she could talk a mile a minute. She was clearly the boss of the two sisters. Annabelle didn't seem to mind; she did her sister's bidding gladly, never seeming to realize when Avery was taking advantage. It was fun to watch their interactions, a little glimpse into their family dynamic.

As Halloween approached, James invited me to join them for trick-or-treating in San Carlos. I'd never spent Halloween with kids before (not since I was a kid myself) and I loved the idea of sharing their excitement.

But we hit a logistical snag. Since I lived so far away and I didn't have a car, there was no easy way for me to get home late at night. The trains stopped running, and James couldn't leave his kids while he drove me all the way back to Oakland. Nor did he want to drag them along.

We decided I'd spend the night. I worried that it was far too early for this, but I really wanted to be there for Halloween and the kids seemed excited to bring me trick-or-treating. James explained to them why I'd be staying over, and they didn't seem perturbed.

But when I arrived, Annabelle spread out a sleeping bag on the floor beside her bed. She thought I'd be staying in her room.

"I think Marie would rather stay in my room," James told her gently. Annabelle looked at me, surprised, and I wanted to shrivel up and disappear. *I knew this was too much, too fast.*

But then she just shrugged. "Okay," she said. "But just so you know, he has race cars on his boxer shorts."

Once they started chasing candy, the girls forgot all about me. Their neighborhood was prime Halloween territory, and they ran from house to house with the other kids, scoring as much loot as they could.

I met Penelope, Avery's best friend, and her mother, Rochelle. They lived down the street and the two girls had been inseparable since second grade. James and Rochelle were good friends who relied on each other for childcare, and along with Penelope's little brother, Mitchell, the four kids practically lived in one another's houses.

Penelope was a brassy little girl with a big personality and a loud voice. She seemed Avery's opposite in every way, but Avery bloomed around her and they chattered endlessly. They wore the exact same Halloween costume: a store-bought Cleopatra ensemble complete with plastic crown and scepter. I watched them mourn the fact that they weren't wearing the same shoes.

Annabelle was dressed as Hermione from *Harry Potter*. On my advice, she'd slept with her wet hair in braids to make it big and wavy. She seemed very pleased by this distinctly feminine tip. It was like I'd brought a new wealth of knowledge into their household.

At bedtime, the kids were all sugared up and hard to settle. They kept calling to each other from their bedrooms across the hall. When Annabelle called out to me, I peeked my head around her doorjamb.

"Don't let Avery take my candy," she instructed me.

"I'm in bed, Annabelle!" Avery called out crossly.

"'Cause I counted the pieces," Annabelle hollered back, "and I'll know if you took any."

Avery made a *pfft* noise.

"Well, good night," I said, edging my way out of her room. I was ready to join James for a glass of wine.

"But you can have a piece," Annabelle went on talking, clearly not done with our conversation. I quickly stepped back inside her room.

"Hey!" came Avery's voice.

"And you can have as many Jolly Ranchers as you want," she offered me. "I don't really like those."

"*I* like them!" called Avery, indignant.

"Okay Avery, you can have my Jolly Ranchers for your Kit Kats."

"No way!"

"Okay, half your Kit Kats."

"Forget it!"

I stepped backward into the hallway.

"Everybody knows that Kit Kats are better than Jolly Ranchers, right Marie? Right?"

Now I poked my head into Avery's room to answer her. "Um, right." She *was* right, everybody knew it.

"Well, I'm not just going to give you my Jolly Ranchers for free," Annabelle said huffily. "You have to give me something. How about your Hershey's bars?"

"Yes," said Avery. "You can have those." There was a small pause. "Except I ate them already."

"Avery!"

"But you can have them next year!" Avery promised.

"All of them?"

"Well, not *all* of them. That's not an even trade. But if you give me two of your Kit Kats now, and all your Jolly Ranchers, then you can have all my Hershey's bars next year."

I wondered if I should counsel Annabelle on this inadvisable trade, but she said happily, "Okay," and the verbal contract was made. I tried to slip back into the hallway.

But the kids just kept talking at me. I couldn't extricate myself; the comments wouldn't stop.

"Last year I was Little Bo Peep . . . "

"She outgrew that dress . . . "

"No, I didn't. I just didn't want to *wear* it, Avery . . . "

"And I was an eighties rock star, and so was Penelope . . ."

"And Mitchell was . . . Wait, what was Mitchell?"

"Darth Vader."

"Yeah, Darth Vader."

"And Dad wasn't anything . . . "

"Yeah, Dad never dresses up . . . "

I saw this could go on all night if I didn't take action. "Okay, good night, girls! Annabelle, I'd better tuck you in." I stepped over to her bed and tucked the blankets snugly along each side of her body, like I was pinching a pie crust. Her arms were pinned to her sides. "I'm just making sure you're nice and tucked in, all safe and sound." I continued tucking around her legs, trapping her securely in place. She was delighted.

As I turned to go, she burst loose from the covers and exclaimed, "I escaped!"

"Oh no!" I said. "This won't do!" I tucked her in again, muttering, "Better tuck her tighter . . . she'll fall out of bed . . . lock her in place . . . just . . . like . . . *that*. Good!" Brushing my hands, I stepped away. Annabelle broke free again, laughing hysterically.

"Do me! Hey, Marie! Do me!" Avery called out.

Having just turned eleven, I was surprised that Avery still wanted to play this sort of game, but she burst out laughing as I tucked her in methodically. For several minutes, I ran back and forth between the kids' rooms, haplessly tucking and re-tucking as they threw off their covers and laughed in glee.

Finally, I said good night for real and escaped to the kitchen, where James handed me a well-earned glass of wine.

"They wore me out," I told him.

"They like you," he said to me and smiled.

But the next morning, Annabelle seemed confused when she found me in the kitchen. It was a weekday and I had to go to work. I was pulling on my jacket when Annabelle stumbled in, pajama-clad and bleary-eyed. She stopped short when she saw me.

"Good morning," I said. She didn't reply, but glared, as though she wasn't sure who I was.

"I'm going to run Marie down the street to the train station," James told her. "I'll be right back, okay? Eat your breakfast."

"She didn't seem happy to see me," I whispered as we walked out the door.

"She's not a morning person," said James.

The four of us fell into the habit of spending Sunday afternoons together, exploring a new neighborhood each week. San Francisco offered up unexpected gems every time we went out: a roller skating derby in Golden Gate Park, or a brass band on a street corner in the Mission. James reported that Avery said to him, "Every time we go out with Marie, something awesome happens."

In a little park in Russian Hill, the girls took turns sliding down a staircase rail. "Marie, watch me!" Avery zipped down the rail with both arms in the air, like she was riding a roller coaster. "Wait, I'm going again!" She raced back up the stairs and slid down the rail once more, this time slowly, waving like the queen. On her third time down, I took a video on my phone. She flew off the end of the railing and into James' arms, burying her face in his neck for a brief, fierce hug.

Annabelle was still young enough that I'd hold her hand while we crossed the street. Sometimes she kept holding my hand after we were safely on the sidewalk, swinging our arms back and forth. Once, she brought my hand to her face and kissed it. I looked at her, surprised, but she didn't even seem to realize she'd done it. She was bubbling over with excitement, thrilled, it seemed, just to be spending the day together.

The girls were happy on these afternoons, basking in our attention, with the city as their playground. We made adventures out of the simplest things: a knotted rope hanging from a tree, or a hopscotch grid painted on the ground. Avery and James would race each other to the top of every hill, their competitive sides emerging. Annabelle, who couldn't care less about claiming first place, would try to get me to run backward up the hill with her.

She still wore her little red coat, though James kept threatening to replace it. I took a picture of her at the top of Lombard Street, leaning on a railing and eating an ice cream cone. An American flag hung behind her in someone's window, and the breeze blew the hair off her face. I knew as I took it that it would be one of those quintessential photos of her childhood. In later years, I framed it.

James' happiness seemed the greatest of all, but he kept it contained. His eyes were alive when the four of us were together, and sometimes the look on his face would make my heart skip. He was falling for us, I could see it. Not just for *me*, but for all of us together.

I waited for the alarm bells to go off in my head, but they didn't.

Passersby would comment, "What a beautiful family you have." That happened quite a few times. James and I would just smile and nod our thanks. If the kids heard, they didn't seem bothered.

It surprised me, because I didn't look anything like the girls. Anyone paying attention would realize I was not their mother. But on those golden afternoons, we sometimes *felt* like a family. We gave off such an air of contentment that strangers around us noticed.

On Thanksgiving, Rochelle and her husband, Gil, invited us to join their family for dinner. They invited other friends, too, so it was a full house, and the kids had a blast running around. Just like Halloween, there was no easy way for me to get home afterward, so I spent the night once again. This time the kids seemed chipper when they saw me in the morning.

We spent the next day relaxing and hanging out. The girls showed me *Dance Off,* a video game where they had to mimic the dance routines on the screen. They were pretty good, and they laughed at me as I fumbled through the steps. Soon we were hopping around the room, trying to outdo one another with silly dance moves. The kids shrieked with delight, their voices echoing off the walls.

When the house phone rang, Avery stopped short, causing her sister to bounce off of her. "Phone!" she said sharply, and Annabelle quickly shut off the TV.

"Is it Mom?" she asked nervously.

But Avery had already grabbed the phone and rushed to her bedroom. "Hi Mom," I heard her say before she shut the door. Annabelle quickly disappeared into her own room. I was caught off guard by their abrupt departure. It was like they were running from the scene of a crime.

"Did you see that?" I said to James, who was washing dishes. His face was stony.

"Yeah."

"What was that about?" I asked.

He shrugged. "They drop everything when Mum calls." But I'd had the distinct impression that they were running from *me,* almost as though they were frightened that their mother could see them through the phone.

* * *

The knitting group met at my house a few weeks later. For once we were all focused on a project; everyone seemed intent on finishing their Christmas gifts.

Katia was studying a pattern. "I think I messed this up. Damn it." She flung the pages down in dismay and started ripping out stitches.

"What are you doing?" cried Alex.

"I screwed up half a page back. I've got to do this whole side over."

"Let me see that pattern." I held out my hand. Katia was knitting a stuffed chicken. I suppose technically she was knitting a chicken *skin,* which she'd later stuff with wool. "This is so complicated," I said. "How are you even following it?"

"Well, I made that little lamb just fine," she said. "Remember? But this chicken is a pain in the ass." I watched the misshapen chicken skin disintegrate into a pile of yarn.

"That's what you get for not sticking to rectangles," Alex said. "Blankets and scarves, girls. You can't go wrong." She indicated the purple scarf that was dangling from her own needles.

"Or you just make the same hat for everyone," Mandy said. She made baby hats that resembled strawberries, complete with little green stems on top. It was the only thing I'd ever seen her knit.

"Hey, how's the new job going?" Alex asked her. Mandy had gotten the job at Roaming Expeditions. She'd been there for a few months now and told Alex that she was enjoying it.

"Are you sick of Marie yet?" Alex grinned. "Now that you live *and* work together?"

"Well, we don't usually commute together," I said. "And she sits way on the other side of the office."

"True. And Marie's been home less and less lately," Mandy said pointedly.

"Oh?" Interested heads turned toward me.

"Yes. She's been spending more nights at James' house." There were a few teasing noises.

"Just some weekends," I corrected her.

"With the kids there," Mandy elaborated.

"Really? How's that going?" Hailey asked. Hailey had two kids of her own.

I paused my knitting. "Actually, I have to tell you guys this story."

"Oh, this is good," said Mandy, who'd already heard it. She rose halfway and reached for the zinfandel. "Can I refill anybody's wine?" Three hands lifted glasses.

"Okay, spill it," commanded Alex, and I described the previous weekend.

I'd gone out to James' house late on Saturday afternoon and we'd passed a nice evening grilling on the deck. Later we watched a movie. The girls' mom called around nine o'clock. Again, I saw the kids switch abruptly from relaxed to nervous. Avery took the phone to her bedroom and closed the door.

Annabelle and I were helping James do the dishes when Avery emerged and passed the phone to her sister. I was in the middle of telling some story and barely noticed when Annabelle took the phone into her own bedroom.

A minute later she returned. "Mom wants to talk to you," she said, thrusting the phone at James.

James frowned. He took the phone and stepped swiftly outside. "Hello?" I heard him say before he shut the door.

But an instant later he came back in. He set the phone back in the cradle.

"What was that about?" I asked, but he shook his head.

The phone rang again and Annabelle made a grab for it. "Hello? Mom?" She took the phone into her room. Avery followed.

"What happened?" I asked again, quietly.

James looked angry. "I said hello and she responded, 'So, you're fucking that tramp who calls herself a Christian?' So I hung up."

"Hold on! She said *what?*" interjected Alex, looking up from her knitting.

"'So, you're fucking that tramp who calls herself a Christian,'" I repeated. There was a moment of stunned silence, then a derisive snort from Mandy.

"What does that even mean?" asked Hailey.

"I'm not sure," I said. "I think it's because we met at church? But it's not like I go around proclaiming myself a Christian. She makes me sound like some pedophilic priest."

"So, he hung up on her?" asked Alex.

"Yeah. And then she called back and told Annabelle, 'Daddy hung up on me because he doesn't want me to talk to you.' Then Annabelle threw a tantrum and went to bed in tears."

"But why would she say something like that? That's just so random." Alex was incensed.

"I think she must have heard my voice through the phone," I said. "It was getting late and she must have been pissed that I was still at their house near bedtime. I guess she figured I was spending the night."

"Which she was," Mandy acknowledged.

"And that's how she handled it?" Alex threw down her knitting, disgusted. "By calling you names and then lying to her kid? That's horrible."

"Yeah, well . . . she's not a very nice lady."

9

A Bit of Background

The story of James and Jessica's marriage had come to me in bits and pieces. He was eighteen and she was nineteen when they wed.

James had had a turbulent adolescence. His father died when he was twelve, and in her grief, James' mother withdrew from her three kids and gave up disciplining them. Their strict upbringing devolved into chaos, with James and his siblings doing whatever they pleased.

When she remarried a few years later, the kids despised their stepfather. He was the contractor who'd put in their new swimming pool, and James believed the man had smelled a lonely widow with money. By age eighteen James couldn't bear to live at home anymore.

For her part, Jessica had woven tales of abuse in her household. She was the eldest of five kids, the youngest of whom was still in elementary school when she and James met. James fancied that he could take her away from that place, so he dropped out of school and they got married. They moved into a little basement apartment and James took a job at Evermore Battery, where he was still employed these twenty years later.

Early on in their marriage, James began to think that he'd made a mistake. Jessica was deeply materialistic, unhappy with their meager lifestyle, and possessive of James' time—although she didn't seem to enjoy being with him. She was rude to his friends and family until they stopped coming around, and she forbade him to enjoy activities without her, so eventually he became cut off from everyone. James' job was the one activity that Jessica endorsed because she approved of his making money. So he buried himself in his work, frequently logging fourteen-hour days.

Over time, James advanced at Evermore and made a fair amount of money. And Jessica spent it. She insisted on a new car every other year. They upgraded to bigger and better houses. She demanded a larger diamond for her wedding ring. James gave in to her requests because she had a terrible temper. He hated conflict, and giving in was the easiest route to take.

The one area where James stood his ground was his refusal to have children until he felt they could financially support them. It was eight years after they married that they had Avery, and two years later, Annabelle. Then Jessica insisted that James have the vasectomy.

A year or so after Annabelle was born, James was transferred from Vancouver to California, and the family took up residence in Dixon. Jessica stayed home with the kids during the day. She joined a Young Republicans group and began spending her evenings in their company.

This was when James first heard Max's name. He was a friend from the group, Jessica explained. Once or twice he dropped by the house to pick her up for a meeting. It became a habit for Jessica to leave the house as soon as James arrived home from work. She began staying out later and later.

James had his suspicions that Jessica and Max were seeing each other; she vehemently denied it. But over time their involvement became obvious. Jessica abruptly decided to become a Catholic and began the process of converting. (Max, it transpired, was Catholic.) She'd stay out until three or four in the morning, purportedly spending her time in a coffee shop, studying for her conversion.

Then she decided to get a breast enhancement. Against James' protests (but with his money), she had surgery to increase two cup sizes. James recalled her unwrapping a towel to reveal her new chest.

"They look fake," he said bluntly. He never saw them again.

James wrote Max a letter saying that he knew about their affair. He reminded Max that there were children involved and implored him to respect their family and step away. Max never responded. James also reached out to Jessica's new priest and asked for his intercedence. Together they tried to engage Jessica in counseling, but she became enraged and refused to speak with the priest.

Instead she moved out, leaving the girls behind with James. She withdrew one hundred and forty thousand dollars from their joint checking account and deposited it in a private account, where James couldn't access it. James was stunned that Jessica would take his inheritance. He said to her, "That money came from my parents. You promised me you would never touch it."

Jessica replied, "That was then, this is now. Now I need it."

James rearranged his life to be primary caregiver to Annabelle and Avery, who were then two and four. Since Jessica showed little interest in parenting and often relinquished her time with the girls, James decided to move them fifty miles south to San Carlos to be closer to his job. Meanwhile, Jessica and Max bought the large house in Vacaville, using James' inheritance as a down payment. They began divorce proceedings.

To garner sympathy from her family, Jessica claimed she'd recovered a memory of James raping her. Sickened by the accusation, James offered to take a lie detector test and said that if he failed it, Jessica could have full custody. Her bluff called, Jessica dropped the issue. She and her family, never close, became further estranged. Her sister Jocelyn flew in from Vancouver to vouch for James at trial, and he emerged with custody of the girls.

When the dust settled, Jessica began a new campaign to malign James. Her methods were subtle but effective. She taught the girls to append their nightly prayers with requests for God to please bless Mommy and Max, Nonno and Grandma (Max's parents), and a long list of others. Daddy didn't make the list.

She told the girls, "Daddy kidnapped you," and "The judge made a mistake," and "I don't feel safe around Daddy." Over the years, Jessica refused to attend any birthday party that James threw for the girls. She avoided all functions where James would be present, missing countless elementary school milestones. She insisted that the kids' school provide separate parent-teacher conferences, so she wouldn't have to attend with James. She never met any of the girls' friends in San Carlos, not even Penelope, whom Avery loved like a sister. She did all she could to instill complete separation between the girls' life with their father and life with their mother.

And she succeeded. The kids were happy enough on the surface, comfortable living with James and content with their home in San Carlos and their visits with their mother. But a sharp divide had been drawn down the center of their lives like an electric fence. It was invisible and dangerous—and at times it would shock us.

10

THREE ATTEMPTS

In the wake of the tramp-fucking incident, I tried to see the situation from Jessica's perspective. I realized that if it were my kids spending time with an unknown woman, I might be uneasy about it, too. If James and I were getting serious—and it appeared that we were—I didn't want to get off on the wrong foot with his ex. I opted to give Jessica the benefit of the doubt.

I would introduce myself, I decided, and let her know that I was a nice, normal person whom she could trust around her children. I was sure she'd appreciate this effort. Perhaps it would even help smooth relations between her and James.

Boy, was I wrong.

* * *

In February, Jessica sustained an injury while on the job. This was not as devastating as it sounded—she was an executive assistant, not a construction worker. She pulled a muscle in her back while lifting three-ring binders from the trunk of her boss' car.

But with her birdlike frame and hypochondriac tendencies, Jessica parlayed her sore back into temporary disability and stopped going to work. Avery said that her mom could barely walk and had to lie flat on the couch all day. She was reportedly in excruciating pain.

James suspected that she was exaggerating the injury. "You know, I'd forgotten about this," he mused, "but when we were married, Jess would occasionally complain about heart problems. We'd go to the ER and she'd get a bunch of tests, but they never found anything wrong. She did it every year or two, whenever she wanted sympathy and attention."

"So, you don't think it's real?" I asked.

"I think she probably hurt herself. But I don't think it's as serious as she claims."

"But she stopped going to work."

He shrugged. "She's an opportunist. She found a way to get paid for a few months without having to work."

"Will this affect her child support payments?" I wondered.

He looked at me, surprised. "Jess has never paid me child support," he said. "Are you kidding? She doesn't even pay her half of the kids' dental bills most of the time."

"But you're the primary caregiver," I said, confused. "Doesn't she have to pay you child support?"

"I never applied for it."

"Seriously? In, what, six years? Seven years?"

"Seven," he said. "I make enough money. It hasn't been necessary. And Jess is so difficult to deal with, I'd rather not bother."

"But James! It's her responsibility."

"Believe me," he said, "Jess is not going to give me any money without grief. She'd probably sue for custody again, just to avoid the child support payments. I'd rather not poke the bear."

Their mother's injury had the girls subdued. They called her every day, sometimes twice, to check how she was feeling. Their time at her house was spent catering to her needs and tiptoeing around her naps.

The weeks went by, but Jessica showed no signs of improving. A month later she was just as freshly injured as ever. The kids' concern hadn't waned, but they were tiring from the effort. They became short-tempered with James and lacked patience with me.

Now when I saw them, it took the girls a little while to warm up to me. It was like the shadow of their mother's house hung over them longer and longer each time they left it.

Avery confided to James that her mother didn't like me. When he asked why—and pointed out that she'd never met me—Avery shrugged. "I don't know why," she said. "But Mom *really* doesn't like her."

I decided that this was my opportunity to reach out to Jessica and try to smooth the path. I composed an email:

> Hi Jess,
>
> I'm writing in hopes that we can meet face to face, and allow me the chance to introduce myself. I think you deserve to know who's spending time with your kids. I also think it would be a relief for the girls to see that the adults in their lives are trying to get along. We don't have to be friends, but we can be cordial with one another. Maybe we could meet one Sunday when you exchange the girls?
>
> I hope you're feeling well again soon.
>
> Take care,
>
> Marie

I could tell James wasn't thrilled by my outreach, but he didn't try to stop me. He gave me Jess' email address and one suggestion.

"Don't call her 'Jess'," he said. "She hates it. She always says, 'My name is Jessica.'"

I thanked him and made the adjustment.

"She's not going to reply," he warned me. "I don't want you to be disappointed."

"I won't be," I said.

But I was secretly sure that I would impress her with my sincerity. I thought maybe I could navigate my way around their bitter history and spark a fresh start.

I was pretty naïve.

Weeks passed and my email went unanswered. Despite James' warning, I *was* disappointed, and a little indignant. But I remained determined. If email wasn't effective, I would introduce myself to her in person.

On Easter Sunday I went with James to collect the girls from Home Depot. We planned to have a nice dinner at my house before he and the kids went home to San Carlos. And I planned to walk up to the car and say hello to Jessica and Max as they dropped off the kids.

James was even less enthused about this idea, but I was sure it was the right move.

"It's ridiculous that we can't say hello to one another," I told him. "It's crappy behavior to model to the kids. I'm just going to introduce myself when they drive up, shake their hands and say hi." I didn't feel quite as breezy as I sounded. "Let's get there early so we can be waiting."

James opted to stay in the car while I stood by myself, leaning against the hood, watching for their arrival. When they pulled up a short while later, Max angled his car perpendicular to ours, so that I was facing him through the closed driver's side window. Jessica wasn't with him—still prone on the couch, I surmised. *No matter*, I told myself. I was going to do this anyway.

I realized I was nervous as I approached his car. My heart was pounding fast, but I kept my voice light. "Hello!" I called, and waved. Max craned his head away from me, toward the backseat. He was saying goodbye to the girls.

"Hello!" I called again. I leaned down to the window and tapped on the glass. "Hi Max!"

There was no way he didn't hear me knock on his window, but Max kept his head twisted in the opposite direction. I saw the kids notice me from the backseat. They both climbed out of the car on the passenger side, but Max didn't turn around.

I rapped a little harder on the window. "Hi Max!" I called, louder. "It's Marie!"

No sooner had the kids closed their door than Max turned to face front, hit the gas, and absolutely peeled out of the parking lot. I jumped back, afraid he would run over my feet.

"Jesus," I said, stunned. The kids and I stood facing each other a car's width apart.

"Are everybody's toes okay?" I asked. They nodded.

James had jumped out of the car when he saw Max speed away. Now he looked over his kids to make sure they were all right. I stood outside as he helped them into the car and closed their door. "Did you see that?" I said in a low voice. "What the hell was that about?"

"I told you. He's a fucking asshole," James said grimly.

* * *

Call me a slow learner, but it took a third attempt to drive the point home: these people didn't want to meet me.

In May Annabelle's class put on a performance of *Gold Rush!*, a musical about early California. For her period costume, I let her borrow an old feather boa that I'd won in a bar on St. Patrick's Day. It was a bright, garish green, and it nearly covered her face, but she loved it. She looked like a pint-sized madam.

The show was scheduled for a Friday afternoon on one of Jessica's weekends. Jessica was still convalescing, but Max planned to attend the show and would collect the girls afterward. We were all a little nervous about how this would go down.

Avery was particularly jumpy. Having us and Max in the same room was almost more than she could take. Throughout the show she sat with us, but kept craning her neck trying to spot him. She spent more time looking around than watching the stage.

The instant the performance was over she stood, searching for Max, anxious about keeping him waiting.

"Where's Annie?" she kept asking. "What's taking her so long?"

"She has to take her costume off," James said. "Relax."

But Avery couldn't relax. "I'm going to see if I can find her," she said and disappeared down the hall.

James was tense, too. "He better not take them before I have a chance to say goodbye," he muttered. I knew he was afraid Annabelle wouldn't resurface. The kids had been agitated about this exchange all day.

"She has to come find us; she has my feather boa," I said. "I told her to return it." I'd done this as insurance because I also feared the kids would bolt. And I'd decided that, hell or high water, I was going to introduce myself to Max this day.

A few minutes later Annie appeared and thrust the boa into my hands. "Here," she said, and turned to go.

"Hey, wait a minute," said James, catching her by the elbow. "Let me say goodbye." We each gave her a hug and complimented her performance. She was rigid and spared us the slightest of thanks. Max stood a few paces behind her, with Avery fidgeting at his side.

I wasted no time, but walked right up to Max, extended my hand, and said, "Hi Max. My name is Marie."

Max turned on his heel, grabbed Annabelle by the wrist, and walked briskly away.

My mouth dropped open. I stood there with my arm out, feeling like an idiot. Avery did a double take worthy of a cartoon character, then quickly trotted off behind her stepfather.

In a flash, my shock gave way to anger. "Excuse me!" I called. I jogged down the hall to catch up with them. "Maybe you didn't hear me," I said, walking swiftly to keep their pace. "I'm trying to introduce myself to you. My name is Marie."

Max's stride increased. Poor Annabelle was dragged alongside him, running to keep up. Avery was in the middle, looking back and forth at us desperately.

"Max!" I raised my voice and saw a few nearby parents raise their heads. "I'm trying to say hello to you! Won't you stop for a minute? *Hello?*"

He didn't pause, but propelled Annabelle through the door at the end of the hallway and didn't look back.

Avery stopped for just an instant and looked at me. Her eyes were brimming with tears.

"I'm sorry, Marie," she whispered, and then followed her stepfather outside.

I stood in the hallway, shaking. When James caught up to me I couldn't speak. I was stunned that a grown man would act that way—pretending like I was invisible, like I didn't exist. And I was aghast that he would do it in front of the kids.

James gathered me into his arms and kissed my forehead. "Now do you believe me?" he asked.

* * *

James and I passed our first anniversary with little fanfare, but we were both in deep.

For months, we'd appended every "I love you" with "a little bit", trying to keep things light. But somewhere along the way we'd dropped the "little bit" and hadn't noticed. Without any big pronouncement, we both knew that we were in love, all the way.

It was a wild feeling—and a new level of commitment that I'd never experienced before. Adding children to the equation made our relationship bigger than any I'd known in the past. There were so many layers to it.

I loved him on his own. I loved when it was just the two of us. And I loved to watch him be a father to his girls. There were moments that made my heart swell, like when he'd sit at the piano and play with Annabelle or hoist the nearly-too-big Avery onto his back for a ride.

And there were times that I caught him looking at me as though I completed the picture. One night he made us spaghetti while the kids and I spun on the kitchen stools. We were all in our pajamas. He paused in the act of grating cheese and gave me a smile so beautiful that I wanted to weep.

I loved him in big, new ways.

Summer was approaching again and we'd been flirting with the idea of a short vacation. With the kids at their mom's half the time, we could steal away for a week to ourselves. We began tossing around ideas.

James was also trying to plan a trip to Canada for himself and the girls. It had been several years since the kids had seen their family there, and James wanted to keep them in touch.

Notably, these were *Jessica's* relatives. Since Jess was estranged from her family, James made an effort to stay in contact with her parents and siblings. It was a strange situation.

"They still call me 'son'," he said, referring to Jessica's parents. "I hate it."

"But you get along with them okay?" I asked. I stabbed a straw into my soda cup. We were grabbing burgers on a rare, kid-free afternoon.

"I get along with her brother and sisters pretty well," he said. "I've known them forever; we all grew up together. I'm not very close with her parents, but they're decent people. It's just weird," he said, making a face. He paused for a bite of his burger. "The last time I was at their house, they still had our wedding picture hanging above the mantle. And right next to it was a picture of Jessica and Max on their wedding day."

I laughed in disbelief. "You're kidding!"

"Nope. They didn't go to Jessica's second wedding, though. I don't think they were invited."

"Did any of her siblings go?"

"Yeah, her brother, Daniel, came down from Canada. But he actually stayed at my house."

"You are incredible," I told him. He just shrugged.

"Family is important," he said. I knew he missed his own parents.

But Jessica proved an obstacle in planning the Canada trip. She held the girls' passports and wouldn't reply when James asked if he could use them.

"She always does this," James said. "She waits until it's impossible for me to find reasonable flights."

"Don't you have legal rights to those passports?" I asked.

"Yes, and she's supposed to provide them if I want to take the kids out of the country. But I'd have to take her to court to make her comply, and then she'd just say that she was planning to give them to me all along." He shook his head in frustration. "It's been four years since the kids have seen their grandparents."

"I just can't get over the fact that this is *her* family you're trying to visit," I said. "You'd think she'd want the kids to see her family."

"You'd think," said James. "Then again, you'd think she might take them for a visit herself."

In the end, he and I decided to go to Canada instead. Not to Vancouver, where Jessica's family resided, but to Quebec City and Montreal, where I had never been.

We had a wonderful trip. Quebec was charming, and Montreal impressed me with cool finds around every corner. We ate wood-fired bagels in the historic Jewish quarter and late-night *poutine* in the old town. Under a highway overpass, close to midnight, we stumbled on a Cirque du Soleil performance in full swing. In the Gay Village ("Is that really what they call it?" I asked), we walked arm in arm under garlands of pink lights and drank beer at outdoor cafés. James flirted with me across the table, and when he pushed his glasses up the bridge of his nose with one finger (like Clark Kent!), I wanted to forget the rest of the city and drag him back to our hotel room.

It was a short week away, but every moment of it was perfect. I hated to say goodbye when we touched down in San Francisco, but it was a Sunday night and real life resumed in the morning.

James called me an hour after I got home.

"Do you miss me already?" I teased.

"Yes," he said, "but that's not why I'm calling." His voice sounded strange. "I came home to a summons," he told me. "Jessica is suing me for custody."

PART II

AN UNCIVIL WAR

11

ACTING OUT

James' lawyer Rhonda reminded me of a bulldog: short, squat, and fierce. She wore a severe black suit and sensible black pumps, but even in heels she didn't come up to my shoulder. Everything she said was blunt and to the point, and sometimes delivered with bite.

By contrast, her assistant Florence was a gentle, elderly lady who offered us candies with wrinkled brown hands when we entered the office. She reminded me of my grandmother.

"Florence, run over to Starbucks and get me my mocha. Do you guys want anything?" Rhonda asked us. We shook our heads. "Are you sure? It's on me." I took this as a nice gesture until James informed me later that Rhonda charged him three hundred and fifty dollars per hour of her time.

But he trusted her, as she had represented him during his divorce and previous custody trial. She knew his history—and she hated Jessica.

"So. You've read Jess' declaration." Rhonda slapped the document onto her desk. "And what do you think?"

"It's a bunch of bullshit," James replied.

"Explain."

"Well for one, she claims that Marie and I are living together part-time."

"And you're not?"

"No."

"So, why would she make this claim?" Rhonda was tough.

I spoke up. "I think it's because I spend some nights at their house. Jessica got wind of it, and it made her angry." I explained about the phone call where she'd accused James of "fucking that tramp" who was me. Rhonda gave a low whistle.

"Always the classy one, Jess. So, how many nights a month do you stay at James' when the kids are present?"

We glanced at each other. "Two or three?"

"Okay. What else?"

James shifted in his seat. "She says that both kids are struggling in school, which is crap. They get all As and Bs."

"Okay. And what about this statement: 'The girls appear to have problems accepting their father's girlfriend.' Any truth to that?"

"No," James said with emphasis. "The kids love Marie."

Now I shifted in my seat. Rhonda glanced at me shrewdly.

"What?" she asked.

"Well, lately, since their mother's injury, they've been a little less . . . enthused about spending time with me," I conceded. "But that's new. For the better part of a year, we had great times hanging out together. I definitely felt a shift."

Rhonda looked at me for a moment, then back down at her papers. "Tell me about this: 'Respondent's girlfriend has engaged in actions that are detrimental to the children. These include a forced exchange at her house to talk about myself and my husband, and scenes in front of the girls where she would run up and bang on the car window, and run alongside the car, striking it.'"

"I didn't 'run alongside the car, striking it,'" I said angrily. "I tapped on the window to say hello. And that 'forced exchange' with the kids at my house was a conversation we had afterward to discuss what happened." I explained the scene on Easter Sunday. "I mean, he did that in front of the kids! Were we just going to pretend it didn't happen?"

"So, what did you tell them?" she asked.

"We said that Marie was just trying to say hello to Max, and we didn't understand his reaction," James put in. "And later I had another conversation with them, after the scene at Annabelle's play." He described it. "I asked the kids why they thought their mum and Max wouldn't talk to Marie." Now he frowned. "And Annabelle said, 'If you don't have anything nice to say, don't say anything at all.'" I looked at the floor.

"I see. So, you think Jess is trying to poison them against Marie?"

"It seems like it."

"And do you think there's any truth to her claim that the kids have been begging to live with her? Thank you, Florence," she added, accepting her mocha.

"No," James said. "They're settled and happy in San Carlos. They like school, they love their friends . . . Avery and her best friend, Penelope, are inseparable."

"Still," said Rhonda, taking a sip of her drink, "a best friend is not a mother."

"But James has never tried to keep them from their mom!" I burst out. "She's the one who relinquished custody. She's the one who left them."

Rhonda stared at me over the rim of her cup. "I'm aware of the history," she said. "Don't get emotional."

There was a moment of silence in which James took my hand.

"So," Rhonda announced, standing up. She was the same height, seated or standing. "Now we draft a response. I want you to jot down any notes you have about Jess' petition—"

"Already done," I said, handing them to her.

She took the manila file and opened it. "Great. And I'll have a legal assistant draft a response for your review. That way I don't have to charge you my full rate." She gave James a little wink.

"Thanks," he replied dryly.

"Actually, I already drafted a response," I said. "I mean, I'm not a lawyer—obviously you'll want to put it in the proper format—but there's a point-by-point rebuttal in there." I tapped the manila file.

Rhonda regarded me for a long moment, then turned her gaze to James. "Looks like you've got an ally this time." She dismissed him with a nod of her head. "I'll call you."

* * *

I wasn't imagining it: the kids were definitely cooling toward me. And they were testy with James. It was always worse in the summer, he told me. The increased time with their mother made her influence more notable.

James bought Avery her first cell phone because he often had trouble reaching the girls when they were with Jessica. She wouldn't answer the phone if she saw that he was calling, and the kids rarely checked in with him.

"I expect you to stay in touch with this phone," James told Avery when he bought it. "If I call or text you, I want a response." Avery said she understood.

But James' calls went unanswered. "I forgot to charge it," Avery claimed, over and over. James drilled it into her to charge her phone nightly.

The following week, after he'd dropped the kids with Max, James came home to discover Avery's cell phone charger on the kitchen counter. He was sure she'd left it behind on purpose.

It transpired that Penelope couldn't get ahold of Avery when she was at her mom's, either. It seemed that Avery cut off all communication with the outside world once she entered her mother's domain.

One Sunday evening the kids came home full of excitement because their mom had bought them a dog.

"Her name is Snowflake and she's *so cute;* she's all white and fluffy, like a snowflake! And she's so little, and she sat in my lap and licked my face, and she's got this little bark like: *Arf! Arf!*" Annabelle rambled on happily.

"That's funny," James remarked. "I thought your mum was allergic to dogs. Doesn't she make you strip and shower before giving her a hug?"

"Snowflake is a Bichon Frise," Annabelle informed him haughtily. "They're hypoallergenic. And Mom doesn't make us shower. Anymore," she added.

"Oh, did she stop being allergic to our cat then?"

Annabelle glared at him and stomped off to her room.

Admittedly, James was a bit testy with the kids as well. He didn't mention their mother's custody petition, but it was hard for him to listen passively when the kids talked about time spent with Jessica.

"I hate that fucking dog," he confided to me on the phone. "Annabelle asked me last night if she could spend an extra week at her mum's house so the dog could get to know her. I swear Jess bought that thing as a lure for the kids."

Avery, too, voiced her desire to spend more time at her mom's house.

"Why not?" she complained angrily when James said no. "You're working all the time and Mom's at home. Why won't you let us spend more time with her during our summer vacation?"

"You've got summer camp," James pointed out.

"So? I'd rather spend time with Mom than go to some stupid camp."

James decided that he and the girls needed what he called "a little daddy-daughter time". He took them to Lake Tahoe for a long weekend, hoping that a few days of fun might ease some of the tension between them.

Since he'd be passing right through Vacaville on his way home, he arranged to drop the kids at a nearby Starbucks, where Max would meet them. But on their return, James realized that he was closer to Jessica's house than the coffee shop and changed course.

As he approached their neighborhood, Avery snapped to recognition.

"Dad, where are you going?" she asked.

James explained that he was going to their mother's house, but he couldn't remember the name of her street. He asked the kids for directions.

The girls became immediately distressed. "You're supposed to take us to Starbucks, not to Mom's house!" Avery said, sounding panicky.

James tried to calm her down. "I'm already in your neighborhood," he pointed out. "Starbucks is another ten minutes away. I just need to know the address."

But both kids erupted in hysterics.

"You're not allowed to bring us there!" they cried. "You're supposed to go to Starbucks! You're *supposed* to go to Starbucks!"

Frantic, Avery called Jessica on her cell phone (which was always charged and ready for a call to their mum, James realized). She put the phone on speaker. "Dad's trying to take us to your house!" she yelled.

Jessica's highly agitated voice came through the phone. "You are supposed to take the girls to Starbucks," she ordered James.

James tried to reason with her. "I know, but Starbucks is another exit down the freeway, and I'm already in your neighborhood. It makes more sense to drop the kids right at the house."

"But Max is already on his way to Starbucks."

"So, call him and tell him he can come home. I just need to know your address."

"No, that is not the arrangement!" Jessica barked.

"I don't understand the problem," James said.

"The problem, James, is that I am confined to the couch with my back injury, and I cannot get up and open the door!"

James thought this unlikely, but he didn't say so. "Okay, so call Max and tell him to come home, and he can let the girls inside. There's no reason to drive them ten minutes down the freeway so they can turn around and drive ten minutes back. I'm right here, Jess. I'm near your house, I just can't remember the address."

"You are to take the girls to Starbucks," Jessica ordered again.

In the backseat the kids were crying. The car was in chaos.

"Dad, why are you making things difficult?" demanded Avery. "Just do what you're supposed to!"

"We won't tell you the address!" shouted Annabelle.

"Yeah, and if you bring us to Mom's house, we won't get out of the car!"

"Just bring us to Starbucks!"

"Girls—"

"Just bring us to Starbucks!"

After driving in circles with two shrieking kids in the backseat, James finally gave up and took them to Starbucks. The girls cried the entire way, and when James parked the car they jumped out without saying goodbye. James watched them run up to Max and throw their arms around him in a desperate hug. He watched Max drive away with his daughters.

Then he drove to my house, crawled into my bed, and with his head on my chest, he cried.

* * *

I went out to San Carlos on a Saturday to spend the evening. James picked me up from the train station and brought me home, where dinner preparations were underway. The house was warm and smelled savory. James resumed chopping asparagus.

"Where are the kids?" I asked.

"Down the road at Rochelle's," he said. He paused to give me a quick kiss. "They'll be back soon. You want a glass of wine?"

I poured myself a glass of cabernet and settled onto a kitchen stool. "Can I help you?"

"Nah, I'm almost done," he said, wiping his hands. "We're having roast chicken with rosemary potatoes and asparagus."

"Yum," I exclaimed. I was not a cook, so every homemade dinner at James' house was a treat for me. When he stayed at my place, we usually brought in burritos.

A few moments later the front door opened and the kids came bounding in. Annabelle stopped short when she saw me.

"Hi Annie, hi Avery," I said, waving.

Avery gave me a half-hearted wave, but Annabelle frowned. "Don't call me Annie. My name is Annabelle."

"Young lady," James admonished.

"My name isn't 'young lady' either." She gave him a challenging stare, one hand on her hip.

"Annabelle," James said warningly. "Manners."

Annabelle flounced off in a huff, and I thought I was about to see a tantrum, but minutes later she was happily engaged in a game with her sister.

Not a parent myself, I wasn't accustomed to the sudden mood shifts of children. Moreover, I hadn't quite figured out how to *like* them when they were acting like jerks. Still, I gave it a shot. Wine in hand, I settled myself on the floor beside the coffee table where the kids were playing. Avery gave a triumphant hoot as Connect Four pieces spilled onto the table.

"I win!" she crowed. Avery, like her father, was very competitive.

"No fair Avery!" complained Annabelle. "You didn't let me put in my last piece!"

"It didn't matter. I'd already won," said Avery.

"Still. You should've let me put in my last piece."

As I shifted the Connect Four box to make space for my wine glass, I saw beneath it one of the delicate paper lanterns that I'd brought the kids from Quebec. "Hey," I said. "Whose is this?" I'd bought them in a handmade paper shop and fitted them carefully in my carry-on, guarding them from rips until I could give them to the children. The girls had been pleased with the gifts and hung them in their bedrooms. Now one had seemingly been discarded.

"It's not mine," Avery said, dropping a black checker into the center space.

"Annie? Sorry, Annabelle?" I asked. "Did it break?" She didn't answer me, but dropped a red checker on top of Avery's black one. "It looks okay," I said, turning it over in my hands.

"My mom can make those, too," Annabelle suddenly informed me. She shot me a defensive look.

"Um, okay," I said. "You know I didn't make this, though. I bought it for you in Quebec."

And no, your mom can't make these, I thought to myself. I was seized by the absurd desire to stick my tongue out at her.

A delicious smell wafted from the kitchen as James pulled the chicken out of the oven. "Dinner in five," he called out.

Then the phone rang, and he grabbed it from the cradle. "Oh, hi Rochelle," he said. "Did the kids forget something?"

I sipped my wine while the kids chattered, and James made murmuring noises on the phone. When he hung up he said, "Avery, come here."

"I'm playing," she said.

"Come here for a minute, please."

With a sigh, Avery reported to the kitchen counter.

"That was Rochelle on the phone," James told her. "Penelope is apparently crying her eyes out. Did you tell her that you were moving away?"

My ears perked up. Annabelle went still. Avery regarded her father with a stony expression.

"Avery?"

"What?"

"Did you tell Penelope that you were moving to your mum's house?"

She didn't answer.

"Avery, talk to me," James persisted. "Why would you say something like that?"

Annabelle dropped a checker with a *click* that seemed to startle her.

"Ave?"

Avery wouldn't meet his eyes. "You'll find out soon enough," she said darkly.

"What do you mean? Has your mum been talking to you about . . . things?"

But Avery had had enough. She turned away and headed for her bedroom.

"Avery, come here please," James called. "I'm not done talking to you."

She called over her shoulder, "Well, I'm done talking to *you.*" She went into her bedroom and closed the door, hard.

"Young lady!" James called. "Come back out here and get ready for dinner."

"I'm not hungry!" came Avery's muffled voice.

James heaved a quiet sigh and looked down into the sink. He seemed to take a moment to collect himself. Then he said, "Annabelle, come eat."

But Annabelle shook her head. "I'm not hungry either," she said in solidarity. She retreated to her own bedroom, but had no door to slam.

James and I stared at the rejected chicken. "Oh well, more for us," I ventured.

He slumped against the counter. "I'm not hungry either," he muttered. I went to him and put my arms around him.

"What exactly did Rochelle say?" I asked.

"Avery told Penelope that she was moving to her mum's and would be starting the new school year in Vacaville," James said. "Apparently, Jess has been telling the kids that when summer's over, they're coming to live with her."

"But she doesn't know that!" I said, appalled. "We've barely begun the process." In fact, we had something called a Meet and Confer scheduled for the following week. The idea was to see if the two parties could reach any resolution before progressing to trial.

"Yeah, well . . . That must be why the kids have been acting all out of sorts." He buried his face in his hands. "I hate her," he said softly. "Why is she doing this?"

It was a rhetorical question, but I thought I knew the answer. "It's because of me, isn't it?" I said. "She doesn't like me being in your lives, and she wants to take the kids away." This seemed the height of hypocrisy after all Jessica had

136

done, but I no longer believed we were dealing with a reasonable woman. "This is punishment for you being happy."

Now James wrapped me in his arms and kissed my forehead. "No," he said. "Well, maybe somewhat, but I don't think that's the entire reason. She's always told the girls that when they were twelve, they could decide where they wanted to live. I thought it was an empty threat; she never seemed that interested in parenting, and the kids were happy here. But now she's got this injury—"

"This fake injury," I interjected.

"Yeah, probably. But she's not working right now, and she's got all this time on her hands. I think maybe she's bored or lonely. And I think a part of her may realize that the girls are getting older, and soon they're going to start to question why their mum didn't choose to live with them." He rested his chin on the top of my head. "Maybe she wants to act before they make that connection."

"Are you scared?" I asked him.

"A little. But I trust Rhonda, and she thinks I have a good case. Still," he said, kissing my forehead again. "It sucks to drag the kids through all this." I knew, too, that it hurt him to see the kids support their mother when there was so much they didn't know going on behind the scenes.

I hugged him tightly. "I love you," I said. It was my balm against this wound.

"I love you, too," he told me.

"Dad?" came a small voice. Annabelle had emerged from her room. "Are we still having dinner?"

I wanted to tell this child to shove off, but James was a better person than I. "Sure," he said, and cut her a piece of chicken. He kissed the top of her head as he handed her the plate, and I marveled at a father's ability to love his child even as she was causing him pain.

12

MEET AND CONFER

The Meet and Confer was utterly bizarre.

James and I took the morning off work, and he picked me up on the way to Vacaville. We parked a few blocks away from the courthouse.

"Thank you for coming," he said. "You didn't have to do this."

"I know," I told him. "But I want to be here."

We walked together toward the building, but James halted suddenly as he noticed who was ahead of us on the sidewalk.

"Is that Max escorting his mother?" I whispered. I could only see them from behind. A slight woman with dyed-black hair was leaning heavily on Max's arm and taking slow, tentative steps.

"No. That's Max escorting his *wife.*"

"That's *Jessica?*" I could barely believe it. She looked like a stooped old woman. She shuffled down the sidewalk with Max taking patient baby steps beside her. There was nothing to do but go around them, which we did without acknowledgement. After the scene at Annabelle's play, I was done extending myself to these people.

We entered the building and took the elevator to the fourth-floor law library, where Rhonda was waiting for us. She wore her usual uniform, a black suit and pumps, and her legal files sat beside her in one of those milk crates on wheels.

"Jess is on her way up," James informed her tersely.

"Okay. I want you to be civil," Rhonda instructed. "We are here to see if we can reach any sort of compromise. We don't want to go to trial if it can be avoided. Did you write up those suggestions for me?" James had drafted a few scenarios that allowed Jessica more time with the kids. He nodded, indicating the folder in his hand.

"Good," Rhonda said. "We'll be meeting in here." She motioned him toward a little anteroom and I made to follow them inside, but Rhonda held up her hand.

"Marie, you're not allowed in." I frowned, ready to protest, but she shook her head. "I'm sorry, but neither is Max. This meeting is for clients and their counsel only. The three of us will talk afterward."

Frustrated, I plunked myself down in a chair and crossed my arms. James shot me an apologetic look, but a moment later his face turned to stone as Jessica and Max inched their way into the library, now accompanied by their lawyer. After helping his wife into the anteroom, Max produced a pillow, which Jessica perched on ever-so-carefully, leaning heavily on Max and her lawyer as she sat down.

If I hadn't been sure before, I knew now that she was faking. It had been five months since she'd strained her back, but she was acting like she'd just been shattered in a car wreck.

The door closed, leaving Max and me together on the same side. I turned to look at him and he froze, then scurried away down the hall. *Run, fucker,* I thought.

I played idly with my phone while the meeting progressed. Forty minutes later the anteroom door opened and Jessica's lawyer was the first to emerge. He was on his way out of the library when Rhonda called him back. "Ben, I think introductions are in order, don't you?"

Ben halted, caught by surprise. "Oh, yes," he said. "I'm Ben Frye." He extended his hand to me and I shook it. "And you're Marie Aaron, correct? Pleasure to meet you."

"And your clients are?" Rhonda prompted.

"Oh yes, my clients are, um, Jessica and Max Mazzeo." He nodded his head at Max, who had just reappeared, signaling him to shake my hand. Max blinked stupidly for several seconds, looking like a deer caught in headlights, and then mumbled, "Hello," to my shoes.

"Hi Max," I said in a cool voice. "I'm Marie. Nice to *finally* meet you."

"And I'm Jessica." She extended her hand, and I looked her in the face for the first time.

She was petite and pretty, bearing a strong resemblance to Annabelle. She wore a tailored black jacket over a white blouse with slacks and very high heels, which seemed at odds with a bad back. Her face was expertly made up, but not garish, and her hair hung loose and skimmed her shoulders. The bad dye job was less noticeable out of the direct sunlight, but still a jarring note in an otherwise flawless appearance. It wasn't black, I realized, but an uneven dark brown.

Unlike her husband, Jessica met my gaze full on. Her hand was pale and limp in my own, and I suppressed a shudder as I took it. My father taught me that a firm handshake makes a good impression. Jessica's flaccid fingers dangled like she expected me to kiss her hand rather than shake it.

"Nice to meet you," I said stiffly.

"And you!" Her tone was conversational, jocular even. She acted like we were meeting at a dinner party rather than facing off in a courthouse. But then her expression turned sorrowful.

"I'm so sorry about my injury," Jessica said. She indicated her hunched frame and gave a rueful little laugh, then looked at me, expectant. For a moment there was silence and she stared at me as though I'd missed my cue. Then I realized: she was waiting for my outpouring of concern.

I'm so sorry about my injury? I thought. *Does she really think I give a shit about her injury? How about: I'm so sorry for this lawsuit? Or: I'm so sorry for turning my kids against you?* She confused me; I wasn't sure if she truly thought I was worried for her welfare or if she was wearing an excellently crafted mask.

"I'll go pull the car around, okay babe?" Max hurried away, clutching Jessica's butt pillow. Ben touched her shoulder, wished her goodbye, and said he'd be in touch.

As James and I made to leave the room, Jessica made a little sound of woe. "Could somebody . . . ?" With a helpless gesture, she conveyed that she couldn't walk unassisted.

"James, give Jessica your arm," Rhonda commanded. I gave her an aggrieved look and she shot me one back that clearly said: *Cool it.*

Stiff as a board and with a face to match, James offered Jessica his arm. With baby steps, they processed down the hall to the elevator. Rhonda didn't move much quicker on her little legs, but she was out of earshot when Jessica remarked casually, "That jacket still looks good on you, James. You're getting good use out of it."

There are some comments that women speak solely for the benefit of other women. That comment was marked for me.

I knew then that Jessica wasn't a poor helpless thing after all; she was manipulative and shrewd. We both glanced at James to see how he'd taken her compliment, but I was pleased to see that James just looked like he wanted to throw up.

There was an awkward exchange on the bottom floor, with James transferring Jessica onto Max's waiting arm. It was like watching their marriages in microcosm. I couldn't help but wonder what Jessica had seen in Max that drew her into an affair. He was portly and baby-faced, but he seemed to have the Stepford Husband act down pat.

The Mazzeos tippy-toed to their car, and we went across the street to Rhonda's office, where she and James filled me in.

James and Jessica hadn't been able to agree on anything. There would be a trial, I learned. Not only that, but there would be a custody evaluation beforehand.

"What does that mean?" I asked.

"It means that a custody evaluator will do a series of interviews with the family over the course of four months," explained Rhonda. "He'll meet with the parents and the kids, together and separately—and possibly with you and Max, if you agree."

"Of course," I said.

"And he'll write up an assessment for the judge with a recommendation as to where the kids should live."

"Any idea how much that's going to cost me?" asked James.

"It won't be cheap," Rhonda said bluntly. "I wish we could have talked Jess out of it. But trust me, it's better to have the four-month, extended evaluation than the standard one-month version. That will give the evaluator time to dig in and see that most of her claims are bullshit." James' brow furrowed, and I imagined that he was remembering Jessica's petition: her assertions that his house was "a slum" and that the girls suffered from poor hygiene under his care.

"This whole process is going to be expensive, James. You know this." James gave a grim nod. "Do you know how Jess is affording it? Is her husband's family loaded or something?"

"I don't think so," said James. "I think they do reasonably well, but they're not rich." Max worked for his dad in the family business—window treatments or something.

"Do you think she expects that James will pay her legal fees again?" I asked.

"Maybe," said Rhonda. "But more likely she expects to win and seek maximum child support. Now that she's not going back to work, she can file zero income against James' salary."

"Wait, what? She's not going back to work?" This was news to me. "Doesn't her disability expire soon?"

"That's irrelevant," Rhonda said. "She doesn't have to go back to work. She can be a stay-at-home mom if she chooses."

And with zero income, James explained, she stood to earn a substantial amount of child support. Each parent's salary was punched into a calculator to determine the monthly payment. James could argue that Jessica should go back to work, but child support was governed by a different court; it would be an entirely separate case.

"You're getting ahead of yourself," Rhonda counseled. "Let's not worry about that now."

"But if Jessica is suddenly able to be a stay-at-home mom, does that negatively impact James' case?" I asked. "I mean, won't a judge see that as being in her favor?" I looked at James and for the first time saw real worry in his eyes.

"Perhaps," Rhonda said evenly. "Which is all the more reason why we want an extended custody evaluation. Let's expose the fact that Jess has been a limited presence in the kids' lives, that she doesn't know their friends, their teachers, et cetera. Her ability to stay at home isn't the only factor here."

Feeling unsettled, we left with assignments to review the three recommended custody evaluators, and a handful of hard candies from Florence.

13

You Could Have Put Her Eye Out

Ken looked a little off-color.

He was slapping labels on the catalogs with a listless air, but stopped to scrutinize one of the mailing addresses.

"How do you spell 'Massachusetts'?" he asked me.

"M-A-S-S—" I began.

"—A-S-S?" he interrupted.

"That spells Mass-ass. It's not Mississippi."

Ken sighed. "I'll finish these later." He pushed the stack to the side of his desk. Just then his stomach gave an angry gurgle.

"Oh God," he said. "Sorry. I feel like I swallowed a live frog and it's trying to jump back out of my mouth." He paused, hand on his stomach. "I think it's from my dinner last night. My girlfriend and I went to Maui Now-ie, and the place smelled like kitty litter."

"What's Maui Now-ie?"

"It's a Hawaiian joint in Japantown. I always liked it because it combines both sides of my heritage, but the food's a little questionable."

"Do you speak Japanese?" I asked, curious.

"Not enough to get me drunk. When you know enough of a language to get yourself drunk—or get slapped by a girl—you're doing pretty good." He wiggled his eyebrows, but without enthusiasm.

A minute later, Ken's stomach gurgled again. "Do you have any gum?" he asked. "I want to go and barf, but then I'm gonna have barf breath." He paused. "That's horrible. I'm sorry I said that out loud."

Ken excused himself to go to the restroom, but came back a few minutes later, still looking green. "I keep dry-heaving, but all I had for breakfast was raisins and coffee, so there's nothing to bring up," he complained.

"Maybe you need to eat something?" I suggested. "There are some leftover bagels in the kitchen. Something bland might help settle your stomach."

Ken considered this. "Good idea. It's a bit early for lunch, but I could do some hide-a-bites." This was code for eating covertly behind his desk. He headed for the kitchen.

When he returned, I caught a whiff of something pungent and saw that he was eating from a Tupperware container. I peeked inside.

"*That's* what you're choosing to eat on a nauseous stomach?"

"What?" he said, defensive. "It's just rice and Spam, wrapped in seaweed."

"Ken, are you eating leftovers from that place?" I asked.

"Yeah. But not the fish. I'm pretty sure it was the fish that made me sick." Another gurgle. "We'll find out in about half an hour."

I did the rounds of each floor of the office, collecting the outgoing mail. When I returned, Ken was slumped over his desk, head in his hands. "Oh God," he said. "It sounds like the Great Calabasas Frog Race in my stomach." He let out a belch that jolted him upright. In the next instant, he jumped to his feet and fled the room.

He came back a short while later looking pale and sweaty, and collected his jacket and hat. "Marie, I gotta go home."

This was not a surprise. "Yeah, okay."

"I'm going to give that restaurant a scathing review. No wonder their Lomi-Lomi salmon was half off."

The next morning, I got an early text from Ken: "MARIE, I STILL GOT THE CRUMMY."

He didn't come into work, so I was alone on the phones all day and it was a busy one. By quitting time, I was wiped out. I grabbed a burrito on the way home and set up camp on the couch, where Mandy joined me half an hour later.

"Long day?" she asked.

"Yeah. The phones were ringing off the hook. It was kind of stressful."

She made a sympathetic face. "Will Ken be back tomorrow?"

"I think so. It sounds like the worst has passed. Oh—he sent me his restaurant review. Check this out." I pulled it up on my phone.

FOOD POISONING!

Both me and my lady got really bad food poisoning here Monday night & we think from eating the same thing . . . The Lomi-Lomi salmon of doom. I miss my island comfort food really bad, but I will never come back here again. Maui Now-ie no ono *unless you want to lose weight the embarrassing way down below, eat backwards up above & smell Jonny Cat litter while eating your* lau-lau!

Mandy laughed in delight. "That guy is a treasure!"

"Yeah, he's one of a kind." I snickered. "Last week he told me that he's been waxing the ends of his moustache with honey from the office kitchen. He said he's waiting for the day when a little bee comes by and lands on it."

Mandy kicked off her shoes and tucked her feet beneath her. She cocked her head at my tortilla chips and I nodded for her to take some. "How's it going with James and the kids?" she asked.

I made a face. "Not great. The kids are still being really standoffish. It's so different from how they used to act with me." I thought about the previous week at church when Avery had point-blank refused to hug me goodbye. "Their mom has told them that I'm 'just another girlfriend' and I probably won't be around long." This report had come courtesy of Annabelle.

"God, she's awful!" Mandy exclaimed. "And what does James say?"

I sighed. "Well, he tells the kids that I'm really important to him and that we're serious about each other. But I'm not sure that's helping matters because now they're afraid we're going to get married. They're just upset and confused." I paused to take a bite of my burrito. "He doesn't want to talk to them about the trial, but Jessica has been filling their heads with crap. I wish he would set the kids straight, but he feels it's better to keep them out of it entirely. It's kind of a mess."

I'd actually been pushing for the four of us to attend family therapy. James and I weren't planning to get married any time soon, but we were seriously involved and our relationship with the kids was obviously suffering. I wanted to regain our easy dynamic—or at least work toward it. James was reluctant, but months of difficulty with the kids were starting to wear him down.

Mandy's cell phone buzzed. "Oops, that's Javier," she said, texting him back with rapid-fire thumbs. "We're going to see his friend's art exhibit and then grab some dinner."

Mandy had met Javier on the shuttle bus to work. After noticing him several days in a row, she decided to make a move. Setting her bag on the seat beside her to discourage anyone from sitting down before his stop, she waited until Javier got on the bus and then discreetly cleared the seat. It worked; he sat down beside her and they struck up a conversation. It turned out that he worked as a feature film compositor at Georgetown Arts, the building next door to Roaming Ex. Originally from Spain, he'd lived most recently in Montreal and was in San Francisco on a temporary work visa, fulfilling a short-term contract. He spoke both English and French with a thick Spanish accent—talk about your International Man of Mystery.

I knew Mandy didn't much like her new commute, but at least she could credit it with bagging a hot guy. This was her third outing with Javier in as many weeks, and although things were still platonic, I had the sense that that might change soon.

"Do you want to come with us to the show?" she asked. It was a genuine offer, but I didn't want to be the third wheel on what sounded like a date.

"No thanks," I said. "I'm hunkered down for the evening."

She looked at me with a friend's concerned eye. "Are you going to be all right?"

"Oh yeah," I said. I indicated my burrito and the remote control. "I've got everything I need right here."

* * *

I was worn out. Being with James' kids these days was exhausting. Our golden afternoons of the previous summer were long gone, and now every one of our outings had an element of battle.

The girls got upset when they saw James and me being affectionate. "You don't hold his hand," Annabelle ordered me when we walked arm-in-arm down the sidewalk. She karate-chopped our hands apart.

"Ow," I said.

"Annabelle," James warned. But she just ran ahead.

If we snuck a quick kiss in front of the girls they called, "Ew! Cut it out!" Avery would grab my arm and Annabelle would grab James, and the two of them would wrench us apart. It was cute the first time they did it. Not so much the subsequent times.

They were no longer interested in spending time with us. Every activity we planned was met with resistance.

"Why do we have to go on a hike?" grumbled Avery when James broached the idea.

"It'll be an adventure!" he said, his tone overly bright.

"Your adventures are dumb," Avery said under her breath.

We waited patiently while the girls assembled their hiking gear: hats, sunglasses, backpacks, water bottles, sunblock, windbreakers, and snacks. "How many days long is this hike?" I whispered to James. He just shrugged.

We drove to a park up in the hills and picked an easy trail. Once on the path, the griping began.

"It's hot."

"I'm tired."

"My feet hurt."

"How much longer?"

"Yeah, how much longer?" I said to James, with a roll of my eyes.

"We just got started!" he said. "Come on girls, lighten up a little."

"Dad, I need a break," complained Annabelle. "I'm already sweaty." That was because she was wearing twelve layers, but whatever. We paused in the shade of a big oak tree, and Annabelle shrugged off her backpack, jacket, and sweatshirt. Avery sat on a tree stump and dug in the dirt with a stick, the picture of utter boredom.

"Fine, take five," said James. He pulled a tangerine out of his pocket and peeled it swiftly, offering me half the fruit.

"Thanks," I said.

"You want another?" He tossed me a second tangerine and I caught it easily.

"No thanks, I'm good," I said, tossing it back to him.

He grinned, took a few steps backward, and lobbed it back to me. Suddenly we were playing catch.

I increased our distance and the tangerine sailed higher through the air. Each catch made a satisfying *thwack* in the palm of my hand. I hadn't played catch in ages. I'd forgotten how fun it could be.

Now the kids were interested. "Hey, I want to play," said Avery, her bad mood forgotten. "Throw it to me!" James gave her an easy toss. She heaved it back at him with force, causing him to jog backwards for it.

"Easy, Ave," he said, throwing the tangerine to me. "Annie, do you want to play?"

She shook her head. "No."

"Are you sure?" The tangerine moved in a circle, from me to Avery to James, and Annabelle's eyes followed it closely. She looked like she wanted to join in.

"Annie, come play," James urged.

"I told you," she said to him, stepping into his sight line, "my name is *not* Annie, it's—"

Whomp!

The tangerine clocked her right in the face and dropped to the ground. It seemed to knock the words out of her mouth, and she stood still, stunned.

"Oh shit!" James and I said in unison and ran toward her.

Annabelle looked dumbfounded for a moment, her mouth open in a surprised little O. But then she began to laugh. The tangerine had hit her in the cheek. It left a bright red circle, but she was otherwise unharmed.

Once we'd established that she was okay, James and I started to laugh, too. She'd looked so funny, like a cartoon character that had been bonked on the head and seen stars.

But Avery wasn't laughing. "You could have put her eye out!" she exclaimed.

Annabelle's laughter abruptly ceased. She looked at her sister and then back at her dad with a frown. "Dad, it's not funny! You could have put my eye out!"

And suddenly the bad moods were back.

"I want to go home," said Avery.

"Me too," agreed Annabelle.

So we gathered all the gear and headed back to the car. As the girls tramped ahead, eager to put an end to the outing, James leaned over and whispered to me.

"I know this is wrong, but I have to say it." There was a little gleam in his eye. "Smacking her with that tangerine felt kinda good."

14

THERAPY

Mercifully, as summer wound down we noticed a new shift in the girls' attitudes. School was fast approaching, and when the kids realized that they wouldn't be moving to their mom's for the new school year, they mellowed out substantially. It was a welcome change.

Jessica, by contrast, decided to crank up her bullshit.

In an effort to be nice, James sent her the details for Back to School Night, with a note:

> *Jessica, I'm not sure how you're feeling. If you're planning to attend Back to School Night, you are welcome to take the girls for a few hours in the afternoon. Let me know.*

In these early days of the custody battle, we still thought that rational compromise could be achieved. But Jessica wrote back:

> *I find it offensive that you would offer me extra time with the girls, knowing full well that I cannot physically travel that far due to my injury. This is not*

a goodwill gesture, but taunting, pure and simple.
Thank you again for showing your true character.

"Is she for real?" I asked, disbelieving.

James snorted. "She loves to bitch about not having enough time with the kids, but she doesn't actually want to *spend* time with them." He shook his head. "For years I've offered to let her take the girls on Wednesday nights while I'm at choir rehearsal. She's never once done it. Her office is right off the Embarcadero; she could have easily met us near Mercy and taken the kids for dinner. But she just didn't want to. I asked the girls why their mum never could meet them after work on Wednesdays, and you know what they said? 'Mum can't come to Mercy because it's in a dangerous neighborhood.'"

True, the Tenderloin was a little seedy, but Mercy was also three blocks from the high-rent Union Square district. Surely James had offered to meet her there?

"Of course I did," he answered. "But then it was, 'Mum needs to go home and go to bed early because she has a hard job.'"

"Well, they were right about that," I quipped. "The job nearly killed her."

"If only," he growled.

"Look," I said. "I really think we should get some therapy with the kids. There are obviously a lot of issues going on here. Let's get someone to walk us through things, and maybe we can invite Jessica and Max to participate." I took his hand. "I think it would be a good thing."

He sighed. "But baby, I hate her." His tone was reasonable, adorable even. "I don't want to do therapy with her."

"I know," I pressed, "but it will be good for the kids. We have to figure out a way to get along." Again, I thought reason was in my tool belt.

Eventually James acquiesced and we began researching therapists. We found a woman we liked named Ilana Samuel who had an office in Noe Valley. The main reason we liked her was because she wasn't yet fully accredited, which meant that her rates were very reasonable. Ilana wanted to meet with James and me alone first, before including the kids, so we set up an appointment for the following week. Meanwhile, James sent Jessica a note inviting her and Max to join us.

Jessica's response was swift. James got a phone call from Ilana that afternoon.

"Jess threatened to sue her," he told me flatly.

"What?" I sank onto my bed in dismay.

"She produced some document from our last custody trial that I'd forgotten about. Neither parent is permitted to take the kids to a mental health professional without written consent from the other parent. She went right to Ilana's supervisor and threatened legal action."

"But why would she do that?" I cried, frustrated. "She's invited to come *with* us. We *want* her to participate. Why would she blow the whole thing up?"

"Because she's nuts," James emphasized. "I keep telling you this."

I rolled my face into a pillow and let out a smothered scream.

"And she must have said something to the kids," James went on, "because they've informed me that they're not crazy and they're not going to therapy."

I stared up at the ceiling. "Of course not." My voice was sarcastic. If anything, this woman was driving *me* crazy.

I took a few measured breaths, trying to calm down. "I want to go anyway," I said to James. "Can we? We still need help; we don't know how to handle this. Let's go get some support."

James sighed and was quiet for a long moment.

"Okay," he said finally. "I don't really want to, but okay."

* * *

"Did I mention that I don't really want to do this?" James asked the following Friday. He had left work early to pick me up at five, and now we were racing to our five-thirty appointment.

"Yes." I kissed his hand. "You've mentioned it a few times, actually."

"Just checking," he said. We lucked out with a parking spot right in front of Ilana's office with two minutes to spare.

The building was a converted Victorian, bookended by a Chinese restaurant and an optometrist. We climbed the narrow, carpeted staircase and settled ourselves in the waiting room. It was very quiet. The air felt awkward.

"This is weird," James whispered.

"Shh," I whispered back. "It's going to be good."

I heard a door open down the hall and a moment later a woman poked her head around the doorframe. "James?"

"Yes," he said, standing.

"I'm Ilana." She came into the waiting room and held out her hand. We each shook it. "Nice to meet you both," Ilana said. "Come this way."

We settled into the room that served as her office, where a squashy armchair faced a leather couch. Absentmindedly I clutched a throw pillow, unaware that I'd become intimately acquainted with it in later sessions.

Ilana looked to be only a few years older than me. She was casually dressed in jeans and a peasant blouse, with a big chunky necklace and clouds of fluffy, light brown hair. Her curls were the crimpy sort, like the edges of lasagna noodles. She had a gentle face and a soft, ethereal voice. I wondered if it was her special "therapist's voice", or if she used it all the time.

"So," she began in melodious tones. "Why don't you tell me a little about why you're here today?" She looked expectantly at James. I did, too.

"Well," he said, then cleared his throat. "Well, you've spoken to my ex-wife."

"Yes." Ilana gave a little smile and wrinkled her nose just the tiniest bit. And suddenly I liked her. I liked her a lot.

"So, uh, she's suing me for custody. And it's been hard on the kids. And on Marie," he said, gesturing to me.

"And on you, too, I'd imagine," said Ilana. "So right now you share custody?"

"I have primary custody," James clarified. "The kids spend every other weekend and half the summer with their mum."

"Okay. And recently she filed to change custody?"

"Yes."

"And the kids are unhappy about it?" Ilana probed gently.

"Oh no. The kids say they want to live with their mum."

"But you don't want them to?"

"Right."

I glanced at the clock and saw that five minutes of our precious hour had already elapsed. I decided to jump in.

"Jessica walked out on them when the girls were little," I explained and launched into the backstory. James fidgeted a bit as I spilled his family's history, but I needed to get Ilana up to speed fast. She may have been reasonably priced, but she still wasn't cheap.

And James' story wasn't short. As I spoke, I felt myself getting heated. I remembered again how it felt when Max turned on his heel and walked away from me, and when Jessica slyly complimented James' suit jacket. I heard Annabelle parroting, "If you can't say anything nice, don't say anything at all," and remembered Avery with tears in her eyes, whispering, "I'm sorry, Marie."

I didn't realize I was shouting until James squeezed my hand. "And she's a horrible person!" My voice bounced around the room. "She's an awful, awful woman who doesn't give a shit about her kids. She just wants to win!"

"Sweetie, you're yelling," whispered James.

"I know!" I hollered. It felt good to yell, and I reasoned that we were paying for it.

"Well, there are other clients in this building," Ilana pointed out, and instantly I deflated. "Not to worry," she said, waving my apologies away. "I can see you're holding a lot of anger."

"Yes," I said, the word seeping out of me like escaping air.

"And what are you hoping to accomplish with these sessions?" she asked.

"Well, originally we were hoping that the kids could come with us," said James.

Ilana shook her head. "Unfortunately I can't see the children without their mother's consent."

James nodded. "We know. By the way, what did she say to you on the phone?"

Ilana paused. "I'm not going to share the details of that conversation," she said in her even, professional voice. "But she was very . . . explicit."

James grinned. "That's Jessica. Very explicit." And Ilana's nose wrinkled again before she smoothed over her expression with a smile.

15

HOT AND COLD

We started seeing Ilana every few weeks, though James remained unenthusiastic. He didn't enjoy dwelling on Jessica in his free time, but I found it such a relief to have someone to talk to. Just having someone bear witness to what we were going through was a comfort to me. I could keep my composure around the kids because I now had a place to put my feelings when they threatened to overflow.

James did take pleasure in the idea that Jessica would've hated Ilana and her boho vibe. He tried to pinpoint the exact element that would've irked Jess the most.

"It's her hair," he finally decided. "It's too big and free."

* * *

In the fall, James lost his job.

His company merged with Kingston Battery and management of his branch was folded into Kingston's South City office. I was shocked that they'd let him go after twenty years, but James' Kingston counterpart had thirty-three years in the business. In the job that he'd dedicated half his life to, James suddenly found himself superfluous.

To his enormous credit, he wasted no time moping. He found a colleague with franchise aspirations and they teamed up to open a retail store. Hassan had the funds and James had the business acumen. Within a few short weeks they'd launched a storefront in Redwood City, and James became manager of a Kingston Evermore battery store.

But the sudden change left us reeling. James lost his flexible hours and began working long days and weekends, trying to get his new store off the ground. His salary was cut nearly in half. He wore neon green branded polo shirts to work, which he hated. They made him look every inch the retail store manager that he now was. It was a considerable step down the career ladder and a terrible time for it.

He began to worry about money.

* * *

The good news, if you could call it that, was that the custody trial was slow moving. James had chosen an evaluator, and true to form, Jessica had refuted his choice. It took some time for them to settle on Dr. Colleen Seeger, and then she couldn't begin right away, so we had a few months of relative peace while we waited.

Life went on in the meantime, and the kids continued to run hot and cold. But with Ilana's support, we leaned into the good times and did our best to create fun when we could.

Our efforts were met with mixed reviews.

For Avery's twelfth birthday, I suggested a slumber party. I couldn't believe she'd never had one before. She was stoked by the idea, but later threw a tantrum when she learned that I'd be staying over, too.

"Dad! She's going to want to *hang out* with us!" Avery wailed, like it was the worst thing in the world. I was offended. I was coming to hang out with my boyfriend, not a bunch of twelve-year-old girls.

But still, I went to bat for her. When James came home with baby carrots, I sent him back out for Cheetos. I insisted that he get a wide selection of movies to choose from, not just two. I even got the guest list bumped up to seven kids— a lot for that little house—but I argued that slumber parties are supposed to be crowded. Avery seemed to chill out as she realized that I was on her side.

With the house crammed full of kids, James and I had nowhere to go but his bedroom. So we set up camp on his bed and watched a movie on the little TV. At my suggestion, James had put up a beaded curtain where his bedroom door should've been—it gave the illusion of privacy.

Halfway through the movie the beads rattled and Annabelle poked her head in. She looked a little forlorn. Avery and the other girls weren't including her, she said.

"Do you want to watch a movie with us?" James asked, and Annabelle nodded. She climbed into bed between the two of us and snuggled against her father.

These moments were now so rare, I was afraid to accidentally touch her and break the spell. I left a gap between us even as I angled my body toward hers, wanting to kiss her still-little face and smooth back her hair. My heart felt too big for my chest. James' hand sought mine under the pillow and I knew he was feeling the same way.

"Um, Mr. James?" came a voice from the doorway. One of Avery's friends was peering through the beads. "Do you have any fruit? Or is it all just Cheetos?"

* * *

For Christmas, I came up with a fabulous idea, if I do say so myself.

"Scavenger hunt!" I declared to James, who looked at me blankly.

"That sounds . . . ambitious," he said. I frowned. "I mean, cool. That sounds cool."

"It's going to be better than cool; it's going to be awesome," I corrected him. "And we can do it on the cheap. You'll see."

"I like cheap," he said.

The Christmas custody schedule was downright stupid. In even calendar years, the girls spent from noon on Christmas Eve until noon on Christmas Day with their mom, and from noon on Christmas Day until noon on the twenty-sixth with their dad. In odd years, the schedule was reversed. The following week, they did it all over again for New Year's.

To complicate matters further, the two-week school break was split in half so that James had the first week (in even years) and Jessica had the second. But the holidays didn't fall neatly into those buckets, which meant that some years, the girls would have to travel between households up to six times over the course of their break—a ninety-minute drive each way.

Never one to compromise, Jessica insisted that they follow the schedule to the letter every year. Even when James tried to shift things in her favor, she wouldn't agree. Jessica knew that the existing schedule interrupted church services at Mercy, and it seemed she'd rather make things difficult for James than agree to a more sensible split.

So Christmas was already a touchy time, and we dreaded the inevitable comparison between Mom's house and Dad's. Max had a large family and the kids enjoyed the festive atmosphere at his parents' house, where they were surrounded by step-aunts, uncles, and cousins. It made James a little glum, and he was already feeling low this year with the custody trial and the loss of his job. But I was determined to plan an amazing holiday for the four of us.

As Christmas approached, I put all the pieces in place. I wrote scads of rhyming clues on little pieces of paper and tied each poem with a bright blue ribbon. The clues would reveal a whole week of Christmas festivities. The kids would have to solve puzzles, make holiday crafts, and gather small gifts along the way. But first, we'd kick things off with an epic nighttime scavenger hunt that would wind through the city.

I put all my efforts into making it a holiday to remember. By the time the scavenger hunt rolled around, I was beside myself with excitement.

"You should take them to the Walt Disney Museum!" suggested Ken, who'd caught my enthusiasm. "I know it sounds totally goober, but it's so cool."

"Maybe another time," I said. "I've already got it all mapped out. James is going to pick me up from work today and we're going to pretend to take the kids to the food trucks. But instead, we're just going to park the car at Fort Mason and then open the trunk to reveal . . . " I gave myself a little drum roll. "Scooters! And we'll scoot all over town, doing amazing stuff!"

"That's so rad!" Ken said. "Did you buy them scooters?"

"Nah, I borrowed them. But there will be other presents. And I wrote all these poems as clues." I scooped up the blue-ribboned scrolls and let them fall through my fingers.

"Man, you are the coolest."

"Thanks!" I *felt* like the coolest. I tucked the clues carefully back into my purse. "You're going to your folks' for the holidays, right? Is Pia going with you?"

Ken leaned back in his chair. "Yeah. She and my mom do *not* get along." He lifted his eyebrows so high, I imagined they'd be hidden by his hair—if he had any. "You know how to make a Molotov cocktail? Put two alpha females under the same roof on Christmas Eve and just add alcohol. *Yowza!* I hope I survive it."

I laughed. Ken's eyebrows descended, then furrowed into a deep V. "Pia's been talking about moving in together."

"Really?" I said. "Do you want to move in with her?"

There was a long pause. "I feel like, if I move in with her, I will probably marry her. And I will never make out with another girl again. Till we get divorced.'"

I didn't know what to say to that, but it didn't matter. Ken glanced out the window and said, "Uh-oh. It looks like it might start raining. That could put a damper on your scavenger hunt."

But I just smiled and held up the four yellow rain ponchos that I'd bought at the drugstore.

"I'm all over it," I said.

The kids were a little moody when they met me after work. They didn't want to go to the food trucks in the rain.

"It's barely drizzling," James said. "We're going to have fun."

We pulled into the parking lot amidst scattered grumbling. James turned toward the backseat. "Before we get out of the car, we have a little something for you." He extended the first clue. "Read this."

Avery snatched the scroll before her sister could take it. "Avery!" Annabelle complained, but Avery was already scanning the poem.

"Read it out loud," I prompted. I was bubbling with excitement.

In a bored voice, Avery began:

> *Hey, what are we doing out here in the rain?*
> *(It altered our plan, but we shall not complain)*
> *We won't let it ruin our evening of fun*
> *Happy holidays, girls . . . OUR CHRISTMAS HAS BEGUN!*

James nodded at me in appreciation of this last-minute stanza change. Avery continued to read.

> *Butholdonyou'rethinkingit'sonlyFriday*

"Hey, slow down," I said. She glared at me.

> *But hold on, you're thinking, it's only Friday*
> *And Christmas is still a good few days away*
> *But why should we wait to enjoy the good cheer?*
> *We're going to do something different this year.*

Avery's voice was monotone. She could not have sounded more bored.

> *We're not going to focus so much on the stuff*
> *(Cause frankly, dear children, we have quite enough)*
> *And Christmas means more than a gift or a toy*
> *It's being together, it's sharing the joy.*

"We're not getting presents?" she demanded. "Dad, are you serious?"

"Just chill out," said James. "Keep reading." Avery frowned.

My enthusiasm was ebbing away. This wasn't the reaction I'd envisioned. "Annabelle, why don't you read a verse?" I suggested. Avery was apparently too cool for school, but I thought Annie might catch the excitement.

But Annabelle put on a nasal, nasty voice.

> *So, we're going to find lots of fun things to do*
> *And you're going to follow each blue-ribboned clue*

"Stop it," James said. There was steel in his tone. Annabelle dialed it down.

> *Through Saturday, Sunday, and Monday, and more*
> *A whole week of Christmas delights are in store!*
>
> *Who knows where this Christmas adventure will lead!*
> *But we should get started now, we should proceed*
> *Put jackets and gloves on, get ready to ride*
> *Then open the trunk and pull out what's inside.*

Both girls stared at us with blank expressions.

"Shall we open the trunk?" James suggested. Slowly, the kids got out of the car.

We pulled out the scooters to absolutely no fanfare. "It's raining," Avery pointed out again.

"It's barely raining," I corrected. "Certainly not enough to stop us from having fun. Plus, I have these." I whipped out a yellow poncho and held it up in triumph. "One for each of us!"

Avery recoiled in actual horror. "I am not wearing that," she said. "Dad, I'm not!"

"Then get wet," he said easily. He pulled a poncho over his head. "How do I look?"

"I think it's very becoming," I said.

"Thank you. It makes me feel very handsome. Plus, I'm so comfortable and dry."

"Oh, let me try mine on." I shrugged into the bright yellow plastic. "Am I beautiful?"

"You are."

"Why, thank you so much!"

"You look like a banana slug," Avery informed her father.

"But I'm so much faster than a banana slug!" James pushed off the ground and sailed away on his scooter, making a big loop around us, then skidding to a stop. "Come on, let's get going!"

"Are we really going to do this?" Avery asked.

"Yeah!"

Avery heaved a huge sigh, as though we'd just informed her that she'd be doing manual labor all evening. She mounted her scooter half-heartedly.

"Here we go!" I called and led the way through the park, bound for Fisherman's Wharf. At the top of the hill I looked back and realized that Avery hadn't moved. She was standing on the path where we'd left her, the scooter on the ground at her feet. We circled back around to get her.

"My scooter is broken," she said angrily. James inspected it. It wasn't broken, but it was impaired, with the front wheel wobbling in an annoying sort of way.

"You're just going to have to make the best of it," he told her.

"Oh great, so I'm only one with a broken scooter? That's not fair!" she cried. "Annie, let me try yours."

"No," said Annabelle, scooting out of reach.

"Dad!"

"Avery, I'm sorry. We didn't realize yours was bent. I'd trade with you, but that's a kid's scooter and it won't hold my weight." Again, he urged her to make the best of it.

"But you guys are going to leave me behind!" Avery was working herself into a fine temper.

"We won't leave you behind." James sounded weary.

"Yes, you will! You already did! You guys were all the way over there before you noticed I was gone!"

"Ave—"

"Why do we have to do this? Why are you making me ride in the rain on a broken scooter? This sucks!"

Something inside me snapped. "If it sucks, then let's go home," I said. My voice was quiet and hard. "I sure don't want to spend time with you when you're acting like this."

I'd called their bluff. Avery stared at the ground. Annabelle nudged her scooter back and forth. "I want to do the scavenger hunt," she said softly.

In the end, we proceeded with the plan, but the shine was off the evening. And my feelings were hurt. I wished I hadn't arranged a whole week of Christmas adventures.

16

THE OLIN FAMILY

In early spring, Jessica's family invited us to join them at Disneyland.

"Wait—they invited me, too?" I asked. I was sure there'd been some sort of mistake.

"Yes, they invited you, too." James smiled at me. "Don't worry, I double-checked."

James remained in sporadic touch with Jessica's four siblings: Jessalyn, Jocelyn, Daniel, and Mary-Margaret. The Olin family.

"Hold up," I said. "The girls' names are Jessica, Jessalyn, and Jocelyn?"

"And Mary-Margaret."

Weird, I thought.

Since the divorce he'd tried to stay connected, and until a few years ago, he took the girls to Canada whenever he could. But Jessica threw a fit the last time, when she discovered that James had left the kids in Jessalyn's care for a few days while he traveled for business. In a fury, she accused

James of "leaving the girls with any Tom, Dick, or Harry that comes along." The story made me giggle, but the result was that Jessica now held the kids' passports hostage.

"And you're sure Jess and Max aren't coming?" I'd already asked this question several times, but I needed to be certain.

"Yup." James yawned. Managing a store was wearing on him, and he tired more easily these days. "I don't think they were invited."

This filled me with secret glee.

"They rented a hotel suite, and we can crash on the floor. All we have to pay for is park entry and food." He yawned again. "It's still more than I want to spend, but it'll be worth it for the kids to see their cousins. Something fun before we start this stupid custody evaluation." Our first interview with Dr. Seeger was finally on the calendar.

So, in late March we drove the seven hours down to Disneyland for some awkward fun with James' ex-in-laws.

To their credit, they were all very nice to me. I met Jessalyn and her husband, Jason, and their two kids, Jase and Juliana, who were Avery and Annabelle's ages, respectively. Annabelle and Juliana flocked to each other immediately and were inseparable the entire trip.

Then there was Daniel Jr. and his wife, Lillian, and their two-year-old son, William. And Mary-Margaret, who reminded me sharply of her eldest sister when I accidentally addressed her as Mary. "I prefer to be called Mary-Margaret," she said. She was perfectly polite, but I still felt a little chill.

The only one missing was Jocelyn, who was heavily pregnant. And, of course, Jessica.

At first I was shy, feeling like the odd man out in this family group. But everyone was welcoming, particularly Jessalyn, who went out of her way to make me feel included. I appreciated her effort.

Even so, it was distinctly unnerving to be around her because she looked so much like Jessica: a carbon copy, but with lighter hair. She was prettier, I thought, but maybe that's because she had an easy smile. Jessica's smile seemed forced and fake, although I was admittedly biased.

There wasn't much talk of the custody trial—not with the kids around—but I got the impression that the Olins were trying to stay neutral. Whatever feelings they had about their sister, they kept mum. I realized I'd been hoping for a little covert trash-talk, but I was disappointed. Daniel made a face when Jessica's name was mentioned, but that was the extent of it. His sisters referred to her in the same way they referred to Jocelyn—as though she was simply not there that day.

"I thought they didn't like Jessica," I whispered to James when I could get him alone.

"They're super Christian," he reminded me. "Forgiveness is a virtue and all that crap."

It was hard to imagine any of these people behaving in the way that Jessica had behaved toward me and James, and this just made my curiosity grow. What had happened in this family to produce several seemingly pleasant siblings and one rogue asshole?

But as the day wore on, the family resemblance began to emerge. Daniel made a crack about their mother and Mary-Margaret grew defensive.

"It's not fair of you to say that Mom never visits, Daniel. You moved all the way out to Fort Mac. That's really far."

"Well, Dad comes out all the time." Daniel took his squirming son from Lillian and bounced him a little.

"Yeah, but Dad goes out there for work. Mom needs to stay at home with the dog. It's not easy to get a dog sitter at a moment's notice." She frowned at him.

"Who said anything about a moment's notice? Besides, she could leave the dog with any of you guys."

"It's not that easy, Daniel. Lucy's getting old; she needs her meds, she needs supervision—"

Daniel shook his head. "I'm just saying, I thought Mom might show a little more interest in her grandson than her dog. But let's drop it."

Aha! I thought. *They've all got mommy issues.* Mary-Margaret turned away, her shoulders stiff.

During lunch at the Rainforest Café, Jessalyn ordered nachos without sour cream, but they botched her order and put sour cream on them anyway. She didn't comment and nobody noticed, but she didn't eat a bite of her meal. When the waiter came to clear the table, he commented on her untouched plate. "Was everything all right?"

"No. I ordered nachos without sour cream, but you put sour cream on them. I couldn't eat any of it." She stared sadly at her plate, then turned doleful eyes to him.

The waiter wasn't sure what to say. The rest of us had finished eating; it was too late to bring her a fresh order. He mumbled an apology and asked if there was anything he could do. Jessalyn hung her head. "It's too late now," she said.

As we left the restaurant, James whispered to me, "That was so much like Jessica, it was creepy. She used to do that kind of shit all the time."

Jessalyn was a bit snippy in the afternoon—hungry, I surmised—and everyone grew a little tired and irritable as the day wore on. Everyone but Avery. She was a fount of good cheer, with energy to spare. What's more, she was acting like I was her very best friend. "Marie, sit with me!" she begged on every ride. She laughed and joked with me all day long and dogged my steps around the park.

I tried to make sense of her sudden change in behavior. Maybe it was because Annabelle and Juliana were two peas in a pod, whereas Jase barely spoke. I hadn't heard him say a word all weekend.

Or maybe Avery felt a little removed from this extended family she hardly knew. She hadn't seen them since she was eight years old. It dawned on me that next to James and Annabelle, I knew Avery better than anyone there. Suddenly she wanted to embrace that. I felt a warm echo of our happy time the year before.

We staggered out of the park at closing time, slept like the dead, and bid farewell to the Olins the next morning. I was ready to go. As nice as they were, our relationship had a clear expiration date.

On the long drive homeward, I sensed an exhaustion tantrum simmering in the backseat. The kids had had a great time, but the magic of Disney wore off at the Anaheim border. So we rode most of the way in silence, trying to preserve the memory of a good weekend. It seemed like maybe things were on the upswing.

* * *

It was a shock the following week when James received a package in the mail: a thick binder from Jessica's lawyer.

"Enclosed for your records are the documents that I will be forwarding to Dr. Seeger," the cover letter read. A long list of materials followed, including: "Notes and pictures from Annabelle sent to Jessica Mazzeo and her husband, Maxwell."

At the back of the binder were dozens of photocopied pages from *The Journal of Annabelle Mazzeo,* written in her own childish hand. James recoiled as though he'd been slapped. Annabelle's last name was de Graaf.

The journal entries had a strange theme, as though they'd been recorded with a purpose.

Dear Mom, I am trying vary hard on my spelling at school. I know you are vary conserned about my father dating her.

Today after dinner I was still hungry so I asked if I could have a snack. Dad said "you can have anything." To make sure I asked if I could have some strawberries and he said "No you may not." It's a good example of our father not telling the truth. I'm not sure if I can trust our father anytime, anywhere. OK so maybe I trust him a little bit but only as much as an electron (a part of an atom.) I miss my mom, a lot. Good night.

Today when I was showing dad my new lunch container he said "Get dressed" and I said "OK". Then he raised his voice and said "Now!" I don't know a certain reason but it scares me, it scares me a lot! Now I am scared for the rest of the day. Good night.

I am not sure if I should be scared of Dad raising his voice or not. I miss mom. Do I have to live here?

Today I found out that Marie isn't the one doing most of the bad stuff. Our dad is. He is lying and saying we like her, and the only problem is him. Dad's why we can't be at our mom's house already. He's the one that lies and says that we should not lie, "Lying is the worst thing you can do." I can't believe our father is lying. Good night. I miss mom! I wish I could be happy and be there.

I didn't hear anything to write today.

Dad said "Wash your coat today or I will throw it away." He raised his voice now I'm scared if he'll just turn around and yell. Hate it here. Hate it at Mercy. Can't wait until I talk to the person who listens.

"The person who listens?" I asked.

"The custody evaluator," James said. He flipped back to the first entry. "These begin in February. It looks like Jess has been encouraging Annabelle to keep a spy journal." He threw the binder on the table, where it landed with a thud. He looked wrecked.

"She's not a very good spy," I said. "What are all these bad things you're supposed to have done?"

"I didn't let her have strawberries?" he said. His voice broke.

17

THE CHILDREN ARE ACTING
LIKE ASSHOLES

Knitting group was being held in Alex's apartment. I stood in her small kitchen, searching for bowls.

"Cabinet on the left, Marie," she directed.

"Thank you." I pulled out four bowls, put them on the table and sat down beside her. "Oh, spoons!" she said.

"I got it." I stood back up to grab them.

"Who made the salad?" asked Hailey, who'd just arrived. "It looks delicious."

"I'll take credit for that!" said Alex. "But everything looks delicious with goat cheese."

Our knitting lay abandoned in the living room while we settled in for dinner. Katia had made a big pot of homemade soup and I'd brought a loaf of crusty bread. Hailey had made brownies for dessert.

"Katia, this is amazing," Alex declared. "I can't believe you brought soup to my house. That's a feat."

Katia shrugged. "It's easy with the slow cooker. I just unplugged it and put it in the car." The soup was a creamy butternut squash, thick and golden and perfect on a drizzly night.

"It is seriously good," agreed Hailey. "Can I get the recipe?"

I felt a flash of old embarrassment as I remembered a knitting night I'd hosted long ago. Cooking is not my forte, and hosting meals tends to fill me with anxiety. After wandering the grocery store for what felt like hours, I'd finally grabbed six cans of chili and tried to pass it off as homemade. Except I'd accidentally bought four cans of beef chili and two cans of vegan chili, with those disgusting chunks of wheat gluten. My friends didn't eat much.

"I'm so glad we're hanging out tonight," Alex said. "I've had a crappy day. These teenagers at work are making me crazy." Alex was a physician's assistant. She worked in the teen health clinic at El Centro, a medical center in a predominantly Spanish-speaking part of Oakland.

Alex impressed me. When we first met she had just graduated from PA school and decided to learn Spanish to improve her job performance. In the evenings she attended language classes, and before I knew it, she was medically fluent and conducting most of her workday in Spanish. This was in addition to her multiple hobbies, including salsa dancing, yoga, masters swim class, and violin practice. Alex was six feet tall and made entirely of energy.

"What's going on?" asked Katia.

"I'm just tired of seeing pregnant kids all day!" Alex exclaimed. "Nobody is teaching these girls that they can do something with their lives other than get pregnant. They all come from these giant families, and it's no big deal to have a baby at fifteen or sixteen—their sister did it, or their auntie did it, and it's what they know. They don't use birth control because it's not convenient or because their boyfriend doesn't want to." She sawed at the loaf of bread, aggrieved.

"Today I had a follow-up appointment with a girl who had an abortion last week. I had told her that she shouldn't insert anything into her vagina for a few weeks, no tampons or anything." Sometimes Alex's stories could get a little explicit. "She comes in this afternoon and I ask how she's feeling, and she says she feels fine. In fact, she and her boyfriend are already having sex again! So I ask, 'Did you use a condom?' And she says, 'Well, no. You told me not to put anything in my vagina.' And I say, *'That includes penises!'*"

The rest of us cracked up. After a moment, Alex joined in, too—although her laughter was more the weary sort. "Oh man," she said. "Maybe I'm just burned out. There are too many pregnant teenagers. I feel like they're multiplying."

"They are," pointed out Hailey.

Alex groaned. "You're right! They're just so incredibly fertile! It's amazing to me how these girls get pregnant at the drop of a hat, when so many women have fertility problems. I mean, if you think about all the *effort*, all the *obstacles* that a sperm has to go through to fertilize an egg, it's a wonder people get pregnant at all!" She shoved a piece of bread into her mouth and chewed furiously. "Where is the justice, I ask you?" she said, spewing crumbs.

"Tell me about it," said Katia. She'd gotten married two summers before and I knew she was trying for a baby.

Hailey reached for the wine. "Well, I'm considering selling my children if you're in the market. They are driving me crazy lately."

"Really? What are they doing?" asked Alex.

Hailey wrinkled her nose. "They're just kind of . . . assholes," she said.

This struck me as incredibly funny. "What are you talking about? Your kids are adorable." Hunter was a science phenom, a certifiable genius, and Poppy was a tiny fireball with a cloud of blond hair.

I'd always admired Hailey. She seemed to maneuver through life so gracefully. She and her husband, Reese, had been together since college, a perfect couple. When we met, she was newly pregnant with Hunter—and then a few years later, she gave birth to Poppy *in the backseat of her car,* with only Reese's assistance.

As if that weren't enough to earn her Superwoman status, she maintained an enviable magazine lifestyle. She always looked put together. She made her kids' Halloween costumes by hand every year and hosted her in-laws for Thanksgiving. Her last New Year's resolution had been to bake a new pie each month, and I was still reminiscing about Coconut Cream Pie July. In short, Hailey seemed to have it all together, and if she weren't such good company, I would have quite disliked her.

So I was a little delighted to hear that her kids were occasionally jerks.

She gave a dry laugh. "Yeah, they're adorable sometimes, but they're getting spoiled. Both kids were griping at me the other day, and I just wondered: How did you get so *entitled?*"

"Do you spoil them?" asked Katia. "That surprises me."

"We try not to, but their grandparents give them a lot of toys. They've got way too much stuff. And they're so . . . *imperial* about it. I was trying to get Hunter to clean his room the other day and threatened to throw out some of his toys if he didn't put them away. And he just said, 'Go ahead, Mom. I don't even like those toys. I'll just get new ones.'"

"See, that's why I don't want kids," said Alex. "I don't have the patience for any of that crap."

"But you're great with kids," said Katia.

"I'm great with other people's kids," said Alex. "But when they start talking like that, I send them right back to their parents. I don't need any tiny assholes in my life."

* * *

That conversation stayed with me for days. I found it quite cheering. It seemed to boost James' spirits, too.

"My kids are assholes," he said, trying it on. "Huh." He paused. "I mean, I love them."

"Oh, of course! Me too," I said hastily.

"But they're assholes."

"Well . . . yeah."

At our next appointment with Ilana, James told the story of Annabelle's journal. Ilana was appropriately disturbed and winced in all the right places. "That must have been hurtful to read," she said. "Now that a few days have passed, how do you feel?"

James pulled out our new maxim. "We've realized that the children are assholes," he said, "but we love them anyway." Beside him, I nodded earnestly. I was proud of our maturity.

But Ilana shook her head, distressed. "Oh no," she said in her soft, musical voice. "Don't say that."

"No, it's okay," James assured her. "We love them—"

"We totally love them!" I chimed in.

"They're just assholes."

"No, no," Ilana protested. "The more you say that, the more ingrained the idea becomes. You start to really believe it. There's a difference between our *actions* and our *being*. Don't misattribute their behavior for who they are." She thought for a minute, fiddling with the beads on her chunky necklace.

"The children may be *acting* like assholes," she said finally. "That's okay to say."

"All right," said James. "The children are acting like assholes."

"But we still love them!" I said.

18

EVALUATION

James and I got into an argument about the custody evaluator. I wanted to send her a binder of materials, too, including a full family history. She needed to know the entire story about Jessica's affair, her desertion of the kids, and the way she'd behaved ever since. But James said we couldn't provide that.

"Why not?" I argued. "It's relevant." I'd already written it all down. I knew I was jumping the gun, but Annabelle's journal had riled me so much, I had to do something proactive. We couldn't let Jessica manipulate this custody evaluation.

"Rhonda says we can't. It's hearsay or something."

"It's not hearsay. It's background. She should know what happened."

James shook his head, no. I made a frustrated noise.

"So, what do we say when she asks about our plans for the future?" I said. "Are we going to tell her that we're moving in together?"

We'd decided to move to San Francisco. James thought we could strike a reasonable custody compromise if we lived that much closer to Jessica. She could be more active in the girls' schooling, and if she ever decided to resume her job in the city, we could even entertain a split-week schedule.

Plus, James had long wanted to live in San Francisco. He appreciated San Carlos for its good schools, but otherwise it didn't much appeal to him. I worked in the city, so it seemed like a good idea all around. We'd even begun hunting for rentals.

James looked uncomfortable. He ran his hand through his hair, making it stick straight up. "I don't think we should tell her that."

"Why not?"

"Because I don't want Jess knowing our business."

I sighed. "Well, it's an in-depth evaluation, James. I'm pretty sure she's going to ask about our intentions. Don't we need to come clean sooner or later?" I didn't like describing it like that, as though we were hiding something dirty. But I felt like we were guarding a secret, in constant fear that Jessica or the kids would find out. "Let's ask Rhonda for her advice," I suggested.

"Rhonda charges three hundred and fifty an hour."

"Just give her a quick call."

"That's a thirty-dollar phone call," he grumbled.

"Babe, this woman is going to be asking us all kinds of questions, and Jessica is going to tell her that I'm just some tramp who sleeps over. Don't you think it looks better for us if we make it clear that we're serious about each other? That we intend to move in together and eventually get married?"

James' features froze. He was quiet for a long moment.

"I just don't think it's a good idea," he finally said.

"Well, I think it's important," I insisted. "Give Rhonda a call. Let's find out what she thinks."

I didn't love the look on his face when I mentioned marriage. I'd been clear from the start about what I wanted in my life; this couldn't be news to him. But there was a bit too much surprise in his expression for my liking.

Rhonda endorsed our honesty. "Marie's right," she said. "There's no point in hiding your plans; everything's going to be laid out in the open during the trial. And if your idea is that Jess could have more time with the girls, we should frame that as an act of compromise. The judge may see it as favorable."

So we stopped hiding our desire to live together. James began to hint to the girls that it was our intention, and a strange thing happened. Avery, from whom we'd expected a tantrum, seemed intrigued.

She began searching the internet for house listings, forwarding her favorites to James with captions like: "Super cute!" and "Too small?"

"I can't figure her out," James said to me.

But I thought maybe Avery was just relieved to know what was happening. She was a high-strung kid by nature and it made her anxious when she didn't know what was going on. James had been close-mouthed about the trial around the kids, and Avery was only hearing her mother's version of events. Now she had something to weigh on both sides.

We printed her emails and added them to our materials for Dr. Seeger. Our binder was considerably slimmer than Jessica's, but at least we had something.

In what was perhaps an act of defiance, I also put together a video. It was a montage of happy scenes of me and James having fun with the kids. Jessica claimed that the girls were uncomfortable around us, but this video showed otherwise. There was the clip of Avery sliding down the railing into James' open arms. There was footage of us choosing a Christmas tree with Annabelle calling, "Come on, Marie! Let's sing a Christmas song!" There were photos of the four of us hanging from trees, smiling in front of the Golden Gate Bridge, and collapsed in a happy pile at the park. The finished movie made me cry.

James thought it was a step too far, but again I insisted that he share it with Rhonda.

"We can't send it to the evaluator," she said. "But let's hold onto it. It may be useful at trial. Good work." I swelled a little with pride.

At this point, James and I were approaching two years together. Nearly half that time had been occupied by the custody battle. I wondered how our relationship might have progressed if Jessica hadn't dropped that bomb. Would we be closer to those milestones of cohabitation and marriage? Or would we be taking our time, allowing things to unfold slowly, knowing that we had all the time to decide?

There was no doubt that this ugly business had left its mark. It had frightened us, hastened our commitment, pushed us closer together. Every thought of playing the field had long ago fled my mind. I wanted to be with James. I wanted to be a family with him and the girls.

We'd talked about having babies. The idea made him light up. "Can we do it soon?" he'd asked. "While the girls are still young?" I knew how much he loved me and how fervently he wanted a life together.

He just always seemed to skip over the subject of marriage.

* * *

The custody evaluation was a lengthy process.

First, Dr. Seeger would meet with James and the girls. Then she'd meet with Jessica and the girls. In the second round, Max would join Jessica's group and I would join James'. Then there would be interviews with each set of adults, and just the kids. Then we'd all have individual interviews, perhaps twice, if time allowed. Finally, there would be a home visit.

"Is that really necessary?" James had argued.

"No," Rhonda said, "but Jess insisted on it. If one parent insists, the evaluator will do it. We won't fight it. Jess has been describing your home as a slum. Let the evaluator see that you live in a nice house, in a pleasant neighborhood, with the kids' friends nearby. Jess will have to do a home visit, too, you know." This wasn't a consolation, given that Jessica lived in a big house on a golf course.

Of course, Dr. Seeger charged extra for home visits. In fact, the entire evaluation would cost thirteen thousand dollars. That was *just* the evaluation, not the trial.

"That's money we could be putting toward the kids' college educations," James complained to me. "God, all of this is so unnecessary! *Why* is she doing this?"

But there was no reasoning with Jessica. James sent her several emails, broaching compromise. They all went unanswered.

James returned tired and cranky after his first visit with Dr. Seeger.

"It was an hour and a half of her asking us pointless questions," he told me over the phone. "Really, I have no idea what she got out of it. Annabelle spent a while describing all the types of fruit that she's allergic to."

I suppressed a snort. Annabelle didn't have any food allergies, but Jessica had convinced her that she could only eat organic.

"I'm serious," he said. "She just listed fruit for about ten minutes. Non-organic apples. Non-organic peaches. Non-organic plums. Bananas are okay." I laughed. "And then she made it clear that Mum buys organic fruit and I buy shitty fruit coated in chemicals. Because all my organic fruit money is going toward this stupid fucking evaluation." He swore a few more times.

"What about Avery? Did she talk about anything?" I asked.

"Yeah. She talked about skiing. She said I drag them up to Tahoe too much." He adopted an airy, teenage tone. "She *kinda* likes skiing, and she's gotten pretty good at it, but she doesn't want to go all the time and it's not fun anymore. She'd rather relax at home, like she does with Mum."

"Okay," I said. "So now Dr. Seeger knows that you take your kids skiing and buy them fruit. Not exactly damning testimony."

"Nope. But it cost me about a thousand dollars."

Looking back now, my sessions with Dr. Seeger are a bit of a blur. It wasn't like therapy with Ilana—there was a distinct sense that we were being judged. But I didn't really understand what the criteria were. Dr. Seeger asked unimportant-seeming questions and left too-long pauses, until our answers bottomed out into uncomfortable silence. She took notes on a yellow legal pad, filling pages with her ballpoint scrawl.

James and the kids and I sat awkwardly in her office-playroom. Avery was reticent. She seemed to dread the whole scene, and she spoke as little as possible. Her enthusiasm for living in San Francisco had abruptly died around the time that her mother received our binder. With a bit of reprogramming, Avery remembered that living with Mom was her chief desire.

Annabelle toyed with the puppets and blocks, talking freely about whatever took her fancy. I almost laughed when she started listing fruit again. I got the sense that she just enjoyed Dr. Seeger's attention. But then she was a bit sassy with James, and I remembered that she, too, had an agenda: to make her mother look like the better parent. James told her to mind her manners, but I could see him second-guessing himself, unsure of how he should discipline his child in front of the evaluator.

I prompted the kids to talk about Christmas, birthdays, fun outings that we'd had. James reminded them about ballet lessons and Taekwondo and school field trips with friends. *Look at our well-balanced lives!* we tried to telegraph. The girls admitted to having some fun on these occasions, but never very much.

James and I each took a written psychological test with nearly six hundred questions. The questions were bizarre, all true-or-false statements like: "I have not lived the right kind of life" or "At times I feel like swearing". I emerged bleary-eyed with absolutely no idea of how I'd scored or what the scoring could possibly mean.

The whole process was terribly depressing. As spring leached away, we spent sunny Saturdays holed up in Dr. Seeger's tiny office, having our lives examined by a stranger. James answered her questions in a straightforward manner, much as he did with Ilana, but again he offered no context. I had to prod him to back up, fill in the holes, make sure Dr. Seeger understood the full story. It exhausted me. Everything we said was the truth, but I felt as though Dr. Seeger had her eye on me, aware that I was driving the narrative.

* * *

My job was exhausting me, too, but for good reason: I'd been promoted! I was now Guest Services Coordinator on the Asia team. This meant I'd assist the Directors with trip planning and client contact. It also meant that I'd no longer be working directly with Ken, which was sad. I'd miss his company—and his updates from the *Bigfoot Times*.

Now they needed to hire someone to replace me on Frontline. In the meantime, I was doing two jobs, training for my new position and covering my old one. It was a lot of work, but my efforts paid off when I was named Employee of the Quarter. The award included a free roundtrip flight anywhere in the continental U.S. Working for a travel company had its perks.

I decided to cash it in and take a short vacation before diving fully into my new role. James couldn't get away; the kids were with him during the school week—and there was no way he'd offer extra time to Jessica right now. But I was going to get out of town anyway. I'd never taken myself on vacation before and I sorely needed it.

I felt excited as I booked a flight to Florida. I planned to rent a car and drive through the state, visiting Miami Beach, the Everglades, and the Florida Keys. Maybe I'd visit James' sister, Rachel, whom I hadn't met yet. I didn't reserve any hotels; I would be spontaneous, traveling wherever my mood took me.

Except, my mood took me downward. As my trip approached, exhaustion filled me, along with a strange kind of dread. Suddenly the idea of coordinating travel seemed an unmanageable task. My limbs felt heavy. I was tired all the time. The situation with the kids, the meetings with Dr. Seeger . . . everything just felt unbearably sad.

The night before I was due to depart, I still hadn't packed. I sat on my bed, staring at my empty suitcase, knowing that I wasn't going to put any clothes in it. I cried a little, not understanding why. And then I crawled beneath the covers, fully clothed, where I stayed until my flight departed the next morning, without me.

It seemed I was depressed.

James was alarmed. "Baby, what's wrong?" he asked me over the phone. "Can I do anything? Do you want to come over tonight?" I told him no. I just wanted to stay in bed. I didn't want to talk to anyone or do anything.

Mandy knocked on my door a few times. She tried to tempt me out of my room with wine and chocolate, but she understood when I refused everything in favor of sleep. She wouldn't tell anyone at work, she promised me. As far as they knew, I was on vacation.

So, I spent a week in solitude, mostly hiding beneath the covers. I slept on and off, and spent hours lying awake in bed, thinking. Sometimes I heard Javier in the house. He and Mandy were officially an item now. They would tiptoe past my bedroom door, trying to keep their voices low. My yellow curtains cast colored shapes on the wall; I watched them slide back and forth as the breeze blew through the window. And sometime during that week, I put pen to paper and began to write.

I think I'm feeling the first stirrings of wishing they were mine.

I came across a picture the other day, tucked into the frame of James' bedroom mirror. It was an old photo of the girls on his lap when they were small; he'd found it in a drawer, he said. The kids were one and three.

I stared for a while at their little faces: Avery's eyes so precious and blue, her lips big and pouty, even as a toddler; Annabelle's face always open and playful. They sat on James' knees, each holding his hand with her own tiny fist.

Looking at the picture I felt a little bit lost. It reminded me how little I know of their lives before. I wasn't there for those years when James was changing diapers, when he could easily carry both girls in his arms. They share a past that I wasn't a part of, and they share it with Jessica. They were a family.

Because of their kids, James and Jessica are forever entwined. There's no life with him and the girls that doesn't have her in it; she's like a weed woven through the foundation of our house—we can't cut her loose without risking collapse.

I've never strived to be the girls' mother; I'm not trying to replace her. But this court battle is like a punch in the gut, a constant reminder that I'm not their mom, not their stepmom, not anything. I envy Max his stepdad title—at least he knows where he stands. I feel like I'm fighting to win a place in their lives.

I'm in love with these kids.

A tear fell onto the page, startling me; carefully I blotted it away. My hand was moving of its own accord, barely able to keep up with the speed of my thoughts.

Not that sweet, fond love of the early days—this is a battle-born love, tested and fierce. It's been growing under the surface all this time, even on tough days, even when I've wanted to throttle them. It's that resilient love that parents have, the kind that survives every hurt. I didn't know I could feel that for children who weren't my own. I thought James had earned it by virtue of DNA.

The fear of losing them is a pit in my stomach. I want to turn back the clock to those days when they were little girls with tiny hands; I want to enter their lives earlier, to love them sooner. I want to turn the clock forward, past this terrible time when James has lost his smile, and arrive safely in a future where I am part of the family.

I want them to be my family.

I put down my pen and wiped the tears off my face. A weight had slid from my shoulders; I felt lighter than I had in weeks. Outside the day was sunny and bright, and I had the sudden urge to be out in it.

From then on I started writing, little snippets here and there, or longer entries as the need arose. I found that it helped me manage my anxiety and sometimes gave me new perspective. It also filled a need I had to document this moment in time and everything we were going through.

Annabelle wasn't the only one who could keep a journal.

19

INDECISION

School ended in early June and the girls resumed their summer schedule, rotating weeks with each parent. Tensions were high all around as a trial date was finally set for the third week of July. But first we had to finish the custody evaluation, and we were having trouble scheduling our home visit with Dr. Seeger.

"The kids are with Jess this week, and Dr. Seeger has no availability the following week," James told me. "And then the kids are with Jess again. And after that, well, we're out of time." Dr. Seeger would need a few weeks to complete her report for trial.

Of course, Jessica refused to compromise. She wouldn't swap weeks and she wouldn't allow James to keep the kids an extra day during her scheduled time, even if he offered her two days in return.

"She can't shift one day to accommodate the evaluator?" I grumbled. "It's not like they're actually doing anything over there." Jessica never sent the kids to summer camp. They just lolled around the house all day.

Eventually Rhonda had to get involved, prompting Jessica's lawyer, Ben, to coerce his client's cooperation. Jessica offered to let James have the girls for an hour and a half on one of her days. "The home evaluation is only ninety minutes," she emailed him. "We will drop the girls off prior to and pick them up directly after."

"That's bullshit!" I exclaimed. I was furious. The home visit was supposed to be an opportunity for Dr. Seeger to observe the kids on a regular day at home. How did she expect the girls would act with their mother waiting outside in the car?

Again, Rhonda intervened, pointing out to Ben that the trial would likely be delayed if Jessica didn't offer a suitable compromise. Finally, she conceded to swap one day, allowing us to sync up with Dr. Seeger.

It still wasn't ideal. Our home visit was scheduled for a Monday, an unusual time for me to drop in on the household. I had to leave the office early and take the train down to San Carlos, where James and the kids picked me up from the station. The girls had been at Taekwondo and were still wearing their uniforms.

We spent a nervous half hour waiting for Dr. Seeger to arrive. James busied himself with dinner preparations and I tried to distract the girls by asking for a Taekwondo demonstration.

As the kids showed me each move, I mimicked it badly, prompting their laughter. "You're doing it wrong!" said Annabelle in delight. She corrected my form as Avery modeled each move, and I copied her, deliberately mucking it up.

The girls snapped to attention as Dr. Seeger's car approached the house. Annabelle ran outside to flag her down, her nervous energy almost resembling excitement. She led Dr. Seeger inside with an air of importance, reminding me of the younger girl, who, nearly two years before, had been excited to show me her home for the first time.

Avery had a better handle on her mission. She arranged her face in a stoic expression, determined to show the evaluator that she was unhappy in her father's home.

But Avery was still just a kid—and a crappy actress. As Annabelle led Dr. Seeger into her bedroom, Avery turned to me and resumed my martial arts lesson in whispers. "Now, this is a roundhouse kick." She demonstrated and I copied her, badly. She was smothering a giggle as Dr. Seeger reentered the room.

"The girls were teaching me Taekwondo," I explained. "I'm not very good."

Dr. Seeger smiled at us. "Would you like to show me some moves?" she asked the kids, who suddenly became very shy. They shook their heads.

But as James showed Dr. Seeger the kitchen, Annabelle said in a carrying whisper, "Marie, this is a side kick. *Yop-chagi!*"

We probably couldn't have scripted it better. It was clear that the girls weren't intimidated by me, that in fact, we laughed and had fun together. What's more, I think it came across that they were putting on an act, trying to show that Dad's house was inferior. They just did it so badly.

"This is our weird bathroom," Annabelle said proudly, showing off the moonscape interior.

"And we have a miniature train in the backyard," Avery added. "It came with the house; it's so random. Want to see it?"

We invited Dr. Seeger to stay for dinner (what were we supposed to do? It was dinnertime), but she demurred. She did, however, accept one of the chocolate-chip cookies that Avery and James had baked the night before.

"Do you like to bake?" Dr. Seeger asked Avery.

"Yeah. Dad and I bake a lot." She caught herself. "I mean, Mom and I bake a lot, too."

Oops.

We all exhaled a bit after Dr. Seeger left and had a mellow dinner of pasta. Avery seemed aware that she'd botched her mission. "You probably scheduled the home visit for the end because you knew I'd be more comfortable," she said to James. But it was an empty accusation; she didn't seem to care all that much. I think she was just tired of the whole thing. By contrast, Annabelle genuinely did not seem to know that she'd screwed things up in our favor.

Dr. Seeger's report would be done ten days before the trial. "I guess now we wait," I said to James as I snuggled against him in bed. I'd have to get up at the crack of dawn to get to work, but it was nice to have this extra night with him.

"Yeah," he said. "Now I just have to figure out how to pay for all this." He gathered my curls in absent fists, his fingers tightening and loosening in my hair.

* * *

The rest of the week was kid-free, but unlike previous summers, there was little joy in it. James was worn out. His store was understaffed and he was filling in the gaps himself, working long hours and six-day weeks whenever the girls were with their mom. He hadn't been to my place in ages, but that Friday evening he drove up to Oakland to have dinner and spend the night.

We went to a little wine bar in my neighborhood and sat on the heated patio, ordering two glasses of zinfandel and a few tapas. It should have been lovely and romantic, but James' stress was palpable.

"How'd it go at work today?" I asked him. James had worked a ten-hour day, opening and closing the store.

"Les called out again," he said. "This time his niece's best friend died, and she was really sad, so he needed to be there for her."

I raised an eyebrow. This was the second non-relative that Les had lost in a month, and the degrees of separation were getting further.

"And this is a legitimate excuse for missing work?" I asked.

James shrugged. "Nope. But until I can find someone to replace him, I can't fire him. Otherwise I'll be working every single day."

The problems with staffing a store on minimum wage, I was learning, were endless. James' staff was a rotating cast of characters who seemed to give him more grief than assistance. There was Diana, who wrote erotic novels on the company computer; Ingrid, who was flirting with a nervous breakdown; Monica, who was cheating on her wife—with Ingrid; and Les, who took more time off than he spent in the office. James suspected he had a drinking problem, but hadn't been able to prove it.

He sighed. "I'm going to need to hire another full-time person. I just . . . well, never mind. I'll figure it out." He ran his hands over his face, the picture of exhaustion.

"Sweetie," I said in a low voice. I took one of his hands and kissed it. "It's going to be okay. It'll all be over soon." I was talking about the trial. James' job may have been frustrating, but it was the trial that was wrecking him. He had dark circles under his eyes and he'd lost a little weight. As I looked at him across the table, I noticed that he'd lost some hair, too. The bald circle on the top of his head was spreading, and the tuft of hair above his eyes was thinner now.

I kissed his hands again. They felt rougher these days, and there was grease beneath his fingernails. He'd changed a car battery today, I surmised. "Six more weeks," I said. "Then this awful trial will be over. We just have to hang in there, baby."

James withdrew his hands and wrapped them around his wine glass. He opened his mouth and then closed it again, twisting his lips into a frustrated grimace.

"What is it?" I asked, but the words were stuck in his throat. I watched the fine beads of sweat spring out on his forehead as they did when he was flustered.

"I don't know if I'm going to go through with the trial," he finally said.

My heart stalled for a moment, then leapt back into action with a painful thud. I pressed my fingertips to my chest. "What?" I asked. My voice sounded far away.

"I don't know if I want to continue." He looked sick.

"But James, *why?*" I leaned toward him. "*Why?*" I could hear the shrillness in my voice. I was starting to panic.

"I don't have the money," he told me. "I make less than half my old salary. I'm maxing out my credit cards . . . I don't know how I'm going to pay for this."

I shook my head. "Baby, we'll find a way. You can't give up."

But he was shaking his head. "Even if I took out a loan—"

"Yes! You could take out a loan!" I seized on this. "Or . . . or we could launch a fundraiser. We'll do it online. I know our friends would want to contribute; we have so much support at Mercy—"

"No," he said. His voice was firm. "No fundraisers. Okay?" He looked at me and I promised, I wouldn't launch a fundraiser.

"Even if I took out a loan," he went on, "I'd be in a lot of debt, and I'm not sure I want to do that. I need to think about the future."

"But what is the future without your girls?" I cried. A woman at the next table glanced over at us. I lowered my voice. "James, seriously? These are your kids."

"I know they're my kids," he said in a strangled voice. He looked like he was trying not to cry. "But we deserve a future, too, Marie. This trial will bankrupt me. I will be in debt for years to come. And I need to think about you and the family we want to have together . . . " He swiped at his eyes. He looked heartbroken. "My kids don't want to live with me," he choked out.

"Your kids are brainwashed," I said firmly. "They don't know what they want."

"But they're going to tell the judge that they don't want to live with me. And how do I fight that? Why should I spend forty thousand dollars to fight that?"

"Because . . ." Frustration was filling me, tightening my hands into fists. "Because you *have* to. Do you *want* them to live with Jessica?" My voice sounded accusing, I couldn't help it.

"Of course not," he said. "But I don't know if I can stop that from happening. And I'm not sure I should mess up my whole life to take that chance." He gripped his wine glass so hard I feared it might break.

"You have a strong case," I argued.

"It might not matter," he said.

"So, what are you going to do?" I struggled to keep my voice even. "Are you just going to let Jessica have them? Are you just going to . . . *surrender* them to that household so they can pick up her biases? So they can learn how to judge and ignore people that they consider beneath them?"

I thought about Annabelle, who'd lately been parroting her mother's views on homosexuality. "Love the sinner, but hate the sin." She'd been referring to one of our friends at Mercy. My fingernails dug into my palms.

"We can't do that," I said. "Jessica fills their heads with garbage! We can't just give them up to become little versions of her. Besides, there's no way out of this without giving her full custody. She's not going to negotiate with you, James; she wants it all. If you want compromise, you're going to have to fight for it at trial." I was gathering steam now. "And even if you give Jess full custody, she'll go after you for maximum child support. You'll wind up paying either way; it's a lose-lose."

James grimaced as he accepted the truth of this. "Still," he said. "I might have to pay child support, but I won't lose forty grand on a trial."

"But you'll always wonder if you could have won!" I said hotly. "And your kids will think you gave up on them. Because that's what Jessica will tell them." This felt like a low blow, but it was the truth. This was, after all, the woman who'd told her kids that James had kidnapped them when in fact she'd given them up for a fancy house and ten thousand dollars.

I didn't stop to examine why I was so hell-bent on moving forward. If I had, I might have realized that living without the girls could be better for me. They weren't exactly easy these days. But it just felt so *wrong,* the idea of giving them up. James had put his kids first their entire lives. Jessica had breezed in and out, mothering when it was convenient for her, and launched a smear campaign against us to distract from her own misdeeds. Not for one minute did I believe that the girls would be better off with her. I had to convince James to fight for them.

"If you give up, you will regret it for the rest of your life," I said quietly.

He looked at me, miserable. "I don't know what to do."

"I'm telling you what to do," I said. It was, admittedly, the wrong choice of words. His face hardened slightly.

"Well, it's not your decision to make," he said. "It's mine." And that was the wrong choice of words, too. My temper flared.

"Oh really? Well maybe you should have made *your* decision before you dragged us all through this custody evaluation. You switched jobs eight months ago, James. If you knew back then that you couldn't pay for the trial, why did you wait until now to bring it up? Why did you put us through all that?

"We're *six weeks away,*" I went on. "We're looking at the goddamn finish line. It is *too late* to pull this shit now. So get yourself together, okay? Just . . . be a dad."

I regretted the words as soon as they left my mouth. James stared coldly at me. "What the fuck does that mean?" he asked. His voice was low and scary, his words over-enunciated.

I didn't know what I'd meant. I was just so overwrought by the last year, so filled with panic and fury at the thought of giving up now. I felt desperate to get him back on the same page so we could move forward together with purpose.

I was afraid, I realized. I'd only known James as a father. I was afraid that without his kids, a piece of him would fall away. I was afraid that we would fall apart, too.

20

WHAT CAN YOU LIVE WITH?

James spent the night, but it was subdued. We didn't talk much after we got home from the bar. He left early the next morning to go into work.

Our argument put me in a lousy mood that lasted all day. I was glum and quiet when I met my friends later for knitting at Katia's house.

In fact, the whole tone of the evening felt a little off. Hailey couldn't stay long; her kids were both sick, so we hurried through dinner to get a little knitting in. While we ate, Katia told me that she'd taken my suggestion and applied for my old job at Roaming Ex. She was hoping to get an interview.

"That's great," I said. "I'll put in a good word for you."

I didn't know Katia as well as the other girls. She'd been a late addition to our knitting group, joining as some of the early members were moving on. I thought she was nice, but I'd never clicked with her the way I had with the others.

Katia had grown up on a commune. Her parents were hippies and her older sister had followed suit, but Katia worked hard at being "normal". She found a straight-laced husband and pursued a straight-laced life. That's not to say that she was boring; she loved to travel and she had hobbies—she was an avid road biker, for example. But there was something . . . unapproachable about her. She didn't invite confidences or display much emotion. I found it a little difficult to connect with her.

Even so, I thought she could be a good fit at Roaming Ex. A love of travel was the main thing they were looking for—the rest was just answering phones and translating Ken's wacky patois. I was glad she'd thrown her hat in the ring.

"Thanks," she said to me. "I'm so ready to change jobs. I thought about just quitting, since I'll probably be leaving soon anyway to have a baby. But this job opening sounds ideal." She helped herself to more salad.

I looked at her, frowning slightly. "So, are you saying that you might take the job and then immediately go on maternity leave?" That didn't sit quite right with me.

But Katia didn't pick up on my unease. "Probably," she said blithely, popping a cherry tomato into her mouth. She went on to describe one of her colleagues at work, an unpleasant woman she was eager to leave behind.

I bit my lip, feeling uncomfortable. When she finished her story I said hesitantly, "You know, it puts my company in a difficult position to have to keep re-staffing this role." I knew Ken had been struggling with the temp they'd hired, and that they were looking for a solid replacement for me.

Katia gave me an unreadable look.

"Please just think about whether you can commit to the job before you accept an interview, okay?" That seemed fair to me. I wanted to recommend her in good faith. "I know it kinda sucks," I went on. "There's never a good time to get pregnant, but it's just something we babes of a certain age have to deal with, right?" I'd meant this to be funny, but my joke fell flat. Rather than lightening the mood, the air grew awkward between us.

We moved to the living room and took up our knitting. Alex asked me how things were going with the trial prep.

I shrugged, dejected. "Idunno. We're supposed to have a trial management conference in a couple of weeks. I've been staying up late every night, drafting thoughts for James' lawyer. But now he's not even sure he wants to go through with the trial." I filled them in on our argument.

"Oh, wow," breathed Hailey.

"You can't let that horrible woman win!" said Alex. "You have to go to trial!"

"That's what I think!" I said. My pulse spiked as I thought of Jessica. "She's just so . . . *wretched,* you guys. The stuff she puts in the kids' heads! They don't know which end is up; they want to believe everything she says—she's their *mom.* But she talks such poison, and they soak it right up. Like, the other day, Annabelle said that Mercy isn't a real church, it's a *cult.* Because we 'don't talk about Jesus right'. And Avery doesn't want me to come along anymore when James drops the kids off because she says I cause problems. I try to make her mother and Max talk to me, when I should just respect them enough to leave them alone. Can you believe that? She thinks *I'm* the one—"

"Okay, stop," interrupted Katia. We all turned to her. "I can't listen to you talk about this anymore." She had a white-knuckle grip on her knitting needles.

I was taken aback. "I'm sorry for ranting," I said slowly. "I just need to vent sometimes. There's a lot going on; it's been really upsetting."

"But now you're upsetting *me,*" Katia said. "Marie, I *was* that kid. My parents had a horrible divorce and did all kinds of awful things to each other, and I had to choose between them. And I can't listen to you talk about it anymore, all right? It's enough."

I looked down at my knitting, feeling hurt and a little affronted by the comparison. James and I didn't do awful things to Jessica. The awful behavior was strictly one way. Couldn't she see that?

My throat felt tight when I swallowed. "I just . . . I thought I could talk to my friends."

"Well, talk about it somewhere else, okay? But not at my house." Katia's cheeks were flaming. Alex looked back and forth between us with dismay. I concentrated on the lump in my throat, willing myself not to cry.

There was a moment of uncomfortable silence. Then Hailey spoke. "I hate to say it, but I've got to get going. Reese has his hands full with the kids, and I need to help with bedtime."

I cleared my throat with difficulty. "I should get going, too." We helped Katia bring the dishes into the kitchen and made our goodbyes. The evening ended on a sour note.

Out on the street I turned to Hailey and Alex. "Was I out of line?" I asked. Katia's reproach had come as a total surprise to me. I was sorry to have triggered bad memories for her, but her words had stung. Maybe I was being oversensitive? I just couldn't tell anymore.

They both gave me hugs and told me not to worry about it. We were just having an off night, they said. By the next time we saw each other, it would all blow over.

* * *

But now I had two arguments clinging to me, and I couldn't shake them off. I felt miserable and misunderstood. I'd just been trying to stay the course, but it seemed like I was making wrong moves at every turn. I hated having people upset with me.

On Sunday I went to church by myself, feeling raw. The idea of singing seemed beyond me; I was afraid if I opened my mouth, I would cry. So I found a seat in the back pew and tried to bury myself amongst the congregation. I didn't want to talk to anyone. I just wanted to sit by myself and listen.

As the music rose around me, so did all the emotions I was trying to suppress. While the congregation clapped and sang, I wept quietly. I cried and cried, the tears seeming like they came from a bottomless place. I wasn't sure how I would stop. I sat low among the standing, swaying bodies, thinking myself discreet, like one bent reed in a sea of grass.

But James had seen me. When the music ended he came off the stage and directly to me. He put his arm around me and we sat together like that through the sermon. When the service was over, we found ourselves surrounded by friends who buoyed us with hugs and words of encouragement. "Everything's going to be all right," they said.

If this place *was* a cult, it sure was a nice one.

* * *

The following week we had an appointment with Ilana. We hadn't talked any more about the trial. James was still deliberating, and his indecision was anguish for me. My nerves were stretched to the breaking point, and I was never far from succumbing to tears.

This time I was the quiet one in Ilana's office. I left it to James to explain where we stood, to describe the decision he felt I had no voice in. The lump was back in my throat, big and painful. When Ilana addressed me, I could barely speak around it.

"Marie, you're quiet today." I focused on the faerie-like pitch of her voice, on the clouds of curly hair that floated around her head, untamed.

"You feel very strongly that the girls would be better off with James?"

I nodded. "She . . . doesn't . . . deserve them," I managed to say. Then tears broke loose and ran down my face. It was an unkind thing to say, that a mother didn't deserve to raise her own children, but God, how I meant it. The sentence seemed to burst forth from deep within me. *She doesn't deserve them.*

"And James? Do you think the kids would be better off with you?"

"Yes," he said. "Of course, I do." He gripped my hand. "I mean, I know Jess loves them and she'd keep them safe, and they'd be okay. But she isolates them. Their whole lives will revolve around that house. I'm worried that they won't have friends or participate in any activities. I'm afraid they'll become estranged from their family . . . " He took a deep breath and exhaled hard. "I'm afraid she'll turn them against me." A tear fell down his cheek, and seeing this, I lost all control. I slipped my hand out of his grasp and covered my face to conceal my own sobbing.

"I'm afraid of losing them," James went on. "But I'm afraid of losing everything *for* them, too." We sat together on Ilana's couch and cried.

For a few moments Ilana said nothing, just sat serenely while we worked our way through her box of Kleenex. When my crying was largely under control (James had shed a stoic few tears), she regarded us matter-of-factly. Then she said in her sing-song voice:

"Well, it sounds like you guys are pretty much fucked."

My head snapped up. James' jaw fell open. I looked at her in astonishment. *Was she allowed to say stuff like that to us?*

Ilana sat calmly with her hands folded in her lap. She went on, unconcerned.

"You're fucked if you keep fighting, right? It's going to put you in financial ruin. But you're fucked if you give up because you'll lose your kids." She paused, thoughtful.

"The question is, what can you live with?"

21

THE EVALUATOR'S REPORT

Ilana's question had been like a revelation. *What can you live with?* It made it all plain to me. If I'd had any doubts before—and I hadn't—I was now one hundred percent certain that we needed to move forward with the trial. I didn't think I could live with myself otherwise. I didn't think James could live with himself either.

To my surprise, he wasn't convinced, and continued to hem and haw in the days that followed. My frustration grew as I waited for him to reach the right decision. I abhorred being in limbo. Once my mind was made up, I wanted to act.

The vexation of not knowing left me tense and distracted at work. Supporting four Directors was a big job and required all my attention. Gone were the easy days on Frontline, when I could chat amiably with Ken. Now I was immersed in Southeast and Central Asia, trying to keep track of whose trips were whose and which clients owed us paperwork. I didn't have time to text with James at the office anymore.

When I saw that he'd left me a voicemail in the middle of the workday, I got nervous. My heart thumped as I listened to his message.

"The evaluator's report is finished," he said. "Call me."

I was surprised; Dr. Seeger had finished early! Was this good or bad? "I'm taking a lunch break," I called to my team and hurried outside clutching my phone. With trembling fingers, I dialed James' number.

"I think it's good news," he said when he answered. "I'm scanning the report, and it looks positive for us. In fact," he gave a little laugh, "some of it seems downright shitty for Jess."

I exhaled deeply and sank onto the curb. "Tell me more," I said. "Read it to me." I put my head on my knees and listened.

"It's pretty long," he said. "I'll just give you the highlights. This part is about Avery."

> *Avery has just completed seventh grade. While not particularly eager to talk, she responded to questions with little hesitation. She was much more talkative and active during the home visit at her father's as compared to the visit at her mother's, where she seemed nervous and quiet.*

"Ha," I said.

James went on. "Let me skip ahead."

> *Without being asked, Avery offered at her final appointment that she does not want a 50/50 custody split. She doesn't want to commute. Her mother, who had brought her to that appointment, didn't want her*

to commute either, and that is why years ago she let
them live with her father.

"That's a handy explanation," James interjected. "'Cause obviously she couldn't move houses or anything. Better to give up the kids."

"Keep going," I urged.

"Okay, listen to this," James said. "It's like she's writing from Avery's perspective here."

> *Mom and Max are not fans of Marie. Dad and Marie*
> *are not getting married, so Mom and Max don't want*
> *to get to know her. They would meet Marie if she and*
> *Dad got married. But they don't want to meet her if*
> *she's just a girlfriend.*

"That makes perfect sense," I said dryly.

"It makes Jess sound a bit stupid, doesn't it?" James asked.

"I guess so."

"Okay, I'm jumping ahead to Annabelle's section."

> *Annabelle was more talkative than Avery. She seemed*
> *comfortable and expressed her views clearly. Annabelle*
> *was talking about her journal when she suddenly added,*
> *"All I want to say is that I don't want a 50/50 schedule*
> *like the judge ordered before. I want to live with Mom."*
> *When asked how she knew about a schedule that had*
> *been recommended many years ago, Annabelle*
> *explained that she had asked her mother. This evaluator*
> *noted that within the same hour Avery had broached the*
> *same subject spontaneously.*

Hope blazed through me—it sounded as though Dr. Seeger had seen right through Jessica's coaching. James went on:

> When asked how she had decided to start keeping a journal, Annabelle responded immediately, "It didn't have anything to do with Mom."

James gave a bark of laughter.

> She had not been asked if the journal was related to her mother. The response was odd. It appears that a major purpose of the journal is to report on her father's behavior. It is noteworthy that Annabelle referred once to the diary as "our journal".

"Wow, Annabelle is a crappy spy," I said, laughing.
"Yeah. Listen to this," James said.

> Dad wanted them to see a therapist, but they were worried that the counselor would try to talk them out of living with their mother. It was a weird counselor in San Francisco in a small shack. Since Annabelle never went to this counselor it is not clear how she could have this perception of the office or person.

We both laughed at that.

"There's a lot here," said James. "I don't have time to read all of it now. Let me skim Jess' section."

> Mrs. Mazzeo was cooperative with the assessment process. She expects to be recovered from her injury by the end of this year. At that point she will work perhaps part-time but does not plan on returning to her job in San Francisco.

"Nope, instead she plans to collect child support from me." James made a disgusted noise.

Mr. de Graaf asked them to meet his girlfriend. They declined his invitation to meet Marie because it is inappropriate. Mrs. Mazzeo noted, "I won't justify his girlfriend in front of the kids. Perhaps it would be different if they were engaged or married. But he's trying to use us to put on a show for the girls. He's seeking our approval because the girls aren't accepting of Marie." Mrs. Mazzeo noted that perhaps Mr. de Graaf treats Marie better than he treats the girls, so there are resentments.

"What a load of shit," I said.

"Jess sounds crazy, right?" James asked over the phone. "I mean, she's not coming off well here, is she?"

"I think she sounds totally bizarre, but what do I know?" I said. "What else did she say?"

"Um . . . " I heard him clicking and scrolling. He continued reading from Jessica's narrative.

The girls' father ignores them. He complains to the children that their mother and Max treat him poorly. The girls do not like Marie.

Ouch. That hurt.

The father's house is "like a slum". The kids hate the house and it is not safe. Their hygiene has deteriorated there, and they have bad clothes.

Bad clothes? They wore jeans and t-shirts, like every other kid I knew.

James sighed. "There's more, but it's all the same. I don't really want to read it out loud." He suddenly sounded weary.

I felt frustrated. I wanted to read the entire report right then. "Can you email it to me?" I asked.

"No, Rhonda says I'm not allowed to. I'm sorry. You can see it the next time you come over. But let me cut to the summary, I'll read you some of that." There was a pause while he scrolled through the document.

>Annabelle's journal raises some concerns. In interviews she contradicted what she wrote. It is notable that the girls feared counseling could make them change their minds about where they want to live. It isn't clear what gave them that idea, but no ethical counselor would try to do that.

>The mother and stepfather's lack of support for the girls' relationship with Marie is also a concern. This evaluator usually hears parents complain when an ex-spouse fails to introduce a new partner. But the Mazzeos' reasoning that acknowledging Marie would give the father justification is confusing.

>The girls are caught in a loyalty conflict. To be loyal to their mother, they must be standoffish to their father's girlfriend. Ms. Aaron is not trying to become their mother and liking her should not threaten Mrs. Mazzeo.

>If the sisters were allowed now to move to their mother's home, there is the serious concern that they would align themselves even more with their mother, and their relationship with their father would deteriorate. This matter could be reviewed in a year's

time, during which Mr. de Graaf could sort out his possible move to San Francisco, and Mrs. Mazzeo will presumably heal from her back injury and have clearer plans about her employment. This may lead to more clarity about where the girls should attend school.

James stopped. "It goes on to discuss the specifics, but that's the gist. She recommends no immediate change to the schedule. The kids should stay with me."

I realized I'd been holding my breath. I let it out and felt my shoulders ease away from my ears. "So, will we go to trial?" I asked him.

"Yes," he said.

As I hung up the phone, tears overtook me. I covered my face and wept from relief. Then I dried my eyes and went to the bathroom to splash some cold water on my face. I had to get back to work.

* * *

With the decision made, preparations went into full swing. James borrowed ten thousand dollars from his sister so we could progress to trial. It was only a fraction of what he needed, but it would pay for the court fees, which were due immediately. Rhonda's fee would be billed later and could be paid in installments.

Through a series of strategy sessions, Rhonda sketched out her plan for the weeklong trial. In a phone conversation that must have cost James four hundred dollars, she asked me numerous questions about our relationship, the kids' changing behavior over the last year, and each of my odd encounters with Jessica and Max. As we talked, I paced in the alley behind my office. It wasn't ideal, having this conference on my lunch break, but time was short now.

"Do you think Jessica is a racist?" Rhonda asked me abruptly.

"What?" I was thrown off.

"Do you think she's prejudiced against you because you're half black?" she clarified.

Oh. I thought about it. "I'm not sure how she'd even know that," I said. With my olive-beige skin and loose brown curls, most people mistook me for something else.

"Maybe the kids told her," Rhonda replied. "They've seen pictures of your folks, right?"

As a matter of fact, the kids had met my family the previous fall. My parents and brother had flown out to surprise me for my thirty-fifth birthday. James had arranged the whole thing.

My parents were divorced, but they could get along well for short periods of time. We'd had dinner with James and the girls, and I'd wanted the kids to see that divorced couples could still act kindly toward one another. But I don't think the lesson hit home. Jessica had just dropped the custody hammer and the girls were behaving badly. Annabelle refused to talk to my family throughout the entire meal—but it wasn't like she'd singled out my dad for being black. She'd been an equal-opportunity shit.

"Max is half Mexican," I pointed out to Rhonda.

"Yeah, but don't they emphasize the Italian half?" she asked. She and James must have discussed this before. It was true; the girls always talked about "their" Italian heritage, and Max's Mexican mom seemed to get the shaft.

"How is Italian better than Mexican?" I wondered aloud.

"It's in Europe," she said.

I pondered this. Though it didn't strain credulity to believe Jessica was a racist, I just wasn't sure it was true. I knew she was a homophobe and an elitist, but I didn't feel comfortable making claims of racism.

"Better leave that one alone," I told Rhonda. I heard her scratching it off her notepad.

I went back to work stressed and distracted, now remembering things I'd neglected to say. I ran through our conversation in my mind, not realizing that I'd sealed and addressed a client package without putting the documents inside.

"Damn it," I muttered, ripping open the package. That was the second one I'd ruined today.

I went up to the Frontline office in search of another padded envelope, and walked in on what appeared to be a personal phone conversation.

" . . . they just throw them in a vat of boiling oil," Ken was saying into the receiver. "And that's why, when they serve you guinea pig and it sounds like it's screaming, it's because it is."

Ew. I nearly turned around and left, but Vin the FedEx guy appeared in the doorway behind me. Ken nodded at the both of us and hung up the phone. I used to see a lot of Vin; he made deliveries once or twice a day. I said hi to him, then rummaged through the cabinet, hunting for an envelope.

Vin dropped two boxes on the counter and handed Ken his clipboard to sign. "You got any plans this weekend?" he asked Ken.

"Just packing up the house. I'm moving in with my girlfriend." Ken had finally given in to the inevitable.

"Nice," Vin said. "You guys have been together for a while?"

"Yeah. It's time."

Vin took the clipboard back and initialed it. "Well, congratulations. Are you excited?"

Ken considered this. "Eh. Idunno. I'm used to roaming free. Now I'm going to be cooped up in a little pen and told when I can eat."

"Oh," Vin said. There was a pause while he cast around for something to say. "But she's got a nice apartment?"

Ken shook his head. "Oh no. It's like a dungeon."

With envelope in hand, I escaped to my desk and re-wrapped the client package. "Team meeting," Tracy reminded me as she walked by, jerking her head toward the conference room.

"Coming!" I said. I grabbed my notebook and rushed after her. *Shit, I'd forgotten the team meeting.* I was all over the place today.

I took my seat at the conference room table, the last to sit down. The four Directors, Tracy, Mary, Deena and Tara, were all there, along with Elena, who oversaw our team. Tracy and Mary managed Central Asia, and Deena and Tara handled Southeast Asia. I was supposed to bridge the gap between them, theoretically performing the same tasks for each area, but I was finding that the two halves of the team worked quite differently. It was a big job to support both regions. Some days, like today, I felt a bit overwhelmed.

I listened attentively as Elena outlined a new project. "Mark and the rest of the Affinity team feel they can be more productive if they focus their energies on WE." Worldwide Explorer was our largest Affinity client. Soliciting and maintaining their business took a huge chunk of the team's time, and smaller Affinity clients sometimes drew focus away. I knew that we'd recently lost a WE bid to a competitor, and Mark felt that we could have won the business if other clients hadn't monopolized the team's attention.

"So, we're going to pursue this on a trial basis," Elena was saying. "For a six-month period, we'll have Affinities focus exclusively on WE, and we'll split the rest of their trips among the regional teams." She consulted a short list in front of her. "That means you guys will be taking over two trips in November, to Central Asia and northern Laos.

Deena gave a low whistle. "That's two extra departures during our busiest season," she pointed out.

"I know," Elena said, "but the trips are already set up. All you need to worry about are client questions, payments, and final documents." In other words, all the things I was responsible for. I felt anxiety flare in my chest.

"It'll be a busy few months," Elena acknowledged. "There may be some long days ahead." Tracy frowned and muttered to herself, rifling through her notebook. I stared down at my own to-do list, the words swimming in front of my unfocused eyes. *Shit.* Adding anything more to my plate seemed unmanageable. Unconsciously I ran a hand over my face, willing myself to calm down.

Mary glanced at me. "Are you okay, Marie? You look stressed out."

All eyes turned toward me, and I felt the familiar lump rise in my throat. *Oh God, I was going to cry.* Horrified, I tried to hold the tears back, but then Mary said my name again in her kind, questioning voice, and my eyes spilled over. I covered my face with both hands, burning with humiliation. *For God's sake!* I'd been crying everywhere lately, but to lose control at work was a new low.

"What's wrong?" Elena asked worriedly.

"I'm . . . go-going . . . to have to . . . *testify,*" I said jaggedly, a fresh bout of tears spilling forth. I hadn't intended to say it. *Oh God, this was mortifying.*

"At the trial?" Tara asked. My teammates knew a little about the custody trial. I'd had to plan a week off work, after all, and the time was fast approaching.

"Yeh-yes." The whole sorry story came out: the stressful, four-month evaluation, James borrowing money from his sister to go on, his losing battle to keep the kids off the stand. Jessica had insisted that the girls get their say, and if one parent insists, the court will oblige. Despite Dr. Seeger's positive report, we were afraid of what the kids would say to the judge.

I wanted to testify, of course. I was desperate to participate, to help James in every way that I could. But as the time drew closer, I was starting to feel panicky. *What if we lost?* The odds seemed in our favor—but what if they weren't? What would happen to us then?

In the pit of my stomach I nursed a secret fear, the frightening fantasy of losing the girls. Distraught and bankrupt, James would throw himself into his job. He'd work even longer hours, trying to fill the hole left by his missing children. He'd grow hard and distant. In shutting himself off from the pain, he'd begin to turn away from me. Eventually our relationship would dry out and fall apart, having suffered too much to survive.

The idea filled me with dread. I loved James and wanted to build a life with him. But everything seemed to hinge on this trial.

Poor Elena looked so worried for me. When I finished my story, she seemed close to tears herself. "Why don't you go home?" she said. "It's nearly four o'clock; you can take off early today. Go do something nice for yourself," she suggested.

The others murmured in agreement, several of them patting my hands. That was the nice part about working with a team of women. They didn't make you feel bad when you cried like a sap in the team meeting. I thanked them and assured everyone that I'd be in better shape tomorrow. Then I slunk out, trying not to meet anybody's eye as I grabbed my purse and jacket and headed for the door. I was still crying; I couldn't seem to stop.

I was about to slip past the Frontline office when I heard Ken's voice. "I'm just going to put a little more honey in the ol' moustache before I head out," he was saying. He rounded the corner and bumped right into me.

"Oh, sorry, Marie," he said.

"S'okay," I muttered, trying to navigate past him.

"Hang on." He tilted his head and studied my tear-stained face. "Uh-oh," he said. "You sneaking out?" I twisted my face away and gave a stilted nod.

"Just a sec," Ken said. He ducked back into the office and reemerged with his hat and coat, and a heavy backpack. He must have worked the early shift, if four o'clock was his quitting time. "Lemme walk with you," he said.

I was not in the mood for company. "I'm okay, Ken," I said, trying to wave him off.

"Sure, sure," he said. "But lemme walk with you anyway."

Ken stuck to my side as I walked to the bus stop, followed me onto the bus and rode with me all the way downtown. Dimly I registered that he was on the wrong bus, but I didn't really care; I was too busy trying to stem the tears that kept flowing down my face. Ken sat beside me in silence and offered me tissues from his coat pocket.

When I got off the bus downtown, he got off, too. "You want to sit for a sec?" he asked. He gestured to a sunny patch nearby. I nodded, and we perched together on the edge of a concrete sculpture in the courtyard of a tall office building. People streamed out of its double doors, heading home for the evening. I watched the commuters cross the street to the train station and sink down its escalator, out of sight.

And for the second time that day, I talked. For nearly an hour I yammered on, describing the fear that had been clenching my heart, the agony of waiting. As much as I dreaded the trial, the waiting was the real torture. It had been a year of terrible limbo. My nerves were in shreds, as evidenced by my bouts of tears all over town. I felt like I just couldn't take it anymore.

Ken listened thoughtfully until I ran out of words. Then he spoke.

"This is like that episode of *Magnum, P.I.,*" he said.

I stared at him through my tears. "Huh?"

"Yeah. There's an episode of *Magnum, P.I.* where he finds himself stranded in the ocean and has to tread water for an hour. The whole show, he's treading water. It was a pretty weird episode, actually." He twisted his moustache, remembering. "You kept seeing the thoughts inside his head. But he just had to stay calm. He couldn't thrash around, 'cause then he'd attract sharks, you know?

"And when you think about it, treading water isn't really that hard. It's your mind that makes it difficult." He tapped his head with a finger. "And eventually, after an hour of treading water, the show was over and he was saved." Ken folded his arms and sat back, as though he was a guru who'd just delivered a piece of sage advice.

But strange as it sounded, his story made me feel better immediately. I pictured Tom Selleck—with his own formidable mustache—treading water in a merciless ocean. Of all the things to which I could compare this experience, suddenly nothing seemed more relatable.

"Thanks, Ken," I said. I wiped my face with my sleeve, my tears finally ceased. "That actually helps a lot."

"Good," he said. He hopped down from the sculpture. "All right, Marie, I'm toodley-poos." This was Ken for goodbye.

"Hey, aren't you in the wrong neighborhood? Do you have to catch the bus back across town? I'm sorry for dragging you all the way out here."

"Nah, don't worry about it." He shrugged good-naturedly. "I'm going to walk over to North Beach. I'm hoping to sell some books and make twenty bucks to buy my girlfriend a goldfish." He patted his heavy backpack. "She's talking babies . . . I want to start her off on something that she only has to feed once a week." He waved and set off. "Hasta la pasta."

22

RACHEL

Shortly before the trial, James received another package from Jessica's lawyer. This one contained materials that she intended to use as evidence in the trial. Included were more journal entries from Annabelle, detailing James' every fault. All the entries were carefully date-stamped and entitled: "Today at My Father's House."

Either Jessica hadn't heeded the warning in Dr. Seeger's report or she'd decided that she'd come too far down this path to turn back now. It seemed she planned to lay it on thick with the kids' tales of woe.

Included in this shitty gift was a pointed message from Annabelle: "P.S. Dad if you ever read this, I don't like Marie. And yes I want to live with my mom."

During the custody evaluation, Annabelle was surprised to learn that James had read her journal entries. Obviously, Jessica hadn't described the journal's true purpose to her. Annie was first under the impression that James had gone through her things to unearth the diary, an act of supreme betrayal. When James pointed out that her mother had entered the journal into evidence, Annabelle seemed confused. Her little face wrinkled up as she tried to decide where to file this piece of new information. Ultimately, it became another strike against her father.

Poor, confused, asshole-acting kid.

As part of our evidence, Rhonda decided to send the video I'd made. I could tell James was still uncomfortable with it, but Rhonda advised him, "There's no holding back now."

In a final strategy session, she counseled us to keep our answers short while on the stand. "Do not over-talk," she said. "Just answer the question and stop. Do not volunteer extra information." I thought this was directed at me until she said to James, "You tend to blabber when you're nervous." I'd forgotten, for a moment, that they'd been through this before.

Rhonda continued working through her checklist. "Now, are you in agreement with all of Dr. Seeger's recommendations?" At the end of her report, the evaluator had made several suggestions, most notably that the adults should participate in co-parent counseling.

"Sure," James said.

"Good. Who knows if Jess will comply, but that's her lawyer's problem. You want to come off as reasonable and agreeable, which you are." She scanned through her notes, jiggling a pen between her fingers.

"Now, Marie," she pointed the pen at me. "I'm sorry, but you're not allowed in the courtroom until you testify."

"Why not?" I asked indignantly.

"Because you are not a parent here; you're a witness. A key witness, yes, but just a witness. Your testimony may be colored if you view the trial proceedings."

This really pissed me off. I'd sat through countless hours of evaluation, submitted to a million-question personality test, drafted reams of legal-ish documents, and suffered every step of the way alongside James. And now I couldn't even be in the courtroom? *What bullshit!*

"Is Max allowed in the courtroom?" I demanded.

"It's the same situation for Max," she assured me. "He's not allowed inside until after he testifies."

I was partially mollified. For a minute I'd feared that Max would be allowed inside because he was Jessica's husband, whereas I was just James' girlfriend.

Rhonda seemed to read my mind. She gave James a penetrating look. "Do you and Marie plan to get married?" she asked him.

James seemed taken aback by this blunt question. He blinked at her, that deer-in-the-headlights look stealing over his face.

"This is going to come up on the stand," Rhonda told him. "Jess has made it a key talking point. You cannot hesitate or bluster when you're asked this question. Do you plan to get married?"

I looked at James. Little beads of sweat were forming on his forehead. Once again, the words seemed stuck in his throat.

"Yes," he finally said. But his voice was faint and his face was rigid.

"Do you *want* to get married?" Rhonda asked pointedly.

"Yes," I said.

"Yes," James echoed.

"Then say it like it makes you happy," Rhonda instructed. "Got it?"

James nodded. He took my hand and shot me an awkward, tense smile.

* * *

James' sister, Rachel, flew in from Florida to lend her support.

I liked her right off the bat. In a way, she reminded me of Alex: six feet of raw energy. She was loud and buoyant, the opposite of James, and at first, I couldn't believe that they'd shared the same parents.

But when they sat together at the piano, I could see their similarities emerge. They had the same square jaw, identical smiles, and matching talent on the keys. The girls and I flocked around them, delighted to watch them play. Rachel was like a lighthearted wind blowing through the household, and I think we were all grateful to have her there.

She was also funny, and increasingly more so with each glass of wine. Later, as the kids played video games, we sat in the kitchen, sharing a bottle and catching up on recent history.

A year older than her brother, Rachel had just gone through her own divorce, from a man who sounded almost as unpleasant as Jessica. She, too, had married young— although not as young as James. That's how it was in their small, religious community, she explained. Once you'd slept together, marriage was inevitable.

"See? I wasn't the only stupid one," James teased. Having his sister around had visibly raised his spirits.

"Whatever," Rachel replied, unperturbed. "At least Mum didn't have to write me a permission slip."

They'd moved to the States, settling in Florida, where her husband had landed a job. She and Bill had two kids, and Rachel trained as a nurse, like her mother. She settled into the life she was expected to live.

After years in an unhappy marriage, Rachel decided that she didn't want to be with Bill anymore. He was a dick. Moreover, she wanted to be a doctor, like her father had been. She'd only become a nurse because no one had ever encouraged her to go any further.

So, in her late thirties, and with two small kids, she ditched her husband and started medical school. She steered her life in a brand new direction—and she was enjoying the ride.

"Are you still seeing that guy?" James asked her. "What was his name, José?"

"You mean Julio?" Rachel held out her wine glass so James could refill it. "Naw, that's over. He was fun, but not real bright. Plus, he made these really weird noises during sex. Like, *'Eeuuhhh! Eeeeuuhh!'*"

I snorted into my wine glass. James laughed, but held his finger to his lips. "Rach, the kids," he warned, jerking his head toward the other room.

"Oh, they can't hear me," she said. "And they don't know what we're talking about anyway." The girls had their backs to us, engrossed in *Dance Off,* but I thought they could probably hear us. The back of Avery's head had gone suddenly still.

"They're ten and twelve," James reminded her. "They're not as little as your kids."

"Speaking of which, let me show you some recent pictures." Rachel pulled out her phone and scrolled through her photos. "There's Mya at her gymnastics class. And there's Sam at his birthday party."

Mya and Sam were eight and six now, but I recognized them as the two little blonde children I'd seen in the Mercy balcony a few years before. And Rachel was the tall woman whom I'd mistaken for James' girlfriend. Of course, I'd known this for a while, but it was suddenly clear why I'd pictured them as a family.

"Sam's starting to look a lot like Bill," James commented.

"I know." Rachel slipped her phone back into her purse. "Oh hey! Did I tell you Bill's been screwing the nanny?"

This time I definitely saw Avery's head cock toward us.

"Rachel!" James gave her a pained look. "Remember, I'm going to court next week!"

"Sorry, sorry," she stage-whispered. She launched into the tale of Missy the nanny, who split her time between their two households. It was common for Missy to arrive early and help the kids off to school. But one recent morning, Mya had found Missy asleep in her father's bed.

"She didn't even get up to take the kids to the school bus!" Rachel exclaimed, as though that was the crucial bit. "Can you believe it? So I called the nanny agency to complain, right? And they said there was nothing they could do about it. Apparently it happens all the time." She snorted. "But then the lady said, 'I can help you find a handsome young male nanny, if you're interested.'"

"No!" I laughed.

"Yeah. I said I'd think about it." Rachel grinned and took a sip of her wine. She was forgetting to whisper. "Honestly, I don't care who Bill's sleeping with. I just don't want my kids to know about it." James made a little face, as if to indicate that he didn't want *his* kids to know about it either.

"And this is the guy who had zero sex drive for most of our marriage." Rachel was on a roll. "I remember one night, I came to bed in this fancy lingerie to try and kick things off, you know? Bill rolled over on his back, gave a huge sigh, and said, 'Go ahead and do what you need to do. Just pretend that I'm dead.'"

At this, James and I both let out whoops of laughter. Annabelle turned around, curious. "What's so funny?" she called from the living room.

"Nothing," we called back.

"He's such an ass," Rachel went on. "The nanny can have him. Did you know I took my wedding ring back and got reimbursed?"

"Are you serious?" James asked.

"Totally. I still had the Costco receipt because I bought my own ring, remember?" She rolled her eyes. "But eighteen years later they took it back and gave me a full refund, no questions asked. I just told them, 'I was unsatisfied with my purchase.'"

Oh my God, I loved this woman.

Rachel drained her glass and set it on the counter. "Hey girls," she called. "Are there any hip-hop songs in that game?" She went into the living room to join the dance off.

James and I watched as she tried to teach his skinny white kids how to twerk. "See, you just pop your booty up and down, like this." Rachel gyrated around the girls.

"Your sister is awesome," I said.

James gave a thoughtful nod of his head. "My sister is . . ."

"More booty! Stick it out!"

" . . . on her journey," he decided.

* * *

To everyone's surprise, Jessica agreed to let the kids stay with James an extra day so they could spend more time with Rachel. This was a historical first, clearly engineered to make her seem accommodating at trial.

In a similar stroke, Jess had invited her family to come visit, presumably so she could tell the judge that James' claims of her estrangement were bogus. Her tactics weren't entirely successful, however. Since most of her siblings had recently come to Disneyland, they weren't eager to make a second trip to California. Her mother didn't come either. But Jessica's father did fly down for a few days shortly before the trial. Avery and Annabelle were having some awkward family reunions.

Since I wasn't allowed in the courtroom until my testimony, Rachel and I spent the first day of the trial hanging out with the kids. I felt badly sending James off to court by himself, but he wanted to make the day as lighthearted as possible for the girls. Rachel and I took them on a hike, and then shopping, and in the late afternoon we all drove up to the courthouse in Vacaville.

James was in the parking lot, leaning against his car. He looked as though he'd aged years since that morning. As we spilled out of my car, I spotted Jessica and Max down the block, tiptoeing toward us in little injured steps. The girls froze, uncertain of which parent they should go to.

Rachel took control. "Watch this," she said under her breath to me. "Come on girls, let's go see your mother. It's been *years* since I've seen her!" She waved to the Mazzeos with apparent delight. "Hel-*lo!*" she called out to Jessica. Her voice was saccharine sweet. "How *are* you?"

I turned away. I knew Rachel was making sport, but I couldn't handle watching this bullshit tableau. The very sight of Jessica made my stomach hurt. She matched Rachel's over-bright tone with ease, the two of them chatting like old, fake friends. Jessica even waggled her fingers in my direction and called out a chipper "Hello!"

Fuck you, I nearly replied.

The girls stood trapped between their mother and aunt, captives of the weird scenario. When the conversation ended, they looked ready to flee, but Rachel held them each by a shoulder. "Go give your dad a hug goodbye," she said firmly. It was clear they weren't planning to, but they did as they were told.

"I hate that bitch," Rachel said in the same smiley tones as we watched them walk away.

"Me too," James said wearily.

"Do you want to grab some dinner nearby?" I asked, putting my hand on his arm. "You can tell us how the day went?" The poor guy looked beat.

"No. I want to get the hell out of this shithole town," he said.

23

TRIAL

To: Friends & Family
Subject: Today in court

It's the second day of the weeklong trial, and today the kids gave their testimonies. I'm not allowed to know the specifics until after I've testified, but I'm told that they were well spoken and very clear. Neither kid cried; both expressed in no uncertain terms that they want to live with their mom. James bore up pretty well throughout that part.

Jessica's new stance is to make it seem like everything has been just an unfortunate misunderstanding. After reading the evaluator's report (and probably at the suggestion of her lawyer), she and Max "had therapy" to learn how to be better communicators. They went exactly one time—but apparently that's all it took! Their therapist must be better than mine.

To prove how much they've changed, Jessica made several overtures to me today. I bumped into her in the courthouse bathroom and she acted like we were old friends. "I love your sweater—such a pretty color! How's your job going? Any fun trips coming up?"

She later declared on the stand that we've worked out all our differences. Even Max tried to buddy up to me in the hallway. Remember, these are the same people who wouldn't say hello to me for the past two years. But bygones, right?

As expected, the kids stayed glued to Max's side while their parents were in the courtroom. They ignored me, and I let them. I was too nervous to force a conversation. After the kids testified, Max took them home. He waved goodbye to me; they didn't.

James' lawyer cross-examined Jessica for a long time. At two o'clock, the doors opened, and I thought I was going to be called in. It turned out they were just taking a break. At three o'clock, I thought maybe they'd bring me in for the final hour.

But instead, the doors to the courtroom burst open and Jessica came stumbling out, crying. She was alone. She collapsed onto a nearby bench, heaving with sobs. It was late in the day and the hallway was otherwise empty—it was just her and me.

A security guard stepped out of the courtroom and said to Jessica, "Do you need medical assistance?" Jessica stopped crying long enough to say in a tortured voice, "No. It's just . . . the pain . . . is so bad." The guard said simply, "Okay. I'm just *required to ask." Then he went back inside. Nobody else came out to assist her, not even her lawyer.*

Jessica has been milking her back injury for a year and a half. I don't believe she's nearly as hurt as she lets on. She was walking around just fine this morning—in quite high heels!—but when she enters the courtroom, she hobbles. She makes a big show of sitting on pillows and mentions her injury whenever possible. So her sudden burst of tears seemed engineered to halt her cross-examination.

She sat in that empty hallway, gasping and spluttering, strangled by tears. It was quite a performance—but I was the only one there.

I tried to ignore her, but that didn't feel good. So I walked over and offered her my bottle of water.

"Oh, no, thank you," she said. She gave me a brave, wobbly smile. "It's just . . . the pain. It's so bad . . . "

But I walked away. I don't give a shit about her pain.

When Jessica realized that she had no audience, she went back inside. Five minutes later they all came pouring out. The judge had adjourned an hour early to accommodate Jessica's injury. I will testify tomorrow.

So, I spent the entire day in the hallway when I could have gone to a movie. But that's okay. I'm glad I was around for James. And it's been so great having his sister Rachel here for five days. She is awesome. She taught us how to Soulja Boy and made us sit and watch while she rapped to Eminem and Lupe Fiasco. Like, for a long time. She was awful: so white, so Canadian. I totally love her.

* * *

To: Friends & Family
Subject: More from court

Day 3. I spent the morning in the hallway, while Jessica continued her cross-examination. She made a big show of wearing flip flops, rather than the high heels she'd had on yesterday.

James and I were dismayed to see her enter the court with the kids in tow; they'd already testified and there was no reason for them to be there. James asked her why she'd brought them along, and Jessica was indignant: "I need them to help carry my things, James! I can't carry them myself!" Annabelle carried her mother's butt pillow. Avery was empty-handed.

We had an awkward exchange in the hallway. The kids pretended that they couldn't see us—even though we were standing right in front of them. James and I said a pointed hello, and Avery feigned surprise and mumbled, "Oh, hi."

Avery's been really weird this week. She's acting like court is a grand adventure and she's having the best time. Annabelle has been a brick wall: won't look at us, won't talk to us. She follows her mother diligently through the hallways, holding open doors, walking alongside her in baby steps, a ten-year-old bodyguard. I wish the judge could see all that goes on in the hallway of the court.

After Max and the kids departed, I settled myself down to wait. Cross-examination took about an hour, and afterward James and Rachel filled me in. It seems that Jessica spent a great deal of time explaining why she'd refused my efforts to meet. It came down to her confusion between the terms "meet" and "meet up". You see, she was agreeable to "meeting" me. But she was not agreeable to "meeting up".

I would have laughed if it weren't all so dismal. She'd better pray the judge is an imbecile.

I took the stand next, finally allowed to enter the courtroom. We started out by playing a video that I'd made of our earlier happy times with the kids. I didn't think we'd ever wind up using it, but boy, am I glad now that I put it together. The judge was inscrutable as he watched it, but Jessica put on a big smile, as though the content of the video delighted her.

I don't remember much of what I said on the stand, but I was surprised that neither attorney seemed to dig into me that much. Jessica's lawyer asked me if Jess had spoken to me in court this week. I said yes, she had. He asked me how many times the children had hugged me in the last year. What the hell? I told him that I couldn't possibly answer that accurately, and he looked disappointed.

His argument seems to be that Jessica misunderstood my intentions to meet (versus "meet up"), but now that she understands, she is making an effort, and my relationship with the kids is thereby improved. I think he was hoping for some hug statistics to back that claim.

James' lawyer ended by asking me: "Do you love James? Do you love Avery and Annabelle? What do you want out of your relationship with the girls?"

I answered that yes, I love them all. And that all I wanted was for the girls to feel free to care about me in whatever manner they choose.

* * *

It was sad saying goodbye to Rachel on Wednesday, but she had to get back home to her kids.

"Jessica's lawyer seems like an idiot," she said, hugging us both. "I'm sure everything is going to be fine."

We dropped her at the airport for her evening flight, and although we were both exhausted, we decided to go to Mercy and catch the end of choir rehearsal.

It was the right move. Our friends' support reinvigorated us. We were met with hugs and prayers and so many questions that I added a host of names to my email distribution list. Writing the daily digest was therapeutic for me.

"What can we do?" asked Russell. "Can we come to the courthouse and support you? I bet the judge would be impressed to see the whole choir turn out as character witnesses! Maybe we could sing a song." Others murmured their agreement. I bit back a smile as I imagined the choir descending on the courtroom singing "We Shall Overcome".

"I'm glad we went," James said later, as we walked to the car. "It was a good reminder that despite everything, we're blessed."

I put my arm around his waist and matched my steps to his. "We're lucky to have good friends," I said. "Can you imagine going through all this as a couple of assholes? It almost makes me feel for Jessica and Max."

* * *

To: Friends & Family
Subject: Thursday and Friday in court

THURSDAY:

Jessica began the day by complimenting my outfit. "What a lovely pink shawl! Look girls, isn't that pretty?" (Barf.)

Once again, she'd brought the kids with her. Avery paraded by on Max's arm, giggling like he was her prom date. Annabelle marched past us in military formation, eyes straight ahead. "Why are they here?" James asked Jessica in a low voice. She looked at him like he was slow. "Because I need them to assist me, James." Annabelle carried her mother's pillow again.

Thursday was a half day, and James spent the entire time under direct examination. He did really well at first, answering questions clearly and concisely, and I was pleased that his attorney Rhonda started way back at the beginning, in the days before James and Jessica's divorce.

By contrast, Jessica's lawyer, Ben, did not have his act together. Every time Rhonda referenced a document in evidence, he whispered to her, "Which one is this?" Then he made an objection but didn't state on what grounds. We all sat waiting while he fumbled through his binder. He'd made the objection, and he didn't know why! Finally, he confessed, "I'm drawing a blank, Your Honor. Objection withdrawn." The guy doesn't seem too smart.

For all that I'd hated sitting in the hallway the day before, I realized quickly that an hour in the courtroom feels like forever. By ten-thirty I was exhausted, and James was visibly flagging. He neglected to provide context on several occasions, causing Rhonda to re-ask the question until his meaning was clear. I could see Rhonda getting frustrated and the judge becoming irritated. When the judge tried to clarify the timeline of an event, James, who was trying to be helpful, spoke over him in response. The judge snapped, "Mr. de Graaf. NEVER interrupt the Court. Is that understood?" James flushed with embarrassment.

Rhonda had James read aloud a string of emails wherein he asked repeatedly for Jessica to provide the girls' passports. He read them in a speedy, dull monotone—I wanted to holler at him, "SLOW DOWN!" Several times Rhonda and the judge broke in to ask questions, and James would lose his place. The whole process was painful to sit through and took a long time, but I think, ultimately, it came across that Jessica was creating obstacles to prevent James from traveling with the children.

We adjourned for the day at one o'clock. I was loitering in the hall, waiting for James and Rhonda, when the court reporter came out of her little room.

She caught my eye, grinned and said, "I've never seen so much bullshit in all my life."

That took me by surprise, and I laughed for the first time in days. She went on, "I think the whole passport thing really clinched it for you guys."

I put out my hand to stop her from walking away. "I like you very much," I said.

And that was Thursday.

FRIDAY:

James was on the stand for most of the day. Once again, he did really well in the morning. He answered Rhonda's questions directly and came across as honest and humble.

During a ten-minute break, James found himself in the bathroom with Jessica's lawyer. His water bottle fell out of his jacket pocket and hit the floor with a loud bang, making Ben jump. As they were washing their hands, Ben said, "You scared the hell out of me, James. I thought you'd shot me."

Back in the courtroom Ben began his cross-examination. There was nothing particularly potent about it, which surprised me. I got a little bored. I doodled for a while. At one point James said something rather brilliant, and I couldn't help myself; I shot Jessica an ultra-bright smile. But she, far more practiced in the art of fakery, matched me watt for watt.

We broke for lunch and went to the deli across the street with Rhonda.

"How am I doing?" asked James.

"You're doing well," said Rhonda. "Just keep telling the truth. But for God's sake, if you feel yourself talking for a while, look at me to see if I'm giving you my shut-the-fuck-up face, okay?" (Yes, she really said that.)

I mentioned that Ben's questioning seemed rather weak. "He may not have wanted to get into anything heavy right before lunch," Rhonda said. "We don't know yet. But the writing is on the wall, you know. Eventually these girls are going to go live with their mother, especially if Jess gets her head out of her ass and starts acting cooperative."

I froze, staring at her.

"These girls want their momma," she went on. "They made that very clear on the stand. Now, whether the judge gives their testimony much weight, we'll see. But now that Jess and Max have agreed to go through that co-parenting program with you guys, it's possible that you'll be revisiting custody next year—even if you win this time around. This is not an issue that's going to go away."

James grunted. I sat mute, staring at the table.

We finished our lunches and James went to the men's room. I sat in silence across the table from Rhonda. As she scrolled through emails on her phone, she asked, "How are you?"

"I'm a little upset," I admitted.

She looked at me. "The problem is, the door to court is always open. Jess can do this again and again. That's just the situation until Annabelle turns eighteen. You understand that, don't you?"

I tried to nod. James rejoined us, and we walked back across the street to court.

Back on the stand, Ben's cross-examination didn't get any sharper. Three times in a row he referenced "the girls" when he meant to say "Avery", and Rhonda objected: "Mistakes testimony."

James was getting tired. Each time Rhonda objected, James was supposed to stop talking. But three times in a row he tried to answer the question anyway. After the third time, the judge thundered, "Mr. de Graaf! When there is an objection in the court and I have sustained it, you DO NOT SPEAK. Do you understand?" James apologized, but then he giggled

*nervously, which gave the unfortunate impression
that he was laughing at the judge.*

*Ben wrapped up his questioning, and I don't think
he hit on anything truly significant. But then the judge
asked James a question. "In your estimation, do you
believe that Avery and Annabelle are mature for their
ages? Their progress reports, the evaluator's report,
and their testimony suggest that they are well-adjusted
and mature for the ages of ten and twelve. Do you
agree?"*

*James said, "Absolutely." He added a bit of
commentary that further underscored the girls'
maturity.*

*My stomach sank like a stone. All along Rhonda
has been saying that our biggest challenge will be the
kids' testimony. We knew they would align firmly with
their mother, but the question is, how much weight
will the judge give to their words? And James just told
the judge that his kids are incredibly mature for their
ages. I felt like he'd gift-wrapped the verdict for
Jessica—and he didn't seem to realize he'd done it. I
wanted to cry.*

*With that, the trial concluded. Both lawyers are
to turn in their closing arguments in writing by July
31st. We reconvene on August 5th for a ruling.*

I went straight to the ladies' room to have a few minutes
alone. When I emerged Rhonda and James were sitting in
the hallway. They both looked up at me.

"You okay?" asked Rhonda.

"It didn't seem to end very well," I said quietly.

She shrugged and got to her little feet. Together we walked out to the curb.

"James," I said urgently, "why did you tell the judge that the kids are mature for their ages?"

He looked at me. "Because it's the truth."

"But it's not the whole truth!" I said. "The kids have a blind spot when it comes to their mother. They are *not* mature where she's concerned. Why didn't you say that?"

James frowned. "Because he didn't ask me that. I was just trying to answer honestly."

Rhonda broke in. "This case is not going to be decided on that question alone." She looked at me steadily. "It's not."

Then she gave us each a hug. "It's over for now. Go get drunk. Celebrate. Have a good cry. I'll be in touch when I'm back from vacation next week."

I began to cry on the way home. I was overwhelmed with frustration and worry. James asked me what was wrong, but I'd worked myself into such a state, I couldn't even speak.

He pulled off the highway to give me a hug, but I wouldn't be hugged. Rhonda had scared the hell out of me. Even if we won, the idea that we could be back in court in a year or two wouldn't leave me. I'd thought this was it. "I'm not doing this again," I said.

I couldn't go through another year like this one. I'd lose my goddamn mind. I knew I should be supporting James, but my thoughts were a self-centered whirlwind. "I'm not doing this again." *Another trial? The door to court is always open?* I didn't realize I was shouting, but I wondered dimly why it was getting so loud in the car as I kept yelling, "I'm not doing this again! *I'm not doing this again!*"

It wasn't my best moment.

James drove to my house and curled up with me as I cried some more. Then he ordered us a pizza. By the time it arrived, I was feeling a little better, but he was feeling worse. I tried to distract him with sitcoms as we ate, but he didn't want to watch TV. He decided instead to read through the evaluator's report again, page by page.

"Did we cover this?" he kept asking. "Did I explain that well enough?" I didn't want to talk about it anymore. I tried to read aloud to him from my trashy magazine, but he didn't seem interested in celebrity babies.

"Forty thousand dollars," he said. "Forty thousand dollars for one week of trial. All this so some judge can arbitrarily decide what's right for my family. I must have spent over a hundred grand with Jess over the years, and what have we gained? Where have we gotten?"

We went to bed early and slept fitfully. James got up at six-thirty the next morning to go into work. It was Saturday. He was exhausted.

I got up and made tea, noting that Mandy's bedroom door was open, and she wasn't inside. I guessed she'd spent the night at Javier's. I knew I should be happy that things were going so well for them, but I just felt hollow inside. I drank my tea and went back to bed.

When I woke up again a few hours later, I texted James:

> *I was hoping I'd feel a little better with the new day, but I don't. How do you feel?*

He wrote back:

> *Whatever happens, we'll figure out how to navigate it. All we can do is move forward.*

I sat for several moments, staring at his words.

And after a while I realized: *I admire the hell out of that man.*

24

DECISION

To: Friends & Family
Subject: The court's ruling

Today we lost.

Rhonda decided not to present her closing arguments aloud. The judge had come prepared to rule, and all that she wanted to say was reflected in her written statement. Ben, on the other hand, wanted to summarize his case. He did a poor job. Six times he referred to Jessica erroneously as "Mrs. de Graaf", and at one point he even called Avery "Angela".

But it didn't matter. The judge gave the greatest weight to Avery and Annabelle's testimonies, noting their maturity and clear wishes—and that they didn't seem to be under any coercion. They want to live with their mother, so they shall.

The girls will move to Vacaville immediately. James will have them most weekends and half the summer, but this is small consolation after raising them himself for the last eight years.

Now the kids will commute every weekend— even more than they did before. They'll be tossed back and forth between households, with little chance to take root in either place.

We are not allowed to discuss the case with the children. So, there's to be no conversation about this sudden change of circumstance, this utter wrenching out of one life, into the next. On Sunday night they'll just go to their mom's. And they'll stay there.

And they will continue to believe that everything that their mother said is true. They will learn that suing people is the way to get what you want. They will never know the results of our custody evaluation because we can't tell them. They will think everything happened just as it should have, just as their mother told them it would. All of Jessica's awful behavior has been validated.

Rhonda was the first one of us to cry. She hugged each of us and said, "You're both good people. I hope you get married, have babies, and live a good life." She was kind enough not to mention James' outstanding bill—though I'm sure she'll send notice by mail.

Avery was a jerk tonight. As James was trying to tell the kids the decision, she just kept asking to be excused from the dinner table, as though she was bored and couldn't be bothered. James was choking back tears and all Avery could say was, "As long as I still get to see Penelope." She's been in her room ever since. And no, she is not sad.

Annabelle has been quiet. She sat alone in the kitchen, while James and I sobbed behind the curtain that is his bedroom door. Now she is snuggled up next to James on the couch, watching a movie. I had to leave the room. Because I couldn't take it, the sight of him silently crying, his tears catching the light of the TV screen, making silver tracks down his face.

Thank you all for your love and support and for your messages. I hope you understand if I don't immediately reply. I can't talk much about this right now. We just have to figure out how to get through it.

Love,

Marie

Part III

Reconstruction

25

ONWARD

"Help me with this?" James asked.

I lifted the other side of Avery's desk and together we tried to back it into the bedroom, but the desk was too wide to clear the doorframe.

"Hang on, I've got it. Step out of the way," James said. I stepped back and he tipped the desk onto its end. There was a crash as the contents shifted violently within the drawer. James pushed the desk easily through the doorway and flipped it right-side-up again. There was a second crash as the drawer fell open and its contents spilled out.

"Oh shit," I said.

James shoved the items back in haphazardly. "Oh well," he said. "Guess she should've taken it to her mum's if she was worried about it." He brushed his hands and went back down to the moving truck.

I watched him go with a raised eyebrow. This new take-no-shit stance was attractive.

Two hours later, we were moved in. Ignoring the boxes and the generous mess, we sank onto my—*our*—bed and made exhausted love.

"Do you think the kids will like the house?" I asked afterward, curled up in his arms.

"I don't really care if they like it or not," he said. There was a slight edge to his tone. I gave his arm a little squeeze.

It turned out, I had underestimated James. I knew that losing custody of his girls was the worst thing that had ever happened to him—and he hadn't led a particularly easy life. Just sharing his grief had been one of the worst things that had ever happened to *me*, and they weren't even my children.

But James didn't turn away from the world, as I had feared. Instead, he did what he'd said he would do: move forward. He'd been hollowed and hardened, and there was a brittle quality to him now. But he wasted no time turning the page, determined to put this tragic chapter behind him.

"Let's move in together," he said to me. "The kids have chosen their lives; let's choose ours." I knew that wasn't easy for him to say. And I was so grateful that he still wanted a life together, even though it looked different now.

So, working with very little money, we started looking at apartments again. Without his kids, there was nothing keeping James in San Carlos. His substantial legal debt meant he could no longer afford the high rent, and I didn't want to live there anyway.

We quickly realized that San Francisco was also out of our price range. The problem was, even though the kids would only be with us on weekends, we still needed a place big enough for four. Affordable options were limited. We expanded our search to the East Bay, and for months we had no luck.

Avery still thought she had some influence. When we looked at an apartment near Lake Merritt, I was tempted to apply based solely on its location. "I think it's too small,"

Avery said. She was trying to be helpful and she was entirely right, but neither James nor I was interested in her opinion.

"You don't get a say," James informed her, and a hurt look swept over her face. I think he felt a little bad, and I did, too—but not that much.

The girls were unprepared for the major changes they had wrought. Although they'd spent a year campaigning to live with their mother, they seemed surprised when their wish was suddenly granted. And *suddenly* was the operative word—their lives were transformed overnight. A week after the judge's ruling, they were thrust into new schools in Vacaville to begin the sixth and eighth grades.

The kids pretended to be happy with their new normal, but they were rattled. They'd had no chance to say goodbye to their school friends. Annabelle, who'd just graduated to San Carlos' middle school, now found herself dumped back into elementary, since Vacaville kids didn't transition until grade seven. And Avery, who should've been enjoying her last year of middle school with her friends, was now the new kid in an unfamiliar junior high. The girls were abruptly faced with the fact that life with mom meant more than they'd bargained for—new schools and no friends.

Avery still saw Penelope on the weekends, since James and Rochelle were neighbors, but Penelope seemed hurt and bewildered that Avery had chosen to move away. Their friendship was undergoing a sea change, and Avery seemed unaware that she had caused it.

If James had won custody, we likely would have waited a year before moving in together, and both kids would have had time to process what was happening. It must have dawned on them, somewhere in those first furious days, that the violent speed behind these changes was entirely their own doing. They tried to act like everything was cool, but they'd been severely shaken. Avery, always prone to temper tantrums, had a shorter fuse than ever, and the once happy-go-lucky Annabelle grew quiet and withdrawn. Their weekends with James were strained.

Then came the news that we were moving in together, and James was leaving San Carlos. And again, the kids were stunned. It was like they didn't expect anyone to follow through on the promises they'd been making all year.

In a way, I could understand it. The trial had seemed to take up years of my life; from a child's perspective it had probably felt like forever. I suppose it was hard to see the end of such a long horizon, especially from the height of a ten-year-old. I felt a pang that we hadn't prepared them well enough for this possible outcome, that we hadn't impressed upon them the weight of their words and actions.

But my empathy was limited. These kids had upended our lives, and the truth was, I wanted them to feel the effects of their work.

I'd been made brittle, too.

In early October we struck it lucky, finding a great two-bedroom house for rent in Oakland. It was near the lake and priced under market, but even so, we could barely afford it. Still, I was thrilled; I loved the neighborhood and the house was beautiful, crammed though it was in a tiny cul-de-sac, overlooking a grocery store.

I dreaded telling Mandy that I'd be moving out, but she took the news in stride. In fact, she was suspiciously upbeat about it. When pressed, she admitted that Javier's lease was coming to an end.

"Are you going to ask him to move in with you?" I asked, surprised.

She shrugged, a little sheepish. "I've been thinking about it. He has to move anyway, so I figure we could try it for a little bit and see how it goes."

"Oh my God!" I said. I gave her a hug. "That's great news!" I liked Javier a lot. I had to concentrate hard when he spoke, because of his thick accent, but if I was understanding him correctly, he was funny and nice.

So, on the one weekend of the month that the girls weren't with us, James and I moved into our new home. He was a bit cavalier with the kids' belongings, upending Avery's desk and dropping a box marked "ANNABELLE—FRAGEL!!!" to the ground with an unnecessary thud. He had some aggression to work out.

By the time I got home from work the following Friday, the kids were already there. James had had to leave the store by midday to meet them for the late-afternoon exchange. The new custody hours were a challenge for him.

I was a bit nervous to show the girls our new home, but they were pleasantly surprised by the house. "It's nice," said Avery appreciatively. I thought they'd gripe about having to share a bedroom, but they didn't. Of course, James had no ear for complaints. He was laying down a new hard line.

"This is our room," he said to the kids, indicating the master bedroom. "You do not come in here without permission from me or Marie. Got it?"

I knew he was just tired of having no privacy, but even I was intimidated by his tone. He wasn't taking any shit.

But I didn't know how to adopt my own hard line. I'd never lived with kids before, and already it seemed I was out of my depth.

"Why are there framed pictures of Penelope hanging in the upstairs bathroom?" I whispered to James on that first night together.

He gave a little laugh. "I guess Avery's been decorating."

I bit my lip. "But I don't want pictures of Penelope in the bathroom of my new house," I said in a small voice.

Penelope wasn't my favorite kid. The brassy quality which had been cute in childhood was less appealing on a teenager. When she and Avery got together now, there was an element of mean girl about them. The last time I'd seen Penelope, she'd smirked at me and whispered something in Avery's ear, then the two of them had dissolved into giggles.

I really, *really* didn't want pictures of Penelope in the bathroom of my new house, but I had a bad feeling that I was going to be overruled. The pictures had been up for a few hours and had somehow gained jurisdiction over the bathroom. I knew there was no way I could take them down without causing a fuss.

"I know it's kind of weird," James said.

"Yes, it's weird!" I agreed. I was glad he recognized this.

"But they're in the kids' bathroom," he pointed out.

"Couldn't they be in the kids' bedroom instead?" I asked.

He gave me a little kiss. "Does it really matter that much?"

Yes, I thought. But I dropped it.

Certain things about the kids mystified me. On Sunday morning we were late to church because Annabelle wasn't ready. We found her on the hallway side of her bedroom door, still in her pajamas.

"Annabelle, why aren't you dressed?" James asked her. "It's time to leave. Where's your sister?"

"In the bedroom," Annabelle said, punctuating each word with a thump on the door.

James knocked, too. "Avery, hurry up. It's time to go."

"I'm getting changed!" came her muffled reply.

"Well, I need to get changed, too!" protested Annabelle, still thumping the door. "Hurry up!"

"Annie, just go in and put your clothes on," said James, losing patience. "We're late."

"No!" came Avery's panicked voice. "I'm in my underwear!"

Annabelle frowned at her father. "We can't get changed at the same time," she said, as though he was stupid.

He stared at her. "But you're sisters."

"So what?" they said from either side of the door.

James looked at me. "Can't sisters get changed in the same room?"

I'd certainly thought so, but both kids cried out, "No!" They sounded scandalized.

James sighed. "Annabelle, we're late. Just go in and get dressed. We're leaving in three minutes."

"Wait! Let me get in the closet!" Avery shrieked.

"Three minutes!" James thundered back. He stomped down the stairs.

"That was weird, right?" he asked me in the kitchen.

"Yeah, that was weird," I confirmed.

But from then on, one of the kids got dressed in the closet, and we stopped being late for church.

* * *

The following Saturday, I set to unpacking the cartons of books that were stacked in the dining room. We had unpacked the essentials, but there were still boxes all over the house. James was at work and had dropped Avery off in San Carlos to play with Penelope. Annabelle was at loose ends, moping around the house.

It was our first afternoon alone together, and for the life of me, I didn't know what to do with her. Annabelle didn't have a best friend like Penelope. She'd had lots of school friends but nobody exceptionally close, and in the three months since moving to Vacaville, she'd let those friendships lapse. James had offered to take her down to Julie or Samira's house, but Annabelle had declined.

Coincidentally, our new house was down the street from Annabelle's old friend Kelsey. The girls had been inseparable during first and second grade, but then Kelsey's father, Lee, had moved the two of them from San Carlos to Oakland, and the kids fell out of touch. James reached out to Lee after we'd moved in, and they'd gone to get a beer and catch up.

"He's a single dad, too," James told me. "His story is actually pretty similar to mine. He's been raising Kelsey alone since she was two years old. Her mum had a drug problem or something and disappeared. I think she's back on the scene now, but Kelsey doesn't see her much. And Lee's girlfriend, Brittany, just moved in with them. Just like us." He gave me a little kiss. "I'm glad those guys are nearby. It'll be good to reconnect."

Now Annabelle sat on the staircase, looking glum as she watched me unload the books.

"Did you finish unpacking your room?" I asked. She nodded mutely. "Can you find a book to read or a game to play?" She shook her head no.

"Um . . . Do you want to help me unpack the books?" Another shake of the head.

I was running out of ideas. "Would you like to see if Kelsey's home?" I ventured.

There was a pause, then a tentative nod.

"Great!" I said. "Let me see if I can set this up." I shot a quick text to James, who put me in touch with Lee, and a few minutes later it was a done deal.

"She's home!" I reported. "I can take you over there in about fifteen minutes." *And then I can finish unpacking without you staring at me,* I thought to myself.

But Annabelle had second thoughts. "I changed my mind," she said. "I don't want to go to Kelsey's."

I stared at her, nonplussed. "Huh?"

"I don't want to go," she repeated.

"How come?" I asked, pointlessly.

She shrugged. "I just don't."

I sighed. *This guy Lee is going to think I'm an asshole,* I thought as I texted him again to cancel the playdate. Then I turned to Annabelle. "Well, what are you going to do with your afternoon?" I asked. Again, she shrugged, slumped miserably against the carpeted stairs. I felt a tiny twinge of desperation.

"Why don't you go watch TV?" I suggested.

That did the trick.

* * *

"I live with children now," I wrote.

I was still keeping a journal. The act of writing helped me process my feelings. But after my courtroom digest, I'd found that writing for an audience was surprisingly gratifying. I turned to social media for an outlet.

> *Marie Aaron*
> *October 5 at 5:32 p.m.*
> *I live with children now.*
> *They yell a lot. They yell for one another, from one room away. They yell for me—when I'm in the bathroom.*
> *They say, "I'm bored." A lot. They beg for playdates. Then I arrange one and suddenly they don't want to go. Then they say, "I'm bored" again.*
> *They say, "I'm hungry." A lot. Then I make them a sandwich and they throw half of it away, claiming to be full. Then they come back 20 minutes later and say, "I'm hungry" again.*
> *They repeat things. A lot. Things they've just said. Things I've just said. If I say, for example, "Where did I put my shoes?", they will say, "You're like: 'Where did I put my shoes?'"*
> *They ate my last piece of birthday cake.*
> *I live with children now.*
> *Pray for me.*
>
> *72 Likes; 36 Comments*

26

FORCING FRIENDS

"Hey girls, I'm going out for a while. You want to come?"

It was another Saturday. James was at work. The girls were holed up in their bedroom. Silence met my inquiry.

I rapped lightly on the door. "Girls! Did you hear me?"

"What?" came Avery's voice. She did not open the door.

"I said, I'm going out for a little while. Would you like to come?"

"No."

"How about you, Annabelle?" I paused. "Annabelle?"

"No."

"But you guys don't even know where I'm going!"

"We still don't want to go."

"I'm going to Disneyland and then I'm going to buy a horse," I said.

"Have fun," came Avery's voice.

Fuck it, I tried.

As the weekends ticked by, I was getting a crash course in Living with Children. And I was thinking about dropping the class.

Here are some things I learned: When a kid asks which mugs are microwave safe, you should not respond with, "Just a minute." Because the next words out of the kid's mouth are bound to be, "Don't worry, I just boiled the milk in the teapot." There are a lot of good phrases to convey disrespect, but an elegant eye roll also does the trick. Buying white furniture is a stupid choice. The simplest way to reconnect with a kid is by laughing when they fart.

The girls and I had our birthdays in quick succession as summer turned to fall. Annabelle's jump from ten to eleven was no major milestone, but Avery was now officially a teenager, with all the attitude and angst that brings. If I'd thought she was a challenge before, I think it's fair to say that thirteen was worse than twelve—by a considerable margin.

One night, while making dinner, I heard a suspicious *clunk* in the dining room. I glanced in there and saw Avery sneaking something out of the glass cabinet that she had no business being in. I didn't say a word, but she cut her eyes at me and spat, "What?"

As we sat down to dinner I realized what was missing from the cabinet: a ceramic ornament that my mother had given me. I asked Avery if she'd taken it. Busted, she admitted, "It fell and the head broke off. I thought I could glue it back on and nobody would notice."

To Avery I said quietly, "You can tell me when stuff like that happens, okay?"

But on the inside I said: *I'm going to break your head off and glue it back on crooked, and maybe nobody will notice.*

I was a little testy. It was hard coming home every weekend to two jaded tweens. Each Friday I'd come in the door and there they'd be, lolling on the couch, watching television. If they acknowledged me with a grunt or a flick of the eyes, it was a good day.

If I had to guess, I'd say that full-time parenting was easier than this weekend crap. We couldn't get any traction. Jumping back and forth between households made the kids irritable. They weren't with us long enough to feel at home, so they weren't comfortable, and they vented their feelings on James and me. But James was still working most Saturdays, meaning the kids were largely in my care. Weekends quickly became the most exhausting part of my week.

The girls acted like time at our house was punishment, a jail sentence that they were forced to serve. I tried to engage them in fun activities, but they wanted nothing to do with Oakland after Jessica told them it was a dangerous place to live.

James and Jessica had begun co-parent counseling. Their therapist was Dr. Ella Sweet, and she outlined a ten-week program designed to help them communicate better. Max and I were supposed to get involved in Week Two, but James and Jessica failed their first session.

I know "failure" is not a term that should be applied to therapy, but they made so little progress that they never advanced beyond the first lesson in the syllabus. Week after week, James would come home frustrated and exhausted.

"This is pointless," he said. "Jessica doesn't compromise, and she doesn't ever admit to being wrong. We can't get through a single discussion."

"What did you talk about?" I asked.

"We tried to talk about Avery's braces. Her orthodontist was ready to remove them, and we were all paid up. But then Jess took Avery to a new orthodontist in Vacaville and decided to leave her braces on." He made a face. "She didn't bother discussing it with me, just sent me the bill. Dr. Sweet tried to point out that it wasn't her decision to make alone, but Jess just kept saying, 'We agreed to this.' In her mind, if *she* agreed to it, *we* agreed to it."

"When do I get to come in?" I asked.

"I don't know," he said wearily. "Dr. Sweet says we're not ready yet. We keep repeating Week One." He sighed. "I don't know why you want to come anyway. It's stupid."

I was frustrated; I wanted to participate. I had shit to say, damn it.

"I should be spending this stupid, wasted time with my kids," James grumbled.

I was determined to get the kids off the couch. I tried to take them to the library.

"Library books are dirty," said Annabelle.

"Since when?" I asked, surprised. "I've seen you read lots of library books."

"Not *Oakland* library books," she retorted.

I tried not to sigh. "That's silly. You love to read and you've been complaining that you don't have enough books." I refrained from mentioning the three cartons of young adult books that my mother had shipped me. I'd always wanted to share my childhood book collection with my own kids, and I'd been excited to share it with James' girls, who were the perfect age. But they wouldn't touch them. It was meant to be an insult, and it worked, but I tried not to show it.

"Come on, it's a beautiful day," I said. "Let's walk to the library and get you both library cards." I willed them to share my fake enthusiasm.

Avery wasn't having it. "We don't *want* library cards here, because we don't *live* here," she said. She turned her attention back to the TV.

Each weekend I tried something new. "Figure skating!" I announced to Annabelle, knowing how much she loved to skate. "Did you know there's a rink just a few blocks away? We can walk there!"

"I'm not skating in Oakland!" she said. "It's not safe." *Jesus, what had Jessica told her?*

"Farmers market!" I tried another day. "We can walk there, too! We'll go right past the lake where everybody's hanging out in the sun, and maybe there will be a drum circle . . . "

This was met with a hard, "No."

"Can I come to counseling yet?" I asked James crossly that evening. I had a bone to pick with Jessica. She should have been encouraging the kids to do things here, as we encouraged them to do things in Vacaville. They still had no friends in either place.

"Not yet," James said. "We flunked our weekly phone call." James had forgotten to call Jessica at the predetermined time, and she refused to pick up the phone when he did call later.

"Get it together, babe," I commanded. "I want my turn to talk."

Despite the tension with the girls, I was so happy to be living with James. I loved having a house that we both came home to every night. James had made a sacrifice for me, in moving to Oakland. His commute to Redwood City was an hour and a half each way, often longer in traffic. He was exhausted every night, but the sweetness of coming home to each other helped to abate it.

I was eager to show off our new house and invited friends to come visit. Hailey, Alex, and Mandy all dropped by, and we hosted an assortment of Mercy friends for our first Thanksgiving. I was trying to show the kids that we could have fun together in our home, but they remained resistant to my efforts. I spent many a Saturday pitching an activity, being rebuffed, and then doing my own thing.

As Christmas grew near, I decided to take a different approach: I would stop asking the kids if they *wanted* to do things, and instead I'd just *force* them to do things.

I saw a flier advertising a holiday craft session at the library. I thought Avery might be interested; I knew she liked to craft—but then Penelope invited her over. Their last two playdates had fallen through, and Avery was eager to see her friend.

So that left Annabelle. Predictably, Annie was mopey when her sister wasn't around. She used to hang out at Penelope's all the time, too, but it was different now that they weren't neighbors. Suddenly she was the annoying kid sister encroaching on Avery's precious time with her friend.

Annabelle had sprouted up over the summer. She no longer resembled the little girl that she was when James and I had started dating—in fact, she was nearly as tall as Avery. But she was still every inch the little sister. She continued to dog Avery's steps and seemed at a loss without her. I looked at her brooding on the couch, flipping channels on the TV.

On a whim, I decided to reach out to Lee's girlfriend, Brittany. We'd never met, but I knew she had recently moved into Lee's house. I wondered if she was going through something similar with his kid.

I felt a bit nervous calling her up, but she immediately agreed to join us for the craft session. We would meet at the library that afternoon.

"Put your shoes on, kid," I announced to Annabelle. "We're going to go make friends and have fun."

I always think that people named Brittany are going to be girly-girls, Barbie-types. It's a stupid notion of mine that had already been proven wrong by my college roommate, also named Brittany, who was anything but a Barbie doll. Still, I was pleasantly surprised to meet this Brittany, or "Brit", as she introduced herself. She had a short, asymmetrical haircut and was dressed casually in a sweatshirt and slouchy jeans. I liked her right away.

Kelsey was tall for eleven, like Annabelle, with long brown hair and a cherubic face. She and Annie greeted each other awkwardly, then lapsed into silence. I could see it was going to be up to us adults to kick things off.

A table at the back of the library was spread with beads and twine, feathers, wires, and glue. "What are we making today?" I asked a staff member.

"We're making jewelry," she said. "Or anything you want, really. You can give them as Christmas presents to your friends and family, or you can keep them for yourselves!"

"Cool," said Brit in her husky voice. She lifted some feathers to her ears. "These would make good earrings, right?" They hung nearly to her shoulders, wonderfully garish in bright rainbow colors. Annabelle wrinkled her nose a bit, but smiled.

"Oh, those look great," I said. "I'm going to make . . . " I scanned the table for inspiration, then seized a pair of hoops. They were the size of soup cans. "I'm going to make earrings, too. With beads and feathers and as much junk as I can hang from them."

We ushered the kids to a table and sat them together, with us a short distance away. Annabelle looked alarmed for a minute, as though I was going to leave her with strangers, but soon became involved in her crafting. She chatted amiably with Kelsey, and we left them to it.

"So, you guys just moved in together?" Brit asked me. She tried to wrap wire around the stem of a giant yellow feather, but it kept slipping off.

"Yeah, in October," I replied.

"How's it going?" She looked at me with a face that knew.

"Honestly? It's been a little . . . challenging." I fiddled with my hoops. "You know about our custody trial?"

"Yeah, Lee filled me in." She tried another feather. "I hear James has a crazy ex, too, huh?"

"*Yes,*" I said, my chest filling with giddy relief. *Had I found a kindred spirit?*

"I've heard a lot about her," Brit said with a grin. "James spilled his guts to Lee over a few beers. She sounds like a real peach."

"Right?" I gave a little laugh. "But the girls idolize her. They think she can do no wrong. Everything she says is gospel, and she's told them that Oakland is dirty and dangerous, so they're determined to hate it here." I sighed. "It makes things difficult for us." Jessica had extended this helpful campaign to James as well, sending him informative emails about the crime rates and registered sex offenders in our area.

"That's a bunch of bullshit," said Brit. "Oakland's awesome. I moved from Daly City and there's way more to

276

do here. Plus, we live right by Lake Merritt, which is the best. Where does the ex live?"

"Vacaville."

"Where the hell is Vacaville? Oh wait, isn't that up near Dixon?"

"Yeah."

"Aw, that town's an armpit."

I laughed gratefully. "So, what's your story?" I asked. "You and Kelsey seem to get along pretty well. Has it always been like that?"

Brit tried stabbing her wire through the fronds of the feather to no avail. "Yeah, we're getting along pretty good these days. It was tough for a while in the beginning. Kels was so used to it being just her and her dad, and she was a little jealous at first. She was kind of a brat for a while." She tossed the wire onto the table. "Man, screw this. Hey, do you guys have any tape?"

"But eventually she mellowed out?" I asked hopefully.

"For the most part. She has the occasional tantrum, but mostly she's pretty chill. Sometimes she acts out after spending time with her mom. Luckily, Yvette's not around that much." Brit shook her head. "That lady's a bad influence."

"Tell me," I said. I was hungry to hear about somebody else's crazy ex.

"Well, she and Lee were never married, so they didn't have to get divorced; they just broke up." Brit wound tape around the stem of her feather. "She had Kelsey initially, but she also had a drug problem and she got involved with her dealer. The guy was abusive to her, but she refused to stay away from him. So Lee took Kelsey, and he's raised her since she was little. Even though Yvette technically has custody, she's never pursued it."

"Does she see Kelsey on weekends?" I asked.

"Sometimes. She's supposed to have Kels on Sundays, but she bails a lot. And if she doesn't cancel outright, she's usually hours late, which makes Kelsey nuts. That's when she acts out the worst, when her mom is late. She's afraid it means she's not coming—and a lot of the time she's right."

"So, she just no-shows?" I asked.

"Yeah. I think she's still on drugs. She bounces around a lot, never seems to have a permanent address. She's got another kid, a little boy, that she can't take care of. He's being raised by a friend or someone, downstate. His name's Oscar, and Kelsey adores him. I think she's got this secret dream that Yvette will get Oscar back and they'll live happily ever after. I don't know where that leaves Lee, but I doubt Yvette will ever get her shit together, so I'm not too worried." She held up an earring, knotty with tape. "How do I look?"

After that day, we four adults were fast friends. Lee and Brit had us over for dinner the next weekend, and we reciprocated the weekend after. Annabelle and Kelsey reconnected like magnets, and the kids played happily while we sat around chatting over beers.

It was wonderful; the effect of having a family of friends right down the street made everything different. And having friends who understood our situation, because they'd lived it themselves, was priceless.

27

DIRE STRAITS

"We probably shouldn't have done that," James said after Avery stomped up to her room in tears.

"Oh, come on, she's overreacting," I said.

He shrugged. "Yeah. But still."

I pursed my lips. "I thought it was funny."

James didn't say anything.

"Come on, it was a little funny."

Master at avoiding confrontation, he kissed my forehead and left the room.

The previous week we'd invited some friends from Mercy over for a holiday dinner. One of them had extreme dietary restrictions, and I'd been determined to make a meal that she could enjoy. So we had a feast that was largely vegan and gluten-free, complete with avocado chocolate mousse for dessert.

I couldn't have paid Avery to try the mousse. She wanted absolutely nothing to do with it and baked an apple pie so she could have something "normal" to eat. This was fine with me, but she was rather rude about it.

Ironically, when all our friends raved about the mousse, Avery thought she might be missing out. Raiding the leftovers, she ate the last cup of mousse—well, only half of it—and left a note on the container that said: "Avery's—Don't Touch!"

It was the "Don't Touch!" that rankled me. I frowned at the note and at the mousse I'd been looking forward to eating.

These children think they can go into my fridge, pull out food that they did not make, and label it as theirs? I thought grumpily. *Well, these children can think again.*

So James and I ate the rest of the mousse, then put the empty container back in the fridge with a note of our own: "Ha ha, good one! Dad & Marie."

Admittedly, it was all my idea and execution. I believed in prank retaliation. Nothing proved you had the upper hand like a little lighthearted, humorous revenge. Like when my brother and I were kids and he used to annoy me, I'd turn his posters upside-down or coat his toothbrush in garlic salt. Or hang his beloved stuffed animal from a noose on the ceiling until he cried. You know, funny stuff.

I felt a little guilty when James took the brunt of Avery's tantrum.

Then again, Avery was having tantrums left and right, and we were all taking turns taking the brunt.

Avery had a temper the likes of which I'd never seen. She could blow a fuse at the slightest provocation, and then it didn't matter what had angered her; she'd draw on every injustice she'd ever borne to fuel her rage. And she was *mean*. She didn't confine her arguments to the matter at hand. She'd conjure whatever hurtful thought she could seize on and hurl it at you. Her aim was maximum devastation.

She didn't care if she took out innocent bystanders. Annabelle was a common casualty; she put herself in Avery's path too often, trying to defend her. It became a pattern: Avery would spew venom at James and he would threaten her with a grounding, Annabelle would jump to Avery's defense with a heroic statement like, "Don't talk to my sister that way!" and Avery would go rogue and attack Annabelle. She was like the Incredible Hulk: both friends and enemies should beware when Avery lost her temper.

Then, once her anger was spent, she'd shrink back to her Bruce Banner form, mild-mannered and oblivious to the emotional wreckage she'd caused.

"You guys want to play a game?" she'd asked the last time, bounding down the stairs, bright and chipper twenty minutes after a screaming fit. No one responded; we were all still reeling from her outburst.

"Geez, why is everyone so grumpy?" Avery asked, then returned to her room in a huff.

"She's so like Jessica," James told me. "That's Jess' temper to a tee. And the other day she did something that freaked me out . . . Jess used to dig her fingernails into my hand when she was mad at me. I'd forgotten about it until Avery did it to me."

"What?"

"Yeah. Jess would take my hand like she wanted to hold it and then dig in her nails until they made marks in my skin. When Avery did it, it all came flooding back. I yanked my hand away and told her, 'Don't *ever* do that again.' It makes me wonder if Jess does that to the girls."

We fell silent, sharing a moment of worry.

The problem was, we knew Jess was hurting the girls, but in small, subtle ways that most people couldn't see. Neither one of us believed she was physically abusive, but her emotional control was disturbing.

On Friday nights, just hours after they'd left her, the girls would call their mom and stay on the phone for ages. James would knock on their bedroom door and tell them to wrap it up, it was time to sleep, but they'd just ignore him. "I miss you so much, too!" they'd say into the phone, over and over. "I love you so much, too!"

On the flip side, when he called them at Jessica's house during the school week, they would never pick up. James would leave messages on Avery's cell phone, on Jessica's cell, and on the house phone, but they all went unanswered. As soon as the girls left our house, they became completely unreachable and it frustrated James to no end. He brought it up in co-parent counseling, and under the guidance of Dr. Sweet, Jessica agreed to have the girls call him the following week.

But they called while he was at work and he couldn't answer. James tried calling back that evening, but again, no one would pick up. For the rest of the week, no one would pick up.

"I had the girls call you," Jessica said at their next counseling session. "It's not my fault if you didn't answer the phone."

They were still on Week One of the syllabus.

Shortly after Christmas, James got a phone call from Jessica's parents, Daniel and Shannon. The Christmas gifts that they'd mailed to Jessica's house had come back to them, unopened. It seemed Jessica had sent them back on purpose.

"Why would she do that?" I asked James.

"They're not sure," he said, "but they think it might be because Shannon didn't go visit Jess during the custody trial."

I thought back. "But Daniel visited." I remembered how surprised we'd been when the girls informed us that Grandpa was coming. It was unlike Jessica to reach out to her family.

"Yeah, but he was the only one. Maybe she felt snubbed."

I doubted that Jessica had been in touch with her family since. Her sister Jessalyn had sent James an email after the judge's ruling: "I'm so upset to hear this news. I just want you to know how very sorry I am. I thought for sure it would go the other way."

So, the girls' presents were sent to our house instead. James put them under the Christmas tree, which was still standing in the living room. (He'd wanted to pull it down the day after Christmas, but I vetoed that, hard. In my house, the tree stayed up through January.)

"What do I tell the kids?" he asked.

"Idunno," I said.

"She's crazy. Right? I mean, the kids will see that this is fucked up. Won't they? They must."

"Idunno," I said again.

When the kids arrived on Friday, James pointed out the packages. "You guys got some more Christmas presents," he said. "They're from your grandma and grandpa."

Excited, the girls knelt to rip open their presents.

"Why do you think they sent them to our house?" James asked casually.

"They always send them to our house," Avery said.

"True, they used to, but now you guys live with your mum. This year they sent them to her house, but the packages were returned. See?" He pointed out the red RETURN TO SENDER stamp on the box.

Avery appeared momentarily stumped. Then she rallied. "They must have gotten the address wrong."

James pointed to the box again. "Isn't that your mum's address?"

Avery frowned at the box. It was indeed the correct address.

James pushed ahead. "It looks like your mum sent them back. Do you know why she would do that?" He looked at his daughters, plaintively willing them to recognize their mother's bad behavior.

But Avery refused to meet his gaze. "The post office must have made a mistake." Her tone made it clear that she was done discussing it. Annabelle, who was pretending not to listen, had already ripped open her present.

"It's a commemorative coin," she said dismissively. "Another one." She left it under the tree.

"Why don't they see it, baby?" James asked me in an aggrieved whisper, behind the closed kitchen door. "Why don't they see the crazy?"

* * *

If Jessica was crazy, she was crazy like a fox. This became clear in early January when James received a letter from the Department of Child Support Services. Jessica had filed for maximum child support, and based on her zero income and James' salary, he would have to pay her fifteen hundred dollars a month.

"But that's like a second rent," I said, feeling sick to my stomach.

"And there's back pay," he said, flipping the letter over. "She filed retroactive to the court ruling, so I owe from August. Seventy-five hundred dollars is considered overdue, and January's payment is due immediately." He looked up at me, stricken. "I don't have nine thousand dollars."

"That's insane," I said. "It's impossible; we have to contest it. Can you call Rhonda?"

He shook his head. "Child support is governed by a separate court. Rhonda has nothing to do with it. They basically just punch our incomes into a calculator and come out with a number. To contest it I'll have to file a brand-new motion with DCSS and wait for a hearing . . . It could take months."

"And in the meantime, you'll have to pay it?" I was aghast.

"Yeah."

"But *how?*"

They garnished his wages, that's how. A full half of his paycheck went straight to Jessica before it even hit James' account. And that didn't even cover the requisite monthly payment. It fell two hundred and fifty dollars short, which accumulated, each month, on top of the seventy-five hundred dollars he owed in back support.

He called and called DCSS, but it was like calling into the void. Nobody picked up the phone. He was routed through the labyrinth of automated messages until the system hung up on him. He filed a motion to modify the order, but it was weeks before he knew if it had even been received. Acknowledgement finally came by letter: a hearing was set for April, three months away.

Meanwhile, the fees mounted. DCSS began sending warning letters that James' payments were overdue. These were printed on red paper in bold type; they used frightening language, outlining the potential consequences for fathers who didn't pay their child support: a revoked driver's license, a lien on property, halted citizenship proceedings, deportation, jail time.

And yet there was no one to appeal to, no one to help James do the right thing in a manageable way. Just one scary letter after the next.

"They act like I'm a deadbeat dad," James said in despair. "Even though I fought like hell to keep my kids and spent all my money doing it. Even though I raised them, for eight years, without asking for a dime of support from Jessica." I could tell he deeply regretted that gallantry now.

His financial situation was dire.

Rhonda's bills were also coming due. James owed her fourteen thousand dollars. He'd begun paying in small installments, racking up interest, but had to stop when his salary was slashed in two. Letters began arriving, polite but insistent, from Florence, Rhonda's deceptively gentle assistant.

Only Rachel didn't immediately call in her loan. James felt awful about the ten thousand dollars he owed her, especially as he realized it would be a long time before he could pay her back.

He was wracked with worry, maxing out his credit cards and bottoming out his bank account. There was a bad day when he went to make a withdrawal and discovered he was down to his last three dollars.

"Avery asked me for money to buy Penelope a birthday gift," he said, "and I couldn't give it to her."

He sold his mother's jewelry, the only memento he had of her. His savings were long gone, but he liquidated the few assets he had and applied for new lines of credit, digging himself into an ever-deeper hole.

Jessica was unmoved when he appealed to her in their co-parent counseling sessions. She was convinced he was hiding money.

"If you have no money, how are you affording that nice house?" she demanded.

"Oh, so now she thinks it's a nice house?" I retorted, when James relayed this to me. "Last week she said we live in a dangerous slum! Which is it?"

James sighed. "It's a nice house with rent that I can't afford."

I quelled a spasm of worry. I loved our house. It seemed a near miracle that we'd found it, and now that I'd seen what was out there, I knew there was nothing else comparable. Bay Area rent was so steep, we'd have to move out to the boondocks to find another house we could afford.

And after living part-time with the kids for four months, it was abundantly clear that somebody would go postal if we were crammed together in a small apartment.

My money was on Avery.

28

TANTRUMS

WHERE are all my spoons? WHAT are these children doing with them?

I learned to do routine sweeps of the kids' bedroom to recover missing articles from the kitchen. It was common for water glasses and the odd plate to migrate to their bedsides. But one day I found a stash of dirty dishes under their bathroom sink when I went looking for toilet paper. It seemed Avery had her own interpretation of "Take care of your dishes."

Avery was a slob. And I say that as one who is housework-challenged myself. Garbage made it near the trash can, but not inside. Discarded underwear lay puddled in the corner of her bathroom, untouched for days.

Annabelle was marginally neater, but that's because she crammed most of her belongings under her bed. When all the towels in the house slowly and mysteriously disappeared, that's where I found them. She would sleep with her wet hair wrapped in a towel, then leave it on her pillow, damp and fetid, while she returned to her mother's house for the week.

The next Friday she would take a fresh towel, push the dirty one to the floor, and repeat.

The dirty house made me despair. I was used to living with adults who took care of their own messes. Kids, it transpired, did not have that innate sense of responsibility. They made messes and just walked away. And they absolutely did not, would not, *could not* pick up an article that their sister had left behind.

"That's not my glass," they'd say.

"Could you please take it into the kitchen anyway?" I'd ask.

"But it's not mine."

The other thing that bewildered me was the kids' seeming inability to see the entire scope of their mess. We'd say, "Take care of your dishes," and they might remove their plate, leaving behind a dirty fork, glass, and napkin. If we told them to try again, they'd pick up one of the remaining articles and leave behind the other two. It baffled me. We practically had to push their noses in the mess, like you'd do to a dog who'd shit indoors.

Friday through Sunday I held my breath, carefully marking the number of times I asked them to pick up after themselves. A weekend could only sustain so many requests before a tantrum erupted. And I lived in fear of the tantrums.

The problem was, as the non-parent in the household, my word held less weight. I couldn't really discipline the kids because they weren't my children. They didn't have to obey me, and I wasn't sure if they'd figured that out yet. So I took care not to create a situation where we went head-to-head. The longer I held the illusion of control, the better.

During one of my bedroom checks, I found a wrinkled note on the floor beside Avery's bed. It was a hand-drawn cartoon of me lecturing the girls to "Clean your room, nag nag nag." The author was Penelope. *Ouch.*

I was tempted to leave the note on Avery's pillow, so she'd know I'd seen it. But instead I put it back where I'd found it. And I confiscated two dirty plates—and the jar of cinnamon—from under the bathroom sink. "This is why I nag them," I informed the picture of Penelope, still hanging over the toilet.

"It's like we're reverse-bonding," I said to Brit one Friday night. The kids were playing upstairs, and James and Lee were in our driveway, admiring the new rooftop storage shell on Lee's car. "The girls will barely talk to me these days. I feel uncomfortable in my own house." I pulled at the label on my beer. It was always so satisfying when I could get it off in one piece.

"Is it really that bad?" Brit asked me.

I thought. "It's harder with Avery," I realized. "We used to be so easy with each other, and now we can't even be in the same room alone. If I come into the living room and James or Annabelle isn't around, Avery will go right up to her bedroom and close the door. I don't know how to talk to her anymore."

Brit made a sympathetic face. I was jealous of her cozy relationship with Kelsey. I'd seen them hugging earlier and it triggered something sad in me. I missed the days when the girls would hug me. It seemed like a million years ago that they begged me to tuck them into bed.

"And she lied to me last week," I went on. "I knew she used my eyeliner because the pencil was dull one day and mysteriously sharpened the next. But when I asked her about it, she lied right to my face." I thought of Avery's eyes, wide and baleful—and lined with the evidence. "And when I told her that I *knew* she was lying, she just doubled-down, bold as hell."

It had been a tense standoff and I was shaken by it. I didn't really care that she'd used my makeup, but the lying upset me. Avery had glared at me with such ferocity, I felt as though she hated me. I buckled under the weight of that anger, muttered something about not lying to me again, and retreated.

Afterward I'd felt stupid. I was the adult, after all. But my authority was a fragile house of cards; I didn't want an eyeliner pencil to bring it tumbling down.

Annabelle and Kelsey bounded down the stairs just as James and Lee came through the front door.

"Hey Dad, can Kelsey spend the night?" Annabelle asked.

James glanced at Lee and Brit, who seemed all too agreeable. "Sure," Lee said. "Absolutely." He and Brit quickly drained their beers, thanked us for a lovely evening, and headed for the door.

"We'll take your kids next time," Lee promised, slipping his arm around Brittany as they left.

Annabelle and Kelsey dragged the air mattress out of the hall closet and up the stairs. A minute later Avery appeared in the living room, looking put out.

"Is Kelsey spending the night?" she asked.

"Yeah," James said.

Avery frowned. "Can I go see Penelope tomorrow?"

James got up from the couch and collected the empty beer bottles. "No, Ave, I told you. I'm not working tomorrow." He had hired a new employee and was finally done working Saturdays. Avery was the only one who hadn't been pleased by this news. It meant he wouldn't be driving past San Carlos on the weekends anymore.

"But can't I go to Penelope's anyway?" She followed him into the kitchen.

"No, not tomorrow." There was the clinking of glass as he pulled out the recycling bin to empty it. Avery followed him to the front door.

"How about next weekend?" she called outside after him. The bottles crashed into the bin.

"No, not next weekend either," he said, coming back inside. "It's a long drive, Avery, and I'm tired. I'm taking a break for a few weeks. But Penelope is welcome to come here." He went back into the kitchen, leaving Avery looking frustrated.

"Invite Penelope over here," I encouraged. "The four of you girls can hang out tomorrow."

But Penelope didn't want to come to our house. She'd made plans with Vivian and Stephanie. Avery chafed with disappointment at being left out.

The next weekend followed the same format, and the next. Annabelle seemed delighted by her friendship with Kelsey. It was sweet to see. Now *she* was the one with the best friend down the street, having playdates every weekend. For the first time in her life, Avery was the third wheel, tagging along behind her sister, their positions suddenly reversed.

She didn't care for it.

Her bad mood burned below the surface, like a pilot light waiting to burst into flame. We all stepped timidly around her.

When Kelsey invited Annabelle to join them for a ski weekend in Lake Tahoe, Annabelle joyfully accepted. She dug out her ski gear from under her bed and danced around the house in her goggles, hat, and gloves. She looked so cute that I reached for my phone, wanting to snap a photo.

"Don't take my picture," Annabelle commanded, throwing her hands over her face. She spun on her heel, presenting me with her back side and ruining the photo op.

I sighed and lowered my phone. This was fallout from the trial. After Jessica had seen the video I'd made, the kids were suddenly, vehemently against having their pictures taken. They didn't want to be captured in any act of fun. Their mother must have given them an earful.

Avery sat on the couch with her arms folded. Whether she was annoyed at being left out or simply in a sulk, her bad mood was palpable. She said darkly, "Don't tell Mom you're going to Tahoe with Kelsey. She might not like it."

The effect was instantaneous; Annabelle's excitement drained away. The smile fell off her face and her little brow furrowed with worry. She turned to James and said, "Actually, I don't want to go to Tahoe."

James was exasperated. He'd seen this scenario play out in various forms over the years: ballet class, field trips, birthday parties—anything that threatened to conflict with Jessica's time was downplayed, dismissed, or even ridiculed.

"Annabelle, don't be silly," he said. "You were excited about it just a minute ago. Besides, it doesn't fall on your mum's time. You'll drive up next Saturday, and Lee can drop you at your mum's on the way back Sunday."

Annabelle stiffened and I could tell she was worried by the idea of someone dropping her at her mother's house. That was not how exchanges were supposed to take place.

"I don't want to go," she said again. She pulled off her goggles and affected a look of disinterest. But James wasn't in the mood to play games.

"You're going," he said firmly. "We already told Lee and Brit yes, and Kelsey's all excited. It would be rude to cancel now."

Annabelle stuck out her chin defiantly. "But I don't *want* to go."

"She doesn't want to go, Dad," Avery echoed.

"Avery, stay out of it please," James said.

"But she doesn't *want* to go. You can't *make* her go." Avery's tone held a note of danger.

"Yeah, you can't make me go," Annabelle repeated.

"But why don't you want to go?" I tried to reason with her.

"Because I don't." Apparently that was reason enough.

"But you love hanging out with Kelsey, and you love to ski," I tried again.

"No, I don't."

"We don't love to ski, but Dad always makes us," Avery put in. *"He's* the one who loves it." *The poor, privileged kid.*

I could see James getting upset. The fact was, he did love to ski and this year he couldn't afford it. He had no patience for Annabelle turning up her nose at a free trip.

"You're going," he said with finality and turned to leave the room. Father had spoken.

Then Avery played her trump card. "I'm calling Mom," she said.

With the mention of Mom, all hell broke loose. James raised his voice as Avery reached for her phone, and suddenly both girls were crying, yelling at us:

"You can't make her go!"

"You can't force me!"

"Mom won't make her go!"

"Girls!" I said, shocked. "What is the problem? You act like we're sending you to boot camp, but this is something fun."

Avery wheeled on me. "It's none of your *business!* Why do you even *care?*" Her voice had reached shrieking level.

"Young lady, watch it," James said warningly.

"She's always trying to make us *do* stuff and we don't *want* to!" Avery cried. She flew up the stairs and into her room and slammed the door, forgetting that Annabelle was right behind her. As Annie wrenched the door open, we could hear Avery already on her phone. "Mom?" she said. Then the door slammed again.

I turned to James, flabbergasted. "What the hell just happened?"

He shook his head, looking grim, then heaved a weary sigh. "I'll bring it up in co-parent counseling tomorrow. Maybe if Jess endorses it, Annie will change her mind."

"This is stupid, James," I said.

"Welcome to my world."

Jessica, of course, was not interested in helping.

"She wouldn't listen," James reported, banging around the kitchen. "She just kept saying, 'Annabelle doesn't want to go.'" He yanked open the fridge. "I tried explaining to her that the kids are always turning things down because they're afraid she'll disapprove. Like when Annie was so excited about ballet—do you remember? It was all she could talk about, and then we found out that the Friday practice overlapped Jess' time by half an hour, and suddenly ballet was stupid and she didn't want to do it anymore." He pulled out the roast beef and mustard. "Do we have any bread?"

"We're out of bread. The kids used it for toast this morning."

"Damn it." His head went back into the fridge. "And all Jess could say was, 'You shouldn't have gotten her excited about an activity that fell during my time.'"

I rolled my eyes. "Okay, but the ski trip doesn't fall during her time. Why can't she endorse it?"

"Oh, because she doesn't know these people, and because Annabelle should be with me during my scheduled time. And if I'm not interested in spending time with my daughter, she'd be happy to keep the kids on the weekends."

"What?" I exploded.

James nodded at the kitchen door, indicating that I should close it. The girls were right upstairs. He started ripping leaves off a head of lettuce with vehemence.

"Yep. She thinks it's inappropriate for Annabelle to be spending so many overnights at Kelsey's. She said I'm 'dumping the kids' with other people and reminded me that she has first right of refusal."

"What's that?" I asked.

James shook his head. "It's irrelevant. It means that if I'm out of town or otherwise can't care for the kids for seventy-two hours or more, it's Jess' prerogative to take them before I arrange for a sitter or stick them with family or something. It doesn't apply here; she was just being a bitch."

"What did Dr. Sweet say to that?"

James gave a short laugh. "Dr. Sweet is pretty useless. She tries to get us to stay on topic, but Jessica only discusses things that she wants to discuss. Like how I'm behind with child support payments." His voice turned bitter as he thought about the mountain of debt Jessica had caused him.

"I think I'm going to quit," he said.

"What?" I was agitated. "Baby, you can't quit! I never got a chance to come to a session. Wasn't the point of this to get all four adults involved?"

I found it so frustrating to be on the periphery of parenthood, never having an opportunity to join the discussions. I had so much to say to Jessica, I was bursting with it. I couldn't wait to get my chance in a counseling session. James would just have to stick it out.

But he was shaking his head. "We're getting nowhere. We've had nine sessions and we're still on Week One. It's only supposed to be a ten-week program."

"Could you maybe skip ahead to the point where I come in?" I tried.

"No, there's no skipping ahead. We're just going in circles, and I can't afford to keep paying for it. I'm wasting money and time that I should be spending with my kids."

I thought. "Look, I know you're frustrated, but don't you think it would be helpful if the four of us could get in the same room and have a real discussion? The girls are struggling. And so much of that is because of this ugly dynamic between our households." I don't know why, but I still had this naïve idea that if we met face to face, I could appeal to Jess on an emotional level, woman to woman. "I'm sure Jessica doesn't want her kids to be unhappy."

James sighed. "Sweetie, Jessica won't admit that the kids are struggling. Or if they are, it's all my fault. And the solution is for them to stay with her full time, since they're perfectly happy at her house."

I stared at him. "But that's garbage. It's not true."

"I know it's not true, but that's her opinion. And her opinion is always right." He took a bite of his roast beef roll-up, which promptly fell apart in his hand. "Damn it," he said, tossing it back on his plate in disgust.

"Please don't quit," I pleaded.

James leaned back against the counter, took off his glasses and rubbed the bridge of his nose. "I hate seeing her every week," he said plaintively. "It's . . . *bad* for me. She makes me so stressed, I get pains in my stomach. She twists my words, makes me out to be a bad father . . . I just don't want to do it anymore." He looked at me, forlorn but resolute. "I think I'm done."

I seized on another idea. "What about family therapy? Could we start that instead?" The judge had ruled that we could take the kids to family therapy—following at least one piece of the evaluator's advice.

James slumped. "Marie, I just can't afford it right now. My bank account is in the double digits. My credit cards are mostly maxed. I just worked out a new payment plan with Rhonda that I'm not even sure I can honor . . . I couldn't afford to keep up co-parenting counseling, even if I wanted to."

I felt a wave of guilt. *Was I supposed to help pay for these things?* I wasn't exactly flush with cash myself.

Then James said, "This is exactly why I didn't want to go through with the trial. Now I'm in a hole so deep, I don't know how I'll ever get out."

The wave intensified and suddenly I was flooded with guilt. I flashed back to that night in the wine bar when I'd given James hell for voicing this very concern. I'd pushed him to go through with the trial. Was it my fault that he was now virtually bankrupt, struggling to keep things together? Did he, on some level, blame me?

I searched his face but I didn't see the answer, just a deep weariness. I felt like crying. Depression was plucking at my sleeve again. I fought the urge to crawl into bed, even though it was the middle of the day.

Then James straightened up, popped the last of the roast beef in his mouth, and put his plate in the sink. "I'm going to the grocery store," he said. "We need bread, and I think we could use some ice cream, too." He smiled and kissed me on the forehead. "I'll be back in a bit."

Watching him go, I thought again how much I admired him. James kept moving forward no matter what. I could stand to be more like that.

But I needed a little help.

29

THANK YOU FOR YOUR EMAIL

"You understand that if I start seeing you individually, I can't see you and James as a couple anymore." Ilana regarded me carefully. "You're sure that's what you want?"

"Yes," I said. James had zero interest in coming back. He wanted nothing to do with therapy for the time being.

"You have fun," he'd said.

Fun. Like we were going out for drinks or something.

We hadn't seen Ilana since before the trial, and as I caught her up, I realized how desperately I needed to talk to somebody. Again, I felt such relief having someone to confide in; I wondered why I hadn't gone back sooner. Ilana's office became my place of refuge. Our Tuesday appointment quickly became the axis of my week.

Dr. Sweet had written a letter releasing James and Jessica from the co-parenting program. It basically said: "You guys are untreatable. Good luck." A copy had been filed with the court and sent to each lawyer. Her parting advice was that they parallel parent.

I looked it up and discovered that parallel parenting was for people who couldn't get along well enough to co-parent. *Co-parenting,* as the name implies, is based around the idea that both parties can cooperate on matters involving their children. *Parallel parenting,* by contrast, advises that high-conflict parents disengage from each other and communicate only when necessary, preferably in writing. Which is essentially how James and Jessica had been interacting all along.

It occurred to me that James might have saved a thousand dollars on counseling if we'd just had a rundown of these definitions first.

Dr. Sweet recommended an online program called Our Family Planner to facilitate their communication. It tracked their messages back and forth and allowed them to post schedules, budgets, and bills. It even had a "tone meter", a function that monitored the tone of each message to ensure civility. I was curious about how that worked, but the tone meter cost extra, so we never found out.

It soon became clear that the Planner would be as effective as co-parent counseling had been. Jessica replied to James' every message with the same short phrase: "Thank you for your email." And nothing more.

When he asked about Avery's braces: "Thank you for your email."

When he requested copies of the kids' report cards: "Thank you for your email."

When he asked that the girls call him during the week: "Thank you for your email."

The Planner allowed for each of us to have an account, but Jessica kept deleting mine. And Max never created one. We speculated that he probably wasn't allowed to.

"Why do you want so much to be part of these conversations?" Ilana asked me.

"Because . . . " I struggled to find the words. "Because I'm in these kids' lives, too. And I'm tired of Jess pretending like I don't exist."

"You want to be acknowledged," Ilana offered.

"Yes! I want to be acknowledged."

"Do you respect Jessica's opinion?" she asked me.

"No." I didn't.

"So, why is her acknowledgement important to you?"

Hmm. Why indeed? I thought about it. "Well, because the kids respect her opinion, and when she ignores me, it teaches them that they can do the same."

"Mm-hmm. I can understand that." Ilana's voice was soothing. I sank back into the pillows of her couch.

"Let's try something," she said. "I want you to put two pillows down on the floor." I did. "Now come sit on one pillow."

I felt a little awkward crouching on the floor while Ilana remained in her armchair, but I sat cross-legged on one pillow, facing the other.

"Now, that pillow is Jessica." Ilana pointed at the free pillow. "What would you like to say to her?"

It struck me that James would be pleased that he'd escaped this uncomfortable exercise. I regarded the pillow warily.

"You're face to face and you have her full attention," Ilana went on. "She can't interrupt you. What would you say?"

I felt like I could have articulated this perfectly well from the couch, but I tried to get into it for Ilana's sake. I looked at the pillow.

"I want to swap pillows," I said, surprising myself.

"Why?"

"Because that one's too pretty. I want Jess to be the ugly brown pillow." I flushed a bit as I said this, but Ilana just smiled and nodded. I switched places.

"I hate you," I said to the squashed brown pillow. I'd surprised myself again; I didn't realize that was going to come out of my mouth.

"I don't think I've ever truly hated anyone before," I went on, "but I hate you. And I hate that I hate you. You've changed me." My voice was quiet, calm. "All I've ever tried to do is be good to your kids. And yet you've convinced them that what I say doesn't matter, that *I* don't matter. I don't forgive you for that.

"I don't forgive you for walking out on them when they were small. You had a chance to share custody and you didn't even bother. And now you've re-written history and brainwashed them to believe it was out of your control, but *you left them.* I hate you for that." I shifted on my pillow.

"But most of all I hate you for taking them now. We could have found a way to share custody, to make things easier for the kids, but that doesn't interest you. I think the child support is what interests you." I could feel heat gathering in my face. "I hate you for taking all of James' money, for making him worry so much that he doesn't sleep. I hate you for making his chest hurt. And I hate you for turning his children away from him."

I finished up by saying something I'd said in this office once before. "They're good girls . . . and you don't deserve them."

I glanced at Ilana. "Anything else?" she asked.

"And your husband's an asshole," I said to the pillow.

Ilana nodded sagely. She didn't tell me that he was *acting* like an asshole, and for that, I was glad.

* * *

I bumped into Ken in the office kitchen while I was making tea. There were leftover pastries from a recent meeting and Ken zeroed in on them.

"My God, what's that? Someone left the cinnamon heart? That's the best part of the cinnamon bun!" He popped it into his mouth.

"I think that's from yesterday," I observed.

He chewed. "Yeah, it's a little stale. But I'm starving." He rummaged through the cabinets, hunting for a snack.

"I feel like I haven't seen you in ages," I said. "How was your trip?" I knew he'd just returned from a week in Hawaii with Pia.

"I got—*gulp!*—engaged. And I saw the new Marvel movie, too!" Ken's hand hit something in the overhead cabinet and a hailstorm of pistachios went cascading to the floor. "Oh no! My nuts!"

"You did *what?*"

"I saw the new Marvel movie!"

"You got *engaged?* Ken, congratulations!" I threw my arms around him.

He grinned. "Thanks. Is that a sympathy hug?"

I laughed. "No, I'm happy for you. I didn't know you were sneaking off on vacation to get engaged!"

"Yeah, me neither," he said. "I mean, I did—I'd planned it. But boy, it came up really fast."

I missed Ken and hearing about his daily life. I'd had no idea he was planning to propose to Pia. I crouched beside him on the floor to help scoop up the mess. "So, when did you do it? At the beginning of your vacation or the end?"

Ken considered a handful of dusty pistachios before tipping them into the trash. "Right in the middle, and it was perfect. We didn't even get in a fight until the last day."

"Oh?"

"Yeah. She said, 'Let's have a baby as soon as we get married.' And I said, 'Okay, then let's not get married for a year.' And she got pretty mad about that." He stood up and brushed his hands on his pants. "But I said, 'You know, we live with your roommate . . . I'd like to live with just you before we have a baby.'"

"You'd have a built-in babysitter," I pointed out.

Ken frowned. "Oh no, I'd never trust her roommate with a baby. She nearly killed my fish. If she can't keep Mr. Sparkles alive, I'd never let her watch Junior."

I followed him down the hall to the Frontline office, eager for details. "So, are you excited?" I asked, and waited—a beat too long—for his response.

Ken twisted his moustache, thoughtful. "Yeah, I'm excited. Totally. It's just that . . . well, I've always been one hundred percent true to every girl I've ever been with. But I like the ladies. And there are a few gals that I've always wanted to smooch that now I'll never get to smooch." He stared into space, and for some reason I imagined a line of forties pinup girls waving goodbye as they sauntered away. "But, you know, it was time. And you gotta get through your first wedding before you can get to your third."

"I guess that's true," I said.

"I'll be like my friend Walrus," Ken said. "He's been married four times. His mom's been married nine times. He loves weddings. Loves proposing, too. He keeps engagement rings in the ashtray of his truck."

30

GROWING PAINS

When my routine sweeps of the kids' quarters started turning up sanitary napkins, I deduced that Avery had started her period. It didn't take any sleuthing—the evidence was all over the floor. Pad wrappers littered the bathroom like ticker tape at a hometown parade. I put the wrappers in the garbage, hoping to illustrate that that's where they go.

But like parade-goers everywhere, Avery didn't seem to care about the mess she left behind. And I was startled one day to find a used pad uncurling near the garbage can. It had been half-heartedly folded up and tossed in the direction of the trash.

"There," I pointed it out to James.

"Oh," he said.

We looked at each other. Neither of us knew what to do. The girls had returned to their mother's house before I'd found this little gift.

"I guess . . . I've gotta pick that up," James said. He looked at me. "Unless you want to do it?"

I put my palms up, the universal symbol for *I'm not touching that.* "No, please, you go right ahead," I said.

"The kid's kind of a slob, isn't she?" James remarked.

I raised my eyebrows. "Ya think?"

A few weeks later I found another used pad languishing even further from the trash can. This one was nearly in the middle of the room.

"Okay, James, you've got to say something to her," I told him behind our closed bedroom door. "This is gross. She needs to know how to dispose of these things properly."

James wrinkled his nose a bit. "Isn't this woman-territory? Maybe you'd like to field this one? I mean, you're her . . . " he trailed off.

"I'm her what?" He must have heard the challenge in my voice, because he altered course.

"You're the lady of the house," he said delicately.

"I'm not her mother," I said. "And I don't think she wants to hear it from me."

But why wasn't she hearing it from her actual mother? I wondered. Presumably Avery was leaving similar messes at Jessica's house. Or had Jess talked to her and the message hadn't gotten through?

"I don't think her mother talks to her about this stuff," James said.

"Seriously?" I asked.

"I really don't. She always thought that periods were dirty."

"Well, they are when you leave the evidence lying around," I said.

I went to the store to buy Avery some feminine products. My idea was to leave them under her bathroom sink, an implicit nod to her blooming womanhood and a

308

silent reminder that I was there to talk if she had any questions. I knew James had only been kidding about having me field the topic, and it didn't seem appropriate for me to step in. As much as I disliked Jessica, there were some areas that I really did believe were her domain. She retained the right to talk to her daughters about their changing bodies.

Also, I had no idea how to handle that conversation.

But the Feminine Care aisle at Target loomed long and daunting. I thought I'd breeze in and pick up some overnight pads and junior tampons. Except . . . junior tampons didn't seem to be a thing.

I was stumped. I could've sworn that I'd seen junior tampons before, but now I couldn't find them. I walked up and down the mile-long aisle six times, scanning the boxes, overwhelmed by choices. Nothing seemed right. Super was out of the question, Regular felt too intense, and Multi-Pack offered Lites, but only a few of them. I'd had my period for twenty-five years—why couldn't I figure this out?

I suddenly remembered a few months ago, when I'd asked James to pick me up some tampons from the store. He'd texted me a photo of this very aisle with the one-word caption: "Help."

In the end, I bought only pads and skipped the tampons entirely. *Let Jessica deal with it.*

* * *

We hadn't had a knitting night in months, and I was trying to get the girls together at my house. I'd even planned to make lasagna—a huge culinary feat for me. Such was my commitment to the cause.

The night before our gathering I texted my friends to confirm our plans: "Are we still on for tomorrow?"

Alex wrote back right away: "Yes! I'll bring salad."

Hailey chimed in: "I'll be there, too. I'll bring dessert."

It was a few hours before Katia replied: "Can't make it tomorrow. Sorry. Plans got shuffled."

I was disappointed. I was hoping the whole group could gather; it had been ages since we'd all been together. I wasn't even sure when I'd last seen Katia, but she hadn't been to my new house yet. We were both so busy, and she'd passed on the last few invitations I'd extended, always citing previous plans.

I tapped back a lighthearted text: "Dude! This is like the 4th invitation to my house that you've declined. I'm starting to take it personally!"

Her response came right away:

> *This time it is just scheduling. Though when you told me that I needed to decide if I wanted to work at Roaming Ex or have a baby, I not only took it personally, but I was shocked at the outright discrimination that "we babes of a certain age" have to deal with.*

I stared at my phone in disbelief. Had Katia been angry with me since *last summer?* Why hadn't she said anything? Surely, I'd seen her since then. But as I ran through the months in my head, I realized that I hadn't seen Katia since that awkward night at her house. I'd been so overwhelmed with the trial and the move that I'd completely forgotten our quarrel. I couldn't believe she'd been nursing this grievance for so long.

My phone buzzed twice in quick succession, and I realized that Katia had sent her message to all three of us. Now Hailey and Alex each texted me privately: Alex with a "Huh?" and Hailey with a wide-eyed emoji.

I didn't reply to Katia. I didn't know what to say.

* * *

The child support hearing was scheduled for early April. James had been waiting impatiently to plead his case before DCSS. The fifteen-hundred-dollar monthly payments were devastating him, and he hoped that the hearing would result in a less severe arrangement.

Three days before the appointment, James got a panicked call from his sister Rachel.

"Sam's been in an accident," he relayed to me. "It's bad."

Seven-year-old Sam had been playing with the little girl from down the street, riding shotgun in her new toy Jeep. It was one of those fun-sized cars that the kids could actually drive, and it went much faster than a toy should. They drove right into the back of a parked car, and seated as they were, only three feet off the ground, they collided with the bumper face-first. Their parents were right there, but it happened so fast, no one could have prevented it.

"Sam's eye is smashed in," James said. My hand flew to my face. "He needs emergency surgery. And the little girl's nose was . . . " he paused, shuddering. "It was pushed into her face."

"Oh my God!" I dropped onto our bed, both hands over my eyes. "Oh God, oh God."

"I need to fly to Florida," James said.

"Of course!"

We both got online and started searching for flights. There was nothing available until the following day.

"I won't get there until late Sunday night," James fretted. "And I've got the child support hearing on Tuesday."

"Can't you move it?" I asked.

"I can try, but Jessica's got to agree."

His phone rang and it was Rachel again. Sam would be going into surgery early the next morning. The bones around his eye were completely smashed in. They would have to make an incision along his hairline and peel back his face to reconstruct his eye socket. I thought I might vomit with this news. James turned a sickly pale color. As soon as he'd hung up with Rachel, he dialed Jessica. He took the phone into the next room and shut the door. I continued searching for flights.

Five minutes later James emerged, now flushed an angry red. "She won't do it," he said. "She won't move the hearing. She says it's out of her hands." Tears slid down his face and he palmed them away. "She said that once the date is on the docket, it can't be moved, but that's bullshit. And she won't call DCSS."

I took his hand. "So, what happens if you don't show up?" I asked, fearing I already knew the answer.

"If I don't show up, DCSS takes her word for whatever I owe her. And I *can't,* I can't keep paying fifteen hundred dollars a month, Marie, I *can't.*" He was crying in earnest now. "What do I do? I don't know what to do."

I pulled him into a tight hug. "It's okay," I said. "It'll be okay. Let's not make any decisions right now. Let's wait until morning and see what the news is."

"I need to be with my sister."

"I know. But by the time you get there Sam's surgery will be over anyway, so let's wait and see what tomorrow brings." I kissed his head.

"I hate her," he sobbed into my shoulder.

"I know."

Sam's surgery was a success, thank God. Since Florida was three hours ahead of us, we heard the prognosis almost upon waking. He had a bunch of metal plates in his head, but he would heal without issue and almost without scarring.

As a doctor, Rachel had a tough constitution. Now that she knew Sam would be all right, she described the surgery to us with fascination. James and I, much more squeamish, held the phone at arm's length for most of the details.

He explained to Rachel about the upcoming hearing and how he wasn't sure what to do.

"Don't come," she told him. "Sam's going to be fine. You go to court and get everything straightened out."

James' eyes filled with tears again. "Love you, Rach."

"Love you, too," she said through the phone.

31

THE MENSTRUAL ARTS

"Surprise!"

The door to our bedroom flew open. "Happy birth—oh!"

Avery and Annabelle froze in the doorway, clutching a breakfast tray. Shock was etched on both of their faces.

Thank God I'm wearing clothes, thank God I'm wearing clothes, ran through my mind like a mantra.

James, who was also wearing clothes—*thank God*—raised up on his elbow and smiled at his daughters. "You made me breakfast in bed?"

The girls didn't answer. Their eyes were big and round and locked on me. Annabelle's mouth hung open.

"You can come in," James said.

But instead they backed out the door and disappeared, taking the breakfast tray with them.

"So much for breakfast in bed." James laughed. "Did you see their faces?"

"Why were they so surprised?" I wondered. "I live here. Where do they think I go at night?"

"Who knows? But good thing they didn't burst in here fifteen minutes ago. They'd be scarred for life." We'd slept naked and had woken early to fool around, and some instinct told me to get dressed afterward. *Thank God.*

James rolled out of bed and pulled on his bathrobe. "I guess I'd better go down and eat those eggs."

I knelt on the mattress and slipped my hands inside his robe before he could close it. "What do you want to do after breakfast? Think we could tell the girls we're taking a nap?"

He leaned down and kissed my neck. "Maybe. Unless they were planning to serve me lunch in bed."

"Just tell them to leave it outside the door," I murmured. "And to make enough for me."

He laughed and kissed me again, then broke away. "Actually, I was going to sort through some paperwork today. I need to find my tax forms before the next child support hearing."

I frowned and tugged at his bathrobe. "No baby, not today. It's your birthday! Forget that stuff. I'll tell you what." I pulled him close again and wrapped my arms around his waist. "You go eat your breakfast, and then we'll go into the city for the day. I've got a few things up my sleeve."

"Nothing elaborate?" he asked with a slight frown. He hated being the center of attention.

"I promise we'll keep it low-key." I swatted his butt. "Now go eat your eggs before they get cold."

* * *

April's child support hearing had resulted in a continuance—which is court jargon for *Come back when you've got your shit together.* Jessica was supposed to provide written updates on her medical condition, workers' compensation case, and disability application. Essentially, the court wanted proof that she remained unable to work.

Instead, she supplied a year-old doctor's note recommending one month's work leave and an invoice from an outpatient rehab center, which closer inspection revealed to be a receipt for a massage.

Rather than calling bullshit on the spot, the court set a second hearing date for the following month. Jessica was to return with the documents requested. James was to supply his Schedule C's from the previous two tax years. And, of course, he was to continue paying the fifteen-hundred-dollar monthly support fee in the meantime.

My respect for our legal system continued to plummet.

James was upset about the hearing's outcome, but more so that he hadn't flown to Florida to be with his sister. He was furious with Jessica, and though he tried to keep it from the kids, they knew what was going on. They were appropriately subdued in the week following Sam's surgery.

But that wore off in the face of a new grievance: church.

Easter Sunday offered an extra service at seven o'clock in the morning. I'd been going to it for years, but James had never forced the kids to go that early.

"It used to be six o'clock!" I pointed out. "You kids are lucky." We weren't going to make them go to all three celebrations, but gave them a choice: early services and then brunch, or sleep in and attend the later services.

The kids chose a third option: full-out mutiny.

"We hate it at Mercy," Avery said.

"It's not even a real church," Annabelle informed us.

"We're not going," they both insisted.

James and I had a whispered conference in our bedroom.

"What do we do?" I asked.

"I think we have to cancel Easter," he said.

Whoa. "Have you ever cancelled a holiday before?" This seemed like the big guns.

"No." He looked doubtful. "Maybe we should check with them one more time."

"Okay girls," he announced to them. "If you don't go to Easter service, you don't get Easter baskets. That's the deal."

"That's not fair," Annabelle protested.

He shrugged. "That's Easter. It all goes together. Either we celebrate it or we skip it. It's up to you."

Avery glared at him. "Skip it," she said.

Annabelle glanced at her sister in surprise. Then she hardened her own face. "Skip it," she echoed.

James and I retreated to our room, where the kids' Easter baskets were hiding under our bed.

"I can't believe they opted to skip it," he said. "I was sure they were going to choose the Easter baskets."

"Too bad for them," I said, my mouth full of chocolate.

* * *

Hailey organized our next knitting gathering. We met at Lake Merritt on a Saturday afternoon. I hadn't talked with Katia since her last heated text, and I was apprehensive as I walked to our meeting spot.

317

Hailey and Alex were already there, spread out on blankets with plenty of snacks. I laid out my offering of Thin Mints and Samoas.

"Girl Scouts attacked me and forced me to buy cookies," I explained.

"Oh good," said Alex, reaching for the box of Samoas. "Hey, these are half gone."

"Um, they forced me to eat them, too." I took a Thin Mint from the box automatically, peering around for signs of Katia.

The three of us had dissected her message at our last meeting over a pan of undercooked lasagna. None of us had realized that Katia bore a grudge against me.

"I don't know what to say to her," I'd told the girls. Of course, I would have apologized ages ago had I known she was upset, but her anger all these months later seemed unfounded. I'd just assumed she'd heeded my request not to pursue the job interview, and I'd been so distracted that I'd never followed up. They'd eventually hired a woman named Christy to replace me on Frontline, and Ken spent his days chatting with her now.

Part of me felt like a bad friend for not checking in with Katia. But another part felt miffed that she'd never checked in with *me*. I hadn't heard from her after the trial. She knew we'd lost custody, but she hadn't said a word.

Maybe it was telling that I hadn't noticed.

Of course, Katia and I had never really been that close. It seemed like we were always getting our wires crossed. I remembered an incident from shortly after we'd met. Back then we'd lived down the street from one another, and Katia had offered me a ride home from knitting. I was surprised when, instead of dropping me off at my house, she pulled the car into her own driveway, bid me good night, and went inside.

As I jogged the three blocks home, I wondered why I hadn't spoken up. It was nighttime—why hadn't I asked her to drive me to my door? But there was something about Katia's manner that stopped me. I never knew how to talk to her.

Now Katia approached from the Grand Avenue path and sat down on the blanket next to Hailey. "Hi guys," she said, studiously avoiding my gaze. "I brought popcorn." She presented it to Hailey and Alex.

The greeting died in my throat. It seemed like Katia was ignoring me. She wasn't outwardly rude, but her eyes never once touched on my face, and she spoke only to Hailey and Alex.

I knew I should say something to cut through the awkward atmosphere, but I couldn't do it. I literally could not make myself speak. And then the moment of opportunity passed, and Hailey leapt in to cover the silence. She told us about the online grad school program she'd begun with the goal of a new career in Library Sciences. We all made exclamations of support, but I realized we were carrying on two separate conversations: the one between the girls and Katia, and the one between the girls and me. Katia and I did not speak to each other.

It was a desperate, twisty tension that I was feeling, but I didn't know how to bridge the gap between us. I looked at Katia whenever she spoke, but she never once looked back at me. It was like I wasn't there.

Alex took over the burden of leading the conversation. "Well, I have news," she said. "I'm taking a seven-month sabbatical from work, and I'm going to travel around South America."

"You're kidding!" we all said and pressed her for details. But my heart sank. With Alex off traveling and Hailey in grad school and Katia . . . well . . . Was this the end of our knitting group? I felt a sharp pang at the thought of losing my friends.

Then again, it seemed like I'd already lost one. Katia made an early departure, waving pleasant goodbyes to Alex and Hailey, and walking back down the path to her car.

I did not go after her.

* * *

James bought Avery her first box of tampons upon request. I was a little concerned that she might not know how to use them, given her general lack of training on the subject, so I pressed James to inform Jessica of this new development. He sent her a brief note on the Family Planner. She responded: "Thank you for your email."

It became clear that Jessica was not giving her daughter any instruction in the Menstrual Arts on a sunny Saturday in May, when the weather was warm enough to take the kids to the beach. With Kelsey along, we drove to Alameda and parked ourselves on a warm stretch of sand. The kids dropped their stuff on the blankets and made a beeline for the water.

"You want some sunblock for your . . . " I tapped the top of my head and offered the bottle to James.

"For my what?" he said challengingly. I just looked at him and extended the bottle.

James seemed to deflate. "I'm losing my hair, aren't I?"

Again, I said nothing. With a sigh he took the bottle and lathered up the top of his head. His hair lay plastered to his scalp.

"Maybe you should get a hat," I suggested.

James flung himself onto the blanket and covered his face with his arm. "She took all my money and now she's taking my hair," he complained.

I stretched out next to him and gave him a kiss. "Relax," I said. "You are as handsome as ever."

With my head on my arms, I watched the kids play in the surf. Kelsey wore a bikini, her eleven-year-old belly poking out between the modest two-piece. I admired her confidence—it had been decades since I'd felt that comfortable in my own body. And I'd never worn a bikini in my life.

Annabelle was skinny as a reed in her own two-piece, her limbs long and gangly. But Avery was starting to develop a shape. I watched her running through the water, slender and strong like a young gazelle, and I felt . . . old. My body wasn't like that anymore. I felt my first brush of envy for her youth.

After an hour a breeze picked up and it started getting cold. James called the girls in from the water, and I began gathering our things. As I picked up Avery's baseball cap, something fell out and rolled onto the sand. I bent over to get it but recoiled—it was another used sanitary napkin.

"Avery, come here," I called. I stood in front of the pad, so the other kids wouldn't see it. I didn't want to embarrass her.

"What?" She stood in front of me, dripping.

"Why was there a used pad in your *hat?*" I said in a low voice. Flustered, she picked it up. "Ave, you've got to wrap these up and throw them—"

"I've got it," she said to me angrily, and ran to the garbage can.

"Avery," I tried again when she came back.

"Just leave me alone, Marie, all right? You're not my mother."

Bingo! I wanted to say. *So why is this my job?*

"Come with me," I said to Avery when we got home. I took her by the hand and led her to the bathroom.

"This is a pad," I said, holding one up.

She glared at me. "I know what a pad is."

"But you don't seem to know how to dispose of one, so let's go over that." She started to retort but I held up my hand. "Just let me get through this, all right? I'm not enjoying it either."

I ripped open the pad and gave her the thirty-second spiel. "You need to wrap up your used pads tightly in toilet paper like this." I demonstrated. "And then it goes in the garbage. Not *near* the garbage, not on the floor—"

"I know where they go, all right?" Avery looked furious—and embarrassed.

"No Ave, you do not. Otherwise I wouldn't be finding these everywhere. And if you think this is embarrassing, wait until your dog Snowflake discovers one and tries to eat it." She flinched. "It happens," I said.

Avery fell silent. A deep blush had spread across her cheeks.

"Isn't your mom talking to you about this stuff?" I asked. She didn't answer.

Goddammit Jessica.

"Well, now you know," I said. "So, don't let me find any more pads lying around. Got it?"

She looked at the floor.

"Got it?" I asked again.

"Got it." She made to leave the room.

"Hold up," I said. "This is a tampon."

Avery looked as though she wanted to shove the tampon up my nose, but at least she stayed and listened.

32

DINNER DISASTER

Mandy stopped by my desk at work. "There are donuts and cookies in the kitchen," she informed me. "That hotel rep brought them in."

"Damn it," I said. "I don't have the willpower to refrain from that stuff! I'm getting round." My self-esteem was also taking a hit, living as I did now with two skinny adolescent girls.

Mandy replied, "Tell me about it. You know how pregnant ladies don't look pregnant until they 'pop'? Well, I felt my thighs pop the other day. Even my Spandex bike shorts feel tight." She gestured with her cookie. "And yet, I've already had two of these."

I felt compelled to make my own admission. "You think that's bad? Yesterday out of the shower, I felt something brush my upper thigh. I kept turning around to look, you know, like a dog searches for his tail?" I dropped my voice to a whisper. "It was my ass."

Mandy snickered, but then looked at me soberly. "You know what it might be time for?"

"Don't say it."

But she said it: "Mike T."

When Mandy and I were roommates we'd jointly purchased a series of exercise videos. I'd seen them advertised on a late-night infomercial. The program was called *Intensity*, and it was hosted by the muscle-bound, indomitable Mike T. For two months we'd sweated profusely in our little living room, running and jumping until our neighbor threatened to call the landlord about the noise. It was hellacious but effective.

So, a few days later, Mandy and I were self-consciously huffing and puffing in the conference room after working hours.

"How's it—going with—the kids?" she asked me jaggedly between jumping jacks.

I shook my head. "Can't talk. You talk. Javier? All good?" We dropped to the floor for push-ups.

"He works a lot." *Down, up.* "Always tired." *Down, up.* "Not so into—" *Down, up.* "—exercise, so—" *Down, up.* "I'm gaining weight."

"Sucks," I commented as we transitioned into basketball drills. I sprang up from the ground, making an imaginary layup. "But otherwise good?"

"Yeah," she labored. "Real good guy." She gave an almighty grunt as she jumped in the air.

"Suicide drills!" Mike T. announced from the conference room television. Mandy started leaping from side to side, touching the floor on each end. I made one grand leap and collapsed in a pile, rolling away from Mandy's running feet.

"Don't give up," counseled Mike T. "You've got to push through it."

"Fuck you, Mike T.," I said wearily from my place on the floor.

"You can do it," Mike T. said, and then I felt bad.

"Hey, do you guys want to go out tonight?" Mandy asked me once the video was over, and we lay in sweaty heaps on our yoga mats.

I shook my head, and even that small movement felt like an effort. "Can't," I said. "The kids will be home and James is making dinner. He likes to spend Friday nights together." In fact, I was procrastinating heading home because the kids were often bumpy on reentry. It said something about the atmosphere at our house that I was choosing to work out rather than go home.

There was something about the dinner table that started arguments.

First, it killed me to spend an hour making dinner only to have the kids race through it in ten minutes and then leave the table. Although in fairness, it was usually James making the dinner; I still found it frustrating.

Second, these dinners were either eaten in silence or filled with forced conversation by the adults. The girls answered questions with as few words as possible and said, "May I be excused?" every thirty seconds until the last person (usually me) was done eating. Then they fled the clean-up.

Despite our tight finances, I was all for ordering in and eating in front of the TV—anything to avoid the two-hour ordeal that was dinner. But James was determined to cook a nice meal, so every week followed the same pattern, featuring a reluctant gathering around the dining room table. I bid goodbye to Mandy and made my way home to the cranky children.

As we set the table that evening, I asked, "Hey, remember how we saw all those kids running around the lake last weekend?" James nodded but the kids just shrugged—they hadn't set foot outside the house.

I'd been fighting a losing battle to get the kids off the couch. It grated my nerves to find them parked in front of the TV on a beautiful day. Annabelle often played with Kelsey if she was around, but Avery hadn't seen Penelope in months. Her bad mood permeated our household, and I was desperate to find her something to do, a reason to look forward to her weekends.

"It turns out, they're a running club. They meet on Saturdays and train for local races. Could be fun, huh?" My voice took on a hopeful note as we all took our seats and started eating.

"No," Avery said flatly.

"But you like to run," James said. "You were the fastest in your sixth grade class. You won the gold shorts, remember?"

"That was fifth grade," Avery corrected him. "But I don't like running."

"Sure you do," said James, in the manner of a parent who's stopped listening.

"No, I don't." Avery stabbed at her chicken.

"Put some salad on your plate." James handed her the salad bowl.

"I'll eat my salad afterward."

"Put some on your plate now." Their eyes met, and after a brief staring contest, Avery put a few leaves of lettuce on her plate.

"A little more, Ave."

She glared at him and took one more leaf.

So, it was going to be that kind of dinner. I should have stayed quiet, but my enthusiasm overtook my good sense. "It could be a good way to meet other kids in the neighborhood," I said. "You could try it out for a while, see if you like it."

"I already told you, I don't like it."

"Me neither," put in Annabelle, supportively.

I sighed. "Okay, Avery, then what do you like? I've been working hard to find some weekend activities for you, but maybe you could help me out. Is there something you're interested in that I haven't considered?"

She lay down her fork and glared at me, already in open warfare. "I don't want to do anything on the weekends." She pushed back her chair and stood up.

"Sit down," James instructed.

"I'm just getting a napkin! Can't I even do that? Geez." She grumbled as she stomped into the kitchen and ripped a paper towel off the roll. When she slumped back into her chair, I tried again.

"You need to find something to do on weekends. I know you're bored and that makes you unhappy, so let's try to fix that." My heart was beating a little too fast, spurred by the conflict, but I tried to keep my voice even.

"You can 'fix that' by letting me stay with Mom on the weekends." *Pow!* First shot fired.

"That's not the solution," James said calmly.

"Why not?"

"Because it's not, Avery. You're with us on the weekends. And I'm sorry if you don't like that, but . . . " He trailed off and shrugged.

"But we want your weekends to be fun," I continued. "And I think a Saturday activity could give you something to look forward to and be a way to make friends here."

Avery heaved an impatient sigh, like she was talking to someone slow. "We don't *want* to make friends here because we don't *live* here," she said, speaking for her sister. "And if you sign us up for a stupid activity, we just won't go." She took a bite of her chicken, pushing the greens to the edge of her plate.

"But you do live here most weekends," I pointed out. "And there are an awful lot of weekends between now and high school graduation. Do you really want to spend them all in your bedroom?"

"Yes," she said in a steely tone, and I believed her.

"But why?" James asked, and Avery's last nerve snapped.

"Because you don't care if I'm having fun or not! You only enroll me in activities to make yourself look good! You do it to show off!"

"Avery," James said.

"It's true!" she cried. "You just want to brag to people about all the things you do for your kids, while their mom does nothing!"

James bristled at this. She'd hit the nail precisely, but on the wrong end. "Well, why don't you do things at your mother's house?" he asked. "Why don't you join an after-school club or a sport? You've been there for almost a year, but you don't talk about any friends in Vacaville."

"I have friends!" Avery said defensively. "I just never get to see them because I'm here every stupid weekend!"

"You were at your mum's for two weekends last month, including spring break," James pointed out. "Did you do anything with your friends then?"

Avery seethed. "I didn't *want* to do anything with my friends then because I wanted to have quality time with Mom. I never get to see her."

"Avery, you're with your mum five days a week," James said.

"But it's not quality time! I have school and I have homework . . . It's not enough time to be with Mom, and it's not enough time to see my friends, okay?" She gripped her steak knife like she wanted to do damage with it.

"You know, you can invite your friends over here on the weekends," I volunteered.

Avery scoffed. "My friends would never come to Oakland," she said rudely. "They're not stupid."

"Yeah, they're not stupid," Annabelle echoed. I looked at her and raised an eyebrow. Her stone face slipped and she giggled a little, then seemed annoyed at herself. Sometimes Annabelle forgot which side she was on.

Avery appealed to James. "Why won't you just let us spend more weekends with Mom?" she pleaded. "That's where we *want* to be. We don't *want* to be here!"

I felt, rather than saw, James crumple a little. "No, Ave," he said quietly.

"But *why not?*" Avery exploded. "You never listen to us! We've said all along that we just want to be with Mom and you don't listen! Nobody listens!"

"Actually," I corrected her, "the judge *did* listen to you. You got exactly what you asked for. Don't you remember?"

She stared at me, confused.

"You told Dr. Seeger and the judge that you wanted the custody schedule flipped, but that you wanted to spend more time with your dad than you used to get with your mom. And that's exactly what the judge allotted."

She was quiet for a moment as this sunk in.

"We agree that this custody arrangement is stupid," I said. "But it's what you asked for." *Pow!* Counter strike.

"Well, the judge misunderstood me," she said finally.

"You were pretty clear," James said, his voice tight.

"Well, then we should go back to court to straighten things out!" Avery proclaimed. Then she quickly thought better of it and recanted. "No, never mind. I don't want to be misunderstood again."

There was a moment of silence around the table. I tried to steer us back on track.

"Avery," I said. "How can we make things better for you?"

"LET ME LIVE WITH MY MOM!" she roared. I flinched; I hadn't seen her draw the breath for that one.

"Try again," I said.

"And lower your voice," James added warningly.

She looked at us in mute misery.

"Avery," I said gently.

"I can't talk to you," she muttered.

"Okay," I said, thinking. *How could I get through to this angry kid?* I tried to remember the parenting articles I'd been scanning on the internet. Avery seemed to read my mind.

"And I'm not using those stupid mailboxes of yours," she said.

I bit my lip. A few weeks back, after a particularly bad tantrum, I'd introduced four cardboard mailboxes, one for each of us. The idea was that we could use them to write letters to each other when we had difficult things to say. They'd gone over like a lead balloon.

"Why not?" I asked.

Avery gave a bitter, *nice-try* laugh. "I'm not going to write down anything for you to use against me." She directed this at James.

He looked surprised. "When have I ever done that?" he asked. "What would make you think something like that?"

"Because I know you," she sneered.

I stared at her in disbelief. It sounded like she was describing the journals her mother had urged them to keep. How had Avery gotten everything so backwards? It was like she couldn't see the things that were right in front of her face.

"Well, we need to find a way to communicate that doesn't involve yelling," I said. "Because yelling will get you grounded."

"Who cares?" she hollered. "You never let me see Penelope anyway!"

Go look at her picture in your bathroom, I thought.

"That's not true Avery, and you know it." James sounded weary.

"It *is* true! You won't drive me to San Carlos and Rochelle won't let Penelope come here because Oakland's too dangerous!" I suspected Rochelle just didn't want to make the drive, but Avery was on a roll. "At least if I spent my weekends in Vacaville, Mom would let me see Penelope!"

"Is that what you think?" James asked.

"Yes!"

"You think your mum's going to drive an hour and a half each way, so you can hang out with Penelope on the weekends."

"Yes!" A little less vehemently this time.

"Avery, has your mum ever met Penelope?"

There was a small pause. "No."

"Even though she's your best friend, your mum has never once met her in all these years." James looked pointedly at his daughter.

Avery glared at him, her eyes wet. I thought for a minute she might soften, but instead she struck out wildly.

"You just don't understand because you don't have any friends! Nobody likes you except Marie and the stupid people at Mercy!"

"Hey! That's enough!" I said sharply. I wanted to point out that James had never had much time for friends, as he'd dedicated the last decade to being a single dad. But Avery was in high gear, maximum damage mode. She wanted to hurt.

"It's true! Nobody likes you, everybody hates you, and you don't understand *anything!*" She was crying now.

It occurred to me that she was testing us, trying to see if she could be rude enough that we'd want to be rid of her and let her stay with Jessica.

"Avery, calm down," I said.

"You don't even want us here!" she accused me.

I looked at her, practically vibrating in her seat, she was so angry. I decided to be honest.

"I'll admit that it's difficult to come home every Friday to two angry kids," I began.

"You see?" she cried. She turned to her dad. "She doesn't want us here!"

"I *do* want you here," I insisted, trying to keep the frustration out of my voice. "But I'm having a hard time knowing how to respond to your temper. It seems like you get angry every weekend."

"So just let me live with my mom," she moaned, hanging her head. "I never get angry over there."

"So, I think," I went on as though she hadn't spoken, "since we're having some problems communicating, maybe we should seek some support around it." I saw James flinch and took his hand under the table. *I'll help pay for it,* I tried to communicate. *We'll figure something out.*

Avery's head snapped up so fast I thought she'd given herself whiplash. "I'm NOT going to therapy!" she yelled. Her fire was reignited.

"Me neither!" shouted Annabelle.

James stayed cool. "That's not your call," he said smoothly.

Avery was agitated. "Therapy is for psychos!" she exclaimed.

"Come on, Ave," I said. "Do you really believe that?"

She did. "Like, eighty-seven percent of people who go to therapy are psycho!" She shook her head to convey that she was not among that number.

"I go to therapy once a week," I said quietly. "Did you know that?"

Avery's wet eyes got big. "I'm not even going to comment on that," she said rudely.

"It's helping me a lot," I said.

"Not going to comment," she repeated, rolling her eyes heavenward.

"And did you know that Marie and I used to go to therapy together? And that really helped, too." James was being a bit generous here; though I'd found Ilana's sessions helpful, he'd said he could take them or leave them. "Even your mum and Max went to therapy once, and she admitted that it helped them, too." Of course, that was a load of bullshit, but whatever.

"I'm not going to therapy with you because you'll choose somebody stupid, like Dr. Seeger," Avery shot back.

"Actually, your mom chose Dr. Seeger," I clarified.

Again, she was silenced for a moment, embarrassed to have her facts wrong. But then she changed tack and said, "Well, Mom only chose her because she was cheap."

James gave a sputtering laugh. "Dr. Seeger was *not* cheap," he said.

"Well, I don't care!" shouted Avery. "I'm not going to therapy, I'm fine! I'm not some psycho! Okay? *You* may be crazy, but I don't need any help!"

My patience finally cracked. "Really?" I quipped. "'Cause you seem pretty messed up to me."

Avery fell silent. Then abruptly she stood up and fled the table. Her feet pounded up the stairs, and a moment later a door slammed.

Annabelle looked alarmed to have missed her cue. She abandoned her dinner and ran upstairs after her sister. The door slammed again.

I put my face in my hands. "I'm sorry," I said to James. "I shouldn't have said that. I lost my cool." I felt wrung out.

Avery locked herself in the bathroom and didn't emerge for hours. I gave her some time, then knocked on the door and asked her to come out so I could apologize. She ignored me. I could hear her crying.

I slipped a note under the door that said: "I'm sorry I hurt your feelings." She ignored that, too, and left it on the floor when she went to bed—without saying good night.

Then I cried.

33

Playing Games
and Having Fun

There were still good times. In fact, the very next day we had a nice afternoon picnicking with the girls at the lake.

But the good times were hours long now, instead of days. And these hours were often bookended with foul moods and tantrums. I knew there would be good and bad days with the kids; I just wasn't prepared for dozens of good and bad days within a twenty-four-hour period. Their moods changed so fast, I was starting to feel schizophrenic.

"It sounds like the girls get upset whenever you point out that they're having fun," said Ilana at our next Tuesday appointment.

I realized that this was true. The kids managed to enjoy themselves if James or I didn't call attention to it. But once we suggested that they were having a good time, they shut right down. They didn't want to endorse any part of our life in Oakland.

"If I could just get them involved in some activities, I feel like their outlooks would change," I said.

"Why is this so important to you?" Ilana asked.

Because they're ruining my weekends, I wanted to reply, but I knew that wasn't the real answer. "Because . . . I'm afraid," I said slowly.

"Of what?"

I clutched one of the throw pillows in my lap. "I'm afraid they'll cry and throw fits until they somehow get to spend weekends with their mom, and then we'll hardly see them."

Ilana looked at me steadily. "And what are the odds of that?"

"Slim," I admitted. I knew James wouldn't just surrender his weekends with the girls, and a judge would need a good reason to reconsider the custody arrangement. But everything still felt so tenuous when the kids were upset. They had managed to upend our lives once before. I wasn't entirely sure that they couldn't do it again.

"Why don't you take some of the pressure off yourself?" Ilana suggested. "You've tried hard to make a good life for the girls in Oakland, but they're not ready to accept it. All you can do now is live your own good life and invite the kids in."

"What does that mean?" I asked.

"Focus on yourself for a while," she said. "Keep seeing your friends and doing your own activities. Lead by example. If you model a fun, fulfilling life, the girls may see that it's something they want for themselves. But you don't have to force it on them. If they want to spend their weekends being bored right now, it's okay to let them be bored."

"So, I should let them spend all day in front of the TV?" That didn't seem like the answer.

Ilana ran her beads through her fingers. "I'm not saying that, necessarily . . . But Friday nights together in front of the TV might be a good idea. If you developed a habit of take-out and a movie on Friday nights, that would be an easy re-entry for the girls that they could come to depend on. You don't always need to interact to spend time together," she said. "Sometimes just being in the same room is enough."

This sounded very appealing to me. I couldn't wait to tell James that the recommended course of action was pizza in front of the TV and *not* talking to the kids.

* * *

May's child support hearing had brought partial relief. Jessica had shown up with the same paperwork she'd brought to the previous hearing—in no way explaining how she was still qualified for disability. But the pressing issue seemed to be James' overdue payments. Despite his garnished wages, the figure he owed Jessica was mounting, and it was clear that he'd never get on top of it. Jessica argued that James was hiding money, but in the end, she was counseled to accept a lower amount. They settled on a thousand dollars a month. It wouldn't apply retroactively, but moving forward.

"A thousand dollars?" I seethed. "That's still ridiculous, James!" I'd thought the amount was going to be at least cut in half. "And nobody scrutinized her paperwork? They didn't ask why she wasn't back at work more than two years after her injury?"

"The Deadbeat Dad defense goes a long way," James said tiredly.

In fact, Jessica was working again—part time, from home, as a remote assistant. But she reported measly earnings of four hundred dollars per month—not enough to move the needle on the child support calculator, but just enough to show that she was making an effort. And she continued to play the injured survivor in court, sitting on pillows at her hearings and wincing with pain at appropriate intervals. The combined effect was powerful.

As was his habit, James was determined to look on the bright side. Rather than dwell on the still-dismal amount of money he was hemorrhaging each month, he decided to focus on the five-hundred-dollar savings. And he took me out for (a cheap) dinner.

But Jessica had suffered dual disappointments: her lowered monthly payout and the indignity of James quitting co-parent counseling. She decided to strike back.

First, she cut off all communication with James, save for one channel: the Family Planner website. She blocked his phone number and email address, so no calls, texts, or emails could get through to her. James had no recourse for reaching out to her in an emergency. She checked the Family Planner only once or twice a week and always responded with the same message: "Thank you for your email."

Next, she set the kids up with profiles on the website and began channeling their correspondence through it. Although both kids now had their own cell phones, neither would answer their father's calls or texts. Instead, Annabelle began messaging James through the website.

Dad, I want to spend next weekend with my mother.

James told the girls that he wouldn't reply to any messages they sent him through the Planner. "I'm your dad," he said. "Pick up the phone and call me. This website is not going to replace our ability to talk to each other." He deleted the kids' accounts and told Jessica why he'd done so.

But she simply made them new accounts, and James received another message from Annabelle:

Dad, I want to spend the weekend with my mother in Vacaville.

And the cycle kept repeating.

* * *

I was just leaving the office when I got a call from James.

"Hey sweetie, what's up?" I said. There was a burst of static from his end. "Are you there? I can barely hear you."

The line crackled again, then cleared. "I'm having problems with my phone," James said. "It won't hold a charge and it's nearly dead. Listen, I'm at Home Depot and I don't know what to do. Jessica just left with the kids."

"What?" I checked my watch. "Weren't you supposed to be there an hour ago?"

"I got stuck at the store and then I hit bad traffic; I was forty-five minutes late. I tried to call Jess, but she's got my number blocked, and then she called me, and my phone died in the middle of our conversation. She said she was taking the kids back to Vacaville—" Another burst of static cut him off.

"—only five minutes down the road, but she won't turn around," he was saying. "What do I do?"

"Wait, I didn't catch that," I said. "Can you repeat it?"

"—irresponsible and that the kids are upset—"

"James, I can't hear you," I called into my phone.

"—follow them to Vacaville?"

"James? Hello?" We'd been disconnected.

I called him back several times, but each call went straight to voicemail. Agitated, I took the bus home, checking my phone every few minutes for messages. Nothing came through.

James left work every Friday at two-thirty to meet the girls at Home Depot by four o'clock. The weekend traffic started early, and it sometimes took more than ninety minutes to get there. It was a lousy arrangement for all involved. Jessica also had to drive forty-five minutes, and now that Max had a new job in the city, she couldn't pawn off the responsibility on him anymore.

We knew Jessica was angry that the exchange location was so close to our house, but it was still a challenge for James to meet her. He rearranged his whole work schedule to allow for these early Friday afternoons, but as manager, there were times when he just couldn't drop everything and run out the door. Usually he'd text Jessica and let her know that he'd been delayed. But now that his messages bounced back, he had no way of reaching her.

It was two hours before I heard from James again. "Where are you?" I asked.

"I'm sitting outside Jessica's house in my car," he said. "She and the kids are inside, pretending that they're not home."

"What?"

Apparently, James had arrived at Home Depot only a few minutes after Jessica left. During their brief phone exchange, she informed him that she'd waited long enough and was taking the kids back home. She refused to pull over and meet him. "If you want the girls, you can come get them in Vacaville," she said. Then James' phone died.

342

So, he'd driven to Vacaville, presumably arriving only minutes after Jessica. Her car was tucked into the garage and the blinds were drawn, giving the impression that she wasn't home. There was no answer when James rang the doorbell, but inside the house Snowflake began barking like crazy, then was suddenly hushed.

James sat outside for a while, alternately ringing the doorbell and trying the kids' cell phones, but they wouldn't pick up. Unsure of what to do, he was debating leaving when his phone rang. It was an unknown caller, a blocked number. James answered, hoping it was Jessica or one of the kids, but it turned out to be the Solano County police department.

Jessica had called the police.

"And then my phone cut out during that conversation," James said. "So, I basically hung up on an officer and I don't have the number to call back."

"I'll text it to you," I promised him. "How are you calling me now?"

"If I leave the car running, I can hold enough charge for a short call, but I'll probably lose you in a minute. What do you think I should do? Should I come home? Should I stay here?"

I thought quickly. "Stay put," I advised. "You don't want to look like you're running from the police. I'll text you the station number; you should call them and find out if they're sending an officer to the scene. Are you—hello?" I'd lost him again.

I sent James the phone number, but I didn't hear back. I paced the house nervously, chewing on my fingernails.

An hour and a half later, James arrived home with the kids. Avery's face was red and blotchy; she'd clearly been crying. Neither kid said hello to me. They went straight to their bedroom and shut the door. They refused dinner.

James and I took a walk around the neighborhood so he could tell me what had happened.

"The cops showed up and Jessica answered the door, all smiles," he said. "They asked if I was the kids' father, and she confirmed that I was. Then they asked if the kids were supposed to be with me this weekend, and she said, 'Yes, officers, but they really don't want to go with him.'"

I sucked air through my teeth to restrain myself from shouting.

"And the cops said, 'That doesn't matter.'" James gave a short laugh. "And that was the end of it. The kids got in the car with me and we left."

"Did the girls make a big scene about leaving their mom?" I asked.

"Not in front of the police," he said. "Honestly, I think they were mortified to have the cops show up at their door. Once it was clear that they were coming home with me, Avery just wanted to get the hell out of there." He took my hand as we walked. "But I was disturbed by the conversation we had on the way home."

"Why?"

"Well, I asked the kids why they hadn't answered the doorbell." He paused, remembering. "And Annabelle said, 'We didn't hear you. We were too busy playing games and having fun.'"

"Wasn't the dog barking its head off?"

"Yep, but Annabelle stuck to her story. So, I asked why their mum made them drive all the way back to Vacaville instead of pulling over near Home Depot to meet me. And then the whole thing just kind of unraveled."

"What do you mean?" I asked.

"Oh, Avery fell apart. She accused me of acting threatening toward her mum, said that I chased her down the freeway, yelling at her on the phone. She said her mum couldn't pull over because she was afraid of me and that she did the right thing by calling the police."

"She really said that?" My heart hurt for him.

"Yeah. And then she said I was just upset because Max had replaced me as their dad, and that they care about him more than they care about me."

"No!" I stopped walking and looked at him.

"Yeah. She was all over the place. You know how Avery gets. When she's angry, she'll say anything." He squeezed my hand and pulled me gently to resume walking. "But then she said that their mum is depressed because she has to deal with me all the time. And it's hard for Jessica to make friends because she's depressed. So that's why the girls don't want to spend time with their own friends or do activities in Vacaville—they need to be at home to support their mum."

This was worrying news. Of course, I didn't give a damn that Jessica was depressed, but she should have the decency to cry to a therapist about it, as I did—not lay it on her kids.

When we got back to the house the girls were watching TV and eating ice cream. They acted like everything was fine. But then Avery's cell phone rang.

"Hi Mom," she said, leaping up from the couch. "I miss you, too. Yeah. Uh-huh. We're okay. Yeah, he did." She shot a glance at her father, then turned away. "I know. I love you so much, too. Yeah, I know. I miss you, too." She padded up the stairs to her room and Annabelle followed suit.

James picked up the sticky ice cream bowls and turned off the TV. Together we shut down the house, turning off lights and locking the door, then went up to our bedroom. From outside the girls' door we could hear Annabelle, now on the phone with her mother. "I miss you so much, too. I wish I was home with you."

James closed our bedroom door and lay down on our bed, fully clothed. I lay down beside him and wrapped my body around his, holding him tightly. For several minutes we just lay there, breathing quietly in tandem.

When he spoke, his voice was so soft I almost didn't hear it.

"Sometimes I hate my kids, baby." The tear slid sideways off the plane of his face and landed in my open palm.

34

TOO GOOD TO BE TRUE

The hits just kept coming.

After the police incident, I convinced James that it was time for some family therapy. He still didn't like the idea, but now he could see the need.

The judge had agreed to therapy on the condition that Jessica would approve our choice of therapist. It was an annoying clause, but ultimately of little consequence. James presented her with two options.

"She'll have to pick one of them," he said to me. "And I don't really care who we go with."

"True," I said. "At least we know Jess can't fuck things up again."

* * *

"I cannot believe that Jess fucked things up *again!*" I shouted.

I was furious. With no response to James' messages—save for the standard "Thank you for your email"—we'd decided to move ahead with our chosen therapist. James had requested an appointment and the therapist's answer had come back that day:

> James,
> Thanks for your inquiry seeking family therapy. I should tell you that I received a call from your ex-wife. She informed me that she does not authorize treatment for your daughters, and her approval is required per your custody agreement.
> However, if you and your partner would like to come in for couples' therapy, I'm happy to discuss an appointment.
> Regards,
> Madeline McDougal, MFT

"What is she talking about?" I demanded. "We have permission to take the kids to therapy; we *won* permission to take the kids to therapy! How can Jessica prevent this?"

James was digging through the fat custody binder, which I'd so painstakingly prepared for trial. He'd made a mess of my carefully labeled sections, shoving notes and printouts in wherever they'd fit. Now he pulled out the judge's ruling and read it aloud.

> Father is permitted to participate in family therapy with the children with a licensed therapist. Father will propose two licensed therapists and Mother will select which one will be used. If Mother does not select a therapist within ten days of being presented with the names, Father will make the selection such that the therapy process can commence no later than December 16th.

His voice trailed off as he reached the end of the passage. "We missed the deadline."

"What?" I grabbed the page from him. "But that's just an arbitrary date intended to make sure *Jessica* doesn't procrastinate! It's a technicality!" I was incensed.

James' face was grim. "Maybe so, but it's in the court order, and we missed it."

Now I was having a tantrum. "This is the *stupidest* goddamn thing I've ever heard! She's exploiting a technicality—meant to *protect us*—to prevent her children from getting help? What the fuck is wrong with this woman?" I was shouting. Thankfully it was midweek and the kids were not at our house.

James dropped the binder on the table. "She's crazy."

"She's more than crazy, she's *deranged!* She's cruel! She's a . . . " Words failed me for a moment. I stomped around the house, looking for something I could break that I wouldn't miss later. *"Why* can't she see that her kids need some counseling? We're trying to *help* them for God's sake! Can we appeal to the judge or something?"

James shook his head. "Not unless we file a new motion and go back to court."

I recoiled at the thought. "So, there's nothing we can do? We just have to live through this?"

James didn't reply right away. I could see him thinking. Then he shook his head again. "There's nothing we can do unless we go back to court."

I stuck my head into the couch cushions and howled with frustration.

* * *

As the school year drew to a close, Avery's eighth grade class held an end-of-year dance. It fell on a Friday evening during James' time, and Avery worried that she wouldn't be allowed to go. It was the first school activity she'd wanted to participate in all year—in fact, it was the first time she'd asked to do anything with friends in Vacaville. James said of course she could go, and he'd pick her up from the dance afterward.

He met Jessica and Annabelle in Vacaville and took Annie out for dinner and ice skating while they waited for Avery. Jessica told him that the dance was over at ten o'clock, and Avery was supposed to text James when she was ready to go home.

But ten o'clock came and went, and there was no text from Avery. James drove to her school, but it was all quiet with no signs of a dance on the premises. Concerned, he called Jessica and Avery, but neither answered their phone.

James drove to the house and found Max standing guard at the end of the driveway. He pretended to be taking out the garbage, but no one else in the neighborhood was putting out their trash cans at ten-thirty on a Friday night. He'd clearly been positioned as sentry.

Max folded his arms across his chest and glowered at James.

"Is Avery here?" James asked through the car window. Annabelle sat silently in the passenger seat.

Max just frowned at him.

James frowned back. "Max, is my daughter here? I drove to the school to pick her up, but there was nobody there."

Then the front door opened and Avery appeared. She had changed out of her party dress but still wore vestiges of makeup, her hair in drooping ringlets.

"Bye Max," she muttered, giving him a hug. Annabelle waved at her stepfather through the window.

"What happened?" James asked her as he pulled away from the house. "Why didn't you text me?"

"Mom came and picked me up. The dance was over an hour ago." She buckled herself into the backseat.

"I went to your school, Ave; it didn't look like anybody was there."

"That's 'cause the dance was at the country club." She refused to meet his eye in the rearview mirror.

"Avery," James said sharply. "Why didn't you tell me that?"

Avery shrugged. "Annabelle knew."

Now Annabelle stared out the window, feigning interest in the darkened scenery.

James was upset. "Girls, that's not okay. You heard me talking to your mum about tonight's arrangements. You knew I was planning to go to the school at ten o'clock. Why didn't—"

"Dad, I had a good night and I don't want to ruin it by talking about this, okay?" Avery interrupted. She leaned her head back against the seat and closed her eyes. Beside James, Annabelle did the same. The conversation was over.

That Sunday, when James brought the girls to Home Depot, Jessica took a photo of him with her phone.

The next Friday she did the same thing. Except now it appeared that she was taking a video. Her phone followed his car as he pulled into the parking lot.

"What's your mum doing?" he asked the girls as they got into his car.

"How should we know?" said Avery.

On Sunday, another video. James wrote Jessica a message on the Family Planner:

> *Please stop recording me at our exchanges. It makes me uncomfortable and puts the kids in an awkward position. Can you explain why you feel the need to do this?*

Jessica responded:

> *Thank you for your email.*

* * *

"She's a nut job," I said to Lee and Brit over beers in their kitchen.

"She sounds fucking crazy," Brit said.

"Wait, why is she taking pictures of you?" Lee asked.

James threw up his hands and shook his head. "I think maybe she's time-stamping my arrival? Who knows? Here, burgers are ready." He handed Lee a platter of hamburger patties and Lee carried them out to the grill. The rest of us followed with the remaining barbecue paraphernalia.

"So, who has the kids during the summer?" Brit asked.

"It's equal time during the summer," James explained. "One week on, one week off."

"Do the kids go to camp or anything?" Lee laid the burgers on the grill.

"Well, at their mom's they just sit around. At our house they'll go to camp, yeah." I pulled a pickle spear from the jar and munched on it. "I'm actually kind of jealous. Annabelle's going to a girl's rock band camp, and Avery is going to row crew on Lake Merritt." I'd been really pleased by these finds, and to my surprise, the kids hadn't protested them. "What's Kelsey doing for the summer?"

"She's going to sleepaway camp," said Lee. "She goes every year for two weeks. It's up in Redding, where my folks live, and she loves it. And Brit and I are going to take a little trip to London." He looked at Brit fondly and gave her a quick kiss.

"That's awesome!" I said. "Aw man, now I'm jealous of you!"

Lee grinned. "When we're back, let's get the kids together. Now that we've got the grill up and running, we can barbecue all summer. Hey girls!" He tapped on Kelsey's bedroom window with the butt end of the barbecue tongs. The window slid up and Kelsey pressed her face against the screen, flattening her nose. Annabelle and Avery flanked her. They looked like the three little pigs.

"Burgers are ready," Lee informed them. "Time to eat."

The following Friday marked the end of school, and we took the girls out for dinner to celebrate. I was surprised to find them in high spirits—particularly Avery, who usually arrived in a foul mood. Tonight she was bubbling over with excitement. Summer had arrived, and she wanted to know what fun activities we had planned.

"Well, Roaming Ex is having a paddleboarding event next weekend in Sausalito," I said. "It's a bring-your-family type thing, so I signed us up." I braced for complaints.

"That sounds awesome!" Avery enthused. "I've always wanted to try paddleboarding."

"And I was going to have some friends over for a *Twilight* marathon," I went on, cautiously. Alex had gotten me into the tween series and was pushing me to watch the movies with her before she left for Chile. "You guys can invite your friends, too, if you want. We can wait until Kelsey's back from camp."

"Oh yeah! Can I make cupcakes that say *Team Edward and Team Jacob?*" Avery was nearly bouncing in her seat.

"Um, sure." I flicked a glance at James, bewildered. I hadn't seen Avery this cheerful in . . . well, *years.*

"What's the matter, Annabelle?" James asked. "Don't you like your dinner?"

We were trying a new Ethiopian restaurant. While Avery seemed to be enjoying scooping up her food with injera, Annabelle looked a little put off. She wasn't so much eating her lentils as she was gently stroking them, getting as little on the bread as possible.

"I don't think I like Ethiopian food," she said.

"Give it a chance, Annabelle," instructed her sister. "You don't know if you like it until you try it." Now James looked at me, eyebrows raised. *Who was this kid?*

"So, do I go to rowing camp next week?" Avery asked me.

"No, the first week you guys will go to the YMCA. But the next time you're with us, Annabelle will do rock band camp and you'll do rowing."

"And I'll babysit for Poppy in the afternoons, right?"

"Right."

Since rowing camp ended at noon each day and we wanted Avery to have an afternoon plan, I'd worked out an arrangement with Hailey. She'd been looking for a mother's helper to spend time with Poppy while she focused on her grad school coursework. Hailey would pick Avery up from rowing camp, feed her lunch, and pay her for her time.

"Cool," Avery said now. "That'll be fun. Poppy's cute."

We gave up trying to make Annabelle finish her dinner and stepped out of the restaurant into a warm summer evening. "It's so beautiful out!" Avery exclaimed. She flung her arms wide. "We're so lucky to live in California."

"Hey Dad, there are food trucks over there," Annabelle pointed.

"Food trucks? We just finished dinner," James said.

"But what about dessert?" She looked at him hopefully and he gave in.

The food trucks were clustered outside the Oakland Museum, and there was a live band playing music. "This is awesome!" said Avery. "Is this, like, a party or something?"

"No," I said. "They do this every Friday night."

"Really?" said Avery. "Wow, Oakland's cool."

I looked at her sharply. *Had I heard her right?*

The girls chose cupcakes from the cupcake truck, and we sat on the concrete steps to watch the band. There was a crowd of people on the makeshift dance floor, from little kids to old folks, and everybody was having a good time. It was a real cross-section of Oakland, people of all different ages and colors dancing together. I felt a swell of love for my town.

The band announced their last song of the night and bade everyone to get up and dance. When she recognized the tune, Avery gasped.

"I love this song! Come on Marie, we've got to go dance!"

Stunned, I let Avery lead me onto the dance floor. We twirled around with the rest of the dancers while James and

Annabelle waved from above. Then we walked home along the lake, the girls chattering happily the whole way.

I couldn't get over the kids' change in demeanor. "I can't remember the last time I saw them so carefree," I told James as we got ready for bed.

"I know," he said. "It's weird. It's almost like they're older versions of the daughters I used to have."

"Do you think they're here to stay?" I wondered.

He shrugged. It seemed too sudden and too good to be true.

35

MUST BE SUMMER

I don't want to babysit for Poppy next week.

Avery's text reached me at work. Exasperated, I dashed one back to her: "Why not?"

She replied right away: "I just don't."

I gave a frustrated sigh.

It's too late Avery; you made a commitment and Hailey is relying on you. You can't suddenly quit.

There was no response.

Later that night she wrote me again:

I need to know Hailey's last name and address.

This sounded suspicious to me. "Why?" I wrote.

Just because.

Because your mother's giving you grief, I surmised. But Jess could suck it. I wasn't giving out my friend's information to her.

Hailey will pick you up from camp and your dad will come get you after work. She lives ten minutes from us. You will be fine.

Avery didn't write back.

The next day she called her father and told him the same thing. "I don't want to babysit for Poppy next week."

James had been briefed. "You accepted a job, Avery, and you have to see it through. You're not going to cancel."

"But I don't want to anymore." Her voice had gone hard and flat. The old Avery was back.

"Is this because of your mum?" James cut right to it.

"No."

"Then why do you suddenly not want to—"

"I have to go." She hung up on him.

By the following week she'd presumably made peace with her situation because she didn't bring it up again. But I watched her carefully for signs that she might flake on Hailey. I didn't want to put my friend in a bind.

By all accounts, the first day was successful. Hailey picked Avery up from camp with no issues, and Poppy adored her, hanging on her all afternoon. Avery reported having fun.

But on the second evening, when I checked in with Hailey by phone, she asked me, "Is Avery a very anxious kid?"

"Well, yeah," I said. "Why, did something happen?"

"No, nothing really," Hailey assured me. "It's just . . . she seems to get really nervous if I'm not there at twelve-thirty on the dot. She'll text me every two minutes, even when she knows I'm on my way. 'Are you nearby? How much longer?'"

I was familiar with this scenario; James went through it every Friday. "I'm sorry," I said. "She does get really anxious around pick-ups and drop-offs. It's a product of all these kid exchanges over the years, with her dad being late and her mom getting angry. I'll try to get her to chill out." I felt a little embarrassed.

"It's not a problem," Hailey said. "Don't worry about it, really. I was just wondering. Otherwise, everything is great."

And things did seem to be okay. If Avery wasn't quite as enthused as she'd been two weeks prior, at least she was mellow. But I did hear her say to Annabelle, "Don't tell Mom about the babysitting." Maybe she'd worked out her problem with a little white lie.

Every evening Avery had long phone conversations with her mother. I hated this. But notably, for the first time, she'd stopped closing her bedroom door. If I made a few strategic trips up and down the stairs, I could catch snippets of her conversations. She lolled on her bed, recounting her days, and to my great surprise, I heard her tell her mother that she was enjoying camp.

"I don't get it," I whispered to James after I'd made him do a covert walk-by. "She's always told her mom that everything about Oakland sucks. What's changed since last month when she exploded at me for trying to make her do some activities?"

James frowned, thinking. "I think it must be summer," he said.

"What do you mean?"

"Well, they've always split their time fifty-fifty in the summer. That's normal for them. And they've always gone to camp at my house. So maybe this is the first thing that feels normal in a long time. Or maybe Jessica sanctions summer camp in a way she won't sanction weekend activities. I don't know." He shrugged. "Whatever it is, I welcome the peace."

For her part, Annabelle seemed to be enjoying rock band camp. The girls were split into groups of four or five, and each got to choose an instrument: guitar, bass, drums, keyboards, or vocals. The kids received instrument instruction in the mornings and worked with their band on an original song in the afternoons. There would be a showcase for the parents at the end of the week.

"It's at a real club," she told me, and when I looked it up I realized that it was a very cool club at that. Local artists vied to get into that venue, I knew, and sometimes they hosted big names.

"Hey, this is awesome," I told her. "Do you have a band name yet?"

"Yeah. We're Queens of Storm," she reported. "We make our band t-shirts tomorrow. Oh, I need a plain white t-shirt."

So, James went out at nearly bedtime to buy a plain white t-shirt, and Annabelle spent half an hour pondering nail polish colors. "My hands are on display while I'm playing the keyboard," she informed me. "So my nails have to look good."

On Friday Hailey only needed Avery's help for a few hours. Her family had evening plans in the city. "Can I drop Avery back at home around four o'clock?" she asked me.

"Of course," I said. "I'll come home from work a little early." I'd barely seen the girls all week, and I thought it would be nice to spend some time with Avery and catch up.

But Avery wasn't interested in catching up with me. Hailey dropped her off at our house, and by the time I'd finished saying hello to her and Poppy, Avery was already in her bedroom, on the phone with her mom. They talked for half an hour, and I lingered in my bedroom nearby, waiting until I heard her hang up the phone.

Finally, I heard the familiar, "I love you, too. I miss you, too. Yeah, I'll talk to you tomorrow." I stood outside Avery's room and rapped on the open door.

"Yeah?" She lay sprawled across her bed and raised only her eyes to me. I should have recognized from her posture that she did not intend to move. She was tired after her busy week and talked-out after her marathon conversations with her mother. But I'd come home early to spend some quality time with her, and I was going to push my luck.

"It's a gorgeous afternoon outside," I began. "I thought we could go for a little walk and you could tell me about your week. I've barely seen you since Monday."

"No, thanks," she said, rolling lazily onto her stomach.

"Come on, I want to hear about camp."

"Camp's over."

I held in a sigh. "I know camp's over, but I still want to hear about it. Did you make any friends that you might stay in touch with?"

"Nope."

"Really? Nobody?"

"No."

"Well, why don't you come tell me about it?" I pointed to her discarded sneakers. "Put your shoes on, let's go out for a bit."

"I don't want to go for a walk."

Now, a smart adult would've let it drop here. A smart adult would've realized that even a walk achieved would not be a walk enjoyed with a teenager in this kind of mood. But I was not a smart adult that day.

"Put your shoes on, Avery," I said, and she heard the quiet command in my voice.

And ignored it.

"No," she said.

We stared at one another, each sizing the other up, each deciding how far we were willing to go to win this argument.

"Avery," I began.

"I'm not going for a walk with you, Marie," she cut me off. "And you can't make me. Okay? You can say whatever you want, but I don't have to listen to you. You're not my parent. You're not *anything*. You're just Dad's stupid girlfriend, and what you say doesn't matter to me."

Something in my chest seemed to shatter into smithereens. Those words pierced from a hundred different angles. God, this kid was devastating! I knew she'd say whatever came to mind in an argument, and often she flailed and chose lesser weapons, but this had been a precision hit. She'd nailed my weak spot. *You're just Dad's stupid girlfriend. You're not anything.*

I didn't know what to say, but I had to say something, so I chose, "You're on the verge of losing privileges."

And then Avery exploded.

She yelled for a long time. Every cruel and hateful thing she could think to say, she said it. She hated my guts. All her friends hated me. She hated living here. I didn't care about her; I only did nice things for her so I could brag to James about it. I had no authority to punish her, and I couldn't take away her privileges. Go on, punish her. Go on. Try it.

"Fine," I said. "Then I'll just tell your dad and he can punish you." *What was I supposed to say?*

This seemed to push Avery over the edge, and she screamed at me in the loudest, most raw voice I'd ever heard her use: "YOU'RE USING MY DAD!"

She was standing now, facing me with fists clenched at her sides. Tears were streaming down her face and snot was bubbling up under her nose. I'd never seen her so upset. "You're just using my dad," she said again, and this time it was like a moan, like the words came from a place of deep sorrow.

"Avery," I said. "I'm not using your dad."

"Yes, you are!" she screamed. "You just tell him what to do and he DOES IT!" The force of her words seemed to lift her up on her toes. I wanted to raise my own voice to match, but I kept my tone calm.

"Well, what am I supposed to do, Avery? You've just said you're not going to listen to me." I tried to reason with her. "I'm not going to let you be disrespectful. So, if you won't listen to me, you can listen to your father."

"He always takes your side!" she shouted. "He always takes your side over mine!"

That was true. James did side with me over the kids, one hundred percent of the time. Sometimes he created sides unknowingly, like when he'd made Avery take her clothes out of the washer so I could get my laundry done first. My mind flashed on a line from Dr. Seeger's report: Jessica's assertion that James treated me better than the girls, causing resentments. It hadn't been true at the time, but there was a shade of truth to it now. A self-fulfilling prophecy.

"You're right," I said to Avery, and she looked at me, startled. She couldn't tell if I was being genuine or if I was boasting about the sway I held over her dad.

"You're right. Sometimes he takes my side over yours, and it might not be fair." How did I explain that James was angry at her? That he'd been so deeply hurt by the kids' actions on the stand and every day of the past two years; that he spent all his efforts trying to submerge that anger to a depth where he could float above it, but it didn't always work? How did I tell this kid that she'd broken her father's heart, but he'd pasted it back together enough to keep loving her?

I didn't.

Instead I said, "The next time that happens, let's talk about it. Can we do that—without yelling?"

Apparently not.

"He takes your side all the time, and you aren't even married!" she shouted. "You aren't even committed to each other! You could be cheating on each other! You could decide to move out any day!"

I looked at her, alert. "I'm not moving out, Avery."

"I wish you would move out," she sobbed. "It was better when it was just Dad, Annabelle, and me. You guys dragged me and Annie into this and you're not even married—it's irresponsible!"

I nearly laughed at that. But as I looked at her tear-streaked face, I wondered about the things she wasn't saying. Was it wishful thinking on my part to imagine that I heard worry in her voice? Was she afraid, on some level, that I was going to leave like her mother had? *You could be cheating on each other,* she'd said. That seemed a strange fear for a kid to have. *You're using my dad.*

"Avery," I sighed, leaning against the door frame. "I know this may be hard to understand, but for your dad and me to move in together, with you kids, was the biggest commitment we could make. I'm not going anywhere. You're just going to have to get used to me." I gave her a gentle smile.

"Would you go away?" she asked.

"No, Avery, kiddo," I reached my hand out toward her, "I promise you, I'm not going away."

She pulled back from my hand. "No, would you *go away?*" she enunciated. "Would you get out of my room, please? Would you leave me alone?"

Oh.

I took a step back. "Okay, I'll leave for now. But how do we resolve this?"

"Just go away, Marie! Please?"

"I'm going. But we are not going to pretend like this fight never happened, okay?"

"Please leave me alone!" She held a pillow to her face and screamed into it.

"Take twenty minutes, cool down, and then let's finish this."

"Would you go?!"

I stepped out of the doorway and the door slammed in my face.

Avery didn't emerge from her room in twenty minutes, and I did not knock. She stayed hidden for two hours, and when James and Annabelle got home, she moved to the bathroom and locked herself in there.

Annabelle was brimming with excitement over her upcoming performance. "I can't wait to hear your song," I said. "I've been looking forward to it all week." I tried to

365

match her enthusiasm, but I was drained from the scene with Avery.

"Marie? Could we take a video of the show for my mom?" Annabelle looked at me hopefully.

"Of course," I said, and she smiled. "Do you want to invite your mom to the show?"

Now she dropped her eyes, suddenly shy. "I told her about it a few days ago, but I didn't have the details." She was twisting her hands.

"Well, I can send her the details," I said. "Do you want to invite her?"

Annabelle hemmed a bit, looking down at the floor. "No," she said quietly. She looked uncomfortable. "I just think it would be awkward."

I was sure it would be awkward, but that didn't matter. "Annabelle, this is your show," I said. "If you want your mom to be there, we should invite her."

She considered this for a minute, still gazing at the floor. Then she said softly, "Yes, please."

"Okay," I said. "Good. I'll send her the details right now."

Annabelle looked up and met my eyes. "Thank you," she said, and gave me a sweet little smile. It touched my heart.

I sent Jessica a message on the Family Planner and a follow-up text to make sure she received it. I was sure she would block me, now that she realized I had her phone number, but oh well.

Avery came down to dinner composed, her face showing no signs of the crying she'd done earlier. The tempest had blown itself out. It dawned on me that the wrong kid had dubbed herself Queen of Storm.

366

During the meal, Avery was on her best behavior. She looked me in the eye and asked questions about my day. I knew she was trying to leave our ugly scene behind, and I wasn't going to let her get away with it.

"Will we continue our talk after dinner?" I asked her.

Annabelle looked at us curiously, while Avery dropped her eyes to her plate and nodded.

When dinner was over we went up to her bedroom and sat across from one another on the floor. Avery seemed contrite. She fiddled with the corner of her bedspread.

"Look, I know this is awkward, so I'll start," I began. Then Avery interrupted.

"I'm sorry for what I said," she let out in a rush. "I was really mad and a lot of it wasn't true. I know 'sorry' doesn't take it back, but I apologize."

I leaned against Annabelle's bed and sighed. She was right. "Sorry" didn't take it back.

I looked at Avery, biting her lip, and saw her through two different lenses. On the one side, I was impressed by her apology. I understood that she was just a kid, angry and confused. On the other side, her words had hurt me deeply. My love for her was bruised.

But I acted like a grown-up and I said all the things I thought I was supposed to say. We worked out a signal to use when she felt her temper getting the better of her. She agreed to try and "take five" the next time she felt a tantrum coming on.

I was proud of both of us when I left her room. I also felt like I'd aged five years.

Before bed, I checked the Planner to see if Jessica had replied to my message. The website indicated that she'd read it, but there was no response.

"You did good today, baby," James said as I crawled into his arms. He pulled the covers over us and I was asleep within minutes.

The next day Annabelle was a little prickly, nervous for her showcase. She carefully ironed her t-shirt and left the house with James at two o'clock, to get to the venue early and prepare. Meanwhile, I checked the Planner website again. Jessica still hadn't replied to my message.

Avery and I set off an hour later and walked to the nearby club. I was impressed by the scale of this production. About eighty girls and their families were crammed into the space, and the noise was already deafening. They gave us earplugs at the door.

The girls ranged in age from elementary to high school and all were decked out in their band t-shirts and their own take on rock-and-roll style: I saw blue hair, black lipstick, pink tutus, Afros, mohawks, and sequins.

"This is awesome!" I shouted to James, once I'd found him in the crowd. The club was dim and windowless, and the floors were sticky with the residue of a thousand shows. I'd been expecting a school auditorium with a talent show kind of vibe. But this place was fucking *legit.*

James gave Avery a few dollars and sent her to the bar to buy a soda. "How's Annabelle doing?" I shouted to him. "Is she nervous?"

"She's a little upset," he shouted back. "Jess just texted her that she couldn't make it to the show because she didn't know about it in time."

"But Annabelle told her about it days ago! And I sent her the details, but she didn't even bother to reply!"

James shrugged. "Apparently she already made other plans."

Like hell she did. "She's a—"

The wail of a guitar and the ensuing cheers drowned out my cursing. Avery reappeared and I turned away from her, trying to get my anger under control.

"When's Annabelle up?" she shouted, peering at the program.

James scanned it over her shoulder. "There she is," he yelled back. "Queens of Storm. They're on fourth."

"Cool," she hollered. "Hey Dad, we have to take a video for Mom." James handed her his phone and shot me a look over the top of her head.

Oh, let's take a video for Mom, I thought meanly. *Let's take a video for precious Mom, who—I would bet a hundred dollars—is sitting at home right now with nothing going on, but just didn't want to come today. Hang in there, Mom. Don't fret. I'll make sure you don't miss a detail of your kid's performance.*

I took a photo of the program, planning to text it to Jessica. I was going to blow up her phone with snapshots. If she hadn't blocked me yet, she certainly would after today.

Just as I was about to hit send, I took another look at the paper.

"James, look at this," I yelled. Each band had their lyrics printed and I pointed at Annabelle's song. "Is this song about suicide?"

Now James and Avery both leaned in and stared at the program.

And if you've ever called me friend
You'll know my misery must end

> *I will no longer be the clown*
> *I'm going down, I'm going down*

"Holy shit!" James said, and Avery raised her eyebrows. When Queens of Storm took the stage, we all watched attentively.

The other girls in the band were a year or two older than Annabelle. She looked young beside them with her still-round face, but she wore the sullen expression of a teenager. Her blue fingernails caught the lights as she moved back and forth between the two chords of the song. I realized that the camp's claim of "instrument instruction" was kind of a generous term.

The lead singer was a morose-looking blonde girl with a pink ribbon in her hair. I could barely hear her over the cacophony of the instruments, but I followed along in the program:

> *I'm going down a hole so deep*
> *I only ever want to sleep*
> *And when the—*

Ba-da-bum-bum-CRASH!

The drummer skipped ahead and launched into her ill-timed solo, making the blonde girl jump. She cast an anguished look at her bandmates—clearly something had gone awry. But the guitar and keyboards kept plodding along between their two chords, oblivious. And when the drum solo was done, Annabelle added a third triumphant chord, thus signaling the end of the song.

"Let's hear it for Queens of Storm!" the emcee shouted, and the place erupted in violent cheers. It didn't seem to matter if the songs were good or bad; these campers were about girl power and volume.

"We're going to take a quick break while the next band sets up," said the emcee. "Remember, you can buy your band photos at the table in the back. Next up, The Five G's!"

Queens of Storm filed off the stage and Annabelle came over to us. We all hugged her and exclaimed over her performance.

"Did you get the video for Mom?" Annabelle asked.

"Got it." Avery held up James' phone.

"So, Annie," James said. "Your song seemed a little . . ." *Suicidey?* "Heavy," he decided. She shrugged.

"Did you help write it?" I asked.

"No. Marisol wrote the whole thing." She jerked her head toward the blonde girl, who was now crying passionately in her mother's arms. "I wanted to write a song about summer."

36

SCHOOL ORIENTATION

Lee and Brit came home from London engaged. As soon as the kids bounded up the stairs, she flashed her ring at me: an emerald flanked by two tiny diamonds.

"You guys! That's wonderful!" I squealed. I threw my arms around Brit, and James pulled Lee into a hug, patting him warmly on the back.

"Details," I demanded.

"He did it on top of the London Eye," Brit said, smiling at Lee.

"I was super nervous," Lee confessed. "But she said yes right away." He gave her a tender kiss there in our doorway.

"That's great, man," James said. "Come on in. You have time for a beer?"

"Naw, we've got to go in a few minutes. We're running late." They were headed into the city for a concert, and Kelsey was spending the night at our place. The thumping above our heads indicated that the kids were already in high gear.

"How did Kelsey take the news?" I asked Brittany.

"Surprisingly well," she said. "I thought she might be a little upset, but she seems totally happy."

As if to illustrate this point, Kelsey flew down the stairs and flung herself at her father. "Bye Dad! Bye Brit!" She wrapped Brittany in a fierce hug and beamed at us. "Did you guys hear the news? Isn't it awesome?" Then she ran back up the stairs to where the girls were waiting.

"Wow," I said, impressed.

"How did you do that?" asked James.

Lee laughed. "I didn't do anything. She just came around." He looked at his watch. "We gotta get going. Sorry to drop off the kid and run."

"No worries," said James.

"Are we still on for a barbecue next week?" Lee asked as they backed out the door.

"You bet. And hey, congratulations again!"

There was another round of hugs, and then they got in their car and drove away.

"I can't believe Lee and Brit are getting married," I said to James later as we got ready for bed.

"Yeah, I know." He pulled a t-shirt over his head, and his hair stuck up adorably.

"They've been together less time than we have."

"Mm-hmm." James peeled back the covers and slid into bed, patting the space beside him. "Come to bed, baby."

I sat down. "It's awesome how Kelsey seems so happy about it."

"Totally. Why don't you lie down?" He tugged a little at my arm and pulled me down to him. I lay on my back as he pressed a trail of kisses down the side of my neck. In one fluid motion, he flipped over and on top of me, smiling down with unmistakable intent.

"Have you given any more thought to marriage?" I asked, and the smile froze on his face.

Come on, I thought. *You had to have seen that one coming.*

James slid off me and landed on the mattress with a little *plop.* I rolled onto my side and faced him, my head propped up on my hand.

"You think now's the right time to get married?" he mumbled.

"Well no, not right now," I said. "We're broke and the kids aren't ready. But I was just wondering when we might get married. Next year? The year after? What do you think?"

James wouldn't meet my eye. "I need to get my work stuff under control first."

"Okay." I stroked the hair on his arm. "How's that going?"

James and Hassan were making a bid to buy a branch of Kingston Evermore. The Hayward branch had been floundering since the merger, too far away to be folded into the South City office, but too small to thrive on its own. There was talk of dismantling it, but James had offered the alternative that he and Hassan might buy it instead, and the company was entertaining the idea. Now they were trying to put together capital, in talks with various banks.

"We're making good progress, but it's slow," he said. "We have a meeting with Wells Fargo next week."

"Well, that sounds promising."

"I hope so. This retail business isn't exactly my dream job." He dropped an arm over his face and exhaled. "But my personal credit is a wreck, and I'll have to find a way to pay down my credit cards before this deal can go through."

How did we start talking about credit card debt?

"So, in a year we'll be in a better position to start planning a wedding?" I said, trying to steer him back on track.

He peered at me from under his arm. "Possibly."

I decided to let it drop. I snuggled up against him and kissed the side of his face.

He rolled over and kissed me on the lips. The look in his eye had returned. "What if we just had a baby?" he asked, running his fingers through my hair.

"Oh sure, 'cause that's a lesser commitment," I laughed.

"I'm serious." He was nuzzling the side of my face now, trying to talk me into the mood. "We don't need to be married to have a baby."

"I know that." I giggled, dodging his kisses. "But I'd like to do one thing in the proper order. We already have teenagers. Let's get married before we add a baby to the mix."

At the mention of teenagers, James stopped. He raised his head and cocked an ear toward the door. "Do you hear that?" he asked. "Is that the girls?"

I listened and heard it, too: a low wail seemed to be coming from beyond our door. But then I heard the crash of grocery carts and the chatter of voices. "It's just the night shift at Fresh Fare," I said. Living above a grocery store meant that all kinds of noise floated through our window.

"Do you think they can hear us, too?" He tickled me and, unprepared, I squeaked.

"James!"

"Shh, quiet. You'll wake the kids."

Near the end of summer, Rachel came for a weeklong visit with Mya and Sam.

Sam looked remarkable. For a kid who'd had his face peeled off and reconstructed just a few months before, there was no sign of trauma beyond an angry red weal that traced his hairline. And his energy was in no way diminished. He ran around the house making a ruckus until "Stop it, Sam!" became the household refrain.

Unfortunately, Rachel's schedule didn't match ours, and she would only overlap with Avery and Annabelle for three days. James wrote to Jessica, hoping she'd let the girls visit a little longer with their aunt and cousins.

Jessica replied: "Thank you for your email."

So we made the most of our short time together, going tubing on the Russian River and having picnics by the lake. But Avery's high school orientation fell during their visit, and James had no choice but to drive her out to Vacaville to register for next year's classes.

He came home angry. Jessica had been there, too. As they walked through the orientation, Jessica grabbed all the paperwork, including the class schedule, extracurricular options, and student ID info.

Avery was tense with both her parents present and followed them around quietly. She lingered at the school newspaper table, seemingly interested in putting her name down, but her mother hustled her away.

"She pushed her right past all the sports and clubs," James told us afterward. "I encouraged Avery to sign up if she was interested, but Jess said she'd be too busy with her schoolwork." Rachel and I both made faces.

"And then at the end, I offered to make copies of the school packet and bring it to Jess at tomorrow's exchange, but she wouldn't give it to me. She said she'd make me a copy instead. And I know she won't; she never does." He ripped open a bag of chips and poured them into a bowl, capturing Sam's little hand as it tried to sneak into the bag. "Stop it, Sam. Go tell the girls that lunch is ready."

Sam bounded away, and James continued, "I started to argue with her in the parking lot, but then Avery begged me to leave it."

"What was in the paperwork?" Rachel asked. "Was it anything important?"

"I don't know. I didn't even get to look at it, but the point is, I should have a copy."

I knew James wanted to play a bigger role in the kids' schooling this year. He'd been blindsided by their abrupt move to Vacaville and hadn't had the time or energy to pay close attention last year. But after Avery's eighth-grade dance, when he'd been caught short without the details, he was determined to be more involved. I hoped Jessica wouldn't create an obstacle.

"Do you have to go?" Mya clung to Annabelle, prolonging their goodbye.

"We're here for four more days. Can't you stay and play?" Sam appealed to Avery with big blue eyes.

"We have to go home to our Mom's," Avery told him.

"But can't you just ask your mom if you can stay here?" he implored. Avery glanced at her dad for help.

"They have to go, Sam," James said. "But you and Mya can come with me to drop them off, if you want."

There was a chorus of "Yay!" Little kids were so easy. Rachel and I kicked back on the couch with a bottle of wine while James piled all the kids in the car for the short drive to Home Depot.

"So, back to Bill," I prompted her.

"Right, Bill," she said. "So, he doesn't even have the courtesy to tell me himself, right? Mya comes home and announces, 'Daddy and Missy are getting married!'"

"Do you think she's pregnant?" I broke in.

"Maybe. I've wondered that. But I can't exactly ask the kids, so I'm just going to have to wait and see. It'd be stupid if she were pregnant, though. She and Bill don't seem that interested in our children. She was a pretty crappy nanny."

"I'll say!"

Rachel took a thoughtful sip of wine. "I just wonder if she's into his freaky sex games."

"What freaky sex games?" I leaned forward, riveted.

"Well, this one time he came home with this big box, right? He said he'd bought me something to wear, and I thought it was lingerie. So, I rip open the box . . . and it's a scuba suit."

"What?"

"Yeah. A fucking scuba suit. With holes cut out for the . . . parts." She made a vague gesture around her lap.

"*No!*"

"Yes! And I was like, 'What is this?' And he said, 'I want you to wear it in the bedroom.' And I said, 'It looks like a scuba suit.' And he said, 'That's because it is.'" She paused for a sip of wine.

"You are *kidding me!*"

"Nope! And I said, 'I'm not having sex with you in a fucking scuba suit.' And he said, 'But this is what I like.'" She put on a forlorn voice.

"Did he cut the holes himself?" I couldn't believe what I was hearing.

"I never found out," she said. "I refused to wear the thing, and either he returned it or he threw it away."

"Or maybe he saved it for the nanny!"

"Maybe!" she agreed. We both collapsed in laughter.

When James came home we could tell immediately that something had happened. Mya and Sam, uncharacteristically quiet, disappeared up the stairs to the girls' room.

"What's wrong?" Rachel asked him. "Wait—hang on a sec." She went into the kitchen and came back with another glass, then poured him some wine. He took it with a hand that appeared to be shaking.

"I pulled up in the parking lot," he said. "And Jess and Max were already there. The girls jumped into their car and they started to pull away, but then I rolled down the window and asked Jessica for the school packet. She told me she didn't have it." He rotated the wine glass in his hand, forgetting to drink from it.

"So, I told her that wasn't unacceptable. She'd promised to make me a copy and she needed to honor that. Then Max got out of the car, like he was her bodyguard or something. And he told me I had no business asking Jess for anything."

"What?" I said loudly.

"So, I got out of the car, too, and I told him that he was being ridiculous. All I wanted was the school paperwork. Did he think this was good co-parenting? And Max said that the girls went to school in Vacaville now, and it wasn't my business to be involved in their education anymore."

"Whoa," said Rachel.

"I reminded him that Avery is *my* daughter, not his. And then he said that I was a useless parent and always had been. He said he didn't have to put up with my crap, and Jess wasn't giving me anything. And if I really gave a shit about my kid, I'd get the paperwork directly from the school."

"He swore in front of my kids?" Rachel looked furious.

"Yeah. And Rach, I nearly hit him." He made a fist with his free hand. "I was so mad, I nearly did it. But then I thought that Jess would call the police again and nail me with an assault charge—and my kids would probably back her up. So, I stopped myself. But I told him, 'You're a fucking asshole, Max.'" He shot an apologetic look at his sister. "In front of your kids."

She waved her hand dismissively. "Oh, they've heard worse."

"Oh my God, they're such awful people!" I punched the couch cushion in impotent fury. "Why are they such awful people?"

"Can you get the paperwork from the school?" asked Rachel.

"I hope so. I'll call them this week," James said. "But I shouldn't have to do this! I don't know why she has to make everything so difficult!"

It was more difficult than he'd even realized, because when James called the school, he wasn't on record as being Avery's father.

"She removed me as parental contact," he fumed. "And they won't reinstate me unless I drive up there during school hours with a photo ID."

"Are you serious?" I asked. "That's the only way?"

"Oh no. Jess could confirm my information—if she wanted to." His voice was bitter. "But what do you think she said to that?"

"Thank you for your email," I intoned.

"Bingo."

* * *

Jessica sent James a message through the Family Planner:

> *Just to remind you, with the new school year, our new exchange time is 6 p.m. on Fridays. You'll recall that is what we agreed in co-parent counseling.*

"We didn't agree on anything in co-parent counseling!" James objected.

"But you're supposed to meet at four. Why does she think she can push back the exchange time?" I didn't understand.

"I guess Avery gets out of school a little later this year." He sighed. "At least, I think she does, but I still haven't seen her damn class schedule."

He wrote back:

> *Jessica, I never agreed to this. I'm happy to talk through some options, but you don't automatically get to have the kids for 2 extra hours each week.*
>
> *Would you consider letting me keep the girls on the occasional Sunday night and take them to school*

Monday morning? It would save you a drive and give me a chance to be more involved.

Jessica replied:

We will abide by the agreement that we reached in co-parent counseling: 6 p.m. on Fridays. If you would like to resume counseling sessions with Dr. Sweet, please let me know.

This useless dialogue went on all week. James sent Jessica numerous messages offering compromise. Her contribution was to copy and paste the same response, six times.

When Friday rolled around, James didn't bother leaving work until four-thirty. But while he was driving, his phone buzzed with a text message from Avery: "We r here. Where r u?"

It was five-thirty. Jessica was half an hour earlier than expected.

"You're late," snapped Avery when James arrived at six. She threw down her school bag and buckled her seatbelt, her mood already filling the car.

"So, what are you going to do?" I asked James later, as we cleaned up the kitchen from dinner.

"Well, she was ninety minutes late tonight, so I guess I'll keep them an extra ninety minutes on Sunday." He handed me a plate, which I stuck in the dishwasher.

"The kids are going to hate that," I said.

He gave a grim nod. "I know."

For the next two Sundays, James kept the kids late by the same amount of time that their mother kept them on

Fridays. Although he'd informed everyone very clearly that he would do this, the girls kept acting surprised.

"Dad, are we leaving?" Avery asked at quarter to six.

"No, Avery, I told you. You're here until eight o'clock tonight."

"But Mom will be waiting at Home Depot!"

"I told your mother eight o'clock. If she wants to wait in the parking lot, that's her business."

She did.

The following week it was the same thing.

"Dad, are we leaving?" Avery asked at quarter to six.

"No, Avery, you know this. You're here until eight o'clock."

"But Mom will be waiting for us! Last week she sat in the parking lot for two hours!"

"Well, that was kind of dumb, wasn't it?" James said.

And Avery lost her shit.

"I can't keep this up," James said after he'd returned from Home Depot. "I can't give the kids a meltdown every weekend. Avery's about to lose her mind. Annabelle's complaining that she doesn't get home until after bedtime. It's not fair to put them in the middle like this."

"Jess is the one who's putting them in the middle, not you."

"No, it's both of us. If I keep the kids late on Sundays, I'm just as bad as she is. We're using the kids as pawns in our grudge match." He uncorked a new bottle of wine. We'd gone through quite a lot since Rachel's visit.

"Well, what's the other option?" I asked. "You can't just roll over and let her call all the shots. It's not up to her." I held out my glass as he poured. "You have a custody arrangement. Somebody needs to hold her to it."

"The only way to hold her to it is to go back to court." He put down the bottle and looked at me seriously.

"Oh no."

"I think we have to."

"No."

"Marie, just listen."

"Listen to what? How are you going to go back to court? With what money are you going to do that? Hmm?" I took a sloppy sip of wine, then dabbed at the spill on my shirt. Thankfully, it was white. "You're in debt up to your eyeballs."

"I know. I'll have to represent myself."

"And say what, James?" I looked at him. "Do you expect to win custody? Rhonda couldn't do it, but you think you can?" I was all wound up.

"No, I don't expect to win custody. But I think I can get them to enforce the four o'clock exchange, and maybe I can get a little more visitation. I want to drive my kids to school sometimes. I don't think that's asking too much."

I was not moved. "So, you want to drive an hour every Monday morning up to Vacaville, then turn around and drive two and a half hours back down to Redwood City for work? That's crazy, James."

"It's not," he insisted. "If I wait up there till the traffic dies down, it's only ninety minutes to Redwood City, and then I'll work a longer day. It'll be worth it if I can stay connected to the kids' schools. She's pushing me out, Marie!" He sounded frustrated. "I don't know their teachers, I don't know their friends. I don't know anything about their lives during the week, and when I ask them questions, they don't tell me. They still want to keep their two worlds separate. But if I could drive them to school once a week, maybe they would start letting me into that part of their lives."

I shook my head.

"I've always known their teachers," he appealed to me. "It's always been me at the school conferences, at the PTA meetings, on the field trips. This is the first time I don't know anything about my kids' lives at school. And Jessica is determined to keep me out."

He took my hand. "It wouldn't be another trial. Nothing like the last time. This would just be a hearing. It's a minor request."

I looked at him. "I said I was never going to do this again."

"You don't have to do anything," he promised me. "You don't have to testify, or come to court, or write any documents. I will do it all myself." He kissed me on the forehead. "But I have to do this." He kissed me again. "I have to."

I pulled back from his embrace. His eyes were resolute.

"Then I will help you," I said.

37

A WHOLE BAG

As was my custom, I drafted the legal paperwork. I knew James said I didn't have to get involved, but honestly, it was hard for me to sit things out. I had so little say in our parenting arrangement that when an opportunity arose for me to contribute, I seized it. Writing the court documents was a way for me to take control.

Our Request for Order was simple; we wanted enforcement of the four o'clock exchange and permission for James to keep the girls on Sunday nights and drive them to school on Monday mornings. We also requested individual therapy for the girls, noting their high anxiety and Avery's troubling temper.

It seemed like a slam dunk. James filed the paperwork and we waited for a response.

Meanwhile, the calendar pushed forward. Avery was now fourteen and Annabelle would soon turn twelve. To our surprise, Annie wanted to have her birthday party in

Oakland. To our greater surprise, her friends from Vacaville agreed to come.

"I thought Oakland was dangerous and dirty and her friends would never come here," I said to James.

"Yeah, well. I don't think her mum's real big on birthday parties."

Annabelle had three new friends at school: Gahar, Luz, and Bibi. Luz couldn't make it to the party, but with the addition of Kelsey and Avery, it was a fair little group. We took the girls to a screen printing shop where they could make their own t-shirts. "It's like rock band camp!" Annabelle exclaimed.

It was sweet to watch her having fun with her friends. Gahar and Bibi looked like sisters, both pretty girls with long black hair and studious manners. Gahar wore little wire-rimmed glasses. The kids laughed and joked with each other in the way that nerdy girls do. (I recognized this from personal experience.)

Later we came home for pizza and presents. The kids were playing in the living room when the doorbell rang.

"Hey, it's another present!" called Bibi. The girls flocked to the door and Annabelle flung it open.

The FedEx guy on our porch seemed startled. He handed Annabelle a large flat envelope.

"Open it!" the kids urged, but James spotted the return address just in time and plucked it out of Annabelle's hand.

"Uh, that's not for you," he said. There was a chorus of disappointed noises, then the kids went back to their games.

James motioned me into the kitchen. "It's Jessica's response." He ripped open the envelope.

"Do you think she had it delivered during Annabelle's party on purpose?" *That'd be a real dick move.*

James shrugged. "I wouldn't put it past her. She obviously paid extra for Saturday delivery."

Avery's head popped around the door frame. "Hey Dad, is there any pizza left?"

"What? Yeah." James dropped the envelope to his side casually.

"Can I have the last piece?"

"Sure, I don't care. I'm going upstairs for a bit." He brushed past her out of the room.

"Me too," I said and followed. Avery shot me a frown, and I realized she thought we were going upstairs to fool around.

Behind our closed bedroom door, James sank down on the bed, reading. "What does it say?" I asked.

He made a face. "'Mr. de Graaf knows that a motion at this time presents undue hardship on Mrs. Mazzeo, as he is more than eight thousand dollars behind in child support. This is forcing Mrs. Mazzeo to have to represent herself.'" He snorted. "Join the club."

I scanned ahead over his shoulder. "'Mr. de Graaf has been late to exchanges thirty times over the past fourteen months, proving that he will be unable to get the girls to school on time. They should not have to suffer tardiness and early mornings because of him.'" I didn't dare say it out loud, but I could see Jessica's point there.

But then she moved into the realm of the ridiculous. "She's requesting *sanctions* if you're more than fifteen minutes late to an exchange?" I hooted in disbelief.

"And she wants to keep the girls on half their weekends." James shook his head in disgust. "She wants the kids to be interviewed by the court."

"What?" I said in alarm. "Where does it say that?" I grabbed the pages from him. "I thought you said this wouldn't be a trial!"

"It shouldn't be, but it looks like Jess is trying to make it one." He caught a glimpse of my stricken face and reassured me. "Don't worry, it won't go to trial. I barely asked for anything."

"Yeah, well she disputes everything you did ask for. She won't do the four o'clock exchange or the Sunday overnights. She forbids therapy. And look, she's requested sanctions here, too, for citing the evaluator's report. She says it's a breach of confidentiality." I pointed out the line where Jessica demanded a five-hundred-dollar penalty for this offense. "Did you know Dr. Seeger's report was confidential?" I felt bad; I was the one who'd referenced it in our document.

"I knew we couldn't share it with the girls or outside parties, but I didn't think confidentiality applied to the court. I mean, it was key evidence at our trial."

I leaned back and nibbled on my thumbnail nervously. "Maybe we should get some legal advice before this hearing," I suggested.

"From who? Rhonda? I think she's about to sue me herself over my unpaid bills."

I thought. "What about Nancy?" Nancy was a friend from church. "She's in family law, right? I bet she'd sit down and talk with us."

James seemed reluctant. "I don't think we need to do that."

"I don't know James, I think we might." I dropped the papers back in his lap. "Jess is good in court," I reminded him. "What's the harm in asking Nancy for help?"

His lower lip stuck out a little, reminding me of a pouty child. "I'll think about it," he finally said.

"Great." I planted a kiss on his cheek. "Now what do we do?"

"Now we get to respond to her response."

"Oh goody." I flexed my hands. "Point me toward the computer, sir. I have some writing to do."

Gahar and Bibi were picked up by Bibi's father around eight o'clock, but Kelsey spent the night. The next morning we'd planned to leave early and drop her back home on our way to church, but it was the usual mad scramble to get out the door on time.

I found Kelsey sitting at the dining room table when I came downstairs. Her arms were clasped around her knees, and she was rocking back and forth in an odd, distressed sort of way. Her phone was clutched in her hand.

"Hey, Kelsey. Are you all right?" I asked her. She was sucking on the end of her hair.

Upstairs I heard James holler at the girls to hurry up and a muffled retort that suggested someone was changing in the closet.

"Kelsey?"

She took her hair out of her mouth and stared at me. "My mom won't answer the phone." She put the phone on speaker and hit redial, and we listened as the call rolled over to voicemail.

"What's the problem?" I asked her. "We're going to drop you off at your dad's in a minute. He and Brit are home, right?" I didn't like the way she was rocking back and forth. There was something spacey about it, almost eerie.

"Yeah, they're home. But my mom's supposed to come get me at ten o'clock. And she's not answering the phone."

I checked the clock on the wall—*shit, we were going to be late to church.* "It's only eight-thirty. Maybe she's still asleep."

Kelsey gave a robotic shake of the head. "It takes an hour to get here on the BART train. If she's not up by now, she's going to be late." She pressed redial again, and I listened to Yvette's answering message.

"Well, she might be in the shower or something." I caught a glimpse of Kelsey's phone display and saw that she'd called Yvette more than twenty times in the last few minutes. "Kelsey? You've got to give her a chance to call you back, okay?"

Kelsey dissolved into tears. "I need my mom to pick up," she said, jabbing at the redial button again. "I need my mom to *pick up.*" She rocked back and forth with urgency.

"Hey, kiddo, did something happen?" I sat beside her on the bench. "Is everything okay?" I was a little alarmed by her behavior. Tentatively I reached out and stroked her hair. She didn't jerk away as James' kids would have done, so emboldened, I did it again.

"My dad gets so mad when she's late," Kelsey moaned. "He and Brit get so upset." She let out a low keening noise.

Ah. I was familiar with kid exchange drama. I wrapped Kelsey in my arms to still her rocking. She let me hug her, and I basked in the feeling of being permitted to comfort a kid.

"Does your dad yell?" I asked her.

"No," she said. "But I just know he's really mad."

"Okay." I smoothed back her hair again. "So, what upsets you more? The idea that your mom might be late, or that your dad and Brit will get mad?"

"That Dad and Brit might be mad." Her voice shuddered on the words.

"Well, can you talk to them about it? Could you tell them that it upsets you when they get mad that your mom is late? I bet they would listen to you. They know it's not your fault when she's late."

I felt Kelsey relax ever so slightly in my arms. "Maybe."

"I bet it would help," I told her.

At that moment, Avery bounded down the stairs and froze at the sight of me cradling Kelsey on the dining room bench. I'm not sure what was more impactful: the unexpected sight of her friend crying, or the fact that I was hugging her in a more intimate embrace than she or her sister had ever allowed from me. Instantly the air turned awkward but I tried not to show it. "You ready to go, Avery?" I asked casually.

"Yeah."

I released Kelsey and patted her cheek. "Everything's going to be fine, okay? Come on, get your shoes on. It's time for us to go."

* * *

Halloween fell on a Friday. We planned to take the kids trick-or-treating with Lee and Brit, but midmorning, James got a call from Avery. They'd been in a car accident on the way to school, she said. Her mother was in the hospital.

"The girls are all right," James assured me. "It was a very minor accident—another car tapped her at a stoplight. The kids just felt a bump from behind. But Jess went to the hospital in a neck brace."

"She went in an ambulance?" I asked.

"It sounds like it. Avery says the police dropped the kids off at school." He snorted. "I guess it was time to refresh the old back injury."

"Just in time for court," I realized. "How clever of her."

"Well, she might really be hurt. Who knows? But Avery didn't sound upset at all, and she and Annabelle are totally fine. They would have taken the brunt of the impact, being in the backseat. Anyway, Max is with Jess, so I'll have to leave work early and drive up to Vacaville to get the kids."

"Oh, no." Now I was dismayed. "Will you be back in time for trick-or-treating?"

"I'll do my best."

James and the girls arrived home at seven o'clock and the kids flew up the stairs to put on their costumes. "Hurry, hurry," I urged them. It was already dark out and we still needed to drive to the high-candy district. Trick-or-treaters never bothered with our neighborhood.

We met Lee and Brit in Trestle Glen and exclaimed over everyone's costumes. Kelsey was dressed as a genie, Avery made a very realistic young Audrey Hepburn, and Lee and Brit were bloody axe murderers. James and I wore big yellow Lego heads that we'd crafted from chicken wire and papier-mâché, and Annabelle was wearing a Chinese *cheongsam* that she'd found at Goodwill. When I asked who she was supposed to be, she just glared at me.

We managed to squeeze in an hour of trick-or-treating, then adjourned to our house for candy and beers. The kids went upstairs to sort their loot and we grown-ups spread out in the living room, the detritus of our costumes littering the floor.

"You guys are truly disgusting," I said to Lee and Brit, who were sipping beers nonchalantly from bloodied faces.

"Why, thank you," said Lee. He smiled at me, a grotesque rictus that made me laugh and shudder.

"So, is Kelsey sleeping over tonight?" James asked, resting his feet on a Lego head.

Lee and Brit exchanged a brief glance. "I think we'll take Kels home tonight," Lee said. "She's had a long week."

"Is everything okay?" I asked. "How's she doing?" I'd called and told him about Kelsey's strange behavior the previous weekend.

Lee sighed and Brit scoffed. "It's Yvette," she said, irritated. "She found out that we're engaged and got all pissed off. I don't know what she said to Kelsey, but she's been anxious and upset lately. She's not excited about the wedding anymore."

"Yeah, and she's been giving Brit kind of a hard time," Lee put in. "She's acting like a bit of a brat."

I was ashamed to feel a tiny bit better that I wasn't the only one taking crap from a kid. I'd been jealous of Brit and Kelsey's relationship since we'd met, but now I could commiserate. "I'm sorry to hear that," I said.

"She wants to spend more time with her mom, which is new," Lee went on. "Yvette was three hours late on Sunday and Kelsey was freaking out the whole time. But once she showed up, Kels was just like, 'Later, Dad.' Totally calm and cool."

"Yeah, and we missed brunch with friends because we were waiting on her." Brit made a sour face.

"So I told Kelsey that it wasn't cool for her mom to keep us waiting all morning," Lee continued. "But then she just flipped out on me."

I frowned. That wasn't the gentle conversation I'd pictured them having. "Can you talk to Yvette?" I asked. "Will she answer the phone if you call her?"

"Yeah, she'll answer the phone, but she usually just tells me to suck a bag of dicks."

James choked on his beer. My jaw dropped open in delight. "Does she honestly say that? Does she honestly say, 'Suck a bag of dicks'?"

Lee nodded. "Yeah, she says it all the time."

"Not 'Suck a dick', but 'Suck a bag of dicks'? A whole bag?" I needed to be sure.

"Yeah."

I fell back against the couch, overwhelmed with laughter. "Who *talks* like that?" I whooped, clapping my hands. I'd never heard such a turn of phrase.

But Brit wasn't laughing. "Yvette talks like that, all the time. It's always: 'Fuck you, go fuck yourself, suck a bag of dicks, you're an asshole, you're a faggot, I hope you die.' That kind of shit."

I stared at her. "And she kisses her kid with that mouth?" Brit gave a disgusted shrug.

"So I get 'Thank you for your email' and you get 'Suck a bag of dicks'," James said. "And for some reason, our kids idolize their mums and can't stand us."

"Doesn't seem fair, does it?" said Lee.

"Why are they such horrible women?" James asked rhetorically.

"Why did you both have children with such horrible women?" Brit asked pointedly.

A depressed silence fell over the room and hung there.

But not for long.

"A whole *bag* of dicks," I said happily, beaming at them. "Such wonderful imagery!"

38

SIDEWALK SHOWDOWN

"Okay, ready? The girls want additional weekends with their mom."

"Um . . . That's not in the best interest of the girls. The judge ruled that I should have the majority of weekends in order to remain a strong presence in their lives . . . There's been no change of circumstance to make him reconsider."

"Good!" I said. "Next one: the girls should be interviewed."

"Strongly disagree . . . extremely stressful for the kids . . . they've already been interviewed by the evaluator . . . et cetera."

"They've already undergone an extensive four-month evaluation," I corrected him. "However, if Your Honor should determine that the girls need to be interviewed again—"

"Then I would request Dr. Seeger. Got it." James sounded tired.

"Right. And then you reference the evaluator's report. Okay, how about . . . Mr. de Graaf says I've never shared school information with him, but my evidence proves he is incorrect?"

James rubbed at his eyes. "Um."

"Come on. You know this one."

Our hearing was tomorrow and I had made a list of all of Jessica's possible allegations and devised rebuttals. I'd given James the list to study, but he hadn't looked at it very closely, so now I was making him practice by lobbing him examples. He didn't seem to be hitting them very hard.

"The emails?" I prompted.

"Right. Look Marie, I think I've got it. That's enough for now, okay?"

I put down my papers, disappointed. "Let's just work on it for another half hour, and then we can call it a night."

But James shook his head. "No, I'm done. I need to watch some TV and relax a little. Then I need to go to bed." He shot me a tight smile and left the room.

I tried to quell my irritation. Despite my aversion to court, I'd done all the leg work for this hearing. I'd written the Request and the Reply, scouring law websites for info, and I'd spent two hours on the phone with Nancy, reaping free legal advice. I learned that Jessica—who was representing herself—had been wrong about the evaluator's report being confidential. She couldn't demand sanctions from James for referencing it. And after doing the math, I realized that if James won Sunday overnights with his kids, it would shift custody to a sixty-forty percent split and could decrease his child support payments significantly.

I was more than a little proud of myself for the work I'd done—and a little frustrated with James for his lack of preparation. In fact, he seemed almost disinterested in the hearing, as though it hadn't been his idea.

Understanding that I wasn't going to get any more out of him tonight, I let the issue drop. We watched TV for a while, then went to bed, where James immediately fell into an exhausted sleep, and I lay for a time, framing more rebuttals in my mind.

* * *

To: Rachel de Graaf

Subject: Fresh Tales from the Courtroom

Well, today's court hearing was underwhelming in the legal sense, but pretty fantastic for the showdown that occurred afterward.

We got less than ten minutes with the judge. He didn't let either party present, but scheduled a settlement conference for March and instructed them to try and work things out in the meantime, ha ha.

Jessica came alone to the hearing; Max was at work and the kids were in school. Which meant she had to carry her own pillow—I don't know how she managed! She moved a little stiffly from her recent car crash, but the judge didn't give her time to exploit it.

We adjourned to the hallway to take that useless swing at working things out. I was surprised that Jessica let me sit in on the discussion, but she was still wearing her polite mask—which she removed just moments later.

"Let me explain why I can't facilitate a 4:00 p.m. Friday exchange," she said. "Annabelle's school bell rings at 2:40, but that doesn't mean she's ready to go! No, she has to walk all the way across the school to reach my car. Sometimes it can take fifteen minutes! Then we have to drive to Avery's school; that's another ten minutes. Then we have to go home so they can have a snack and . . . " You get the idea.

"That makes sense," said James. Or perhaps it was me. I admit to speaking for him at that point. It's

been two and a half freaking years and I never get to talk; I couldn't help myself.

"That makes sense," I probably said. "So, how are you going to let James recoup his parenting time? You've ignored all of his suggestions. Since you're the one in contempt of the court order, the onus is on you to suggest a fair compromise." Her smile turned brittle then. I don't think she liked that I threw the word "onus" at her.

"Onus onus onus," I said a few more times, probably with some other words in there.

Jessica's smile disappeared altogether. "You know, Marie, perhaps you should leave James and me alone to talk," she said tightly.

"No, I'll stay," I replied.

Jess tried a different tack. She rounded on James. "You are significantly behind on your child support payments. Do you know what happens when you reach ten thousand dollars? They'll revoke your driver's license. What will you do then?"

"I'll be out of a job," James said placidly. "How will you expect me to pay child support then?"

"Oh, you'll find a way to pay it," she said. "At least, you'd better. Or you'll be deported. Do you realize that if you don't pay your full debt to me by next month, immigration will get involved and they'll begin deportation proceedings?"

That sounded like a pretty wild shot, but she spoke with certainty and venom. James studied her. "Jess," he said, "why would you pursue that? How is that in the best interest of our kids?"

"It's out of my hands," she said airily. "It's automatic. You'll be sent back to Canada. And you," she said, turning to me, *"will lose your husband. Oh— I'm sorry! I meant your* boyfriend. *Because he hasn't married you, has he?"*

I wasn't sure I'd heard her right. My head was spinning from how fast the situation had turned. I had never seen Jessica drop her composure before.

"Yes, you'll lose your boyfriend, *and what will you do then?"*

I don't recall what I said to that. Perhaps it was *"onus".*

Jessica was gathering a mean head of steam, so to cut her off I said, *"We'll see you at 4:00 p.m. on Friday to pick up the kids."*

"No, you won't," she snapped at me.

"Fine," I replied. *"James will see you at 4:00 p.m. on Friday."*

"I won't be there," she said.

"Jessica, you just heard the judge say that until further notice you have to respect the court ruling, and the exchange time is 4:00 p.m." I couldn't believe her.

"I'll be there at 6:00," she said defiantly.

"And how do you think that will look for you, the next time you're in front of the judge?"

"Oh, it won't matter by then," Jessica retorted. *"Because your* boyfriend *will be in jail."* She turned on her heel and left.

Incredulous, I looked at James. *"What do we do? She just admitted she's going to keep disobeying the court order! Can we go back in and see the judge?"*

He shook his head. "No. We just have to let her do it. It won't look good for her at our next court date, will it?"

"We always think that but she never seems to get in trouble," I said. "How does she keep getting away with this?"

James thought about it as we took the stairs down. "Our next meeting is a settlement conference, not a hearing. It's smaller, I think—like mediation, but in the judge's chambers. He won't be impressed that she ignored the court order. He'll try to talk us through compromises, and she'll refuse every one, just like she did in co-parent counseling. He'll see that she's unreasonable."

As we arrived in the lobby, Jessica came out of the elevator. We couldn't help but fall in step as we all exited the building.

God knows what inspired this next comment, but Jessica tossed it to me over her shoulder. "The sad thing is, if you were half the woman you needed to be, your boyfriend wouldn't feel the need to file motions just to keep me in his life."

That stopped me in my tracks. "What the hell?" I exclaimed. I felt like I'd dropped into a bad teen movie.

"It's obvious that you miss me, James, otherwise you wouldn't keep making these excuses to see me." She gave him a sly smile.

James looked like he'd bitten into a wormy apple. "I do not miss you, Jessica," he said emphatically.

She laughed as though she didn't believe it. "Okay, James. Whatever you say."

The walk sign flashed and for some strange reason we all strolled across the street together. I was caught in her tractor beam; I couldn't break away.

"Well," I quipped as we stepped onto the curb, "it's been lovely spending this time with you. We must do it again." I turned away from her, toward James' car.

"Marie," she said, and I paused. "I actually have no problem with you. I'm sure you're a lovely person."

"I AM a lovely person!" I retorted, very maturely.

The mask of politeness was back on her face. I was mesmerized by her easy ability to slip in and out of character. She was smooth and composed now, no sign of the angry hellcat who'd hissed at us in the hallway. How did she do that?

Suddenly I realized that Jessica was advancing on me. Face to face, she raised an arm and let it hang awkwardly in the air. I blinked at her, confused. Was she going to hit me? Was this some kind of slow-motion karate?

James figured it out first. "Are you trying to HUG her?"

I jumped back. Jessica paused, arm afloat.

"I don't mind giving you a hug," she said beatifically. She was Mother Theresa. She was Meryl Streep.

I was floored. "I don't want a hug from you!" Jesus, I would've preferred the karate.

She lowered her arm and stared daggers at me. The mask was off again and bitch was all over her face.

"Jessica," I began, and I felt all the dammed-up words breaking free at last. "You've been awful to me since day one. You wouldn't even talk to me until we wound up in court! Why would I ever hug you?"

James took a step back and let me fly.

"I've tried and tried," I went on. "I've reached out to you so many times, and you've done nothing but ignore me. You act like I don't exist!"

"You said you hated me," she broke in. "Or don't you remember that email?"

"I DO remember that email," I shot back, "and you should go reread it! I said I was trying NOT to hate you, but you sure were making it hard! And then I invited you to start over, to join us for coffee, join us for church—but you never acknowledged that, did you? You haven't acknowledged any of the efforts I've made over the past three years."

"You said you hated me," she repeated, every inch the victim. "I never gave you any reason to treat me that way."

"PARDON ME," I may have hollered, "but the first thing you ever said about me was that I was a whore! Or don't you remember that conversation?"

"I never said that," she protested, eyes wide with innocence.

"You did, too," put in James.

But Jessica was working a different angle now; she was trying to discredit James. "Have you considered that he's not being honest with you? He's not a truthful man."

I nearly laughed. "Are you trying to get me on your side? Do you think that's going to work? I was there, Jessica!" I shouted. "You said to James, 'So you're fucking that tramp who calls herself a Christian?'"

"I never said that," she lied boldly.

"Yes, you did," James said.

Jessica eyed him, then looked at me. "You know, James has never told me anything good about you." It was an abrupt pivot. I started to see where Avery learned her technique: throw every dart you can and see what sticks.

"We don't talk!" James scoffed. He turned to me. "She was like this for thirteen years of marriage. Lovely, isn't it?"

I shook my head. "You've been nothing but nasty since the beginning, Jessica. And the sad thing is, that's what you're teaching the kids."

"They're my children!" she retorted. "And I have a mother's duty to protect them!"

"Protect them from what? We all share custody of these kids," I said, knowing I was pissing her off, knowing it was not technically true. But I was lost in the sweet relief of loosening my tongue. "They live with me, too. I share them just like your husband shares them."

"Oh no you don't!" she shot back. "He is their stepfather! And you are NOT their stepmother!" She paused and, quick as a flash, changed course. She stepped toward James with a possessive air and made her voice gentle. "Marie, if you want to be a part of our family—"

But James reared back and we roared together like a Greek chorus: "WE HAVE OUR OWN FAMILY!" Honestly, our synchrony was pretty amazing.

Jessica was spitting pissed now. "He's never going to marry you, you know," she sneered. "He'll never put a ring on it, honey. So you might as well just forget it." She tossed back her hair and spun away.

I watched her get into her car and start the engine. I was high on adrenaline; my nerves were popping off. I wanted her to come back so I could yell some more. But the confrontation was over.

James took me by the hand and gave me a beautiful kiss right there on the sidewalk. "I love you," he said softly, and all the fight went out of me. I hooked my arm through his and we started toward the car.

Then Jessica delivered her parting shot. Pulling up beside us, she rolled down her window and called out: "Malcolm never put a ring on it either, did he?" She flashed her own diamond at me.

I stopped short. There's no way that Jessica could have known about my past relationship with Malcolm unless she'd done some serious stalking. Goddamn.

She was idling at the curb. I walked over to her passenger window and stuck my head right inside.

"Did you really just say to me, 'Malcolm never put a ring on it'?"

She smirked. "That's right. Malcolm never put a ring on it and neither will James. So don't hold your breath."

I inched further into her window. "Let me tell you something," I said.

And Rach, in that moment, I was every woman's hero; I was the triumphant end of every film, every book, and every scene you've re-written in your head. "I don't care about your fancy house or your expensive diamond ring. I'm with that man because I love him. You have no idea what you lost." I spoke measured and true. Then I withdrew from her window and stepped away.

Jessica called out to me, "Oh, I didn't lose anything! I threw him away! Like the garbage that he is!" She put her foot to the pedal and peeled off.

James and I stood on the sidewalk for a long moment.

"You know," he finally said, "I think I've done a pretty good job with my kids. Considering that they're half of THAT crazy bitch, they're amazingly well-adjusted."

"Indeed, they are," I agreed, resolving to give the kids more credit. "Indeed, they are."

Back to court in March. The fun just don't quit.

39

GONE GIRL

A few days before Thanksgiving, Kelsey ran away. Maybe we should have seen it coming.

* * *

"Can you talk?" Brit asked when I picked up the phone. It was the week before Thanksgiving, a Thursday night, no kids.

"What's going on?" I said. I'd just gotten home from work and James would be another hour or more. We rarely ate dinner together on weeknights, so I rummaged in the fridge, phone wedged against my ear, searching for some kind of meal. I found a bowl of leftover pasta and put it in the microwave, stepping away from its hum so I could hear Brit more clearly.

"Well, you know that Kelsey and I had been getting along great for months, right? Up until a few weeks ago everything was perfect. She'd hug me when I came home from work; she'd hang in the kitchen and help me make dinner . . . it was all good."

I nodded, forgetting that Brit couldn't see me, but she kept talking.

"But recently, as we told you, Yvette's been kinda messing with her head. And Kelsey gets real anxious on Sundays when she's supposed to spend time with her mom. You guys have seen this."

"Yeah," I confirmed.

"So, this past Saturday night, Kels couldn't get ahold of Yvette. Her phone broke, so she was using Lee's, and she kept calling and calling, but Yvette wouldn't answer. Meanwhile she was getting frantic, like she's never going to talk to her mom again, right? Finally, Lee suggested that she send a text, since maybe Yvette didn't realize it was Kelsey calling from Lee's number. That worked and they made plans for the next morning. Kelsey calmed down, we went back to watching TV, and I thought: crisis averted."

The microwave beeped and I pulled out my pasta and set it on the kitchen counter. Hoisting myself up beside it, I leaned against the cabinets and ate as Brit continued her story.

"So, Sunday morning we got up and made breakfast. Lee wanted an omelet, but we were out of eggs, so he ran around the corner to get some. I was chopping veggies in the kitchen when Kelsey came in, happy and normal, excited for her day. She said her mom would be there in a few minutes and she wanted to see our new puppy. Okay, great. She went off to finish getting ready and I kept making breakfast.

"A few minutes later, Yvette called Kelsey on Lee's phone—he didn't take it with him—and Kels took the call in the other room. When she hung up, she seemed really anxious. She said, 'Mom doesn't want to see the dog right now. She's here, I gotta go, bye.' And then she ran out the door.

"Well, that made me a little concerned, so I went and peeked out the window, and Kelsey was walking away down the street. She disappeared around the corner and I thought: Maybe she's meeting her mom halfway to the BART station. Sometimes she does that.

"Then Lee's phone started to ring. I saw that it was Yvette calling, so I let it go to voicemail. But she called back three times in a row. And suddenly, Kelsey burst back into the house, totally panicked. She made a beeline for the phone and answered it, and I could tell from her side of the conversation that Yvette was *not* happy. Kelsey kept saying, 'I'm sorry, I misunderstood, I'm sorry.' I could tell that she was holding back tears. So again, I was really concerned."

I wrinkled my nose. That sounded a little too familiar.

"When she hung up the phone I asked her, 'Is everything okay?' And she *yelled* at me. 'It's nothing! I misunderstood what she said! She's not here yet!' Bear in mind, she didn't yell at her mom."

Of course not.

"So, I said, 'Is there something going on that I need to know? You seem really upset.' And then she burst into tears and screamed at me, 'No, nothing! Leave me alone! You are not my mom!'"

I felt a deep pang of sympathy for Brit. I knew that scenario all too well.

"I followed her into the other room and said, very calmly, 'I will never try to be your mom. I was just asking you a question because I'm concerned. Why are you angry with me? Can you tell me what I did?' And I kept my voice so calm, Marie, I swear, but inside I was really pissed. And then Kels totally flipped her lid and screamed, 'Nothing's

410

wrong! Leave me alone!' And she ran outside screaming and disappeared down the street.

"Lee came back from the grocery store, and I told him what happened, and he ran outside to find Kelsey. He brought her back and made her apologize, but it was the most insincere apology ever, and I could tell she didn't mean a word of it. Then her mom pulled up in a new Mercedes CLK—no way that was her car—and Kelsey ran out the door and they drove away."

"Geez," I said. "That sounds rough."

"Yeah." Brit heaved a deep sigh. "So, Kels came home on Monday, but she won't speak to me. She hasn't spoken to me all week. For punishment, Lee told her to write a little essay that included an apology and some ideas about how she can better handle her stress on the days that she's meeting her mom."

I made a little noise of approval.

"Pretty good punishment, right? Except what Kelsey wrote instead was an essay about how *I* should have handled things better." I grimaced.

Brit went on, "What the hell? I mean, I know she's just a kid, but I'm really hurt, and I don't understand how this is my fault. Is it because I took her dad away? Because I'm not her mom? What the fuck did I do?"

I sighed in solidarity. "I'm sorry, Brit."

"I don't know how you guys have dealt with this over the last year," she said. "I'm used to Kelsey being a sweet, affectionate kid. She's never behaved like this toward me before. How do you deal with it?"

How indeed? "Well, first of all, I think Kelsey is starting to realize that her mom is not a very good parent . . . and you are. And she doesn't know what to do with that. She loves Yvette terribly and she wants her to be better at mothering, and she probably resents you for treating her well because you're not her mom." I shifted to a more comfortable position on the countertop.

"She's basically crippled with anxiety every weekend because she's afraid that this is the day her mom won't show up. It's happened before. And she lost her little brother, too, right? It's not inconceivable that one day she just won't get to see her mom again."

Brit was quiet, listening, and I warmed to my role as therapist. Countless sessions with Ilana had rubbed off, apparently.

"She can't yell at her mom because you don't yell at the person you're afraid won't come back. So she unloads on you."

"Is she trying to chase me away?" Brit asked. "Does she think I'll split and it will just be her and Lee again?"

"Maybe," I said. "Or maybe she feels comfortable crapping on you because she knows you won't leave." I thought about Avery.

"Sometimes I think about leaving," confided Brit. "It's been really awful here these last few weeks. I love Lee and he's been on my side, but ultimately, he has to put his kid first, you know? And that kind of scares me, the idea of marrying somebody who always has to put his kid first."

"I understand that," I said seriously.

"So how do I handle it? What do I do?" she asked me.

"Get yourself a therapist," I told her.

"You think?"

"*Yes.* I don't know how else I'd get by."

* * *

412

The next day Kelsey didn't come home from school. Police tracked her to her mother's apartment in Daly City—and after confirming that she was all right, they allowed her to remain in Yvette's care.

"Okay, fill us in," James said when we arrived at their house for Thanksgiving dinner. The girls were with Jessica, so we four adults spent a quiet holiday together. Brit cooked a small meal and we gathered around their kitchen table to get the lowdown. "What exactly happened?"

"Yvette pulled Kelsey out of school last Friday," Lee said. "I don't know if she and Kelsey planned it, or if she just came and took her, but Kels never came home. Kelsey's phone is still broken, and Yvette wouldn't answer *her* phone, so I called the police. They found her right away and they told me that she's fine, but I still haven't talked with her. Yvette won't answer my calls."

"Okay, but why is she still there?" I asked. "Isn't she supposed to be with you?"

Lee shrugged. "I'm not going to force her to come home. My feelings are hurt and she scared the shit out of me, but if she wants to spend Thanksgiving break with her mom, well, I guess that's all right. She'll be back for school on Monday."

But Kelsey didn't come back on Monday. She didn't come back the entire week. Or the week after that.

"I don't understand what's happening," I said to James. "Is she going to school?" He'd talked to Lee on the phone.

"I think so," said James. "It sounds like she's been getting herself to school, but she's missed a few days and she's been tardy a lot."

"Why can't Lee just call the cops and have her brought home?" I asked, troubled.

"Because Yvette has legal custody of Kelsey during the week."

I had forgotten this. Apparently, Lee never ironed out his custody arrangement with Yvette, but for years she'd been too strung out or disinterested to claim Kelsey during the week. Now, for the first time, she was asserting her parental rights, and Lee had no legal recourse.

"But what about the weekends? Doesn't he get to see her then?" I was sure Lee must get visitation.

"Yeah, I guess, but it sounds like she won't come willingly. And unless he gets the law involved, there's not much he can do. He'd have to take Yvette to court, but I think right now he's just shell-shocked."

Pain squeezed my heart. I was distraught for our friends. James was affected, too. The situation felt much too close to home.

Annabelle and Avery reacted impassively to the news.

"Do you think they knew?" I asked James behind our bedroom door.

"No . . . I think Annie looked a little surprised."

"What about Avery?" I hadn't been home when he'd told them the news.

"She didn't have much of a reaction, but I think she's less impacted. Kelsey is more Annabelle's friend than Avery's."

I sank onto our bed and bit absently on my thumbnail, a nervous habit. "What did you tell them exactly?"

"Just that Kelsey is living with her mum for a while, and we're not sure for how long. And Lee's hoping she comes home soon, but we don't know what's going to happen."

I looked at him. "You didn't tell them she ran away?"

He shook his head. "No. It seemed like too much."

I wasn't sure I agreed with this, but admittedly I had no idea what to tell them.

James sat beside me on the bed. "The upsetting part was that the girls were totally supportive of Kelsey living with her mum. They both said that's what she wants, so of course she should be with Yvette." A fleeting look of hurt passed over his face.

"Yeah, they would say that. But they have no idea what Yvette is like." I shook my head, upset.

James rubbed his chest, like he had heartburn or something. "I don't like this," he told me. "It hurts all over again."

I knew what he meant.

40

SHITTY CHRISTMAS

Ilana bumped me from her weekly rotation. Now a fully accredited therapist with rates to match, she'd given me the option of paying full price or stepping out of the coveted Tuesday night time slot. Given our financial situation, I cut back to twice-monthly sessions, fitting in wherever she had the space. Sometimes we had a phone session, though I didn't care for these as much—even though I could attend in my pajamas and drink a beer while we talked.

But the weeks leading up to Christmas were busy, and I was stressed enough over the Kelsey situation that I thought a phone appointment might be a good idea. So, on a Thursday night I hunkered down in my bedroom—with a beer—and settled in for Ilana's call.

James was out with Lee and the girls were with their mother. Today marked the start of their winter break and they were supposed to be with us, but Avery had begged to stay in Vacaville an extra day so she could attend a friend's Christmas party. James agreed, as long as Jessica allowed the girls to stay an extra day with us on the other end. Avery never reported back, so we assumed Jessica had consented.

I leaned against the bed pillows and tried to explain to Ilana why I was so stressed about the kid down the street.

"My heart breaks for Lee, but I think it's Brittany's situation that upsets me the most," I realized.

"You relate to her perspective," Ilana said.

"Yeah. It's hard to step into someone else's family. And she's done everything she can to love that kid, but Kelsey's just lashing out." I told her about the notes that Lee had found in Kelsey's room: "Brit is an ugly dyke" and others like it.

"This is supposed to be the happiest time of her life. She's supposed to be planning her wedding, and instead everything is on hold while they—"

I was interrupted by the doorbell. Surprised, I asked Ilana if she would please hold. Padding down the stairs in my sock feet, I looked out the window to see Avery and Annabelle standing on our doorstep. Jessica's car idled in the driveway.

"The kids are here," I said into the phone.

"I take it you weren't expecting them?" Ilana asked.

"No, this is a total surprise. I'm so sorry, I'm going to have to go."

"No problem," she assured me. "Let's reschedule for next week—just give me a call, okay?"

"Thanks." I hung up and opened the door. The girls filed into the house, mumbling hellos, and went straight up to their bedroom. As soon as she saw me, Jessica pulled away.

Confused, I followed the kids upstairs. "Uh, hi guys," I said, standing in their doorway. Annabelle was sitting on her bed, arms crossed, leaning up against the wall. She was still wearing her coat, a graying white jacket that sorely needed a wash. She looked mutinous.

Avery was kneeling on the floor, busying herself with her schoolbooks, stacking them in a tidy pile. She didn't look up at me.

"This is a surprise," I said. "We weren't expecting you tonight."

Avery shrugged. Annabelle just stared at a spot on the wall beyond my head.

I wasn't sure what to say. "Um, what are you doing here?"

"Mom said we're here tonight." Avery's voice sounded funny, as though she'd been crying. When she lifted her face, I saw that her eyes were red and blotchy.

I made my voice gentle. "Well, yes, that's what the schedule says, but I thought you were going to spend the night in Vacaville so you could go to your friend's party tomorrow." There was no response. "Also, isn't it your mom's birthday today?"

"Yeah."

"And didn't she know that we were fine with you guys staying there tonight?"

"Yeah."

"So, why are you missing the party and your mom's birthday?"

"Mom said we're here tonight."

Avery's strangled tone suggested that more tears might be on the way, so I thought I ought to leave her alone. I glanced at her sister, still sitting motionless against the wall. "You okay Annabelle?"

"Fine."

I eased my way out of their room. Downstairs, I gave James a quick call to let him know the kids were home.

"I know," he said. "Avery called me from the Home Depot parking lot, wondering where I was. I told her I wasn't expecting them tonight and I was out, so their mother could either bring them back tomorrow or drop them at the home with you." *Ah, so that was why she'd come directly to our house.*

"Do you think she ruined Avery's plans on purpose because she didn't want to compromise with you?" That seemed like a risky move—and a shitty thing to do to her kid.

But James said, "I'm sure of it. Avery said her mom had approved of the party—until I told her I expected an even time swap. She didn't want to give me a day back with the kids on the other end."

"So she ruined her own birthday?" This seemed preposterous to me.

"She's a professional martyr, remember?" A burst of noise came through the phone, sounds of the rowdy bar around him.

"How's Lee doing?" I asked.

"Not so great. He hasn't said much, but he looks terrible."

I frowned. "Well, give him a hug from me."

It was a subdued Christmas. James and I hadn't bought gifts for each other, and the girls didn't have anything for us, so we spent Christmas afternoon watching the kids open their presents. I took little joy in it this year. Every time the girls opened something from me, they gave me a cursory hug with all the warmth of a robot. It felt so fake I could hardly stand it, and after a few of these empty embraces, I told them to stop. James looked at me, surprised. I could see the gentle reproach on his face and I felt terrible. My nerves were tangled up like Christmas lights, but that wasn't the girls' fault.

Up the road, Lee and Brit's holiday played out like a bad dream. Kelsey had spent her Christmas break with Lee's sister, Karen, in Redding. I was surprised that she wanted to spend the holiday with Lee's family when she seemed to want nothing to do with *him,* but the plans had been made ages ago, and Karen worked hard to keep them in place. She made nice with Yvette and convinced her that she was a neutral party, so she could keep her connection with Kelsey intact.

Karen reported to Lee that Kelsey did not seem well. She was high-strung and jittery; she'd put on weight and was prone to bouts of crying. At the end of the week, Lee spoke to Kelsey for the first time since she'd run away. He reminded her that school started on Monday, and Kelsey freaked out, certain that she'd had another week off.

The next morning, a Saturday, Karen called Lee again. They hadn't been able to get ahold of Yvette, and Kelsey was in a panic. She took the phone, crying, and begged her dad to come get her.

So Lee drove the six-hour round trip to pick up Kelsey in Redding. She cried much of the way home, pausing long enough to leave Yvette a voicemail: "Don't bother getting out of bed. My dad came to pick me up." It took Lee hours to calm her down, but after a good talk, Kelsey seemed to unwind.

Later that evening, Yvette finally called Kelsey back. They argued, and Kelsey said she was at her dad's and she wanted to stay there.

Then Yvette said the words that shattered her daughter: *"Fine. I don't want you anymore."*

Kelsey unraveled. She cried herself sick. She followed Lee and Brit around the house, unwilling to be left alone for even a moment. Unsure what to do, they pulled an air mattress into their room and let her sleep at the foot of their bed.

The next day, Sunday, Lee and Brit did everything they could think of to distract Kelsey. They took her to the dog park and signed her up for programs at the YMCA. They even promised to buy her another puppy if it would only make her smile, make her calm, make her stop crying. She spent another night at the foot of their bed.

"I don't know what to do," Brit texted me from the bathroom. "This is serious shit. I can hear her crying, 'I want my mom' as I type this. I'm afraid she might be suicidal."

But the next day Kelsey seemed a little bit calmer. Lee drove to her to school, and before he dropped her off he asked her, "Are you home for good?"

Composed and apologetic, Kelsey said, "Yes, I'm home for good." She gave her dad a hug and waved goodbye as he pulled away.

The moment Lee was out of sight, Kelsey borrowed a phone and called Yvette, who arrived an hour later and pulled her out of school.

"Is she okay? Are you guys okay?" I stood in the hallway outside my office, spurred to call Brit after the torrent of texts she'd been sending.

"Kelsey's okay. Lee is a mess. She just called him and asked him to send her birth certificate so Yvette can enroll her in school in Daly City."

"*What?*"

"Yeah. She was totally nonchalant. 'Oh, hi Dad. Can you mail my birth certificate?'"

"What did Lee say?"

"He said, 'Kels, I don't think this is the right time for you to be asking for that.' And then Yvette got on the phone and started cussing him out."

"I don't believe this. I just don't believe it!"

"Yeah, well, it's happening. I had to leave work to go comfort Lee. Now *he* won't stop crying."

Kelsey was truant for the rest of the week. On Friday, Lee filed a police report when Kelsey didn't come home. This was on the advice of his lawyer, who urged Lee to file a report every time that Yvette withheld his visitation. Finally spurred to legal action, Lee was challenging Yvette's custody and the lawyer seemed to think he had a slam dunk case. Between the truancy, her intent to switch schools without Lee's consent, and the withheld visitation, Kelsey's situation was less that of a runaway than a kidnapping, and Yvette was clearly at fault. So, as the weekends clicked by, Lee filed report after report with the police, hopeful that this mounting evidence would count in his favor at the court date, which had been set for early April.

But Yvette was amassing evidence, too. She had Kelsey write out a list of reasons why she didn't want to live with her father. Kelsey alleged that Lee was neglectful and Brit was abusive. She claimed to be afraid to return to their home.

Lee was heartbroken, shuffling through the days like a sleepwalker. And Brit was in a dark place, a place that I recognized. I tried to help her, but I didn't have the means.

"Did you find a therapist yet?" I asked her.

I could almost hear her shrug over the phone. "I don't really see how a therapist can help. It's just a god-awful situation. Lee is an absolute wreck, a shell of himself. Sometimes he talks about giving up, and I've been encouraging him to keep fighting, but . . . " Her voice caught a little. "After hearing what you and James went through, I just know, deep down, that he's going to lose."

"Brit—"

"It's never going to be about you and me, Marie! We will always be second to those kids. I can't live with that, and there is no therapy out there that can convince me otherwise. This is my *life*, and I don't want to spend the good parts waiting for someone else to figure *their* life out! I know it's selfish. I know it is. But it's my life."

Her words sliced through me and I felt their pain so acutely that I didn't know where her grief ended and mine began. Could I live with a love where I always came second? *Was that what I had?*

"I'm thinking about moving home to Chicago," Brit was saying. "My family and my best friends are there; I have a much better support system back home. I love Lee and I want to be with him, but I just don't know if I can make it through this. I don't see it ending, you know?" She sniffed a little, and I realized that she was crying.

I was silent for a moment, waiting for the right words to arrive. "Brit," I finally said. "I really hope that you don't go. But I know that you have to do what's right for you.

"But before you make any decisions, please talk to Lee. Make sure he understands how you're feeling and what you're thinking of doing. He's a good guy and he loves you so much. He's just been dealt a shitty hand. He's got to make his own choices, too, but he deserves to know what he's choosing. And don't forget—that man proposed to you. That's more than I've gotten." Brit made a small noise of acquiescence. "Don't walk away from that without talking, *really talking* it through with him, okay? You both deserve that."

Now Brit was silent, waiting for the words to come to her.

"I want to say one more thing," I went on. "If Lee loses . . . well, there's life after losing. I didn't used to think so. You didn't know us during the actual trial—that was really the worst part. I thought that if James lost his kids, he'd be broken. I thought we'd break, too. And I stressed so hard about it, because I didn't want to lose him.

"But he did lose his kids, and life went on. We didn't break up; we moved in together. And there's been a lot of tough stuff in the aftermath, but we've survived. We have a home together, we're carving out a life together. Soon enough the kids will be moving on, but we still have lots to look forward to in the years ahead. That's worth remembering. Okay?"

After a pause, Brit said quietly, "Okay."

"Good," I said. "Love you, my friend."

"Love you, too."

* * *

Annabelle was depressed.

In the weeks that followed Kelsey's disappearance, Annabelle maintained staunch support for her friend. But as the weeks turned to months and it became clear that Kelsey wasn't coming back, she seemed a little lost. Over the past year the girls had become as close as sisters, spending nearly every weekend together, and Kelsey had left without saying goodbye. Annabelle was hurt, but she couldn't show it. It was like a throwback to our custody verdict—she seemed confused and utterly unprepared for the reality of the situation she had championed. Once again, she'd backed the wrong team.

She moped around the house, clearly lonely, but when we asked if she was missing Kelsey she denied it haughtily. She masked her sadness in arrogance.

Avery, by contrast, seemed positively chipper. She liked Kelsey, but as James pointed out, Annabelle and Kelsey were closer, being the same age. Avery had not enjoyed being the third wheel in their games, and she was not distressed when Kelsey stopped coming around every weekend. Avery would come into her maturity, but at barely fourteen she was still very much the center of her own world. You could tell she thought that circumstances had been unfairly weighted toward Annabelle this past year, and equilibrium had now been restored.

"Your sister seems down," I noted one evening after Annabelle had slunk off to her bedroom. "It's a lot quieter around here without Kelsey, huh?" Avery just shrugged.

"Are you sad that Kelsey's not around?" James asked her. I'd been hesitant to ask this question. I had a feeling the answer would be *no.*

Again, Avery shrugged. "Not really. Kelsey wants to be with her mom. I'm happy for her. And honestly, I'm glad for a little peace and quiet. Kelsey was over here a lot."

"Penelope used to be at our house a lot," James pointed out.

"Yeah, but Penelope never had screaming fits in our closet."

James and I looked at her sharply. "What are you talking about?" he asked.

"Kelsey. Sometimes she shut herself in our closet and screamed and cried." Avery spoke casually, as though it was no big deal. "Honestly, I'm surprised you never heard her."

Suddenly I remembered a night months before, when I thought I'd heard wailing coming from beyond our bedroom. We'd chalked it up to noise from the parking lot outside, but that must have been Kelsey, crying in the kids' closet.

"Why didn't you tell us, Ave?" I felt sick that I hadn't known. But Avery just shrugged again, and lifted her hands as if to say, "What would have you done about it?"

What indeed?

41

ENTER THE ICE QUEEN

Ken's wedding was less than two months away and the preparations were in high gear. As I walked past the Frontline office, I saw that Tracy and Felicia were gathered around his desk, watching him open a package. Curious, I joined them.

"This just came in the mail," Ken said, holding up a small box. He slipped off the lid and we all leaned in to see.

"Wow, your wedding ring!" I exclaimed. "Try it on!"

Ken slid the ring on his hand and held it out, opening and closing his fist experimentally.

"Huh," he said. "I've got hairy knuckles like a Hobbit."

The phone rang and we left him in peace to answer it. "I can't wait for this wedding," said Felicia as we walked back to our desks. "It's going to be like a glimpse into Ken's mind."

"It's outside, right?" I asked.

"Yes," said Tracy. "And we're all sitting on picnic blankets, so don't wear heels."

"Got it. What else do you know?"

"Well, there will be pineapples with googly eyes at the food stations. And the groomsmen are wearing blue capes. Actually, he's calling them 'knights'. Ken has knighted them all."

I grinned. *Of course he has.*

"Apparently the capes are Pia's breaking point," Tracy went on. Friends with both bride and groom, she was privy to the wedding details. "She asked her mother to 'lose' them on the way to the ceremony. At first her mom agreed, but now she's not sure she can do it. She said, 'Oh honey, after spending more time with Ken . . . well, he just seems so excited about the capes, I'm not sure I have the heart to misplace them.'"

Felicia snickered. "Like I said, I can't wait for this wedding."

* * *

Avery's good mood persisted. In early spring, it suddenly dawned on me that it had been months since she'd thrown a tantrum. The revelation surprised me, and I tried to pinpoint the last time I'd seen her upset. It was before Christmas, I thought, but I couldn't quite remember when . . .

And then I landed on it: Jessica's birthday. The night that Jess had dropped the kids off at our house unexpectedly and Avery missed her friend's party.

The connection seemed too neat. I wondered if that was reason enough for Avery to flip off her tantrums like a light switch, but it appeared that's what she'd done. The more I thought about it, the more I realized that Avery had been well-behaved—arguably *pleasant*—for months. We'd just been too distracted to notice.

I continued to walk on eggshells around her, too conditioned by her hair-trigger temper to relax in its absence, but as time went by I couldn't deny that Avery appeared to be a changed kid.

Unfortunately, so was Annabelle.

It was like the departure of Avery's temper had made room for Annabelle's anger. But where Avery had been all wrath and firestorm, Annabelle was an ice queen.

She would make her face a mask of detachment. Annabelle rarely cried, but she *removed* herself, shutting the door on you with a look. And when she turned that look on me, I'd curdle, just as I'd done when faced with Avery's tantrums.

I realized that both girls had inherited aspects of their mother's personality: Avery with her rages, her fingernail-gouging, acid-tongued furies, and Annabelle with her absence, her cold, blank eyes and her withheld affection. Her mask made her unapproachable. She was *Thank you for your email* personified.

But I worried about her. Without Kelsey, she dragged through the weekends, miserable. I tried to get her to invite Bibi or Gahar over to play, but she refused.

"How come, Annabelle?" I asked.

"Because I don't want to," she said.

"But you seem bored."

"Well, I'm not." She flashed me a frosty look.

"I know it's a little lonely without Kelsey around," I said, pushing my luck.

"No, it's not. And I don't want to invite my friends over, so stop asking." She got up and left the room.

Once again, I hunted for a weekend activity that would give her something to do. Choices were still slim, but to my delight I found a spring session of the rowing program that Avery had done last summer. It seemed like the perfect thing.

Annabelle wanted nothing to do with it.

"No," she said flatly.

"Are you sure? I think you might really like it," I pressed. "Avery enjoyed rowing camp last summer, didn't you, Ave?"

"Yup," she said, ever cheerful.

"I don't care," said Annabelle.

"Annie," I said, "I'd like to—"

"My name is *not* Annie."

I sighed. "Annabelle. I'd like to get you involved in something. You need to make more friends, kiddo. Kelsey may not be coming back for a while, and I don't want you to be so unhappy. Why don't we give this a shot?"

Annabelle stood up like she intended to leave the room, which was no surprise. But I was taken aback to see tears in her eyes. Maybe I'd hit a nerve when I'd said that Kelsey might not be coming back.

She ran up the stairs and shut herself in the bathroom, slamming the door as her sister used to do. When she hadn't emerged after twenty minutes, I went upstairs to talk to her. As I approached the bathroom, intending to knock, I heard Annabelle's muffled voice from behind the bathroom door. It sounded as though she was talking to somebody. Quietly I approached the door and listened.

She was crying. In between tears I could hear her saying, "Yeah. Uh-huh." I realized that she was on the phone.

Then, in a furious whisper that carried right under the door, Annabelle exclaimed, "But Mom, she's trying to make me *do stuff!* She wants me to *have fun!*" And then she burst into fresh tears, crying as hard as I'd ever heard her.

I drew back from the door as though I'd been burned. Still I could hear her, murmuring assent to whatever Jessica was telling her on the other end of the phone. "Okay. I know. I'll try to."

You'll try to what? I wondered. *You'll try to bear with me and all the awful fun I'm forcing you to have?*

What was Jessica saying to her? What possible response could any rational mother have, except to acknowledge the effort I was making? Somehow, I didn't think that was it.

I crept away from the bathroom door, angry and hurt. And I thought, not for the first time: *Screw you, kid.*

On Monday, James got a message from Annabelle on the Family Planner:

Dad, I want to spend next weekend with Mom.

"Not this again," he complained and deleted Annabelle's account. The next day it had been renewed.

Dad, I want to spend next weekend with my mother.

James called Annabelle, who didn't pick up. "If you want to talk about something, call me," he said to her voicemail. "But this website is not going to be how we communicate. Got it?"

She didn't get it. The next day she sent another message.

"Fuck this," James said. "This is ridiculous. Her mum puts her up to this. I could delete her account a hundred times, and she'll just keep recreating it."

So James deleted his own account instead. He sent one last message to Jessica, explaining exactly why, and then he cut the digital cord, setting himself free.

"How are you going to stay in touch with her now?" I asked. "You still have to coordinate around the kids."'

"We've got our settlement conference coming up soon," he said. "I expect the judge will tell her she's got to unblock me. She can text or call me, like a normal person."

* * *

On a Sunday afternoon without the kids, James and I walked arm in arm to a little bakery in the neighborhood. We were meeting Lee and Brit for coffee—and cheesecake, if I had my way. As we approached the bakery from across the street, I saw that Lee and Brit had already claimed a table on the sidewalk. Looking closer, I realized there was somebody with them. "Is that Kelsey?" I asked.

It was. My eyes met Brit's and she gave a little shrug. She and Lee greeted us with hugs, but it was clear that they couldn't talk about the elephant on the sidewalk: the runaway teenager, returned.

I hadn't seen Kelsey in months. She seemed a different kid: older, and harder, somehow. I noted the chipped black polish on her bitten nails, the streaks of fading blue in her long, unbrushed hair.

Lee gave us a half-smile that indicated he'd fill us in later. I assumed Kelsey's return was a surprise since he and Brit hadn't mentioned it when we'd made our plans. They really wanted to see us, Brit had said. It had been a little while since we'd gotten together.

Now we crowded around the small table, with Kelsey sitting awkwardly off to the side. Once she realized the kids weren't around, she busied herself with her phone.

"We have some news," Lee said. *Clearly,* I thought, glancing at Kelsey, but Brit gave a small shake of her head.

"We're pregnant," she said.

I was stunned. I looked from her to Lee, whose smile had grown broader. Brit was smiling, too. Joy flared in my heart, a new hope blooming for my friends who had been through so much.

"You *guys,*" I said, feeling tears gathering in my eyes. I threw my arms around Lee, who was closest, then made my way around the table to Brit and wrapped her in a hug. James was grinning broadly; Lee was laughing. Kelsey continued to stare at her phone.

"How do you feel?" I asked Brittany.

She glanced at Kelsey, and I knew she was tempering her reply. "I'm really excited," she said, but she kept her tone measured. *"We're* really excited." She nodded at Lee, who reached over and took her hand.

"I am so happy for you!" It was true. The bloom of hope was still unfurling in my chest, making me feel light and almost giddy.

Brit glowed at me. "Thanks. We're really glad to have you guys as friends. We hope you two can be a part of our baby's growth." I glanced at James and saw that his eyes were wet.

"Now we just need to come up with a really good name. Like, an awesome name," said Lee.

"Why don't you just call the kid Awesome?" I suggested.

"Awesome Sampson," mused Brit. "I like it."

It seemed that Kelsey had come home of her own volition the previous Friday night, just turning up as though it were a regular weekend occurrence. Lee was afraid to ask what had prompted her return, so he too acted like it was no big deal. Kelsey returned to Yvette's on Sunday night—but the following weekend she went back to Lee's house, in accordance with their custody arrangement, which they had never followed.

"Do you think this is a ploy for court?" I wondered. Lee and Yvette's trial was next month. "Is Yvette trying to appear compliant?"

James frowned. "I don't know." I knew what he was thinking: it didn't seem to take much for a woman with a grudge to pull one over on a judge.

* * *

Our own court date rolled around the following week. Once again, I pestered James to prepare with me, pulling out my notes from the previous hearing.

"I think we summed it up pretty well in this document," I said, referring to the short brief with the long name: Reply to Petitioner's Responsive Declaration to Request for Order.

"It hits all the main points. But it's not exactly conversational, so I've re-written it as more of a presentation." I indicated the papers in my hand. "Now, it's been a few months since the last hearing, so it's probably best if you can offer the judge a recap. It's all here, so all you have to do is read it, okay?" I started to read it out loud to him.

As I turned the page I realized that James was wearing a tight expression. "What?" I asked him.

"Nothing."

But as I returned to my reading, he lay his hand over the paper, forcing me to trail off. "What are you doing?"

"I know what to say, Marie. I'm just going to put it in my own words."

I frowned, remembering that James' own words hadn't always served him well in court. "But I've already written everything down for you." And it was good, I knew it was. "Why don't you just refer to this?"

"Because it's too . . . " he paused, searching for the right word. "Long," he decided.

I bristled. "It is not too long. It's two pages."

"I just don't think I need to talk that much. The judge knows what I'm asking for. It's a reasonable request. I expect he'll just ask some questions and we'll answer them."

I felt a flicker of frustration. "Babe, that's not how Jessica operates and you know it. She's going to go in there with plans to make you look bad and you need to beat her to the punch." I stopped. I hadn't meant to say that, exactly. "I just mean you have to be prepared to defend yourself. You need a clear argument that puts your points forth right away, before she has time to twist the situation."

I knew I was being pushy, even a bit condescending, but I couldn't help myself. I got like this every time a court date approached. I had a desperate need to be in the driver's seat, to have control over something.

But James didn't like being controlled. "I've got it, thanks." He left the room, signaling the end of our discussion.

The next night, the night before the hearing, I found him in our little office at bedtime, rifling through papers. "What are you looking for?" I asked.

"We were supposed to Meet and Confer," he said, flipping through the binders I'd carefully prepared for our previous court dates.

"Well, that's a laugh," I replied. "I assume Jessica told you to shove it?"

"Yeah, but I can't find that letter. I need to show evidence that I at least made the attempt." He tossed the binders on the floor in a heap.

"Is it in the Family Planner?"

"Oh yeah. Shit," he said, remembering that he'd closed his account.

"It's okay, I printed everything." I handed him a binder with all the Family Planner materials, including sixty-four messages from Jessica that said only: "Thank you for your email."

He took it from me, absently, but did not say thank you.

"Are you coming to bed?" I asked.

"Soon."

"Can I help you?"

"No. Thanks."

I didn't go with James to court the next day. I wasn't allowed to be part of the settlement conference, so there didn't seem any reason to take off work.

He sent me a text midafternoon:

Lost.
Again.

I found him that evening sitting on the couch with a beer in his hand, flipping channels on the TV. He looked exhausted, which was the norm, but he greeted me with a weird, caustic grin.

"What happened?" I asked, shedding my coat and kicking off my shoes.

James muted the TV. "Well, I don't exactly know," he said.

"But you lost."

"Yep, I lost. I lost across the board. I lost shit I didn't even ask for."

"What are you talking about?" *How could he lose something he hadn't asked for?*

"Oh, Jess complained that the exchange point wasn't halfway between our houses anymore, so now on Sunday nights I have to drive the girls all the way up to Vacaville instead of ten minutes to Home Depot."

"Shit!" I sank onto the couch beside him. "That sucks! Tell me you don't have to drive both ways."

"No, she's gotta drop the girls at our house on Friday nights. The idea is that the kids can let themselves inside if one of us is a few minutes late, so that's good, at least. I'll give Avery a house key."

"But what else happened?" I asked.

"Well, Jess argued that she couldn't get the kids to Oakland by four o'clock because of Avery's class schedule, and the judge agreed to set the exchange time at six o'clock."

"But that's crap!" I exclaimed. Avery got out of class only ten minutes later than last year. We'd finally learned this once James had proved his identity to the school and been allowed to see her schedule.

"Yep. Let's see . . . I lost the request to keep the kids for Sunday overnights. Jess said that the commute to school would be too long on Monday mornings, and the judge agreed." James took a long pull on his beer.

"So how does he plan to adjust your parenting time, since she's stealing two hours from you each week?"

"He doesn't."

"What?"

"And I lost the bid to get the girls therapy. Oh, and Jess doesn't need to reply to my texts or emails, according to the judge. We should just pass messages back and forth through the kids." He gave a bitter little laugh. "I'm sure that's healthy for them."

I was incensed. I sat up straight and put my hands on my hips. "James, did you stick up for yourself at all?"

"I tried."

"Well, did you read the remarks I prepared?"

He stared beyond me at the silent television. "I didn't really have a chance to read them. That wasn't how it worked."

"Well, how did it work?" I persisted.

"I told you . . . the judge asked a few questions and we answered them."

"And did Jessica have remarks prepared?"

There was a pause before he answered. "Yeah."

I stood up and walked out of the room before I could say something that I'd regret. But I was furious. Once again Jessica, with her flimsy arguments, had trounced James in the courtroom. But this time I felt that James hadn't prepared. I was upset that he'd resisted all my efforts to help.

Dimly it occurred to me that if I hadn't pushed so hard, James might've come through on his own. I hadn't been supporting him so much as directing him. But I didn't give the thought room to mature. I was too angry that I'd been emotionally drawn into yet another battle that I wasn't allowed to fight.

Thus began a new chapter in Jessica's Passive Aggressive Handbook. On Friday evenings she would bring the girls to our house by five-thirty—despite having campaigned for a six o'clock exchange. Then she and the girls would sit in our driveway for half an hour, with Avery sending us nervous texts every few minutes: "When u home?"

"I don't understand; why won't you use the house key we gave you?" James asked her.

"Just because," said Avery. She made a little face like she was embarrassed.

"Because why?"

"Because Mom doesn't want us to be home alone in a dangerous neighborhood," Annabelle supplied. Her tone suggested that not only was this obvious, but that she agreed.

James shot her an exasperated look. "Have you told your mum that you've been home alone before?" Silence greeted this question.

"Look, I can't get home before six," James said. "I scheduled my work hours around this new custody arrangement. So why don't you guys leave Vacaville a half hour later?"

But the following Friday they were there again at five-thirty. "U home soon?" texted Avery.

And again, the following week. "How far out r u?"

"If you're going to arrive so early, why don't you go to a coffee shop or hang out at the lake?" James was baffled by Jessica's behavior.

"Mom would never hang out in Oakland. It's too—"

"Dangerous. Yeah, I know. So, your mum would really rather sit in our driveway for half an hour than go spend time with you guys?"

"She is spending time with us," Annabelle said, defensive.

"You two were reading in the car," James pointed out.

"It's still quality time together," she retorted.

"Annabelle, it's silly. Don't you ask her why she insists on sitting in the driveway?"

Annabelle gave him an icy look. "No, I don't. That's her business, not mine." She went up to her room.

Some Fridays James would get stuck in traffic and I'd be the first one home. Walking from BART, I'd approach the house from the back, up the long staircase that led from the road below. As I climbed, nerves would steal over me and my heart would begin to pound double-time. Sometimes I would have to stop and hold onto the railing until I could catch my breath. If I knew Jessica was waiting in our driveway, I would begin to feel physically ill. I finally understood how James felt when he faced her. She had hurt us so often that we'd become afraid of her, and now she was the first thing we saw when we came home on the weekend, blocking us from entering our own driveway.

One Friday I got off work early and was ascending the staircase at five-thirty. Right on time, Avery's text lit up my phone: "How far out?"

I saw the back of Jessica's car and felt the familiar nausea, the racing pulse. I paused at the side of the house and leaned on the railing until my breath returned to normal.

Avery's text flashed again and I shot back a reply: "Use your key."

Stand up to your mom is what I meant.

Her response came immediately. "But how far out?"

I peered around the corner. I could see the backs of both girls' heads through the rear window of Jessica's car. Retreating a few steps down the staircase, I sat down where they couldn't see me, banking on the fact that the girls wouldn't get out of the car.

This is ridiculous, I thought. *If they want to sit in the driveway, they can sit in the goddamn driveway.*

"I'm about 20 minutes away," I wrote to Avery.

Then I pulled out my book and enjoyed a nice read.

42

MISCARRIAGE OF JUSTICE

Annabelle's misery was so palpable that against our better judgement, James and I suggested a visit with Kelsey. The girls hadn't seen each other in months. Annabelle knew her friend was home on the weekends now, but neither girl seemed willing to initiate a visit.

So James and Lee made good on a threat they'd been batting around for ages: a foot race around Lake Merritt. It seemed like a low-pressure way to get the kids together. We met on the green, where the guys ribbed each other good-naturedly.

"Prepare to be crushed," warned Lee. "I go running every week."

"Oh yeah? Still smoking those cigarettes?" James asked with a grin and Lee frowned.

They squared off on the lake path, facing away from each other.

"You're going to run in opposite directions?" I asked.

"I'm doing James a favor." Lee took his mark like an Olympic runner. "I don't want him eating my dust the whole way."

"I'm going to make you eat your words," James retorted.

"All right gentlemen, I want a clean race!" I said. "You're going to do the whole lake, including the inlet. The girls will follow you on bikes to keep you honest." Annabelle and Kelsey were wheeling back and forth in the dirt, waiting for the signal.

"On your mark . . . Get set . . . *Go!*"

The guys took off in opposite directions, but both girls followed Lee, quickly overtaking him and biking right past him. Within seconds they were out of sight.

"Huh," I said. "I guess we didn't think that through."

"They'll be fine." Brit gave a dismissive wave. "The path goes in a circle and they're together."

"True." I guess that was the point of this outing anyway.

"Where's Avery?" asked Brit.

"Oh, she's at home, watching makeup tutorials online." *And enjoying an hour of peace and quiet,* I surmised. The girls so rarely got privacy from one another. I sat down on a low tree branch and Brit sat beside me. "So, how's it going at home? Fill me in."

She gave a little snort. "It's weird." Her eyes followed Lee's retreating form. "We can't figure out what Kelsey is doing. She's been coming home on weekends like everything's normal, like she didn't run away four months ago. We never even learned *why* she ran away—I mean, I know her mom was behind it, but Kelsey never explained or apologized." Brit pulled off some loose tree bark and tossed it in the dirt. "Lee's so happy to have her home, but he's wary of her, you know? Kelsey does whatever she wants at Yvette's house. She doesn't have any rules. Last weekend Lee tried to make her clean her room and Kelsey just walked out! Just hopped on the BART and went back to her mom's."

"She goes back and forth on BART by herself? She's only twelve." Kelsey suddenly seemed years older than Annabelle, whose mother kept her locked safely in the car, even in our driveway.

"Yeah. Lee puts money on her transit card so she can always get home. We didn't think she'd come back after that, but she turned up last night like nothing had happened. And Lee didn't bring it up. He's afraid of scaring her off again."

I sighed. *What an awful situation.* Our house often felt out of control, but at least James knew his kids' whereabouts. There was no easy public transit option from Oakland to Vacaville, thank goodness.

"So when she's home, is she nice to you?" I asked. "Are you guys getting along okay?"

"Nah, she pretty much ignores me," Brit said. "And to be honest, I'm avoiding her—which is hard to do in a small house. But it just seems . . . prudent, I guess, to give her and Lee some space. I'm trying to avoid setting her off before our trial." Brit kicked at the dirt, scuffing her shoe. "But it sucks, man. I can't get any time alone with Lee. When Kelsey's home, he's fawning all over her. I don't mean to sound like a jerk, but I thought this was the time he'd be fawning all over *me*, you know?" She put a hand on her stomach, absentmindedly.

"How've you been feeling?"

Now Brit smiled. "Pretty good. A little bit of morning sickness, but nothing too bad." She chuckled. "We've been kicking around some names. Lee really likes Awesome Sampson. We're going to have to think of a real name that he likes better, otherwise I'm afraid he might try to use it."

I laughed. "Maybe you could use it for a middle name."

"No way!"

"Well, no matter what you name it, it's going to be one lucky kid." I smiled at my friend, and she smiled back.

"Thanks." Then a shadow crossed her face. "We've just gotta get through this god-awful trial and then we can focus on happier things."

"How's Lee doing? Is he ready for it?" Their trial was in two weeks. I had impressed upon Brit the importance of Lee being fully prepared.

"I think so," she said. "Kelsey's sleeping on the couch in a tiny apartment that her mom shares with her ex-drug dealer. It shouldn't be so hard to prove that Lee deserves custody." But she sounded uncertain.

Lee was the first to cross the finish line (hastily drawn in the dirt with a stick), but James came in just a minute behind him. I was secretly impressed; I'd thought Lee would clobber him. Lee staggered around, clutching his side, but James dropped straight to the grass and lay in a heap.

"You did pretty good, James," Lee allowed, breathing heavy. "You're faster than I thought. Just not fast enough." He smirked, then coughed.

"Maybe I should take up smoking," James said weakly from the ground.

"No, you shouldn't." Lee dropped to his knees beside him. "I feel like I'm gonna die."

"Where are the kids?" I wondered.

"They're doing another lap around the lake," said James. "They look like they're having fun."

They *were* having fun, I noticed, when they turned up on their bikes a short while later. But neither girl asked if they could extend the outing. The easy comfort between them had dissolved. We waved goodbye and headed home, slowly, James already discovering new aches and pains.

* * *

"Holy shit. You want a taste of crazy to make you laugh?" I was texting Brit.

> *Remember how I told you that James quit that Family Planner website? Well, tomorrow starts spring break and he and Jessica need to talk about schedule. But rather than answer his emails or texts, Jess wrote him a message on the Family Planner, printed it out, and MAILED IT TO HIS OFFICE.*

I laughed, I couldn't help it. Jessica had paid eight dollars to send the letter via priority mail. The woman had some twisted principles.

I popped off another quick text to Brit: "How are you feeling?"

She responded a few minutes later.

> *Wow, that lady is nuts.*
> *I'm good. Had a miscarriage.*
> *It's ok. We'll give it another shot.*

I gasped; my hand flew to my mouth. *Oh no!*

> *We found out last Wednesday when we went to the doctor. No heartbeat. I started bleeding this week. It's ok though. A shocker, but not the end.*

Tears pricked at my eyes. I didn't know how to reply. Brit's texts kept coming.

> *We were so excited, too. Still talking about baby names.*

446

Things with Kelsey are getting bad again. She ditched school on Friday. The police pinged her phone and found her at the Daly City fair. Yvette got to her first, and apparently Kelsey said that she ditched school because she didn't want to go back to her dad's. Lee went to the police station to pick her up, but the cops said Kels should be allowed to stay with her mom. So Yvette took her home. It wrecked Lee. Kelsey will be suspended for a day for ditching.

My heart felt like a rock in my chest. I still couldn't find the words to respond. Finally, I wrote: "You want to talk?"

Nah, I'm going to take a nap. These cramps are the worst. But if you or James don't have any plans later, could you maybe reach out to Lee? He's really upset and I'm in no condition to help him right now.

After promising Brit that we'd check in on Lee, I slumped against the couch and closed my eyes against tears. I felt like bawling. That baby had seemed like such a miracle, a bright spot in a dark time. It was like a promise that everything was going to be okay, a lifeline for Brit, just when she needed it most.

And now it was gone. I was devastated for my friends.

* * *

When Lee lost his custody trial, it felt like the world was coming down around our ears all over again.

It should have been a slam-dunk case. That's what his lawyer kept saying; that's what we'd all dared to believe.

447

But everything went wrong. None of the evidence seemed to matter: Kelsey's truancy, her plummeting grades, Yvette's failure to enforce any kind of discipline. Lee had tried to have Yvette drug-tested, but her lawyer refused it. He suggested instead that *Lee* get a drug test—and Lee's lawyer *concurred,* calling it a gesture of goodwill. But when Lee declined, somehow it was twisted against him. He came off looking like he had something to hide.

The most damning testimony was Yvette's assertion that Kelsey was cutting herself because she was so afraid of her father.

"Is she cutting herself?" asked James.

"I don't know," fretted Lee.

It was entirely possible, we all agreed. Kelsey was certainly acting erratic; she could have been hiding scars under long sleeves or pants. But the judge didn't request proof, and the case mediator boiled it down to the bones: whether or not she was cutting, Kelsey clearly had high anxiety. The best thing they could do was remove the source of that anxiety—and that was Lee.

"Bull-fucking-*shit* that's Lee!" I was furious. "Goddammit! She's anxious because her mother is making her *choose* between her parents! Why doesn't anyone see that?" I wanted to push over the table, to throw my beer bottle against Lee's kitchen wall. I remembered Kelsey's Christmas meltdown, sparked by Yvette's cruel words, *"Fine. I don't want you anymore."*

James looked like he might cry. Lee was crying, quietly, brushing tears from his lashes with a brusque hand. Brittany sat in the corner, dead silent. She looked dangerous, explosive.

"So what does this mean, Lee? Yvette maintains custody?" James looked at him, questioning.

"Yeah. Yvette will keep her. And I'm not allowed any contact with Kelsey."

"*What?*" I exclaimed.

"I can't call, text, or email my kid. The only thing I'm allowed to do is write her 'love notes' with pen and paper. And maybe in time I'll 'regain her trust'. That's what the judge said."

"Jesus Christ, Lee!" I hung my head, tears falling onto my lap. "Jesus Christ."

"But what about visitation?" James asked. "You must get her sometimes, right?"

Lee shook his head. "Not right now. That's to be revisited down the road."

"When?" I demanded.

Brit spoke for the first time. "Inconclusive." Her voice was gravelly. She twisted her engagement ring round and around her finger. The emerald caught the sun and threw little green prisms across the wall.

In bed that night James wept. I lay like a stone, heavy with feelings I'd hoped to never feel again.

It didn't matter that Kelsey wasn't our kid. Losing her ripped open all the old wounds and laid them raw.

Twice in two years I'd seen a judge separate a good man from his children despite his doing everything right. While the mothers did drugs and had affairs and walked out on their families, Lee and James had been pillars of love and stability for their daughters. And this is what they got for it. If I'd had any respect left for the family court, this destroyed it.

I wondered how Kelsey was feeling. Was she happy? Sad? Did she lay confused on the couch that was now her bed, questioning what she'd done?

I'd always been curious if the girls had any idea how rare it still was for children—girls in particular—to be raised by their fathers. Especially when their mothers were healthy and lived nearby. Why had they never made the connection that there was a *reason* they'd been raised by their dads? Why couldn't these kids see that their fathers had always been there for them, while their mothers came in and out of their lives?

I had a sudden flash of memory: "These girls want their momma." Rhonda, staring at me with her no-nonsense gaze. "The writing is on the wall, you know. Eventually these girls are going to go live with their mother."

I wrapped myself around James' shuddering form and held him tight, thinking that down the street, Brit must be doing the same for Lee.

We tried to see them every weekend, wanting to show our love and support, but it was hard. We couldn't help sharing their pain—couldn't even distinguish, sometimes, between their pain and ours—and each visit left us wrung out. James and I found ourselves arguing problems that weren't ours to solve.

Brit wanted to move to Portland. Lee's company had an office there, and he could put in for a transfer. "We need a fresh start," she said. "Kelsey made her choice. We're not allowed to see her, and we deserve lives of our own now."

Lee was stunned and indecisive. He nodded as Brit spoke, but seemed reluctant to leave Oakland. What if Kelsey needed him?

"I don't know, babe," I said to James later that night as we put fresh sheets on the bed. "I see both sides, but I think Brit might be right. They need a fresh start."

450

James shook a pillow into its case and dropped it on the bed. "You don't leave your kids," he said simply.

Another flash of memory assaulted me: "It's never going to be about you and me, Marie! We will always be second to those kids."

* * *

A life-sized statue of the Jolly Green Giant greeted us as we entered the meadow. Ken's wedding was already living up to its promise.

I spotted my colleague Felicia waving at us. The lawn was bedecked with beautiful, Indian-print blankets, and Felicia had chosen one under a big oak tree. Long, colorful scarves waved from its branches, and painted Mason jars full of flowers hung from the boughs as though suspended in midair.

"This is lovely," I said. Pia had obviously had a hand in the decorating. Each blanket held a wooden crate containing picnic gear, a vase of flowers, a chilled bottle of wine—and a pineapple with googly eyes.

"Nice headdress," said James, remarking on the crown Felicia was wearing. It was made of felt and liberally coated with glitter. "Did you bring that from home?"

"Oh no, they were provided." She rummaged in the wooden crate and came up with handmade creations for the both of us. I chose a delicate lace band with a turkey feather, and James got stuck with the pipe-cleaner tiara.

"Look, there's Tracy." I pointed across the lawn to where Tracy was playing croquet with her boyfriend, Brian.

Both of them were wearing headdresses drooping with beads. "Anybody else here from Roaming Ex?"

Felicia shook her head, still poking through the crate. "Just us three."

"Wow, I feel so privileged." I accepted a Mason jar full of wine and leaned back against the thoughtfully provided throw pillows to take in the scene.

It was a perfect clear, blue day. The vibrant blankets made a patchwork of the lawn, and with the rolling hills beyond, the scene was picture-worthy. A band was setting up in the corner of the field under a canopy tent. Over the keg hung a pirate flag and a hand-lettered sign that read: "Ye be warned. 7.5% alcohol. 'Tis a sipper, not a gulper."

Ken's groomsmen—er, knights—were romping around in shiny, blue capes, each fastened at the neck by a cardboard badge. One of the knights (Sir Bob, by his name badge) was also the videographer, recording the day for posterity on an old-fashioned Super 8 camera.

"I see the capes made it to the venue," I commented, counting at least fourteen knights. "I take it Pia's not pleased?"

"Uh-uh. But she got lucky, really, because the Star Trek uniforms made their debut at the bachelor party, so they couldn't be worn again." Felicia grinned. "This wedding is everything I'd hoped it would be."

When the chorus of kazoos rang out, we realized the ceremony was starting. James grabbed my hand and hoisted me off the blanket. "Come on," he said. "I think the knights want us to follow them."

Indeed, the knights were beckoning folks to join them in a parade across the lawn and up a stone staircase, where they

452

parted to reveal the place of ceremony. The clever choreography made an aisle out of the wedding guests, and the bride and groom marched through with Sir Bob hot on their heels.

It was a charming ceremony. Pia was gorgeous in a white lace dress with bell sleeves, and Ken's moustache was twirled to perfection. I wondered if he'd dressed it with honey and snickered at the thought of a little bee landing on it.

After the "I do's", the wedding party took pictures. Pia looked like she was drowning in a sea of blue capes, but when Ken took her by the hand, she smiled and kissed him. An accordion player and a violinist were waiting on the lawn, and as twilight fell, we danced to old-timey tunes under a pink and purple sky.

* * *

I fell asleep on the car ride home and woke up with a feather indent in my forehead. "You look cute," James said, kissing the spot. "Let's go to bed."

As we snuggled together under the covers, I replayed the day's events in my mind. "That was a really sweet wedding, don't you think?"

"Mm-hmm," murmured James.

"What was your favorite part?" I'd enjoyed the pineapple lawn bowling, myself.

"Oh . . . it was all nice." His hand was sneaking up my shirt, stealing over my belly. I giggled, ticklish.

"Maybe we should do something like that," I mused. "Without the Jolly Green Giant, I mean. Would you want an outdoor wedding?"

James' hand stilled. "Mm."

"It was a beautiful venue," I said, looking at him carefully. "And I'm sure it was cheaper than a hall. See? We could do this thing economically." He didn't reply.

Suddenly I was wide awake and annoyed. "James," I said.

"What?"

"When are we going to get married?"

There was silence.

"James."

His mouth was dry; I heard his tongue stick when he tried to speak. "We will get married," he said weakly.

"But *when?*" I knew I sounded demanding and I didn't care. A fine spray of sweat broke out on James' forehead. He worked his mouth, but no words came out.

"Oh, come on!" I threw back the covers and sat up. I'd gone from zero to pissed in no time flat. "Are you really surprised by this question? You've got nothing to say?" James tried to take my hand, but I pulled it away. "Talk to me," I said.

"I—I want to be with you forever," he stammered. "And I want to have more kids with you." He swallowed. "But marriage isn't something I need."

I glared at him. "Marriage isn't something I *need* either. But it *is* something I want. You've known that from the beginning."

"I know." He sounded strangled.

"So what are you saying?"

"I'm saying . . . that we'll get married when the time is right." He patted me awkwardly, looking like he'd rather be anywhere else in the world. James hated confrontation. "I just . . . I need to get my work stuff under control—"

"Forget work!" I batted the idea away. "I don't need a big fancy wedding. I would marry you under a tree in the park." I looked at him, hurt. "James, we've been together for four years. Does the idea of marrying me scare you that much? You're sweating bullets and you can barely talk."

James made an effort to pull himself together. "I'm sorry," he said. "Marriage . . . wasn't good for me. And I know," he went on hastily, "you're not Jessica. I know you would always treat me with kindness. But it's still a little scary, I guess."

I sighed, softening. "I'm *not* Jessica. I'd never act like her. But it bothers me that she gets to call me 'just a girlfriend', like I'm nobody important."

"Why do you care what Jessica thinks?" he asked.

"I don't care what *Jessica* thinks; I care what the *kids* think. And they think what their *mother* thinks." I punched the covers in frustration. "There's a difference between a girlfriend and a wife, and it means something to them, James. It affects how they treat me and how they feel about me. It's not fair that I have no control over it. I have no control over anything."

"That's not true," James protested.

"It *is* true. I'm not a parent. I'm not involved in any of the decisions. I don't get to do co-parent counseling, I don't get to talk to the judge—I write all your arguments and you don't even read them! You suck me into court battles that I'm not allowed to fight, and then you don't even prepare, so you keep losing!"

James looked hurt, but also guilty. The little voice of conscience whispered that I wasn't being entirely fair, but my frustration drowned it out.

"All these things impact my life," I said. "And I don't get a say in any of it. The only thing I have control over is whether I stay or go."

Now James looked stricken. "What are you saying?" he asked in a small voice.

I sighed again. "I'm not leaving. I'm not saying that." Relief flickered in his eyes. "But sometimes I wonder: why am I working so hard on a relationship with two kids who couldn't give a shit and a man who doesn't want to marry me? And how long do you expect me to do it?"

"Baby," James said gently. "You've been wonderful. You've been more amazing than I ever expected you to be. And I know you deal with a lot from us." He tried to pull me down beside him. "I appreciate you, and I love you. And . . . I want to give you everything that you want."

"But do you want to marry me?" I asked him pointedly.

James gave me a pleading look. *Oh my God, he couldn't say it.*

"I want to *be* with you," he said instead. "For the rest of my life. I want to have babies with you." He tried to put his arms around me, but I pulled away.

"*No*, James!" I cried. "You can't . . . *snuggle* me out of this! I don't want to make love or talk about babies—" A sob escaped me, taking me by surprise. I was thinking of Brit's miscarriage.

"You don't know what it's like to be the one on the outside of the family," I said, choking up. "To just want to live your own life with the man you love, and instead have everything derailed by a crazy woman and an angry kid. I mean, kids." I was crying now, confusing Brit's story with mine. The grief I'd been trying to hold at bay came rushing at me, and suddenly I couldn't bear it. I bent in half and cried like my heart would break.

"They should be planning their wedding," I sobbed. "They should be getting ready for their *baby!* But instead everything's fallen apart. It's just loss after loss and I can't . . ." I trailed off, covering my face with my hands. "I can't take it anymore."

"Marie." James sat up and wrapped his arms around me. "It's okay."

"It's not okay," I wept. "It's her *life,* James, but she has no control." I looked at him through my tears. "And I have no control over mine."

43

CHAPERONE

At Ilana's urging, I decided to put the topic of marriage away for a while. James' response always upset me, and as neither of us seemed ready to take action, she thought I should spare myself the angst.

She also suggested that James and I take a little break from Lee and Brit.

"I know you want to support them," she said in her soothing voice. "But you also need to take care of yourself. Their problems bring up a lot of grief for you. I'm not saying you should disappear, but it's okay to take a little space. Let yourself heal."

So, we tried to take a step back from our friends' troubles down the street—and refocus on the ones in our own house.

With the end of the school year approaching, Annabelle was excited for her seventh-grade field trip. All the kids in the music department were going to Rushing Waters amusement park for a day of fun. Annabelle had been talking about it since the first week of school, when she joined Concert Band. She couldn't wait to go—until she realized it was on a Saturday.

"What's the problem?" I asked, confused.

The problem was that Annabelle was in Oakland on Saturdays, and the field trip bus would pick the kids up and drop them off in Vacaville.

"You can still go, Annie. Annabelle," James amended quickly, seeing the look on her face. "I'll just bring you to Vacaville in the morning and pick you up that night."

"That's too much driving," Annabelle said staunchly. "It would be better if I spent the weekend there."

"I don't mind swapping weekends with your mum," James said. But at the word *swap*, Annabelle's face shut down. We all knew that Jessica didn't swap.

"Just bring me the details," James said. "I'll work it out with your mum."

Annabelle kept "forgetting" to give James the details. A week went by, and then two. She was going to miss the field trip entirely if they didn't act soon, so James emailed the band teacher. Her response came back quickly.

> Hi James,
> Annabelle told me that she's not allowed to go on the field trip. If something has changed, please let me know. We'd love to have her.
> Sincerely,
> Louisa

James heaved a great sigh. "This shit never ends." He dashed off a response.

Louisa,

Sorry for the confusion. Annabelle is in my custody that weekend and she has my permission to attend. If you can send me payment details and a permission slip, I'll get those right back to you.

Also, do you need chaperones?

Thanks,

James

"Are you sure Annabelle wants you to chaperone?" I asked him.

He shrugged. "I used to chaperone all the kids' field trips when they were little. She used to like having me there."

I kind of doubted she would this time, but I didn't say so. I knew he wanted to be involved.

Annabelle's email came the next day.

Dad, my band teacher told me you paid for my ticket. Am I spending the whole weekend at Mom's house? Yes or No.

P.S.—You should be using the Family Planner.

And when he didn't respond immediately, a follow-up:

Am I spending the weekend at Mom's house? YES OR NO.

"She has such a charming way with words," I said dryly.

James didn't have an answer for her because, predictably, Jessica wouldn't respond to his messages, and Annabelle wouldn't prompt her to.

On Wednesday evening, Annabelle had her spring band concert. James and I usually missed these because they were always held midweek at an inconvenient time, like five o'clock. But it was the last concert of the year, so James left work midday and drove to Vacaville—three hours in ludicrous traffic—to watch his daughter play the flute.

And to try to talk to Jessica.

As luck would have it, he wound up directly behind Jessica and Max in the entry line. Max's parents were there, too—Nonno and Grandma, as the girls called them.

"Jessica. Can we talk about Annabelle's field trip?" He addressed the back of her head. She remained facing forward, pretending not to hear him.

"Jessica." Max made a growl of disapproval, but James ignored him. "Can we please talk?"

At this, Jessica cocked her head to the side like she was listening intently. "Is someone talking to me?" she said.

"Jess," James tried again.

Now Jessica looked to and fro, wide-eyed in mock confusion. "Max? Do you hear someone calling my name? I *hear* someone talking . . . but I don't *see* them." She looked right at James, blank-faced, then looked away.

Max's parents looked uncomfortable. James flushed with embarrassment.

"Do you want to swap weekends for Annabelle's field trip? Or should I just drive her to the bus?" The words came out in an angry rush.

Jessica didn't answer. Instead she shrugged, all cartoon whimsy. "Must be a trick of the wind," she said. Taking Max's arm, she led him into the auditorium, leaving James standing there with her in-laws.

"So what did Max's parents do?" I asked when he got home later.

461

"They were nice," James admitted. "I think they were a little embarrassed. His mom invited me to sit with them."

"I assume you didn't take her up on it."

"No, I sat on the other end of the room, as far away as I could get." He dug in the freezer for a pint of ice cream. "And after all that, the kids only played three songs."

"You mean Annabelle only played three songs," I said. "The flutes."

"No, I mean the *whole concert* was only *three fucking songs.*" James stabbed at the carton with a spoon. "I drove four hours to hear *three fucking songs.*"

"Oh," I said. "Were they any good?"

He spoke with his mouth full of ice cream. "They were not."

Annabelle wasn't pleased with the way things panned out. She complained again that it was too much driving, and she had a point—the amusement park was halfway between her two houses. She'd be driving right past it, and then again on the way home.

"Well, if I chaperone the field trip, we can just meet the group at the park," James suggested. "What do you think?"

"Can I have one field trip without my parents?" she retorted.

So James wrote to the band teacher to revoke his offer to chaperone. He was taken aback when Louisa replied:

> Hi James,
> Thanks for your message. I understand that Annabelle's mom will be chaperoning instead. Glad you worked it out.
> Louisa

"That sneaky bitch," I marveled. Sometimes I almost admired Jessica. She was crafty as hell.

"Why didn't Annabelle just *tell* me she wanted her mum to chaperone?" he wondered. "I would have been fine with it."

"Well, she's about to get what she wished for. I'm sure little miss fragile, bird-bones Mom is tons of fun at the amusement park."

I was sad when my snarky prediction came true. Jessica's chaperoning amounted to sitting on a deck chair near the kiddie pool, underneath a wide umbrella. And Annabelle, so conditioned to stay by her mother's side, did the same.

"You didn't hang out with any of your friends?" I asked gently. "What about Bibi and Gahar?"

"Bibi's not in Concert Band, and Gahar couldn't go. So none of my friends were there anyway." She shrugged, affecting indifference. "I did hang out with Mirabel."

"Oh?" Mirabel was a new name. "Did you guys go on any rides?"

"No. Mirabel and I don't like fast rides. We did the lazy river a couple times. But mostly we hung out with Mom. It was fun," she said defiantly, her chin in the air.

"Well . . . I'm glad you had fun," I said.

But I wasn't glad; I was worried. Annabelle used to be such a happy-go-lucky kid, with lots of friends. Where had that girl gone?

44

ROAD TRIP

"Are you pregnant?" Avery met me at the door with a flushed face and wide eyes.

"Well, hello to you, too," I said. "Um, can I come inside?" It was Friday evening and I was just getting home from work.

She stepped out of the doorway so I could enter but didn't cease her questioning. "Are you having a baby?" she demanded as I kicked off my shoes and padded into the living room. I greeted Annabelle and gave James a kiss. "Are you?" Avery repeated.

"No, Ave—those books your aunt brought home were just free samples." Rachel had been in town last week for a medical conference and brought us an armload of schwag, including *What to Expect When You're Expecting, What to Expect Before You're Expecting, What to Expect the First Year,* and for some reason, *Qué Puedes Esperar Cuando Estás Esperando.*

"I met the author," she'd explained.

She'd also brought me a handful of fertility pamphlets and lectured James about "fixing his junk", but the girls didn't know that part.

"Did you guys adopt a kid? Did you adopt *more* than one kid?" Avery was practically vibrating with her need to know.

"Of course not," I laughed. "Do you really think we would just adopt a kid without telling you?"

"Maybe," said Annabelle dryly.

"Marie!" Avery hollered. "Why did you buy a minivan?"

I glanced at James. "Should we tell them?"

"Oh my God, tell us!" Avery was jumping out of her skin.

"We're going on a road trip," he said.

My aunt and uncle had bought a cabin in the north woods of Wisconsin and invited the entire family to come visit. Well, *cabin* was the wrong word—it was a five-bedroom lakeside home, probably twice the size of our house. They had a yard and a private dock and enough space to host a family reunion for dozens of people.

James wanted to bring the girls, who'd never met my extended family. We thought they might have fun playing with my cousins' kids and swimming in the lake. But we couldn't afford four plane tickets to Wisconsin.

"We could rent a camper van and drive," I'd suggested, scrolling the internet for ideas. This summer, for the first time, we had the girls in two-week blocks. It was the one good thing James had wrested from his pitiful settlement hearing.

He came and looked over my shoulder. "Or . . . we could buy a minivan and *convert* it into a camper van," he'd said.

"How is that any cheaper?"

465

"Simple. We'll build our own and then we'll rent it out." He showed me a website where people could rent out their vehicles. I hadn't known such a thing existed. "In a couple months, it'll pay for itself."

That seemed like a pretty good idea. "Do you know how to do that kind of build?"

"Sure. It'll be easy."

"Really?" I was impressed. "Well, aren't you Mr. Handy?"

"*If the women don't find you handsome, they should at least find you handy,*" he'd said, quoting some Canadian TV program from his youth. "I can have it done in two weeks."

"Seriously?"

"Yup. Two weeks, tops."

Eight weeks later, we had ourselves a camper van.

* * *

Post to: Classified Ads

Meet Minnie.

She's a sleek, sexy camper van who wants to take you for a ride.

Minnie's candy-apple red exterior and mint-green rooftop tent portray a stylishness that belies her versatile functionality. She seats 5, sleeps 4, and comes with everything you need.

Take a gander at her interior. From her flirty cowgirl curtains to her perky polka dot mattress, everything about this girl says pizazz.

Minnie includes all the listed amenities free of charge.

*Crabby teenagers rented separately. Please inquire for details.

* * *

I was afraid the kids would balk at the idea of a visit with my family, but they actually seemed excited by the prospect of a road trip. We planned a route that would take us through Yellowstone, Bighorn, and Mount Rushmore. On the way home we'd stop in the Wisconsin Dells and Arches National Park.

I worried that Jessica would make trouble, but James didn't need her permission to travel with the kids domestically. He just had to provide her with an itinerary. Jessica made the girls promise to call her every night—but they already did that.

So we set off in July with a camper van crammed to the gills, en route to adventure.

The first day we didn't make it very far.

"We're sleeping in a Walmart parking lot?" Annabelle was incredulous.

"It's an adventure," I said firmly. We'd had a late start, it was eleven p.m., and we weren't going to reach our campsite. "Okay, everybody out! Let's set up the beds."

I braced for complaints, but to my surprise, there weren't any. "Cool," Annabelle decided.

"This is so random," said Avery. "Wait till I tell Penelope." She reached for her phone.

"Uh, just don't tell your mum," said James.

Avery looked at him knowingly. "Don't worry, Dad. I'm not stupid."

* * *

Marie Aaron
July 6 at 9:37 p.m.
Greetings from Yellowstone National Park! As we rolled into the campsite I made a joke about bears and picnic baskets. The park attendant said seriously, "You know, humans in sleeping bags are the soft tacos of the bear world."
Then he said he was just kidding, but now the kids and I can't sleep.

44 Likes; 9 Comments

Marie Aaron
July 7 at 9:14 p.m.
Much discussion tonight over the perfect degree of toasting required for a marshmallow. The kids call my marshmallows "carcinogen bombs", but to each her own.

23 Likes; 4 Comments

Marie Aaron
July 9 at 3:22 p.m.
The backseat of my car looks like a frat house. I reached back for the Oreos and came up with a handful of somebody's underwear.

61 Likes; 13 Comments

Marie Aaron

July 10 at 8:19 a.m.

We're 5 days into the 2-week road trip and everything was going well. The kids were behaving beautifully, despite long days in the car. We were seeing America and everybody was having a good time. Until last night.

Unable to push through to our destination, we pulled off the highway into a roadside campsite. It was pitch black and infested with mosquitoes. By the time we made camp, our car (where the kids sleep) was filled with bugs, and the girls were basically bat-shit spastic.

It was a night straight out of hell. For hours we did battle, swatting, slapping, and swearing. (I'm pretty sure I heard the 14-year-old use the F-word, and she said it with such precision and venom that I don't think it was her first time.) James and I were in the rooftop tent, and the entire van was swaying with the kids' exertions. At one point they sprayed half a can of bug spray into the car, and then we had to climb down and open all the windows so they wouldn't asphyxiate. 'Cause that's good parenting.

At first it seemed that James and I were well protected in the rooftop tent. But then it became clear that the bugs were finding their way inside. We'd settle down toward sleep and then one of us would spring up shouting, "In my ear! It's in my ear!" and we'd have to turn on the flashlight, perform a tiny murder, and then search for the breach in our protective canvas. From the thrashing below us, we gathered the girls were doing the same.

The hours dragged on. The killings got sloppier. At one point James lurched drunkenly out of sleep, waving feebly at the air; I spotted the mosquito on his forehead and, without warning, smacked him right across the face.

He loomed over me in the lantern light, looking deranged. The tent wall behind him was smeared with mosquito blood. "Where are they COMING FROM?" he whispered in desperation. He traced the perimeter of the tent with the flashlight but found no answer. There were dead bugs scattered everywhere.

Meanwhile, I was wrapping myself up like a mummy, dragging the sleeping bag up to my chin and pulling a pillowcase over my face. I left only a tiny hole for my nose. "You'll suffocate," James said, but we were both kinda past caring. He kicked the covers off, brazenly exposing his legs. "I'll draw them away from you," he mumbled gallantly, then immediately started snoring. For a few moments there was peace.

And then a mosquito flew up my nose.

James told me later that he cried just a little bit. "I felt like I was going insane," he said. While I was rolling around, freaking out with a finger up my nose, he finally spotted the gap in the canvas and sealed it. We shuddered into sleep, my feet against his face, and remained unmolested until the sun came out, approximately 2 hours later.

Now it is daylight and we are back on the road. No one is having fun anymore. We're sleepy. We're itchy. We're positively bitchy.

It's time to introduce them to my family.

105 Likes; 51 Comments

Marie Aaron

July 17 at 10:11 a.m.

There is no privacy on a road trip with children. The girls have followed me into every public restroom from California to Minnesota.

Last night we claimed 3 adjacent stalls in a nondescript Nebraska truck stop . . . whereupon we discovered that the toilets were actually fancy bidets with a multitude of options for all our hygienic needs.

Thus began the most fun I think you can legally have in a truck stop restroom with someone else's children.

It was probably 10 minutes before I realized that there were other people waiting for the bathroom. I flushed the toilet to signal to the kids, but they were slow to catch on; the younger one was still shrieking with joy, "Should I use the turbo function?!?"

Back in the car the kids went straight for their travel journals to record this most awesome experience—the first account they'd written all week.

Based on the giggles, I think there may have been illustrations involved.

68 Likes; 18 Comments

Marie Aaron

July 18 at 5:06 p.m.

Captured on film! Teenagers hugging! Admitting fun and expressing gratitude! Story at 11:00!

70 Likes; 6 Comments

Marie Aaron

July 19 at 8:47 p.m.

Day 13. The kids are over it.

And I am over them.

Moab, Utah. 8:00 a.m. Kids still in bed (car) but awake. James and I making breakfast. Sky opens up. We tell kids to hurry, fold up bed so we can get in car, out of rain. Kids refuse to open door because they are 1) in pajamas, 2) brushing hair. (Pause for expletive.) Adults prevail. Kids set their moods to Extreme Bitchy.

8:30 a.m. Kids disdain the much-anticipated bacon-in-pancakes breakfast, proclaiming it "meh". Adults have to sing the "Bacon Pancakes" song by themselves.

10:00 a.m. Arches National Park. Complaints begin. The 12-year-old is tired. Hot. Bored. Sickly. The 14-year-old is pissed 'cause we're hiking too slow.

10:30 a.m. James cautions kids against walking too close to cliff's edge. 14 decides she's old enough to do what she pleases. James corrects this notion with order to "Get your ass over here!" (Shouted.) Angry tears. Accusations of inferior parenting. Silent treatment lasts for duration of hike.

10:45 a.m. 14 trips over her own feet, proving that she is not as coordinated as she claims.

10:55 a.m. James Googles "death by falling at Arches National Park". Stats exist; 14 not impressed.

11:30 a.m. 12 reminds us that she is, in fact, hating this.

11:35 a.m. James and I start walking really slowly on purpose.

12:10 p.m. Temps in the high 90s. Tempers nearly as high. Hike concludes. Kids declare they're done for the day.

12:40 p.m. Kids are proven wrong.

1:15 p.m. 14 deliberately hides inside an arch, causing us to worry and search for her. When found she snipes, "Was right behind you," and "Guess you'd better keep a tighter leash on me, Dad."

1:25 p.m. I pretend to be really interested in a lizard and make kids stand in sun for many minutes watching it.

1:30–3:30 p.m. More of same.

3:35 p.m. Sun shows no promise of setting. Everyone at their limit. I propose we take our books into a shady arch and read for a while. Kids protest. They'd prefer to read in 100-degree van. Adults are monsters for not allowing this.

4:15 p.m. 14 drops her water bottle into a canyon. Spectacular clang as it falls. 14 revealed to be quite a klutz, as it turns out.

5:25 p.m. Kids still crabby. Adults give up. Return to campsite to drink beer, feed bitchy children.

6:00 p.m. Sudden gust of wind blows beer into my lap. Pants soaked. Kids laugh.

6:10 p.m. Kids decide they're quite cheerful now and ready to chat and play. I can't even.

7:45 p.m. 14 says casually, "Thanks for the fun hiking today." James and I snort and spit our beer. 14 looks wounded, then suspicious. Demands: "Are you guys drunk?"

Vacation over. Aaron out.

92 Likes; 52 Comments

45

PROLOGUE REDUX

It was a good summer with the kids. Having the girls with us for two-week blocks proved beneficial. With less back-and-forth they were able to relax more and were better behaved as a result. For the first time in a long time, things felt comfortable between us.

I embraced summer with gusto because it was the one time I was allowed to do parent-type things. Summer camp was my project—dare I say, my *masterpiece.*

With the first breath of spring, I began hunting for camps that fit our custody schedule. I made spreadsheets of all the options, color-coded by kid. If it served ages eleven through sixteen within a ten-mile radius, you can bet I knew about it.

When the girls had questions about their summer plans, they came straight to *me.* I wrangled all the details. I made sure the lunches got packed, the alarm clocks got set, and the swimsuits got washed. I was good at it. And I relished it.

Avery, who was enrolled in cooking camp, delighted in showing us what she'd learned each day. I came home one evening to find her expertly sautéing chicken breasts, looking quite pleased with herself.

Then she said, "I don't want to kill you guys, so I microwaved everything first." Dinner was chewy.

She loved to be in the kitchen—and to use every single pot and pan we had. She was also quite skilled at disappearing when it was time to do the dishes.

Annabelle was doing another session of rock band camp. This year she chose the drums. At the start of the week she was excited and giddy, practicing her part endlessly (with a pair of chopsticks) and deliberating over her outfit and nail polish.

On the morning of the showcase she woke up aloof, disdained her chosen outfit, and rolled out of the house in grungy jeans and unkempt hair, looking like she just couldn't give a damn. Looking, for all the world, like a motherfucking rock star.

I had to say, this camp was highly effective.

Part of the reason for her attitude may have been her mother. This year I sent the performance details to Jessica well in advance, but once again she pretended not to see them and didn't turn up. Annabelle didn't say anything about it, but I thought she was a little hurt.

Thankfully, her spirits lifted the next week at sailing camp. She came home on the second day with wet hair, damp clothes, and a big smile on her face. "They made us tip our boats over!" she crowed. "We had to dump ourselves in the water and prove that we could climb back into the boat!" She stank.

"You jumped into Lake Merritt? The Lake of A Thousand Smells?" That had actually been its nickname once.

"Yeah. It was so gross." But she was grinning from ear to ear. "Smell my towel!" she said, thrusting it at me.

"Ew, get away!"

"Where's Avery? I'm going to go give her a big hug." She ran up the stairs.

"Go get in the shower!" I called after her. Above my head, Avery shrieked. "You know what—take two showers!"

Summertime made it feel like we were a family again. We never returned to those early halcyon days, but these days felt more . . . real, somehow. We'd been in the trenches together—we still were—and that family feeling was hard won. I savored it.

Later that night, after showers, dinner, and some TV, the kids went upstairs to bed. "Good night!" we called after them.

"Love you!" I added hesitantly.

That was new. I didn't tell the girls I loved them. I used to, back in the beginning, but then Avery told James it made her feel uncomfortable, so I stopped. I hadn't said the words "I love you" out loud to them in years. I wasn't sure how to work it back into the conversation.

The kids didn't respond, though they may not have heard me. But James shot me a look of surprise. Then he smiled that beautiful smile.

I remembered one of our early dates, when James had said to me seriously, "My kids don't need another mum. They've already got a mum." I'd been impressed at the time, and I was even more so now, knowing all that Jessica had put him through. He never tried to supplant her in their hearts.

I knew full well that I wasn't their mom and never would be. But they still felt like mine. I'd fought to love them, and I'd earned it. They weren't my daughters, but they were my kids.

However, the next day, when Annabelle's camp counselor informed me of the Friday potluck and invited me to "bring a healthy snack that feeds twenty kids," I laughed in her face.

"Sorry," I told her. "I'm not a real parent."

* * *

On Labor Day weekend I took Minnie out for another spin, but this time with my girlfriends. Despite our pleasant summer, I needed a break from my household, and a quick girls trip seemed like just the thing.

At our campsite on the Russian River, we unloaded three carloads of supplies, including four camp stoves, a bevy of pots and pans, a dozen folding chairs, and enough flatware to start a catering company.

"Huh. Maybe we should have coordinated before we left," said Alex.

"I can't believe how much gear we have." Hailey surveyed the spread with hands on her hips. "And I left half my stuff at home."

"I guess we've got the bases covered," Mandy remarked. "But did anybody bring alcohol?"

Half a dozen voices spoke up: "I did."

"Oh." She looked around in approval. "Then I guess we're all set!"

There were seven of us on this weekend getaway, including Naomi, Gia, and Amber, friends from our days at New Trails. I was surprised that Gia wanted to come, being seven months pregnant, but she jumped at the chance for a getaway before her third baby boy was born. "There's going to be so many of them," she said, looking a tad overwhelmed. "So many boys."

While Amber and Naomi erected the tents, the rest of us put together lunch. Hailey sliced rounds off a crusty French bread while Gia chopped tomatoes and basil for a rustic bruschetta. Mandy opened jars of hummus and olives, and I produced a few bottles of moscato, which had been chilling nicely in Minnie's handy fridge.

"Well, this is not too shabby!" said Amber, wandering back over to accept a glass.

"We camp in style, ladies," Naomi declared, and I had to agree. This beat the hell out of ham and cheese sandwiches in the Walmart parking lot.

Alex, recently returned from her adventures in South America, regaled us with travel tales as we ate. Energetic as ever, Alex had done a yoga immersion program in Chile and emerged as a certified instructor.

"You never cease to amaze me," I said, giving her an impromptu squeeze. "I've missed you!" It felt like she'd been away for ages.

"I've missed you guys, too," she said, squeezing me back. "And I missed my family. But I did *not* miss work." Sabbatical ended, she'd gone back to her job as a physician's assistant—and immediately regretted it. "I think I'm burned out on healthcare. Medicine feels like a bad boyfriend that I just keep going back to."

"Will you teach yoga now instead?" Gia asked with interest.

"Maybe. We'll see." Alex speared a strawberry from her salad and held it up to the sun, contemplative. "But first, I'm thinking about going to farm school!"

After lunch we put on our swimsuits and traipsed to the nearby river. There was some talk of cruising with the current, but ultimately we decided to plop our inner tubes in a shallow pool and just float. It was a gorgeous, hot day, and fireflies skipped over the water, little flashes of gold and green. Lashing our tubes together, we formed a circle and passed around a bottle of wine—except for Naomi, who could never sit still for very long. She wandered the riverbank, chatting up strangers.

"That girl is always networking," commented Amber. She passed the bottle of wine to Gia, then thought the better of it. "Oops, sorry G."

But Gia, who had lived in Italy, took a European approach to pregnancy. "A little wine won't hurt him," she said, taking a small sip. "And if this kid is a little calmer than his brothers, that's probably not a bad thing."

"How did the boys react when you told them they were going to have a baby brother?" I asked.

"Oh, they were adorable." Gia smiled. "Honestly, they made me feel so much better about it. We were only planning on having two kids," she explained to the others. "And I cried for days when I found out I was pregnant again. But the boys were so excited that it totally turned me around." She patted her belly fondly. "Anyway, that was months ago. Now he's almost here! And I guess we'll just have a big old happy family."

"Didn't your sister-in-law just move in with you, too?" asked Mandy.

"Yup. And she brought her dog. So now we'll have two cats, two large dogs, three little boys, Conner, Susan, and me." Gia looked up at the sky and sighed. "And possibly my mother-in-law."

"Wow. That *is* a big old happy family," said Amber.

"Mm-hmm." Gia stared off into the distance, cradling the bottle like a newborn. I reached for the wine but she didn't seem to want to let go of it.

Hailey plucked a second bottle from where it lay cooling in the water and handed it to me. "Did you hear that Katia's pregnant?"

"Really?" said Alex, intrigued.

"Oh, I knew that," said Gia, coming back to attention. I looked at her in surprise. "Katia Kahn, right? She's in my book club. She's due a few months after me." She touched her belly again. "I'd forgotten that you guys used to knit together. We should have invited her this weekend!"

Hailey, Alex and I exchanged glances. I hadn't spoken to Katia since that afternoon at the lake—well, before then, since we hadn't actually spoken. Our knitting group had unofficially dissolved that day, and Alex left the country soon after. Hailey had tried to stay connected, taking Poppy to see Katia's pet chickens, but described the afternoon as awkward. They didn't get together again, but stayed in sporadic touch through social media.

I felt bad that the girls' friendships with Katia had fallen apart, and I felt a pang now at hearing her name. But before I could digest the news, Mandy spoke up shyly with news of her own.

"Javier and I are getting married." Her cheeks pinkened as five surprised faces turned to her. With the sun glinting off her golden hair and her rose-tinted complexion, she looked angelic, every bit the blushing bride.

For a moment we were suspended in surprise; then the silence broke and we all whooped in delight. Down the riverbank, Naomi turned her head sharply at the noise and came splashing back to us. "What did I miss?" she demanded, and Mandy repeated her news to a second round of cheers.

"Congratulations!" shrieked Naomi, and fell on Mandy with open arms. Her sudden hug capsized Mandy's inner tube and sent them tumbling into the water. Alex and Amber, who were connected to Mandy on either side, fell in also. Hailey skittered to safety, but Gia and I went spinning into the current, each clutching a bottle of wine and laughing.

That night I lay in my sleeping bag, thinking. Hailey and Alex were above me in the rooftop tent, and I could hear them giggling. It was cozy inside the car and I was comfortable. I gazed at the curtains that I'd sewn out of cowgirl-printed fabric, and studied my feelings.

I was truly happy for Mandy. She was one of my closest friends, and we'd shared enough boy drama that I was thrilled to see her wind up with a wonderful man. Her very own International Man of Mystery. *Well done.*

But after hearing about Mandy's engagement, Gia and Katia's pregnancies, and Alex's farm school—whatever the hell that was—my own life felt . . . stalled. I knew Ilana would tell me that "to compare is to despair" and that my life was on a different trajectory than those of my friends. But I was about to be thirty-eight years old. Some comparison was unavoidable.

A soft blue glow lit Minnie's interior. I glanced at my phone and saw a text from James. "Miss you," he wrote. "Hope you're having fun."

I was about to reply when a second text lit the screen.

Just got home from Lee and Brit's. Kelsey came back again, out of the blue. No explanation. Lee seems happy but Brit looks stressed. I think they're in a rough place.

"Ya think?" I muttered, annoyed. Of course they were in a rough place. Brit's life bounced at the whim of a twelve-year-old kid.

I began punching out a reply, but then paused. I didn't want to have this conversation now. Nor did I want to think about Kelsey on my weekend away. I pushed the phone under my pillow and closed my eyes. I'd pretend I hadn't seen the message.

* * *

When my birthday rolled around a few weeks later, James asked me what I wanted to do. "Nothing fancy," I said. "Why don't we take the ferry into the city and wander around?"

It was a Thursday, but we both took the day off work, which was nice. I wore a long black dress in an effort to be cute, but regretted it early in the day, as the sun was hot. We walked around North Beach, reminiscing about our early dates, but my heart wasn't really in it. I was never at my best in the heat, and it was slightly irritating to recall just how long ago those early dates had been.

James kept trying to hold my hand, but his grasp was too warm and I was overheating. I slipped my hand out of his and gathered my hair on top of my head, holding it so that the weak breeze might cool my neck. We turned toward Embarcadero, slowly making our way back to the ferry building.

"So, how's it going at work? What's the latest progress?" I could've bitten the words back as soon as they left my mouth. It was a loaded question and James knew it. He shot me a sidelong glance.

"Uh, well . . . Wells Fargo turned us down—but you knew that." *Yeah, after stringing you along for a year,* I thought. "And I told you that we're trying to get a smaller loan from Umpqua Bank, which looks promising."

The Umpqua loan did *not* look promising from where I stood, but I didn't say so. By all appearances, this deal had died on the vine. Kingston Evermore had not leant the support that James had counted on to buy the Hayward branch, and it seemed clear to me that he was stuck in his retail management post.

James had done a good job with the store. They were pulling decent profits and his financial situation had improved somewhat. We still worried about money, but it wasn't the constant soul-sucking, everyday fear it had been. But James was overqualified for his job, and he longed to do something bigger. I wished he would cut himself loose from the company and find somewhere else to work, but that was part of the problem—James didn't want another boss; he wanted to work for himself.

"I've got a meeting with Whit lined up in a couple of weeks," he was saying. I knew Whitman Hames led the distributor business; I'd heard his name entirely too often over the last few years. I also knew that he'd postponed this meeting three times already.

"If I can get Whit to co-sign this loan, then things will start happening." He reached for my hand again.

"But didn't you already ask him?" I said.

"Yes."

"So this meeting is about changing his mind?"

A pause. Then, "Yes."

I went silent, but James could read my thoughts on my face. I was sick of this goddamn deal.

I didn't care what James did for a living. His job held no prestige for me. I just wanted him to be happy and to support himself without worry. But every discussion we had about our future, about marriage and children, harkened back to his job and to this deal. He'd made the rest of our lives contingent on his gaining the next foothold on this particular ladder. What he wouldn't see is that this ladder wasn't leading anywhere.

"What?" James said, seeing the look on my face. There was a hint of a challenge in his tone.

"Nothing." We'd arrived at the ferry building but had just missed our boat. I could see it pulling away. No matter, there'd be another in half an hour.

"You look like you want to say something," James prompted me. He tried to steer me toward a picturesque bench in the sun, but I was too hot; I slipped my hand from his and wandered toward the shade.

"You know that Whit is screwing you around, right?" James frowned, and I backtracked a bit. "Maybe not intentionally, but babe, he's not going to co-sign that loan.

If he was, he would have done it already. Kingston Evermore doesn't care enough about this deal to push it through." Someone had dragged a pair of hard-backed chairs up to the railing and I plopped down in one, looking out at the water. An intrepid seagull plucked at the garbage can beside me.

James remained standing. "I think we still have a shot," he said stubbornly. He sounded upset.

I looked up at him, shielding my eyes from the sun. "Sweetie, I know this is what you want to do, and I support that—but not at the exclusion of everything else. It's not just your life on hold here, James." He looked hard at me, and I looked away.

When I saw the diamond coming at me, I threw up my arms like I was blocking a punch.

"No!" I barked. James flinched, but persisted. "Don't do this now! *Please* don't do this now!" *Who proposes in the middle of an argument?*

James dropped to one knee beside the garbage can and held the ring out toward me.

"Please, can we do this later?" I asked in shrill tones. I averted my eyes, as if not looking at the ring would make it disappear.

"I'm doing it now." His voice held a spark of anger. "Marry me, Marie." It wasn't a question.

In our attic I had a stack of wedding magazines. I had spent hours poring through their glossy pages and imagining. I must've planned hundreds of weddings in my head, envisioning every venue, every dress, every detail. The only thing I'd never let myself imagine was the proposal. That was his to design, his gift to give, and I didn't get to dissect it in my mind. I knew it would be magical, however it happened.

And *this* was it??

For a long moment I looked at James, kneeling on the pavement beside a splotch of seagull shit. His outstretched arm wilted a little, and his determined expression flickered. I saw the deep well of feeling for me in his eyes and I was torn by indecision. I'd been basically begging this man to marry me for years. And now he was on his knee in front of me and I could not say yes.

I felt dazed, panicked. I knew that every second I spent searching for the right response was widening the gulf between us. My mind flashed to Mandy and Javier. On the drive home, after we'd dropped off the other girls, she'd told me more about his proposal. It turned out Javier had proposed months ago.

"I didn't know what to say," Mandy confessed. "I didn't feel ready—but it's yes or no, right? There's no in-between. You don't get to pick 'not yet' and expect that it won't . . . *change* things between you." She'd said yes, but didn't share the news until she was sure that she really meant it.

But what was I supposed to say now?

"James, I . . . " I stole a glance at the ring. It was a princess-cut solitaire, a sizable diamond in an ornate setting. Surprisingly, anger flared within me again. I'd always told James that I wanted a simple ring. *Wasn't he listening?*

A woman stopped and offered to take our picture; James growled and she scurried away. I took a deep breath. "James, sweetheart. Get off your knee, please. Sit beside me." Slowly he lifted himself into the adjacent chair. I gave him a hug, burying my face in his shoulder. "I love you," I said.

"I love you, too," he said. "Marry me."

You're not asking me, you're telling me, I thought desperately. This was so unlike gentle James that I knew he was riled, knew that neither of us felt good about this moment. I wished he hadn't done it this way.

We sat for a time, holding hands, eyes locked together. We sat so long that another well-meaning passerby offered to take our picture. This time I waved him away. James seemed to be out of words. I felt like crying.

"It must be time to catch the ferry," I finally said. "It's been half an hour. Shall we go?"

"Can I put the ring on you?" he asked me in a small voice.

I shook my head. "Put the ring away."

When we got home James climbed into bed, fully clothed. I followed. Daylight still streamed through the windows, but neither of us could face any more day. I lay on my side, my back to James. Closing my eyes, I willed sleep to come and wipe this strange scene away.

There was silence for a time, and then rustling. I felt James turn toward me. He stole a cautious arm around me, and when I kissed it, he wrapped his whole body around mine, hugging me tight. His breath was ragged in my ear, and I thought maybe he was crying.

"I'm sorry," he whispered. "I didn't do that well."

"No," I agreed softly. He *was* crying. A teardrop fell on the back of my neck. I felt tears gathering in my own eyes.

"I messed it all up." He sniffled. "I should have just waited, but I wanted to propose on your birthday. I told your dad I was doing it today."

"What?" I twisted my head around to look at him. "You talked to my dad?"

"Of course," said James. Face to face, his soft brown eyes were huge and wet. "I called him last week to ask for his blessing."

I hadn't been expecting that. Funny, that was a detail I'd never imagined—but I *should* have. I knew it must've meant a lot to my father for James to ask, and I was touched that he'd thought to do it. "What did you say to him?"

James reached for a curl that lay over my face, gently lifting it out of my eyes. "I told him that you were the kindest woman I'd ever known," he said softly. "And that you had the biggest heart. And I trust you with my daughters in a way that I've never trusted anyone." He stroked my hair. "I said that I was the luckiest man in the world to have you love me and my girls. And that I just wanted to love you, and be with you, every day for the rest of my life." He gave me a watery smile.

"You said all that?" I breathed.

"Yeah."

I rolled over to face him. "Oh, James. I think you proposed to my dad."

There was a beat of silence, then a snort of laughter. I'm not sure if it came from him or from me. Suddenly we were both in hysterics, laughing and crying at the same time. "You're right!" he wheezed. "I proposed to your dad!"

I wiped tears from my eyes, hiccupping. "Damn, I'd have said yes if you'd asked me like that! That was beautiful!"

James took my hand, suddenly serious. "Is that a yes?"

"You still haven't asked me," I pointed out.

"Oh right. Sorry." I snorted again, but James didn't laugh. He pulled the ring box from his pocket and opened it. "I love you, Marie," he said, looking at me intently. "Will you marry me?"

"Yes," I said and kissed him.

James' face lit up like the sun. He opened his mouth wide in that soundless laugh, like his joy needed a way out of his body. I could understand; I felt like my own heart might burst. I couldn't stop crying, but they were tears of happiness, and I let them flow.

As he slipped the ring on my finger, I admired the delicate filigree. "This ring is just a placeholder," James said, to my surprise. "I know it's not what you wanted, and we can replace it. But I had to get you something, and it had to be good."

It *was* good, I admitted to myself, admiring my sparkling hand. The diamond was lovely, and I felt it seducing me. "How did you afford this?"

"I didn't pay for Annabelle's braces," James confessed.

I hooted with laughter—unaware that I'd be writing a check for orthodontia next week.

James touched his forehead to mine. We were still lying face to face, holding hands. The afternoon sun bathed us in its warm, golden glow.

"Thank you for choosing me," he whispered.

PART IV

REDEMPTION

46

THANK YOU FOR CHOOSING ME

After all that, it only took another two years to make it down the aisle.

Yeah. *Two more years.*

* * *

It was a good time for us, though. I'd been right about the girls—making our relationship legal did mean something to them. They celebrated our news with an enthusiasm that surprised me. Annabelle was perhaps a bit quieter than Avery, but she'd always looked to her older sister for cues. On the whole, they were supportive and sometimes more helpful with the wedding planning than James—who, having uttered the magic words, seemed to think his role was complete.

But getting engaged had an extraordinary effect on James. Perhaps I didn't realize the size of the fear he'd conquered, because the emotional onslaught that followed nearly swept me off my feet.

He became unaccountably weepy, following me around the house and touching me in wonderment, like he couldn't believe I was really there. The morning after our engagement I woke to find him gazing at me. I smiled and his face crinkled up with emotion. "Thank you for choosing me," he said and burst into tears. I cooed and kissed him, and it was lovely.

After a week of it, this daily ritual felt less adorable. "Thank you for choosing me," he wept, clinging to me, and I patted his back in an absentminded way.

"Okay sport, time to get up. You're making me late for work."

* * *

Lee and Brit were among the first people we wanted to tell, but we couldn't seem to get together. They postponed on us twice, and a month slipped by before we met for dinner.

We chose a pub-and-pizza place with outdoor seating, but it was a Friday night and the restaurant was packed. We couldn't get a seat in the garden and finally claimed a little table inside near the bar, where it was too loud for a proper conversation. James and I resorted to shouting, "We're getting married!" and I flashed my ring at them. Their faces lit up, and they mouthed some words we couldn't hear—presumably "congratulations"—and came around the table to hug us.

While I was showing Brit my ring, a couple of guys approached and gave Lee friendly slaps on the back. It transpired that they were friends from work, and Lee and James wandered with them up to the bar. Brit and I were left alone at the table.

"So, when are you guys going to do this thing?" I shouted, pointing at Brit's ring. They'd been engaged for some time now. I looked up at her face—to read her lips— and was startled to find that she was crying. She quickly turned her back on the bar, not wanting the guys to see.

"We fight all the time now," she said, wiping her eyes. I leaned forward, straining to hear her. "Kelsey's been coming around every weekend and Lee drops everything when she's home. He's so intimidated by her that he's been acting like some dumb boyfriend, buying her stuff, taking her out to fancy meals with her friends . . . anything to keep her coming back." She paused to blow her nose. "And then last week we found out why she's been coming around so much. Yvette got evicted. They were couch-surfing for a while, but then they wound up on the street."

I gasped. "Yvette let Kelsey sleep on the *street* rather than send her back to Lee?" A wave of rage swept over me. "What kind of mother *does* that?"

"She's on meth," Brit said flatly. "And probably some other shit, too. Kelsey didn't want to tell Lee, but he knew something was up, and he finally got it out of her. Yvette's a mess, and Kelsey admitted that she wants to come home."

"Holy shit." I couldn't believe it. "So she's back for good?" I didn't waste time wondering about the courts. They wouldn't bother to enforce their arbitrary ruling; they never did.

Brit nodded. "For now, anyway. At least until Lee tries to make her do chores or something, and she runs away again."

"Oh, Brit." I reached to give her a hug, but she pulled away.

"Don't! That's going to make me cry harder, and then I won't be able to stop."

"Sorry." We sat quietly for a moment, though the noise of the bar roared all around us. I looked at my friend. "Maybe it'll be okay," I ventured. "Maybe Kelsey's learned something from all this."

Brit shook her head. "She still won't talk to me. And so much has happened, we can't ever go back to the way things were." She shrugged, looking utterly dejected. "I don't think there's room for me in that house anymore."

* * *

A week later Lee and Brit broke up.
She texted me:

> *I'm moving out. I found a place in South San Francisco, closer to my job. Lee needs to focus on Kelsey right now and I get that. But I need to focus on me.*

In bed that night I cried as though my heart would break. "Thank you for choosing me," I sobbed, clinging to James. I didn't want to let him out of my arms. "Thank you for choosing me."

47

LOVE YOU

After soloing at church one Sunday morning, I was approached by a young woman. As the choir was filtering off stage, she made a beeline straight for me.

"You have a beautiful voice," she gushed and threw her arms around me. I was unfazed. Mercy was full of huggers.

"Thank you," I said, hugging her back. "My name's Marie. What's your name?"

"I'm Raelin." She looked at me adoringly, arms still wrapped around my waist. "Are you single?"

I detached her grip and took a step back, frowning. "Um . . . " *How old was this kid?* She looked about fourteen.

"Don't freak out, she's asking for me." A short, smiling woman was climbing the steps. She stopped in front of me and pointed to my left hand. "She's got a diamond on her finger, kiddo. And a handsome man coming up behind her." She winked at James.

"I'm Jo." The woman extended her hand, and as I shook it, she pulled me into a hug. "And I see you've met my daughter. We're new here." Raelin was now hugging James without a trace of self-consciousness. These people were not shy.

"I'm Marie, and this is my fiancé, James." It gave me a little thrill to say that. "And these are his daughters, Avery and Annabelle." The girls were heading toward the stage, clearly hoping to hasten our departure.

Raelin put herself right in their path. "Hi!" she said in a bright voice, and before they knew it, she'd hugged them both. The girls appeared stunned. Most of our friends at Mercy knew they didn't care for hugging, but Raelin didn't have that information yet. She plowed ahead. "How old are you guys? I'm fourteen. I'm in ninth grade at Benicia High. Where do you go to school?"

"Vacaville," managed Annabelle.

"Cool! You're not that far from me. Are you a freshman? Sophomore?" Like Annabelle, Raelin was tall, all legs and hair. She had a cute little Afro and friendly brown eyes that must've put the girls at ease because they suddenly found their voices.

"I'm a sophomore, and Annabelle's in eighth," said Avery.

"We're thirteen and fifteen," Annabelle added.

"Oh, perfect! You fit right between them, Raelin. You guys will be great friends," Jo proclaimed. Raelin nodded like it was a done deal. James' girls looked at each other, slightly baffled. They didn't seem to have a say in the matter.

"We all will," said Jo confidently, and James and I shot each other the same surprised look.

She was right, though. The kids hit it off right away, and so did we three adults.

Jo was a bundle of energy. She had more hobbies than even Alex did. Within a few short weeks at Mercy she had joined the choir, offered herself up as tambourine player,

498

hopped on three or four planning committees, and taken over the kids' program. She also taught dance classes, played on two different softball teams, and called the games as announcer for her local league. If Alex was a tall cup of coffee, Jo was a double shot of espresso.

Raelin took right after her mom. She was on the swim team, color guard, honor roll, student council, and every committee that her high school offered. I was impressed at how Jo managed both their busy schedules as a single mom—maybe she used spreadsheets, too.

Jo and her ex-wife, Lindsay, had also had a messy divorce, and I wondered if that helped the kids to bond. I assume they talked about it in some of their marathon gab sessions. Raelin was a talker, and when she and Avery got going, they could set Olympic speed records for chitchat. It was really quite remarkable.

What was also remarkable was the effect that she had on both the girls. Raelin was the most unselfconscious kid I'd ever met. She liked what she liked, and she didn't apologize for it. She didn't worry about what was popular or cool. She simply did her thing.

For ages, James and I had been battling with the girls over Mercy. They hated going and they made no secret of it. On Sunday mornings we would argue over who would wake the kids because it came with a fifty-percent chance of a tantrum. Even Avery, who was pretty well-behaved these days, had no compunction about rebelling over church.

But Raelin loved Mercy, and she took for granted that her new friends did, too. In much the same manner that she'd befriended them—by taking no heed of their hesitations—she gently strong-armed the girls into participating at church.

I was astonished the day Avery took the stage in a Mercy Kids sash and addressed the congregation. "Hi, I'm Avery," she told the crowd timidly. "I'm one of the Mercy Kids teachers." Across the risers, James and I looked at one another in shock.

"Mercy Kids is a program for kids ages three through, um . . . whatever." She gave a nervous laugh. "We read stories and do crafts, and, uh, have a lot of fun. So if you have a kid who wants to participate, find one of us wearing these sashes"—she gestured offstage to where Raelin and two of the adult staff were waving proudly—"and we'll take your child upstairs. Uh . . . I guess that's it." She fumbled the microphone back into the stand and started to leave but then stopped short. "Oh! And don't forget to come get your kids after service. 'Cause we like them, but we don't want to keep them all day." The crowd laughed.

I turned to Jo, who was sitting beside me on the risers. "How in the hell did you get her to do that?" I whispered. Like her father, Avery hated to be the center of attention.

Jo shrugged, but a little smirk played at her features. "I just asked."

With a job to do, and a friend to do it with, it became a whole lot easier to get Avery out the door on Sunday mornings. Annabelle was too young to officially participate, but she was the resident sidekick, helping the girls mind the younger kids and tidy the room afterward.

"It's like a miracle," I said to James when they hopped in the car on Sunday mornings without complaint. If Annabelle was a little less enthusiastic than her sister, at least she'd stopped referring to Mercy as "a cult". I would take it as a blessing.

* * *

"Shannon and Daniel want to come visit," James said.

"Who, us?"

"Well, the girls. But yeah, us, too."

I hadn't met Jessica's parents and never really thought I would—but then, I never thought I'd go to Disneyland with her siblings either. I guess this wasn't any weirder.

"And they're asking if they can stay with us," James said.

Okay, that was weirder.

"Like, in our *house?*" I stared at him. "Why don't they stay with their daughter?"

We both knew the answer, but James explained it anyway. "Because Jessica won't talk to them. And they haven't seen the kids in . . . I don't know, seven years?" He paused, thinking. "Well, I guess Daniel saw them when he visited before the trial, but Shannon didn't. And since Jess always blocks me from taking the girls to Canada, visiting us is the only way they can see their grandkids."

"Yeah, okay. But why can't they stay in a hotel?"

His voice went up an octave. "I don't know? And I was too uncomfortable to ask?"

"You sound like you're asking *me,*" I said.

He gave me a sheepish look. "Maybe I could tell them that you're not okay with it?"

"And make me the bad guy? Uh-uh. If you don't want them to stay with us, just tell them."

James frowned. When Avery bounded down the stairs he wheeled on her. "Hey Ave, your grandparents want to come visit. Should they stay with us or in a hotel?"

Avery instantly took on the look that James was wearing, one of extreme discomfort. "Oh gosh. I don't know?" She looked at me in supplication. "What do you think, Marie?"

"I think you guys are on your own! Leave me out of it."

And that's how the Olins came to stay with us.

They brought Juliana, which was a good idea. As she'd done in Disneyland, Annabelle flocked to her cousin immediately, which was something of an icebreaker for the rest of us. A petite twelve, Juliana looked like a little version of her mother, Jessalyn. But it was Shannon I couldn't stop looking at, for she looked just like Jessica—in another thirty years. The Olin family resemblance was strong.

Shannon and Daniel were incredibly grateful to us for hosting them. They were lovely to me, and they were delighted to see the girls, but even so, our first evening together was a tough one.

"They keep calling me 'son'," whispered James in the haven of our bedroom. "I hate it when they call me 'son'."

"Listen up, 'son'," I threatened. "If you leave me alone with them again, that'll be the *least* of your problems." James had gotten stuck in traffic on his way home from work and left me to play the graceful hostess. To my credit, I had done a damn good job. I'd bought everybody dinner and made small talk like a champion. When the conversation turned political, I'd put on a pleasant, vapid smile and pulled out a board game. And then another one. And then *another* one.

Now I flopped back on the bed with a huge sigh. "I better be going straight to heaven after all this."

"Amen," agreed James.

The next day at the farmers market Daniel made us pose for pictures. All thoughts of heaven and my rightful place there fled my mind as I stared at the photo of myself with Jessica's parents and her children. I had an almost uncontrollable urge to text her the image with a note: "Having a wonderful time. Wish you were here."

The angel on my shoulder shook her head: *no.*

But the devil on my other shoulder cocked an eyebrow and said, "Worth it."

* * *

What a weekend.

It transpired that the kids' grandparents were anti-gay, anti-refugee, anti-tattoo, anti-Muslim, and anti-Roman Catholic (go figure). In fact, I wasn't sure how they'd fallen out of favor with their daughter since they shared most of the same opinions.

For two days we managed to avoid most talk of religion and politics. Then on Saturday night, James mentioned that we'd be going to church in the morning. Shannon and Daniel were welcome to come with us, or not. At the mention of Mercy, they fell silent—until the wine was opened after dinner. Shannon, as it turned out, loved her wine.

"I'll just be frank with you," she said. "I don't agree with the gay lifestyle and I'm never setting foot in that church of yours again." I raised my eyebrows—not with surprise at her opinion, but upon learning that she'd been to Mercy before. "The last time we were there they had a slideshow of the Black Panthers, and the man next to me smelled absolutely atrocious. I had to hold my breath for the whole service!"

I refrained from saying that Mercy helped the underserved community—not unlike the Black Panthers—and instead asked when they had visited.

"Oh goodness, when was it Daniel?" she wondered.

"I think the girls were . . . five and seven?" he said.

"Something like that. Five and seven, six and eight, I'm not sure. We came down fairly often back then. And we always stayed with James because—" she snorted "—our *daughter* certainly never invited us to stay with her."

I shot James a look. *They had stayed with him before? He hadn't mentioned that!* But I didn't have time to investigate, because I didn't want to miss a word Shannon said about Jessica. She was in her cups and off her guard.

Unfortunately, James didn't pick up on my hunger for gossip and steered her the wrong way. "I'd forgotten you came to church with us. Wow, that feels like so long ago."

"Right, your church." Back on track, Shannon took up her point with great zeal. "Now, I'm not homophobic, okay? I have gay friends. But the homosexual practice is simply an abomination against God." Daniel nodded his agreement.

It went on like that for a while. Daniel listed all the verses in the Bible where God said gays were bad; Shannon told us about all her gay friends—who completely respected her opinion of their deviant lifestyle—and more wine was drunk.

At one point Shannon accused Daniel of being a homophobe. Daniel turned scarlet and James' face suffused with absolute glee. "More wine?" he offered, refilling Shannon's glass.

For half an hour James spoke calmly in defense of LGBTQ rights, refuting his ex-in-laws' arguments with simple, compassionate words. He made me proud.

I was a little less eloquent.

"Just think about the anatomy," argued Shannon, making lewd gestures with her hands. "The human anatomy doesn't support homosexuality. Two men just can't fit together!"

"Um, yes they can," I said bluntly.

504

I swear, there was a small sucking noise as Daniel's butt hermetically sealed itself shut.

Just then, the doorbell rang. James and I glanced at each other: *What impeccable timing.*

Jo and Raelin had gone to a concert that evening at a venue close to our house. They'd invited us to come, but we suggested instead that they join us for ice cream afterward. And now here they were.

James stood up to answer the door. With his hand on the knob, he paused and turned back to face Shannon and Daniel. "Oh, by the way," he said, "our friends are gay."

I could almost see the thoughts whizzing through Daniel's head as we welcomed Jo and Raelin into the house. *Dear God, are they both gay? Is the* kid *gay?*

The kid actually *was* gay. Or bi, anyway. Raelin talked easily about her crushes on both boys and girls, and at first I think Annabelle was a little taken aback. Despite her long exposure to Mercy, she still spent five days a week in her mother's home, steeping in her strong opinions. But after a little time to digest, Annabelle accepted the situation freely. Just as she'd done with Mercy, Raelin made being gay okay.

I wondered if she'd have similar powers over Shannon and Daniel.

They did have *some* kind of powers, I mused, watching Jo and Raelin win over the room. I marveled at how naturally they did it; they simply assumed that everyone around them wanted to be friends. Within minutes, the four girls were engrossed in Monopoly, and Jo and Shannon were gabbing like they'd known each other for ages. James kept pouring the wine, and after another glass, Shannon rose from her chair to show off her dance moves.

There was no music playing.

But Jo, the dance instructor, didn't let a little thing like that stop her. She shimmied up to Shannon and the two of them bumped hips and spun on their heels. "I've still got the moves!" Shannon called out in delight.

Daniel primmed his lips, disapproving. "That's my wife you're dancing with," he said to Jo. Emphasis on *wife*.

Shannon waved his words away. "Relax, Daniel. See, I told you he was a homophobe!" She put her hands in the air and twirled in a tipsy circle. Jo raised her eyebrows at me and I turned my laugh into a fake fit of coughing.

When the dance party burned itself out (and the wine was gone), Jo gathered her purse and her daughter and they made their goodbyes. As was their custom, she and Raelin hugged everyone in the room. Daniel accepted his hugs stiffly, but Shannon, who was generously lubricated, kept trying to bump hips.

As Jo hugged me goodbye she whispered in my ear, "Another half hour and I think I could turn her."

Come morning, when the wine had worn off, it was a whole different scene. Sober Shannon was a lot less fun.

"We promised Jessalyn that we would keep Juliana safe . . . and not bring her anywhere near that church of yours," she said. (I suspected Daniel had had words with his wife—maybe he thought the gay was catching.) "So, if you don't mind dropping us off at the train station, we'll just head to the airport a little early."

Nine hours early.

After a whispered conference, they conceded to come with us into the city and go shopping while we went to services. But as we pulled off the freeway, God winked. A

506

man stood at the red light with a sign asking drivers for change. He was dressed in a halter top and a tight skirt.

I thought Shannon would have a stroke, especially when Annabelle commented, "I like his boots." It was all I could do not to kiss her.

We pulled up to Mercy, and as soon as we parked the car, Shannon, Daniel, and Juliana took off like three shots from a gun.

"I'm ready for them to *go home,*" James whispered to me.

"I think they feel the same way." We watched them hotfoot it down the sidewalk.

But later we met up for lunch, and Daniel insisted on paying for all of us. And when we said goodbye that afternoon, the hugs they gave me were real. "Thank you for inviting us into your home," said Shannon sincerely. Daniel slipped me a little USB drive—which turned out to be an audiobook version of the Bible.

As the girls hugged their grandparents, I felt a fierce bloom of pride fill my chest. The kids had been amazing all weekend. They were polite and respectful, but they did not yield their own beliefs under pressure. They were deciding whom they wanted to be and choosing their own influences. They were growing up.

Most impressive, they were *kind* to their grandparents, even when they clearly found them ridiculous. And Shannon and Daniel were kind to *us,* even when they clearly thought we were going to hell.

I mused on this for a while, thinking how unlikely it was that I should ever have even met these people, let alone spent a cordial weekend with them in my home. But seven of us—who disagreed on nearly everything—spent three days crammed together in a little house and nobody acted like an asshole.

How about that?

* * *

James insisted on going away the next weekend. I think he felt claustrophobic after enduring a stretch with his ex-in-laws.

"I need to get out of the house," he said. "Let's go camping."

I was a little sick of camping by then, but the girls seemed willing enough, so we planned a quick two-day getaway up to Tahoe. We'd drop the kids at their mother's on the way home.

"Ahhh." James sighed with pleasure as he sank into a camp chair beside the fire. He reached for his beer and took a long sip. "Isn't this cleansing?" he asked.

"Um, *cleansing* might not be the word I'd use." The mess we'd achieved in one short day rivaled our two-week road trip. We'd gone swimming and tracked beach sand all through the van. "But it is pleasant." The girls were roasting marshmallows and chattering amiably. It was a lovely warm evening, and I sat down beside him and clinked his beer with my own.

"So very pleasant," he agreed, closing his eyes.

Later that night, before the campfire died, before the skies opened up and drenched our drying laundry, before the kids crawled into the sandy shambles of our camper van and drew closed the cowgirl curtains, Annabelle put her arms around me.

"Good night," she said. "Love you."

For the first time ever.

48

THE WINDS OF CHANGE

I woke up sweating from my first wedding nightmare.

"What is it?" James asked sleepily.

"Bad dream," I muttered. "About the wedding."

"Mmm?"

I rubbed my eyes. "The ceremony went so long that we ran into Jessica's time and had to ask the guests to wait while we drove the girls back to their mom's house."

"Mmf."

"On the way there, I got a message from the caterer we forgot to cancel, who charged us two thousand dollars for paella. Then I realized we forgot to plan a reception, and our guests were going to be so pissed." I sat up and pushed off the covers, now fully awake.

"*Then* I realized we'd forgotten the children . . . and were just driving around aimlessly."

* * *

Choosing a wedding date was unaccountably difficult. It had to fall within our custody time, obviously, but that meant a host of subsequent decisions that James never seemed ready to make.

Summer felt like the obvious choice—then we didn't have to deal with the dramatic weekend kid-exchange—but that begged a new question: did we intend to honeymoon right away? Did we want the kids with us for a while, or did we want to be alone? Every time I posed these questions, James murmured, "We'll figure it out."

I pored over the custody calendar, making absolutely sure of the schedule. "We could do it over a long weekend," I said doubtfully. "Or maybe spring break?" Christmas was out; that holiday was already too complicated.

"We'll figure it out," James said absently.

I'd come to hate this catch phrase, he said it so often. "Are you going to *help* me figure it out?" But he'd already drifted away.

"Fine!" I hollered across the house. "Then we're getting married next July! Put it on your calendar!"

The reason I fretted so much about the date was because I knew Jessica would make no allowance for any mistake we made with the schedule. My nightmare wasn't baseless, after all—that was just the type of thing she did. There were gaps in the court-ordered schedule, spots where the language was unclear. Any reasonable set of parents should have been able to navigate these together, but Jessica always had a different interpretation than James. Which meant that every school break came with a hassle.

I wanted, above all, a wedding free from Jessica's hassles. If I had to wait another year to get it, so be it.

Once the date was set, the months blew by with surprising speed. And the winds of change seemed to be blowing, too. Jessica's bad behavior was starting to catch up with her.

I think she'd become so accustomed to the girls' unwavering loyalty that she'd overlooked one important thing: they were growing up. It took a lot more effort to manipulate a teenager, but Jessica hadn't upped her game. She still behaved like they were children who wouldn't question anything she said or did.

She wasn't entirely wrong—the kids knew better than to question their mother. It would take an act of God to inspire a rebellion in that household. But what Jessica failed to see was that the girls were seeing *her* with new eyes.

And she didn't always impress.

* * *

I was stunned when Annabelle agreed to sleepaway camp. I figured she'd veto two weeks in the Santa Cruz mountains, but to my astonishment, she was intrigued. Before she could change her mind, we signed her up, and she spent a happy few days poring over the glossy camp brochure.

"Marie, should I list you as a parent or a guardian?" she asked casually, while filling out her camp forms.

"Oh, put me down as guardian," I said, trying to match her easy tone. But my heart swelled.

The hiccup came when we discovered the medical forms. Annabelle needed to provide proof of a recent physical.

"Can you get that from your mum?" James asked. Jessica held all the girls' medical information and assiduously guarded the relationships with their doctors.

"I'll ask her," said Annabelle, but she looked worried.

The weeks passed and Annabelle came up empty-handed. I didn't understand how Jessica would ignore a direct request from her daughter, but Avery admitted, "She gets mad every time Annabelle asks her for it." She didn't have to add: *And you don't push Mom when she's mad.*

In the end, James took Annabelle to a local clinic and paid out of pocket for a new physical, even though she'd just had one. I worried Annabelle would suddenly decide that she didn't want to go to camp, but she seemed grimly determined—if understandably grouchy.

The night before she was due to leave, Jessica and Max dropped the girls at our house. Annabelle burst inside and clomped up the stairs to her bedroom, clearly in a foul mood.

"What's with her?" I asked Avery, whose raised eyebrows indicated that something had just gone down.

"Mom figured out that Annabelle's going to sleepaway camp. She got really upset."

"What are you talking about? She knows Annabelle's going to camp."

"Yeah, but she thought it was *day* camp. She didn't realize Anabelle's going to be gone for two weeks." Avery's eyebrows climbed even higher. "And she didn't like that *at all.*"

Through the window I watched Jessica back out of our driveway. She wore a pinched expression. "How on earth did she not know that?" I wondered aloud. "Annabelle showed her the forms, right? She's been trying to get your mom's help for weeks!"

Avery shrugged. "I have no idea. But I don't think Mom ever read the forms because every time Annabelle mentioned camp, she just got mad and left the room." She allowed herself a small giggle. "Even Max said, '*We* all knew it was sleepaway camp.' Now Mom's mad at him, too."

* * *

When Annabelle started high school, she got a haircut to mark the occasion: a short, swingy bob that looked adorable on her. I'd never seen her with short hair before. (I gathered this had something to do with a hair mishap sustained years earlier on James' watch—perhaps the reason he was not allowed to take the girls to the salon.)

New hair and new opportunities put Annabelle in a brand new frame of mind. She was thrilled to be starting high school, and I couldn't get over the change in her. For two years she'd been moping around the house like Eeyore, but now she seemed ready to take on the world.

That first weekend after school began, she came home bubbling over with stories. She kept us captive for hours, telling us about her new teachers and classes, the subjects she liked and the ones that seemed boring. She was particularly excited about Concert Band—which she loved—and Marching Band, which she couldn't wait to join because then she'd get to play at the pep rallies!

The sheer enthusiasm that Annabelle infused into *pep rallies* made me wonder if she was going to have a very different high school experience than her sister. Avery had entered high school without fanfare and was continuing the same way. She had a few quiet friends whom she didn't see outside of school, and she rarely attended dances or events. I had the feeling that she wanted to, but it wasn't worth the fuss it inevitably caused. It couldn't be easy, attending high school in one town and spending all your weekends in another.

Annabelle looked set to smash that pattern, and I hoped she'd do it. While I worried that it might spawn arguments for more weekends at their mother's house, I wanted the kids to have full lives with lots of friends, and this seemed to be Annabelle's moment. Maybe she'd take her sister along for the ride.

But Marching Band died a quick death. It didn't get Mom's seal of approval.

"I don't understand. Why is Concert Band okay, but Marching Band isn't?" I asked her.

"Concert Band is third period, but Marching Band is after school," Annabelle said. I noted that she was considerably less animated this weekend. "Mom would have to pick us up at two different times, and she can't do that."

I wasn't sure why not; Jessica still only worked a few hours a week, and they lived just ten minutes from the school. Even if she didn't want to spend her afternoons driving kids around—which I could understand—surely they could work out a carpool or something.

But Annabelle was already talking herself out of it. "It's fine; I didn't want to do it anyway. They make you wear a dumb uniform." With a shrug, she dismissed the idea as stupid.

After that, her new enthusiasm seemed to drain away. She didn't try to join any other school clubs or activities. When the first pep rally rolled around, she skipped it.

* * *

In the fall, the girls turned fourteen and sixteen. It was handy having the kids' birthdays in the same season; it made it easier to plan surprises.

I *loved* surprises.

This year I'd hit on a birthday idea that felt like a winner. The Solano County Fairground was hosting a mud run in early October, smack in between the girls' birthdays. I was tickled to find it; James and I had done a mud run last year with Lee and Brit, and we'd had a blast. The kids loved looking at the pictures of us crawling on our bellies through a field of sludge. (Slender James had nearly lost his pants.) Ever since then the girls had wanted to do a mud run, so I felt pretty confident in my idea.

But then I came up with an even *better* idea. "Let's make it a campout!" I said to James, full of excitement. "The girls can invite their friends. After the mud run they can go swimming, roast marshmallows, stay up all night . . . They'll love it!"

So I booked a campsite and bought eight tickets for the mud run. "You can each bring three friends!" I announced proudly, when we presented the girls with their gift. I beamed at them and waited for their happy response. But the kids just stood there, frozen.

It was too big of a gesture. I knew almost immediately that I'd overstepped, because rather than looking excited, the girls appeared worried. "It's okay, we'll do all the driving," I assured them. "And the mud run is up near Vacaville. Nobody will have to come to Oakland."

But I'd only grasped half the problem. "I get Raelin!" Avery blurted out, then gloated while her sister looked upset.

Understanding dawned. *They don't have enough friends to fill this party,* I thought. *Not enough close friends, anyway.*

I felt terrible. I'd been so excited by my idea that I hadn't realized—hadn't *remembered*—that the girls didn't do slumber parties in their mother's world. They didn't have the kind of easy friendships that developed from sleeping over at each others' houses or hanging out every day after school, because they didn't do those things anymore. And my big gift, though kindly meant, was forcing them into uncomfortable territory. I didn't realize until that moment how much pressure I was putting on them.

The problem took care of itself a few weeks later when the mud run was postponed—to one of Jessica's weekends.

"Oh shit," I muttered when I saw the email. "I guess that's the end of that."

I tried, of course. I sent Jessica all the details—and the eight non-refundable tickets—and urged her to take the kids herself. To no one's surprise, she ignored all my messages, and the day of the mud run came and went.

I thought the kids were a little relieved. I didn't try suggesting that we have the campout anyway. It didn't seem like such a great idea anymore.

But the incident made me pause and reflect. The kids didn't like surprises, I realized. Nor, for that matter, did James—their lives had enough unpredictability, and they were wary of anything they couldn't see coming. What's more, I had a way of putting them in difficult positions. Even when I didn't mean to do it, I was forever forcing them to confront the uncomfortable in their lives.

This realization left me subdued. I almost wished I hadn't planned anything for their birthdays. I hadn't meant to turn this one around on their mom.

But Avery surprised me. "I'm sorry my mom didn't respond to you," she said after the mud run had safely passed. "She shouldn't have ignored you like that." She gave me a little half-smile, and the twist of her lips conveyed more than she knew how to say.

49

GOOD DEEDS

"When's dinner?" Avery bounded down the stairs and into the kitchen. "Hey Marie, when's dinner?"

"Mm?" I turned to answer her but stopped short, surprised by the look on her face. Or rather, the look *of* her face.

"When is dinner?" she enunciated through scarlet lips, then caught me staring. "What?"

"Uh, nothing," I said. "Dinner's in five minutes. Can you please set the table?"

"Okay." She opened the kitchen cabinet and reached for the plates.

Now age sixteen, Avery was allowed to wear full makeup. Her mother's rules for cosmetics were complex. At thirteen, the girls were allowed nail polish. At fourteen, lip gloss was permitted. At fifteen, foundation, blush and mascara were added to the mix. Now, at the coveted age of sixteen, eyeshadow and eyeliner were authorized, and lip gloss could graduate to lipstick.

"What do they get at seventeen?" I wondered.

"Married," James said dourly.

Being color blind, James wouldn't have noticed if Avery went out with a face full of clown makeup. But I didn't care for this mature new look. She looked far, far older than sixteen, and I found it difficult to avoid staring at her bright red mouth across the dinner table.

While we ate, the kids chatted about school. Annabelle complained about her French teacher. "She gives us the easiest, dumbest assignments," she said. "It's like, eighth-grade stuff. And we keep telling her that she can skip ahead, but she won't do it. It's annoying."

"Aw, but Madame is so nice," protested Avery.

"Yeah, she's *nice,* but she's wasting our time. I kinda wish I'd stuck with Spanish." A scheduling mishap had put Annabelle in Spanish for the first two weeks of the school year. She'd seemed a little regretful when it was straightened out.

"It'll get more challenging, trust me," Avery promised. She took a careful bite of chicken, dabbed her lips daintily with a paper napkin, inspected it for lipstick, and continued. "Besides, you have to stick with French so you can come visit me in Paris!"

"You're going to Paris?" I asked. This was news to me.

"Yeah! I mean, I hope so. Mom said I should apply to AUP." I gave her a questioning look.

"The American University of Paris," Annabelle supplied. Clearly, she'd already sat through this discussion.

"Oh." I tried to keep my voice neutral.

I'd been wondering how Jessica was going to handle the college situation. We couldn't even work together on summer camp, so I didn't hold out a lot of hope that college would bring our two households together. I thought it more likely that she would do one of two things: enroll Avery in an expensive, private university and expect James to pay for it or ignore college altogether.

In fact, I'd been so afraid of the former that I'd secretly consulted a lawyer after James and I got engaged. I was relieved to learn that his financial responsibilities ended with high school. Of course, I knew James would make sure his kids could go to college. They'd just have to work together to find an affordable option.

Somehow I didn't think AUP was that school.

James was clearly thinking along the same lines. "You should look at some schools in Canada," he said. "There are some great universities there, and we'd get a break in tuition as Canadians." The kids had dual citizenship.

Avery made a little crimson moue. She clearly didn't consider Canada to be as glamorous as Paris. I wondered briefly why Jessica thought Paris was a good idea for a kid who still wasn't allowed her own house key.

The doorbell rang, and we all exchanged looks of surprise. Annabelle leaned back in her seat to peer out the window. "It's a man," she reported. "A stranger."

James, who was closest to the door, got up to answer it. "Hi," he said to the man on our porch.

The man's mumbled voice didn't carry far, but I made out a few words: " . . . sorry to bother you . . . any food . . . sorry . . . "

"Uh . . . just a second," I heard James say. "I'll be right back."

The door closed and he reappeared in the dining room. "What does he want?" Avery asked.

James raked his hands through his hair, making it stand on end. "He's hungry. He asked if we can spare any food." He looked at me with raised eyebrows.

Oakland had a lot of hungry people. This wasn't news. Tent cities sprung up in parks and under highway overpasses like mushrooms after the rain. I passed homeless folks every day and I gave out money when I could. But in thirteen years, I'd never had anybody ring my doorbell and ask for food. I could tell James and the girls hadn't either. For a moment there was silence as we stared at each other.

Then James snapped to and strode into the kitchen. He looked at the chicken carcass that had been dinner. "I guess I could make him a sandwich."

"Good idea." I pulled a wedge of cheese and a head of lettuce from the fridge and handed them to him.

"Better make it two sandwiches. And some fruit," Avery said. "He might be really hungry." The girls were rummaging through the cabinets, hunting for supplies.

"I'll get granola bars," offered Annabelle. "Hey, can we give away this Tupperware?" She held up a plastic container for my approval.

After a few minutes of hustling, James was able to present the man with a package of food. He gave weary thanks and moved off down the road, the girls and I watching from the window.

As we returned to our meals, Annabelle said, "We should buy a bunch of disposable containers and keep them ready, in case this happens again. He might have friends who are hungry, too."

A lump sprang up in my throat and I looked down at my plate to hide my face. The pride I felt was so fierce I could barely swallow. I'd thought the girls might take this as evidence of our neighborhood being dangerous or at least undesirable. I wasn't prepared for their easy generosity, their immediate kindness. In that moment I loved them so much, I scared myself.

Inspired by that event, we decided a few weeks later to make a second Thanksgiving meal and bring it to one of the tent cities near our house. I won't pretend the girls were *enthused* by this idea, but they agreed.

It was a clumsy good deed and we made a few rookie mistakes. Namely, we started too late in the day, so by the time the food was ready, it was dark outside. And there's a reason why people don't go under the overpass in the dark.

It's scary as hell.

Even the folks who *live* under the overpass don't hang around when it's dark. They go inside their tents and zip up the doors—making it difficult to distribute food and good intentions.

"What do we do?" I asked James as we stood on the concrete median, traffic whizzing above our heads. Inside the car, the kids pressed their faces to the windows.

I'd thought we'd give out twenty meals in five minutes and head back home, but instead, we wound up driving all over town. For hours we scoured the streets, hunting under freeways and poking through parks, the kids cheering us on from the backseat. We wouldn't let them out of the car, but they handed us meals and called out directions: "Over there, Dad! I think I see someone over there!"

When we finally delivered the last of the food, everyone was elated. There were no complaints about our brief outing having turned into an all-night affair. Once again, I felt exceptionally proud. And exhausted. If I never saw the underside of another overpass, it would be too soon.

Then Annabelle spoke up. "We should do that again at Christmas," she said.

So we did.

After that, everyone's altruism wore off. "No more good deeds for a while, okay?" grumbled Avery.

But then I saw her quietly put her own money in the collection basket at church.

* * *

On a Wednesday night during the kids' winter break, we dragged them with us to choir practice. To stave off the protests, Jo brought Raelin, and the young trio curled up in a corner of the sanctuary, gossiping and giggling.

There was a knot of people on the risers, and as I climbed onstage, I saw that they were centered around Perry, a fellow soprano, who was sporting a black eye and a split lip. "What happened?" I asked, drawing closer.

"Beat up," he said tersely. "Again."

"Jumped at the BART station," Angel put in. "On Sunday, after church." He hovered protectively around his friend.

"Oh no," I murmured, as understanding dawned.

Perry was a neighborhood fixture and well known throughout the Tenderloin as someone who'd survived its mean streets. He ran one of Mercy's recovery groups and was respected in the church and among the people outside.

Most days he wore a black hoodie and a knit cap over nubby dreads, his gold tooth winking every time he cracked a smile. But on Sundays, Perry dressed in drag. He came to church in full diva regalia—and even in the flamboyant Mercy crowd, he stood out.

I'd grown so accustomed to seeing him in a dress that I'd long forgotten that there was anything unusual about it. But even in San Francisco it wasn't always safe to be out and proud. Perry's bruised face was a stark reminder.

He was quiet during rehearsal. He hadn't come to sing, it seemed, but rather to be in community. I knew that feeling and held his hand for a while, just to let him know someone was there.

When rehearsal ended, we gathered around him to pray. But Perry didn't want prayers for himself.

"Please y'all, pray for Princess. Pray for my dog," he asked. Princess was Perry's constant companion; she went with him everywhere, even to church. She was a small dog, but abundant feeding had made her quite round, a little canine blimp. She didn't walk well on her own, so Perry often carried her.

"I dropped her," he said, a catch in his throat. "When those boys jumped me, I dropped my dog and she broke her leg." He stopped and pressed his lips together, unable to go on. He was crying.

Hands reached out to comfort him. "Take your time," somebody said, softly.

Perry swiped at his eyes. "Please pray that they don't need to amputate her leg," he finished.

As we adjourned for the evening, James and I communicated with a look. "Hey Perry, can we give you a ride home?"

In the car, I squeezed into the backseat between the girls, allowing Perry to sit up front with James. He held Princess in a basket on his lap, the little dog's bandaged leg jutting out awkwardly from its porcine body.

"So this happened in broad daylight?" James asked, stealing a glance at Perry's battered face.

"Yeah. Broad daylight, in the busy BART station. It happened so quick, I didn't even have time to shout for security. These three men came up on me. One of 'em jumped on my back, another one punched me in the face. They called me 'a nigger in a wig'." Behind him, I sucked in my breath.

"When they grabbed me by the arms, I dropped Princess." He stroked the top of her head with his finger. "She fell halfway down the stairs—you know, that long flight of stairs? And I was so scared for her, I managed to break away from those boys, and I just ran. They couldn't catch me, I was running so fast. I grabbed up Princess and jumped on the train, just as the doors were closing. And we got away."

"Oh, *Perry.*"

He flapped his hand. "It ain't nothing new. Same shit, just a different day." He caught Annabelle's eye in the rearview mirror. "Excuse my language."

She shrugged back at him, indicating: *I've heard worse.*

"'Course, I used to get beat up all the time, back in the day. Back on the street. That was a hard life, man, you know." His voice took on a faraway sound. "The street will suck the life right outta you. Ain't that right, Princess?" Princess gave a yippy little bark of assent.

"That's why Mercy means so much to me," he went on, absently. "When I first walked through those doors, I was a mess. Whacked out, cracked out, ho'd up, miserable *mess,* child! But they didn't turn me away. Reverend Lewis, he just told me, 'You keep coming back. We need you here.' And when I got cleaned up, they offered me a job." He nodded at the memory. "They gave me a job and they let me be *who I am*. Didn't nobody care if I wore a dress and high heels, as long as I did my job. And nobody called me 'faggot'." His voice trailed off and he stared out the window. For a while, we rode in silence.

Annabelle shifted beside me and I sneaked a peek at her face. Not long ago, a monologue like that would have sent her into nervous spasms, but she was listening calmly. In fact, both kids wore compassionate expressions.

We pulled up to the curb outside Perry's apartment. "Thank y'all for bringing me home. I didn't want to mess with no BART tonight." He struggled to get out of the car with Princess' basket.

"Let me out, Ave, I'm going to help him." I nudged her and she opened the door, letting us both out onto the sidewalk. "Here, I'll take her." I held Princess so Perry could climb out of the car and gather his things.

"Are you going to be okay?" His black eye looked worse under the streetlamp, shiny and hollow. Silver tears leaked down his face as he looked at me.

"Is it because of who I am?" he asked in a ragged voice. "Will it be like this my whole life?"

I had no idea what to say. What balm could I possibly offer against that anguished question? I stared at him, my heart breaking, my arms aching under the weight of his dog.

And then Avery stepped forth and hugged him.

50

SPRING SHOWCASE

I bumped into Ken in the office kitchen, where he was microwaving his lunch.

"Hey, Daddy-O!" I exclaimed. "You're getting close to the big day! How much time is left?" Pia was heavily pregnant.

He shrugged. "Supposedly nine days, but the doctor says she needs to start walking more, or nothing's going to happen. There's been no sign of any action."

"And she's so tiny, too!" I'd seen Pia at the farmers market a few weeks before, sporting a cute little bump. She looked like me after a big meal.

Ken shook his head. "Nah, she's getting big now. The baby practically doubles in size during the last month of pregnancy. I saw her getting out of the shower this morning and I was like, *whoa.*" His eyes bugged out. "She's a zeppelin. Don't quote me on that."

The microwave pinged and Ken pulled out his bowl and gave the contents a stir. "You know, it's taken me almost thirty-five years of my life to realize that I love eating with heavy utensils," he mused. "Especially soup. I really feel like I'm getting more food when I eat with a heavier spoon." He blew across the bowl and took a careful sip. "Hey, you want to come out for drinks tonight? Me, Edward, and Felicia are going to this tiki dive bar in Chinatown to celebrate my last days of freedom. The drinks are stiff and cheap."

I made a disappointed face. "I'd love to, but I'm taking the girls shopping tonight. It's our last chance to find bridesmaid dresses." Otherwise they'd be walking down the aisle in blue jeans. "Rain check?"

"Sure. Although pretty soon I'll be up to my elbows in diapers. I'll see you at the wedding, though!"

* * *

"How about these shoes?" Avery held up a pair of pumps that would daunt even the bravest of strippers.

"Um, I think those heels are a little high."

"No they're not. I can totally walk in them," she insisted.

I held in a sigh, trying not to let on how tired I felt. I hated clothes shopping. "They're a little too adult."

She frowned. "But you're wearing high heels."

"Yeah, well, I am an adult. And I'm the bride." *Duh,* I wanted to add.

"So how high am I allowed to go?"

I scanned the shoe display and picked up a nice, modest pair. "How about a kitten heel?"

"A *kitten* heel?" she exclaimed. "Geez Marie, you're worse than Mom! Even she lets me wear heels this high."

Patience sapped, I retorted, "Great, then you can wear them to your mother's next wedding."

Oops.

After hours combing the racks, we'd finally found a bridesmaid dress that both girls could agree on. It was pale pink and lacy, sleeveless and simple, ending just above the knee. In a stroke of good fortune, it also resembled my wedding dress, making it look as though we'd coordinated on purpose—rather than hit it lucky in a Macy's basement sale mere weeks before the wedding.

Yes, despite our two-year engagement, we were doing it all at the last minute. James had been indecisive about everything. I couldn't get him to make up his mind on venue, menu, or anything else—and he'd been banned from uttering "We'll figure it out" under pain of death.

I knew he didn't want a big event, and things were quickly getting out of hand, but I was frustrated when I had to prod him into planning the ceremony. To me, it was the most important part of the whole affair. I envisioned us walking down the aisle with our families, saying our vows in front of everyone we loved . . .

But James was hesitant. "I'm not sure I want the girls to walk me down the aisle," he finally admitted.

"Why not?" The plan was for him to walk down the aisle with his kids and his sister, and I would follow with my parents and my brother. I hoped he wasn't going to ruin my symmetry.

"I'm not sure I want the kids in the wedding."

Oh.

I was surprised. It hadn't occurred to me that James might not want the girls to stand up with us.

He looked at me, shame and guilt scrawled on his face. "They haven't been very supportive," he said.

"Not always." I sat down beside him. "But they came around. Eventually."

He shrugged. "I guess. I just . . . I need to think about it some more." I could tell he felt bad.

"You're still angry," I surmised. "About the trial."

"Not *angry* . . . Hurt, maybe. From the trial and everything that came after." He looked at me. "Aren't you?"

I considered this. "Well, yeah. But I've spent the last three years in therapy, talking to throw pillows as though they were your kids." He gave a little laugh. "It helps, you know."

"I'm not going to therapy." He shook his head, decisive on this point at least.

"Well, now you sound like your daughters." I pushed myself off the couch and planted a kiss on his head. "You need to work through your feelings, babe. And soon, so we can finish planning this thing. We're running out of time."

"I know. We'll figure it—"

"Don't say it."

"Sorry."

I remained a big advocate of therapy, even though my sessions with Ilana had dwindled. I didn't like doing them over the phone and she couldn't fit me in as often as she used to—unless I wanted to pay full price. Besides, things were so much better these days, I didn't need to go as often. I had a feeling that my time with Ilana was coming to an end.

Nevertheless, it seemed like a good idea to schedule one more session before the wedding. I was pleased that she could see me in person on a Thursday after work. I couldn't remember when I'd last seen her face-to-face.

Longer than I'd realized, apparently, because when Ilana welcomed me into her office, I was stunned to find that she was at least eight months pregnant.

"Holy shit," I blurted out. I couldn't help it.

"Marie, it's so good to see you." Ilana's warm voice poured over me.

"You are very pregnant," I stammered.

She laughed, a musical tinkle. "Yes, I am. Come on in, I'll tell you about it." I followed her into the room and stared as she lowered herself heavily into the armchair. My old friends, the throw pillows, were wedged behind her back.

"I didn't want to tell you that I was pregnant over the phone, so I'm glad I got a chance to see you." She rubbed circles on her belly, smiling. "I don't normally discuss my personal life with my clients, but I'm going to share a little bit with you today."

I leaned forward, listening intently. It suddenly dawned on me that I knew absolutely nothing about this woman to whom I'd been pouring out my heart for the last three years.

"I am choosing to have this baby alone," Ilana said. "My partner already has a ten-year-old son and he doesn't want any more children. I've told him that he can be part of this, or not, as he wishes. But I'm ready to be a mother."

I was agog. "Are you married? Do you live together?" She didn't seem to be inviting questions, but I couldn't help myself. "How long have you been with him?"

"We're not married, but we do live together," she said. "It's been almost five years."

"Wow." I sank back onto the couch. "So, you've basically been a stepmother for the last five years?"

"I suppose so." Nothing about her tone or expression indicated that she recognized a kinship with me.

"Wow," I said again. "That's . . . wow. I wish I'd known."

She gave a dismissive little shrug. "Yes, well. It wasn't relevant to our work together."

I gaped at her. *Not relevant? You mean all this time we could've been common-law stepmom pals—and instead you had me talking to throw pillows??*

Ilana deliberately changed the subject. "So, how have you been doing? Is there anything you want to discuss today? I know your wedding is coming up soon."

There was actually something I wanted to discuss, although it had nothing to do with the wedding. Pushing aside my curiosity over her domestic drama, I started to tell her about Annabelle's Spring Showcase.

* * *

We wouldn't normally have gone, it being on a workday afternoon, but it was the year's final concert and it came with an awards banquet. Of course, the kids only played five songs—and Annabelle sat two of those out—but what can you do?

The concert took place in the school gymnasium. I spotted Jessica as we entered the room, sitting in the bleachers with Avery. Max wasn't with them; he must've been at work.

We chose seats on the other side of the gym. But the kids were coming home with us for the weekend and an interaction with Jessica seemed inevitable. Sure enough, when the music was over, she and the girls approached.

"Hel-*lo!*" she called out gaily, all smiles. Beside me, James went rigid.

She didn't spare him a glance, but came straight to me, gushing as though we were old friends. "Congratulations on your engagement! I just think it's wonderful!"

I remembered the last time I'd seen her, spitting venom on the courthouse sidewalk. That was not the sentiment she'd expressed that day! But now her kids were watching. Eyes on my shoes, I muttered thanks.

"So, what's the plan?" Avery asked, in that nervous, brittle voice she used when both her parents were in the same room. It was clear she was eager to leave.

"It's up to your sister," I told her. "If she wants to stay for the awards ceremony, we'll stay." I was sure she wouldn't want to; she never did.

But Annabelle surprised us. "Sure, let's stay," she said.

Jessica's face flickered. "But your things are in my car." Avery looked anxious. Annabelle shrugged, a hint of defiance in the set of her shoulders.

"Okay, we'll stay for a little bit," her mother conceded. "But not too long, because I need to go home and rest." Jessica was always resting from something.

It was awkward now to part ways, so the five of us sat down together on the bleachers, a strange little group. Jessica tried making small talk with me. "So, how's your job at the travel agency? Do you have any trips coming up?" She sounded so pleasant.

There was a time when I would have appreciated this gesture, but by now she had done so much damage in our lives, I could barely look at her. James actually, physically, could not look at her. He sat on my other side, in a visible sweat.

It angered me that Jessica only played nice when someone else was watching. She chirped along while James and I sat stiff as mannequins, trying to ignore her. I knew we probably looked like assholes—but for once, I think the girls had an accurate read on the situation. Avery gave her mom a little swat, signaling her to stop talking.

Jessica's voice rose to a shrill pitch. "Do *not* hit me! I am just trying to be *polite!*" She turned to me with a wounded expression and stared, as though she expected me to roll my eyes and chuckle, "Kids, huh?" But I ignored her.

With no audience for her dramatics, Jessica was ready to leave. She kept pestering Annabelle to wrap things up. "Do you even know these kids? Do you really want to stay for this?"

Annoyed, Annabelle turned and growled at her. "I already told you, *yes!*"

I was stunned. This was the first time I'd ever seen—or even *heard of*—the kids standing up to their mom. Unfortunately, James missed it; he was leaning so far away from his ex-wife, he was almost in a different zip code.

But Jessica had a point. Annabelle didn't seem to know any of the other kids.

There were long tables set up on one side of the gym. A banquet dinner had preceded the concert, and now most of the kids were hanging out at these tables with their friends. Our kid was the only one sitting with her parents.

"Did you go to the dinner?" James asked Annabelle.

She shook her head. "It was for Marching Band only."

I was starting to put the pieces together. That was why Annabelle had skipped two songs—because they were Marching Band songs, and she didn't know them.

When Annabelle learned that she wasn't allowed to join Marching Band, she'd rebranded it as "lame". I knew she was just masking her disappointment, but I hadn't realized that she was one of only three or four kids who weren't in both ensembles. She'd made them sound entirely separate, but it turned out they weren't. I hoped she hadn't been missing out on things all year.

We sat on the hard wooden bleachers, watching the section captains give out superlative awards. These had silly titles like "Most Saxy" and "Most Broken Drumsticks". When they called the flute section, James and I urged Annabelle to go up and join them.

There were a lot of flutes—there must've been twenty kids up there. Each one got a certificate, a silly title, and a good-natured ribbing from her friends. Annabelle stood slightly apart from the others. One by one they called up the kids, the group growing smaller and smaller, and still she stood there. My chest started to tighten as I waited for them to say her name.

And waited.

And then the flutes were done, and they moved onto the clarinets. Annabelle was the only one without a certificate. They'd forgotten her.

She walked back to the bleachers, where the four of us had no idea what to say. It was excruciating. My heart was pounding painfully and I was sure James' was, too. Nobody spoke.

We continued to watch the awards. As I sat between James and Jessica, I wondered if we were all on the same page for the first time in history. Watching your kid suffer a humiliation is a sickening feeling.

But then Jessica said to her daughter, "Can we leave now?" And I wanted to *claw* her.

"No," Annabelle replied stonily. On the inside, I shouted: *Good for you, kid!*

James and I feigned great interest in the rest of the ceremony. We made it clear that we were in no hurry to leave, but after a short while, Annabelle's mother wore her down.

"We have to leave soon," she told me, as though I couldn't hear Jessica harping in her ear. "Mom needs to go."

I didn't see the big deal. Jessica could leave, but we didn't have to. "Why don't you just get your stuff from her car? Bring it in here." Each kid had one bag; it's not like they were moving house.

Annabelle just shrugged at me, beaten. "We need to go."

So they got up and left. James and I remained, unsure what to do. It seemed clear that we were supposed to follow them, but I wanted to stay and talk to the band teacher. Frankly, I wanted to inform her that it was her goddamn job to make sure *every* kid got a certificate.

So we stayed behind. And after a moment, the panicked texts began.

> *Pls bring your keys so we can put our stuff in your car*
> *U coming?*
> *Where r u???*

"Ignore it," I said. "They can bring their bags inside."

But then James' phone began to ring. The kids were clearly starting to freak out. He gave up and trudged off to the parking garage, and after accepting that I wouldn't get an audience with the band teacher, I followed.

We pulled up alongside Jessica's car, where the kids were looking agitated. As she grabbed her bag from the trunk, I could see that Annabelle had been crying. She held her head high and her expression was frosty, but her eyes were red-rimmed and puffy.

In that moment, I saw that her ice queen exterior was more than just an annoying pretension. It was a mask of protection.

I wasn't sure what to do. She did not like being hugged. "The ceremony is still going on," I said. "Would you like to go back inside?"

"No."

"Are you sure?" her sister asked. "We don't mind." This was kind, as Avery was angsty enough to gnaw off a limb, but Annabelle just shook her head.

So we drove home. And we didn't talk about it.

But behind closed doors James and I despaired, because the things we'd feared had come to pass. Our kid was the outcast, the one who didn't participate, who didn't know anybody. The one who was literally forgotten.

"This is why I fought so hard to keep my kids," James said to me in the dark.

We stayed up late, remembering the happy little girl who used to have lots of friends. Remembering the confused girl who was made to choose sides. And the angry girl, who thought life with Mom was going to be so much better and spoke those words to a judge. I'd wanted so badly for her to understand the future she was choosing.

Sadly, I thought she understood a little now.

51

WEDDING BELLS

Behind the old train station, where the pockmarked walls were scrawled with graffiti, I stood in my wedding dress and waited for the man who was about to become my husband.

James approached from the vestibule. A smile lit his face when he saw me—the kind of smile that made me glad we'd planned for this moment alone.

I watched him walk across the empty platform. He was dressed in a handsome gray suit with a vest (no jacket) and a crisp white shirt, open at the collar. His beard was neatly trimmed, more silver these days than brown, and a gray flat cap hid the top of his head and the evidence of time gone by.

He'd been adamant about the hat. But I loved every hair that was (and wasn't) on his head. I loved his soft brown eyes behind his wire-rimmed glasses: older now, deeper. I'd shared some years with this man.

"You look beautiful," James said. He touched one of the curls that framed my face. (I had deftly plucked the silver from my own hair.) Then he leaned in and whispered something secret in my ear. I heard a soft *click* and knew our photographer had captured my look of shocked delight.

My dress was simple: a champagne-colored halter that tied at the neck in a pussycat bow, lace with a sheer overlay. My shoes had little flowers on the straps that matched my bouquet, and the bloom pinned behind my ear.

I had always pictured myself in a floor-sweeping white gown, but when the time finally came to choose one, I discovered that I *hated* wedding-dress shopping. It was just like regular shopping, only worse. In the end, I ordered my dress online. It fell well above the knee—which startled my mother and surprised even me—but there was nothing conventional about our wedding, so I didn't waste time worrying about it.

The venue we'd chosen was a historic old train station in West Oakland. Once the terminus of the transcontinental railway, the grand building later fell into disuse and disrepair. It had elegant bones under its graffitied face—and we could rent it for cheap.

Because the building had no electricity (see: cheap), we decided to have the reception outside at Lake Merritt. And, in keeping with our tendency to do everything backwards, we'd held the party the day before.

It was a perfect, sun-filled, blue-sky day. In fact, it was a perfect *everything* day. It was the best party I'd ever been to in my life.

We invited everyone: all of our friends, colleagues, the entire Mercy choir, and both our extended families. After much debate, we even invited the Olins, but they were sensible enough not to come. Instead they sent us a lovely card—and a surprisingly large check.

We laid blankets on the lawn beside the lake and hired a taco truck to feed people. A live band played under the gazebo, and when they took their breaks, one of our friends jumped up to DJ. For hours there was music, dancing, and joy with all of our loved ones.

I wish I could replay the day over and over and see it from a hundred different angles. There was Alex, chatting with Hailey and her husband Reese, while Poppy and Hunter ran around. Mandy and Javier sat with Gia and her brood, cooing at new baby Emerson. My mother and father held court across the lawn, catching up with the family; I was touched by how many aunts, uncles, and cousins had flown in from out of state. On the dance floor, Naomi and Amber hula-hooped to the band, while a crowd from Roaming Ex cheered them on. New daddy Ken was rosy to the tips of his moustache, as friends kept plying him with drinks. Pia had successfully delivered a baby girl just the week before, and she and Lulu were at home, resting. Ken was showing off baby pictures on his phone. "That little critter came out of my nuts," he said fondly.

Because we were in a public space on a sunny Saturday afternoon, plenty of strangers joined us, too. Cyclists rode by and waved, picnickers joined the fringes of our party, and passersby stopped to listen to the band. But the best, most *Oaklandish* thing of all was the group of dancers who set up a portable stripper pole to practice their clumsy moves. Mercifully, they left their clothes on.

This sent the kids into spasms of laughter. "Dude, I'll give you five bucks if you get on that stripper pole." Penelope wore a devilish grin.

"Omigod, no!" Avery kicked at her friend with a bare foot. "You do it."

"You guys, this wedding is amazing," Raelin said.

"Yeah, why are you always saying that Oakland sucks?" Penelope punted Avery with her own bare foot. "This place is awesome."

"Because Mom filled our head with lies," Annabelle replied—and I nearly walked into the lake.

Alex flagged me down. "Hey, is that your handsome brother over there?" She and Hailey shot covert looks in Theo's direction.

"Uh . . . yeah." I was a little tired of hearing about my handsome brother. Alex was at least the third woman to comment on him that morning. Even Jo had said, "I'd flip for him."

Theo had been a slightly heavy, asthmatic kid, but he was always good looking. After years of CrossFit, martial arts, and vigorous tattooing, he'd grown into quite an attractive man. Women were always giving him the eye. In fact, he'd once told me about a college class where he'd fallen asleep with his mouth open and drooled all over his shirt. The girl next to him tapped him awake, pressed her number into his hand and said, "Call me."

Single Alex was looking at Theo appraisingly. I sent her silent vibes: *Please don't sleep with my brother.*

"Marie."

I turned around to find Brit smiling at me.

"Oh, you came!" I threw my arms around her. I hadn't seen Brit in ages. We'd tried to stay in touch, but things just weren't the same after she moved away. Our two families had been so close, but we no longer had that family life in common. I missed her and I told her so.

"Have you seen Lee?" I asked, pointing to where he sat chatting with James and his sister, Rachel. The guys had done a better job of keeping up their friendship. They still got together every couple of weeks, but I didn't often join them. Without Brit there, I felt a little sad.

"Yeah, I saw him earlier. We're cool." I gave her a hopeful look, but she shook her head. "Nah, that's not happening."

I still nursed a secret wish that Lee and Brit would get back together. I wanted so much for them to have the happy ending that James and I were getting. But I knew that too much time had passed and too much had broken between them. Besides, Kelsey was only fourteen. There were years yet before she'd be out on her own, and poor Lee continued to struggle with her. She lived with him now, but still disappeared from time to time, presumably crashing with her mother. In fact, Lee didn't know where she was that day. She'd been invited to the wedding, but hadn't shown up.

To make matters worse, Yvette was pregnant again. I didn't mention this to Brittany.

"Anyway, I'm moving back to Chicago soon," Brit was saying.

"Oh no, are you serious?"

"Yeah. I've given San Francisco a fair shot, but it's time to go home to my family."

I gave her a huge hug and prayed with all my heart that her happy ending was waiting for her in the Midwest.

* * *

Shafts of light filtered in through the train station's tall, arched windows. James and I stood facing each other in the cavernous room.

"Marie." He sounded nervous. "I love your big heart. I love your kindness toward me, my children, and the stranger in need of help. And I love your smile; it puts joy in my heart every day."

There was a murmur of appreciation from the crowd. We were encircled by chairs, surrounded on every side by people who loved us, watching as we spoke our vows.

He continued, "I promise to always treat you with kindness and love. When times get hard, when life sets us back, I promise to work together to make things better. And to always be committed to *us*—" he looked me straight in the eye—"to our family, every day of our lives."

There was scattered applause, which was quickly hushed.

"You can clap," I said, and everybody laughed.

I looked at the man who would soon be my husband.

"James . . . I love your laugh, like a seal barking." There was more laughter from the crowd, and James gave an unwilling demonstration.

"I love your kindness, how it's always the path you choose, even when you don't want to. And even when it bites you, you choose it again." My throat tightened and tears gathered in my eyes. "I love how you risked everything for your children. And then I love how you risked everything for me." I was crying now. "Thank you for marrying me."

James leaned in to kiss me, but the reverend interrupted, "Not yet, now." There were more chuckles.

I swiped hastily at my eyes and went on. "I promise to look after your girls for the rest of my life." Now James was crying. "And I promise you a house full of love." They were the two biggest gifts I could give.

The reverend spoke. "Marriage is not to be entered into lightly, but with certainty, reverence, and joy. We are here to affirm Marie and James in their relationship, asking God's blessing on their lives together." He paused to look around the room, and so did I.

The first person I saw was Perry, resplendent in a lime-green dress and cinnamon wig. He winked at me with lashes like butterfly wings. Beside him, Henry grinned, the proud smile of a matchmaker. Jo and Raelin beamed at us from the row behind.

Our Mercy friends filled the room. They had sung us down the aisle, *hallelujahs* coming from all sides, and every pair of eyes shone with love. I looked around at our friends who'd helped bring us together and felt a deep sense of gratitude.

The reverend went on. "And so I ask you, their community: Will you continue to support and care for them? In times of sorrow, but also in times of joy? If so, say, 'We will!'"

A loud *thwap* split the air, and every head spun toward the back of the room. Angel surveyed the crowd from behind the red silk fan he'd just snapped open.

"We will," he said, with emphasis.

And the room, obediently, repeated it.

I was already kissing my husband as the reverend proclaimed us man and wife. And in that moment—which may have lasted hours—there was nobody else in the world but him and me.

We emerged from the kiss to cheers and applause. Music started to play and the people nearby began reaching for us, wanting to give their congratulations. I hugged my parents, my brother, my new sister-in-law, and everyone within arm's reach.

Then I turned and saw the kids and—*holy shit, I forgot about the kids.*

I had literally *just* promised to look after them for the rest of my life and within seconds I'd forgotten they existed.

Hopefully they hadn't noticed.

They were standing with James, marooned on a little island by themselves. The three of them were holding fast to one another and crying.

I was surprised; I hadn't expected the girls to get emotional. Annabelle in particular was sobbing hard, washing away all the makeup that her sister had applied that morning.

I joined their little cluster and put my arms around my new family. We held each other and murmured *I love you's,* and it was perhaps the sweetest moment in the sweetest day I'd ever known.

Even though we'd partied the day before, there were cocktails and cupcakes and more dancing. Theo approached and nodded toward the center of the room.

"Your friend's name is Alex, right?" She was dancing with Poppy, looking fetching in a black strapless dress. "Is she single?"

Please don't sleep with my friend, I said silently.

But I was saved from having to answer by the wedding paparazzi. Being the bride was a demanding job.

Later, when our guests had drifted away, we convened with our families for a private dinner. James also invited Lee, reasoning that he was almost like family—plus, he'd helped us tremendously in setting up the event.

I worried briefly that Lee wouldn't know anyone, but he was irrepressibly social and within minutes was chatting with both of our siblings. At the end of the night he took charge of the cleanup and even offered to drive Rachel and the kids home. She was going to stay with the girls while we spent the night at a hotel.

"I got this," he said to us. "You go enjoy your wedding night."

"Thank you for everything." I gave Lee a big hug and a kiss on the cheek.

"You're a good friend, man." James embraced him and clapped him on the back. When they let go, both men's eyes were wet.

"I love you guys," Lee said sincerely. "You deserve this more than anybody I know."

Except for you, I thought. And as James and I embraced our friend again, I sent up a prayer for his happiness.

Then I stole away with my husband—*my husband!*

Which just goes to show that prayers do get answered.

* * *

We came home the next morning rumpled, tired, and blatantly post-coital. We smelled like booze, to boot; James had spilled champagne on our bag of clothes. If "walk of shame" could be applied to one's wedding night, we were walking it.

"I'm a little embarrassed to come home this way," I said as we climbed the front steps. "What will the kids think?"

"I'm sure they know we didn't go to a hotel to play Scrabble." James grinned at me as he unlocked the door.

No sooner had we stepped inside than Avery came flying down the stairs. "Omigod you're home!" She was wringing her hands. "Auntie Rachel left!"

"What?"

"Auntie Rachel *left!*"

James frowned at her, confused. "What are you talking about? Rach?" he called out. "Hey, Rach?"

"She's not *here!*" Avery was bouncing up and down.

"What do you mean she's not here?" I put down my bag and walked into the living room, expecting to see Rachel and all her belongings. But it was empty.

"I'm *trying* to tell you! She *was* here, but then she left—in the *middle* of the *night!*" Avery seemed ready to burst out of her skin. "Lee dropped us off and he went home, and the three of us watched a movie, and then Annabelle went up to bed, and then we watched *another* movie, but Auntie Rachel was falling asleep on the couch, so I went upstairs to bed, right?" She was talking a mile a minute. "But I didn't fall asleep, and a little while later I heard a noise like the front door closing and it scared me, so I went downstairs and Auntie Rachel *wasn't there!* And all her stuff was gone! So, I looked out the window and saw Lee pulling away in his car—with Auntie Rachel in the *passenger seat!*"

She sucked in a huge breath while James and I stared at her, dumbfounded.

"So, I texted her, *'Where are you going?'* and she wrote back *'I don't want to miss my flight, so Lee's bringing me to the airport early.'* But Dad, it was *four* in the *morning!*"

My eyebrows shot up. Rachel's flight was at two p.m.

"So, I ran upstairs to tell Annabelle, but she just said, 'Leave me alone, I'm sleeping.' So, I texted Penelope and Raelin but nobody's written me back yet, and oh my God I'm so glad you're home, I've been *dying* to tell somebody: *Auntie Rachel hooked up with Lee!*" Her face shone with the pride; it was the greatest speech of her young life.

James looked stricken. "But . . . she was supposed to be babysitting you."

Avery scoffed. "We don't need a babysitter, Dad." A wicked grin spread across her face. "But Auntie Rachel does."

I snickered. I couldn't help it.

"It's not funny," said James. He turned to me, betrayed. "Why are you laughing?"

I tried to wipe the smile from my face. "It's just that . . . well, yesterday I was praying for Lee to find happiness." I stifled a giggle. "I just didn't think he would find it *so soon.*" Avery snorted and that's all it took; suddenly I was seized by hilarity, laughing so hard that I could barely breathe. Avery was beside herself with glee.

"Aw, you guys, stop." Poor James sounded woebegone. But I couldn't stop. Tears were rolling down my face.

"I was afraid . . . that Alex . . . was going to sleep with my brother." I hitched in a big, raggedy breath. "But instead . . . *Lee* slept with *your sister!*" I was howling. I was on the floor.

James sagged against the wall, the picture of a man in shock. He stared at the two of us, convulsing with mirth.

"My sister is . . . on her journey," he said weakly.

52

WELCOME TO THE FAMILY

"If I hear the word 'Paris' one more time, I think I might scream," I whispered to James. We were at church and Avery stood at the center of a little knot of people, happily explaining that she'd been accepted to the American University of Paris. What she failed to explain was that we weren't actually going to send her there.

It was the autumn of Avery's senior year and college was on everyone's mind. College was the only thing that people knew how to discuss with a seventeen-year-old kid. "Where are you applying to school?" was the mandatory question. And no matter what the kid said, people responded, "Oh, that's great! Good for you!" So Avery was getting a lot of positive feedback about her half-baked plan.

"We don't have forty thousand dollars a year to send you to college," we kept telling her, but she was deaf to such details.

"I'll get loans," she said. "Mom will help me."

Somehow I didn't think Mom would be so helpful—she'd already refused to drive Avery to the SAT test. Still, Jessica was pushing hard for Paris. She and Max had once taken a short trip there and she'd been enamored by the city, forever promising the kids that she'd bring them one day. But supporting the *idea* of Paris was not the same as *paying* for it—something that Avery could not bring herself to see.

We implored her to apply to other schools, to give herself some reasonable options. So she applied to the American University of Rome.

For a smart kid, she wasn't always bright.

"Look, I support you going away to school," James kept telling her, calmly. "In fact, I really think you need to get some distance from your Mum and me and all of our . . . stuff. But you need to pick a place we can afford."

James was now the manager of two retail battery stores. The Kingston Evermore deal had indeed fallen through, but true to form, James hadn't wasted time moping. He and Hassan opened a second store in Hayward, which did decent business. But he wasn't making Paris money. That forty grand price tag didn't even include room and board. Unless Avery got a full ride, AUP was way out of our budget.

James tried to steer her toward the path of reason. "What about one of the Canadian schools we saw?"

After the wedding, we'd taken the kids with us on the first week of our honeymoon, going to Ottawa and Montreal for the express purpose of visiting colleges. (Such is the second wife's honeymoon: instead of Bellinis on the beach in Bali, it's college campus tours in Canada.)

"You loved Montreal," I pointed out. And she had. Montreal in the summer was wonderful, full of outdoor concerts, street art, and fireworks. Avery had been enthralled.

She shook her head. "Montreal is not Paris."

"They speak French."

"Yeah, but it's gutter French," she said scornfully.

"Gutter French!" I bit back a laugh, remembering Avery's attempt to order a bagel *en français.* The guy behind the counter couldn't understand her, and she'd left Tim Hortons looking mortified. "Where did you pick up that term?"

"From Grandma."

* * *

Grandma was the source of our current dilemma. James had gotten a phone call from Daniel; Shannon was in the hospital, seriously ill. It was pancreatic cancer.

"I'm so sorry to ask you for this," Daniel told him. "But we're trying to get Shannon's affairs in order, and I need Jessica's Social Insurance Number. I called her to ask for it, of course, but she refused to give it to me."

I frowned at the implication that Shannon might not make it. The girls were somber as they took in the news.

"Grandma wants to see you guys," James told them. "Do you think your mum might take you up to Vancouver? We can shift the schedule however we need to, but I really think you should go. Soon."

But Daniel called again that night; apparently Jessica wasn't interested in visiting her mother. "We'll offer up a Mass for you in church," she'd informed Shannon coolly over the phone.

"Isn't that what they do for dead people?" I asked, shocked.

James shrugged. "How should I know? You're the one who was raised Catholic."

"Yeah, but I'm lapsed," I reminded him. "So, what else did Daniel say?"

"He wants to know if *we* can bring the kids to visit."

"Oh wow." I consulted my mental calendar. "Do you think we could take them out of school for a few days?"

James scoffed. "Jessica won't visit her own mother on her deathbed. I don't think she's going to let me take the kids out of school. No, we'll have to wait for their winter break." He frowned. "I just hope it's not too late."

We planned a trip to Vancouver after Christmas. Always in doubt about whether we'd receive the kids' passports from their mother, we employed the same strategy we'd used for our honeymoon: booking a flight to the northernmost U.S. city and renting a car to drive across the border. If Jessica refused to produce the passports, we'd simply vacation in Seattle. And if Shannon died without seeing her grandkids, well . . . Jessica was assured a spot in hell.

It didn't come to that, though.

As we drove to their house, I entertained a sorrowful fantasy of the scene that awaited us. Shannon would be in her bedroom, surrounded by her kids and grandkids. I would stay in the background, making myself quietly useful: washing dishes, tidying up. One of the sisters would say to me, "You've been so helpful, Marie. We can't thank you enough."

I was actually quite sad at the idea of Shannon's passing. She'd been kind to me and she was too young to die. Plus, I ached for her, knowing that her eldest daughter didn't care enough to say goodbye. I couldn't imagine what that must feel like. I wondered what the girls thought of their mother now.

Avery had been brave enough to ask Jessica if she minded them going to Vancouver. Jessica had simply shrugged. "They're *your* grandparents," she said—as though she herself had never met them.

We were all stunned when Shannon answered the doorbell, looking hale and hearty and positively glowing with good health.

"Come in, come in!" she cried, taking our coats and wrapping the kids in hugs. "It's so good to see you!" Daniel appeared, proffering a tray of salami and cheese. James and I exchanged confused looks. We'd come expecting bereavement, and here we were at a cocktail party.

"Full remission," Shannon declared, once we'd been greeted and seated. "It's nothing short of a miracle. We thought I was at the end of the line!"

"We really did," agreed Daniel. "We planned her funeral service and everything."

"I gave away all my clothes!" said Shannon. "I got out of the hospital and I had nothing to wear! Thankfully the girls held onto some of my stuff, but I still had to go out shopping because I'd lost a bunch of weight."

"You look great," I told her truthfully. "You don't even look like you were sick."

"I know. It really is a miracle." She smiled beatifically upon us. "Of course, I have to change my diet now and give up my wine, but that's small potatoes." She did look a bit rueful at the mention of wine. "And I tell you, I have a whole new outlook on life. It's too short for the—" she mouthed the word *bullshit.* "I don't have time anymore for petty squabbles or any of that nonsense. You've got to forgive and forget."

Her sincerity touched me. She really did look like she'd found a new lease on life.

Suddenly she clapped her hands. "Come on girls, let me show you around. You haven't been to visit since we moved into this house."

I trailed behind while Shannon gave the house tour. I've always loved looking at other people's family photos, and of course here—in the bosom of my enemy's family—I was fascinated. Daniel caught me looking at the mantle. "You need to give us a wedding picture," he said meaningfully. I wondered if he meant to display it beside Jessica and Max's. Her first wedding photo with James was no longer in evidence, and I couldn't decide if I felt relieved or disappointed.

Then Shannon unearthed James and Jessica's wedding album. "Have you girls ever seen this?" As they flipped through the pages James looked uncomfortable. I was captivated.

"You're so young!" I exclaimed.

"Well yeah, I was eighteen," he reminded me.

"And you have so much hair!" These pictures were very different from our own recent wedding photos.

"Who's that?" Annabelle asked, pointing to a young girl in the wedding party.

"That's Mary Margaret," said Shannon.

"Really? She's so little!" The girls were surprised.

"Well, if I was eighteen, she would've been what . . . ten?" James looked at Shannon for confirmation.

"Ten! You guys were just babies!" Avery grabbed the photo album for a closer look.

"Yes, we were," James said firmly. "Which is why you shouldn't get married until you're at least thirty-five."

I looked over Avery's shoulder as she flipped through the glossy pages. Jessica wore a demure, white wedding gown with puff sleeves and a beaded collar. Very early nineties, but lovely. Her hair was done up in elaborate ringlets and secured with a seed pearl tiara. She looked very much like Annabelle.

Shannon was on her hands and knees, sorting through the other photo albums. "I made one of these for each of my kids," she said, "with their baby pictures and shots of them growing up. Oh, here it is." She sat back on her heels, an album cradled in her arms. "This one is your mother's. I was hoping to give it to her myself, but maybe you girls could give it to her for me?" She handed the album to Avery, who took it reverentially.

"Of course," she promised.

We were invited to dinner that night at Jessalyn's house. With the exception of Daniel Jr., who lived in Alberta—and, of course, Jessica—the entire family was there. Everyone was thrilled to see the girls, and they welcomed James and me warmly.

Jocelyn was the only sibling I hadn't yet met, and I was intensely curious about her. She was, after all, the one who'd testified against Jessica in court all those years ago.

I'd expected another Olin clone, but Jocelyn didn't look much like her sisters. She had dark hair like Jessica and Mary Margaret, but her face was her own.

"It's good to see you James," she said, hugging him. "It's been such a long time."

James had a real fondness for Jocelyn, and I knew he'd be forever grateful for what she had done for him. Whether or not she'd known it at the time, she sacrificed her relationship with her sister by speaking out for James. I was surprised when she started to talk about it—I didn't think she'd want to air the dirty laundry in front of me—but she seemed ready to gossip, and I leaned in eagerly. She reminded me a bit of her mother.

"I haven't talked to Jessica in ten years," she said. "I thought things were okay between us after that trial. She came up here for Christmas that year to show off her new husband, and she brought gifts for everybody, including me." Jocelyn kept her voice low as kids went running in and out of the room. She had four little ones who'd never met their big cousins, and Annabelle and Avery were chasing after them merrily.

"But it was such a weird visit," she went on. "Max wouldn't let her lift a finger; he waited on her hand and foot. Mom made some comment about how chivalrous he was. And Max said, 'Jessica shouldn't have to do any housework. She spent her whole childhood cooking and cleaning for your family.'" She snorted. "You should've seen Mom's face!"

"I can imagine," James said dryly. I remembered that he, too, had been taken in by Jessica's tales of childhood abuse.

"And after that visit, I never heard from her again. She cut me right out of her life. My brother and sisters at least get Christmas cards from her." She pointed to Jessalyn's refrigerator, where I was surprised to see a photo of the girls with their mom and Max. "Merry Christmas from the Mazzeos," it said. I'd never seen a picture of the four of them before; it stung a little bit.

"I send her a card every year," Jocelyn said, "but I never hear back."

At that moment, Annabelle, who was racing past, skidded to a stop. "Oh yeah. Mom throws your card in the garbage every year. She doesn't even open it."

She looked startled when everyone stared at her, as though she wanted to pull the words back in. Since it was too late to undo her blunder, she straightened her shoulders and said, with new maturity, "I don't understand why she acts that way about family."

I was quietly impressed.

After dinner, everyone gathered in the family room to talk. Jessalyn's husband, Jason, told stories of his exploits with James back in high school, much to the kids' delight. I hadn't realized that they'd been such good friends back then, but as the sisters chimed in with memories of their own, it dawned on me that James had known these people for most of his life. They'd shared their youth together. And with his own parents gone and his extended family scattered, the Olins really were family to him—whether he liked it or not.

Whether *I* liked it or not.

As Shannon basked in happiness, grateful for her second chance at life, understanding washed over me: she hadn't told us about her remission for fear that we might not make the trip. I was glad that we had.

To my surprise, I was glad to be part of this little tableau—however weird it was. In fact, as more photos emerged, I was taken aback to find myself in an album from our Disney trip, five years earlier. *How about that?*

The girls were also happy to be with their family. While Annabelle played with her little cousins, Avery gravitated toward her three aunts, eager to be part of their adult camaraderie. However, when Jessalyn asked her where she planned to go to school next year and Avery boasted, "Paris!", the Olin sisters frowned.

"Paris?"

"Well, that doesn't seem smart."

"That sounds very expensive."

"You know, your cousins are getting jobs."

James and I smothered our grins. Avery made hasty attempts to change the subject.

"Actually, we're going to visit UBC while we're here," James said. The University of British Columbia was nearby.

"Now, that's a good idea!" Shannon exclaimed. "You'd be so close! We could see you all the time."

I saw Avery's expression falter. Although she was enjoying her visit, I knew that living near Jessica's family was bound to cause conflict with her mother. This trip was already putting the kids on thin ice.

"If you go to UBC, we will pay for your tuition," Shannon promised boldly. Avery looked distinctly uncomfortable.

Before the night could end, Daniel gathered the family for photos. I offered to take them, but he insisted that I be *in* the pictures. Then, awkwardly, I wound up front and center. I wondered if I'd come across those photos in a future album.

As we made our goodbyes, Shannon cornered James. "Seriously," she said. "Let's talk about college. You call me." Avery looked at her anxiously.

Shannon gave me a hug. "It means so much to me that you guys came up here," she said with feeling. "Thank you, truly." And Daniel congratulated us again on our wedding.

"Welcome to the family," he said to me.

Welcome to the family?

I stared at him for a moment before cold realization hit.

Oh shit. I think I've got in-laws.

53

SEX EDUCATION

The months ticked by, but Avery came no closer to choosing an affordable college. James was ready to let her fall on her face.

"So she spends a year flipping burgers," he said. "If that's what it takes for her to figure it out, then that's what it takes."

I took a slightly different view. I thought we hadn't done enough to persuade Avery to increase her options. She needed to understand that her mother might not come through for her financially. But as a stepparent, I was never really sure when to step in. I'd tried in Vancouver. Avery put on a great show of disinterest as we toured UBC. When we stopped for lunch afterward, she preempted conversation by saying, "I'm not going to school there. I know you and Grandma want me to, but I hated it. It's not for me."

"I liked it," Annabelle said mildly. I noticed she'd collected all the literature and even made some notes. But Avery was shaking her head, determined.

"I would be miserable," she said, looking at her dad with pleading eyes. "You can't make me go there."

"No one's going to make you go anywhere, Avery," I reassured her. She shot me a grateful look, then reached for her menu as though the conversation was over. But I wasn't finished.

"It's January though, kiddo. The application deadlines for most colleges are next week. And you've only applied to two schools that we cannot afford."

A stubborn look crossed her face. "I'm going to Paris," she said.

"Okay, Avery, but how are you going to get there?" I pressed. "Even with loans, we don't have the resources to send you. I know you've said your mom will help you, but is she actually going to pay for—"

"Excuse me." Avery stood up abruptly, tears threatening to fall. She bolted from the table and ran for the ladies' room.

I sighed, slumping back in the booth. This was not the first conversation about Paris that had ended in tears. "What are we doing wrong?" I asked Annabelle. I expected her to shrug and look away, but was surprised when she actually answered.

"I think Paris is Mom's dream," she said wisely. "And she's made Avery think that it's her dream, too. So she won't consider any other options."

James and I glanced at each other, impressed by the kid sister's insight. Annabelle went back to her college brochure. "If Grandma wants to pay to send *me* to UBC, I'll go."

Under duress, Avery finally applied to one university in Montreal, but Annabelle later revealed that she botched her application on purpose. It seemed clear that Avery was trying to give herself only one option—and she believed her parents would come through for her if there were no other choice.

"There is another choice, though," James told me cheerfully. "It's called McDonalds."

"You're really not distressed about this?" I asked.

"I'm really not. We've done everything we can do. Now we wait and see."

It occurred to me that of the four parents, I might have been the most invested in Avery's attending university. Neither James nor Jessica had gone, nor any of the Olins, and Max had started in community college before switching to a four-year school. I knew there were other pathways forward in life. But Avery was a smart kid, a good student, and eager to launch into the world. I wanted to see her go off and find herself. I wondered who she'd become when she broke free of her parents' influence—particularly her mother's.

* * *

There were also other things on my mind. James and I were trying to have a baby.

Well, almost. First he had to have his vasectomy reversed.

"Are you sure you want to do this?" I asked him. It was a rare Friday night that we were both home before the kids, and we sat together on the living room couch, my feet in his lap. "There are other ways to make a family, you know. And the chances of success are pretty slim." We'd been reading up on the viability of getting pregnant post-vasectomy. After a decade, the chances declined significantly.

But James was certain. "It's not just about a baby," he said. "It's about . . . fixing a part of me that's broken. I never should have done it in the first place." He rubbed one of my feet absently. "It feels like one more thing that Jessica took from me. And . . . I guess I want to get it back."

"Yes, but what if you go through this surgery and it doesn't work?" I poked my other foot into his hand.

"Oh, it'll work," James said confidently. "Jessica and I hardly ever had sex. I'm pretty sure I know exactly when each kid was conceived, and it only took one try. I'm very potent." He gave me a cocksure grin and I raised an eyebrow.

"What about the cost?" I'd read that the procedure could run up to ten thousand dollars.

"That's the best part!" He lifted my feet off his knees and leaned over to grab his laptop. "I found a doctor who does budget vasectomy reversals."

"Budget vasectomy reversals?" I made a scandalized face. "That sounds like a back-alley abortion. I don't think that's the kind of surgery you want to get on the cheap, babe!"

"No, check it out." He angled his laptop toward me. "There are some doctors out there who see vasectomy reversal as their Christian ministry. They help men who want to put their fertility 'back in God's hands'." He made air quotes. "But they're real doctors with successful practices. Look, this guy in Texas has been doing it for twenty years."

I scanned the website. "Huh. And you're *sure* you want to do this?"

"Positive." He leaned in and planted a soft kiss on my mouth. "I want to make you pregnant," he said.

The sound of a car pulling into the driveway broke our reverie. I peered out the window. "The kids are home."

"Who's driving?"

"Just Jessica tonight." I let the blinds fall. I didn't want to make eye contact with her.

The doorknob rattled and the kids burst into the house, laden down with bookbags and convulsing with giggles. Avery closed the door and leaned against it. "Oh my God, that was so weird."

"What was weird?" James called out. "Hi."

"Hi." The girls dumped their bags and kicked off their shoes in the hallway. They were unusually giddy for a Friday-night exchange. "It's Mom," Avery explained. "We're driving along and out of nowhere Mom says, 'Foreplay is important, girls.'"

"She said *what?*"

"'Foreplay is important, girls,'" Annabelle mimicked. They both burst into fresh giggles.

"What brought *that* on?"

"I have no idea." Avery threw herself on the couch. "We were literally just riding in silence and she said it out of nowhere. And we were like, 'Uhhh . . . okay.' And that was the end of it."

James laughed uncomfortably. "Um, was that the extent of your mother-daughter sex talk?" he asked, his voice going a little high pitched. "Do I need to buy you guys another book?"

"No, Dad," they chorused, but given the breadth of Jessica's schooling on menstruation, I had my doubts.

When Avery turned sixteen, I had offered to answer any questions she had about sex. She thanked me awkwardly, but never took me up on it, and I didn't push. If they were my own kids, I would've started a lot earlier, but I still believed that this was Jessica's domain. I remembered, though, that

Jessica forbade the girls from participating in their middle school health class. Foreplay *was* important, but I hoped she'd gone over the basic mechanics.

Annabelle put my mind at ease by digging into her bookbag. "We're doing Sex Ed in health class," she said. She handed over a surprisingly robust worksheet that far surpassed anything I'd learned in school.

"You guys are talking about sexual identity in class?" I was impressed.

"Oh, we're not just talking about it. They showed us this weird video of these ice cream cones—"

"Oh my God, you guys have got to see this video," Avery interrupted. "Can I borrow your laptop, Dad?" I saw James hastily close the tab before pushing it over.

"Watch this." Avery pulled up a video of a bunch of ice cream cones in a group therapy session. The vanilla cone was trying to convert the other flavors to vanilla, insisting that his was the only natural flavor. But the others disagreed. The mint chocolate chip cone, boasting two flavors, suggested that she went "both ways". And then the strawberry and chocolate cones tried to pressure the vanilla into a Neapolitan.

"You watched this at *school?*" James blurted out.

"I think her teacher's been reading *The Sensuous Woman,*" I murmured.

"Huh?" said Annabelle.

"Nothing."

"Keep watching," Avery instructed. "Look! They all jump into a bowl and have an orgy!"

"*What?* How do you know what that is?" James' voice was very high pitched now.

"Come on, Dad." The girls laughed at him. "We're in high school."

"I need to call your teachers," James said weakly.

I glanced at the girls, speculative. At fifteen and seventeen, they were at an age where a lot of kids started dating and having sex. I knew Jessica kept too tight a leash on them for anything risky to happen, but I wondered what Avery might do next year if she succeeded in going off to school. It was often those quiet, sheltered kids who wound up going bananas.

In our room later that night, James left a voicemail for the doctor in Texas.

"So you're really going to do it?" I asked.

"I'm really going to do it." I knew he was making the decision as much for himself as for me, but I was still touched. I kissed him on the cheek.

"I'm going to be out of commission for a little while," he said. "You should probably take advantage of me while you still can." He angled his hips toward me, suggestively.

"Oh really?"

"Yes, really." He undid his buckle and slid the belt out of his pants in one smooth motion. "I would suggest taking advantage of me as many times as you can." He put a hand directly on my breast. I frowned in mock dismay and removed it.

"Slow down there, mister. Remember: *Foreplay is important.*" I closed my eyes and leaned in for a kiss, but my lips met empty air. "Hey, where are you—aw, come back!"

"Nope. You ruined it." He went into the bathroom and shut the door.

* * *

In May, Avery had her senior prom. I didn't think she would attend—she hadn't been to a dance in all four years of high school—but she surprised me by planning to go with a group of her friends. After weeks of fussing, she settled on a long, pale-blue dress with baby's breath pinned into her upswept hair. She looked lovely, and she was unusually excited.

Strangely, Vacaville's prom was held in Oakland; we could walk to the venue from our house. I had half a mind to wander past and see the kids in all their finery, but James talked me out of it. Avery wanted to go back to Vacaville after the dance, to hang out with her friends at a diner. She wasn't asking to stay with her mother—on the contrary, she thought Jessica probably wouldn't let her go. She was hoping James would drive her back and forth.

"That's silly," I said. "Why doesn't she just invite her friends over here?" I would have been happy to open the house to Avery's friends for the evening. I'd always wanted us to have the kind of home where kids ran in and out. But she didn't want to do that. The fact was, we'd never met any of Avery's Vacaville friends, and it seemed too late now to gain entry into that part of her life.

As it turned out, the dance was a bust and the post-prom plans fell apart. Avery came home around eleven o'clock, a little deflated but not depressed.

"It was just okay," she said. "None of my friends really wanted to dance. We spent most of the night dealing with Kathleen's relationship drama." I gathered that Kathleen had been dumped shortly before prom.

"So you didn't dance at all? Nothing good happened?" I was disappointed for her.

"Well, some stuff happened. Nothing too interesting. I'll tell you about it later; right now I just want to go to bed." I watched her go up the stairs, her dress billowing behind her.

Poor kid. I'd so hoped she'd have one incredible high school memory to look back on.

Then I remembered my own senior prom: getting drunk on Zima and hooking up with my boyfriend at a friend's house, while our chaperone—"cool Aunt Leslie"—lay passed out drunk on the front lawn.

It occurred to me that maybe we'd gotten off easy with the kids' high school experiences.

The following weekend, Avery kept hinting that there was more she wanted to share about prom, but every time I asked, she demurred. I didn't push. It sounded like something to do with her friend's relationship drama, and though I would have loved to be drawn into her confidence, I couldn't summon much interest in Kathleen's breakup.

On Saturday evening James and I surrendered the TV to the kids and went upstairs to read. As we lounged on our bed, propped against the headboard, there was a knock on our open door. I looked up to see Avery standing there. "Can I come in?" she asked.

"Sure." After a moment's hesitation she sat gingerly at the foot of our bed. "I came to finish telling you guys about prom."

"Okay. Did something happen?" I looked at her curiously. It was highly unusual for Avery to come into our room, much less sit on the foot of our bed. There was a kind of sweet intimacy about it, but I worried that it presaged some grim announcement.

"No, nothing happened."

"Okay. Well, what did you want to tell us?"

She launched into a rambling story about Kathleen and her girlfriend that I couldn't quite follow. I willed my eyes not to stray back to my book, but I was quickly losing interest.

"Dad! Are you listening?" James' eyes had glazed over. I gave him a gentle kick and we both refocused on Avery, who continued to jabber on aimlessly.

Several minutes later I had completely lost the thread and floated away in my own mind. Which is why I didn't register Avery's abrupt conclusion: "So, I'm bi."

"Hmm?"

"I'm bi," she repeated. "I'm bisexual."

James snapped to alertness. Alarmed by his sudden movement, I looked back and forth between them. "Wait—*what* did you say?"

"I said, I'm bisexual." She gave a nervous little shrug. "I'm mint chocolate chip."

A moment of stunned silence lay between us. And then I let out a whoop of laughter so loud they must've heard me down the street.

"Oh my God!" I laughed and laughed. "I'm sorry. I'm just—I'm absolutely stunned. I never saw this coming in a million years!" Avery looked wary and I rushed to reassure her. "Oh, kiddo. Thank you for telling us. I'm super happy for you, I'm just—" Another burst of giggles overtook me. "I'm just so surprised!"

"Dad?" She looked at him. James looked a little whey-faced. "Are you all right?"

"Yes," he said croakily.

"Where are you going?"

"I'm going to get a stiff drink. I'll be right back." He walked out of the room like an automaton.

"Is he all right?" she asked me. "I didn't really think he'd have a problem with me being bi." She looked a little worried, but I shook my head.

"Don't worry. He's got no problem with 'bi'. His problem is with 'sexual'." I slipped into another cascade of giggles.

Armed with a large bourbon, James returned and Avery began to tell her story. How she'd known since she was twelve but tried to deny it, leaning more and more toward the Catholic church. How she slept with a rosary under her pillow and decided to become a nun, even choosing a convent.

"That didn't work because I kind of liked the idea of being locked away with a bunch of girls." She grinned, a little naughtily, and I abruptly got up and stumbled toward the kitchen.

"Bring the bottle," James called.

By age fifteen she'd come to terms with it and spent the next two years sitting with her secret. By then she had a few gay friends: Raelin and Kathleen.

"Wait . . . Kathleen is a lesbian . . . But you're bi, right?" I was a little confused.

"Yes, but I'm still gay. We're all under the gay umbrella." I paused to digest this and Avery beamed at us. "Thank you guys for asking questions. I was so nervous about coming out to my friends, but when I did, they were like, 'Oh. Cool.' Like it was no big deal! So I haven't had a chance to, like, *explain* to anybody."

"Who have you told?" James asked.

"Well, Annabelle. She's known for almost a year. And I told my close friends a few weeks ago. And now you guys. So far, that's it."

I was intensely touched and I could tell James was, too. He hugged her and told her that he loved her. I followed suit and there was no awkwardness between us, no hesitation in saying the words. She hugged me back with real affection. "I love you guys, too." I found myself a little teary.

But then Avery said, "Man, I've been dropping hints for *months*, hoping you'd just *ask* me, but you never figured it out! How did you think I knew what all the different gay flags were? And why do you think I wear so much plaid?"

"That's not fair," I protested. "I came of age in the nineties. Everybody wore plaid."

"So you haven't told your mum yet?" James asked.

"Not yet, but I plan to tell her soon."

His tone was measured. "Okay. But you know, you don't need to tell her right away if you don't want to."

Avery caught his meaning, but waved away his concerns. "Mom will be fine with it. Max has a few cousins who are gay and everybody loves them."

I had my doubts, but I didn't voice them. James kept his face carefully neutral.

Then, out of nowhere, another burst of laughter assaulted me. I tried to stifle it, but it escaped out my nose in a loud snort. "I'm sorry," I said, giving way to the giggles. "Sorry."

"What's so funny?" Avery turned her big blue eyes on me and I shook my head trying to contain myself.

"I really shouldn't say."

"Well, now you have to." She and James looked at me expectantly. "Come on Marie, why are you laughing?"

"Okay. Forgive me." I steadied myself. "It's just . . . for years, I've had this little fantasy of what would piss off your mom the most, and I always pictured you coming home with a big, dreadlocked Rastafarian guy." I snorted again. "And your *sister* coming home with a chick!"

54

THE BAD GUY

Happy to be out of the closet, Avery spent the next few weeks trying on her new identity. By this I mean she took pains to point out every attractive girl she saw.

Annabelle didn't care much for this. James and I tried to support Avery's free expression, but there's a limit to the number of times you can hear your kid say, "Oh my God, she's so hot!" James was going through a lot of bourbon.

She even did it when we were watching TV. I could understand why Annabelle found this annoying—after all, she lived with Avery all week and we only saw her on the weekends. But one night, as Avery was drooling over an actress on the screen, Annabelle abruptly got up and abandoned the movie we were watching. She went upstairs to her bedroom and shut the door.

I was a little surprised. Avery had described her sister as being fiercely protective when she'd first told her the news, but once she'd come out to her friends—and received nothing but support—Annabelle began to withdraw.

"I think she thought she'd have to stick up for me," Avery admitted. "But there was no one to fight against. Everybody's been cool about it."

Even Jessica had been benign, to my astonishment. "I figured," she reportedly said. "I've seen you looking at girls." It didn't sound like a particularly warm and fuzzy conversation, but then again, we were the ones who'd blown through half a bottle of bourbon, so I really couldn't judge.

Jessica continued to mystify me. I wanted her to be one-hundred-percent villain, but frustratingly, she wouldn't oblige. I'd been so certain she would kick up a fuss when Avery came out—in fact, I worried she might kick her out of the house. But she'd been cool as a cucumber, and I . . . well, I had to admit it: I was disappointed.

It irked me when she was reasonable. It messed with my head. She was so often awful, so reliably ruthless, that when she *wasn't,* it was disorienting.

"Did you think Jessica would be so cool with all this?" I asked James that night as we got ready for bed.

He paused in the act of brushing his teeth. "I don't think she actually *is* that cool with it. I think she's probably talking shit behind Avery's back. But yeah, I expected there to be more drama." He rinsed out his mouth and climbed into bed. "I don't think Jessica—"

"Hey! No breaking the rules!"

"Okay. Never mind."

I frowned. "Well, you can't start and not finish."

James and I had made a New Year's resolution: no more talk of Jessica in bed. It may sound strange, but often it was the only place we could go to talk privately, without the girls in earshot. It became a bad habit though, and I realized we

573

had an unhealthy fixation based on the number of times we were hopping in and out of bed.

"Fine." He flung off the covers and stood up. "I don't think Jessica actually supports this, but it's kind of abstract, right? There's no girlfriend in the picture, and I doubt that Avery is ogling girls in front of her mother. So Jessica can kind of ignore it."

He lay back down and I climbed in beside him. "Did you kind of *want* there to be more drama?" I asked.

He thought. "Maybe? It feels like Jess is always—"

"Get up!"

"Damn it." We both stood up. "It feels like she's always stopping just short of doing something that makes the kids see her clearly. Like she flashes her true colors to the world but not to them."

"Or maybe she's changed?" I ventured. "I mean, you're different than you used to be." James had grown up with the same religious dogma and had once held similar views. He'd made a remarkable transformation. Of course, he'd had Mercy and the benefit of friends who were different from him. But it wasn't impossible that Jessica might have come around on her own.

"Maybe," he conceded. "I don't really think so, but maybe." We lay back down.

"One more thing." We stood back up.

"I'd really like to go to sleep now," James said pointedly.

"Okay, okay. But do you think . . . maybe . . . we just *want* her to be the bad guy?" The idea unsettled me, probably because I recognized some truth in it.

"Could you blame us?" James asked reasonably.

"No. But I *am* us."

James leaned against the bed, thought the better of it, and took a step back. "I know that I can be paranoid when it comes to Jessica," he said. "I always assume the worst of her because that's usually how she behaves. But we should be glad that she's supporting Avery, even if it's just on the surface." He sighed. "I will work on that."

"Me too." He sank onto the bed but I urged him back up. "Hang on, I've just got one more thought. Do you think—what are you doing?"

"I'm just going to sleep on the floor."

The next morning I took Avery out to brunch, just the two of us. It wasn't something we normally did and I felt a little awkward suggesting it, but I wanted to hear more about her coming out. Was she fully public now, or had she told just friends and family? Did she have a crush on someone? There was so much I was curious about.

Avery was happy to talk, so pleased by my interest. It was really sweet. She had had a crush on a girl, I learned, and had hoped something would happen at prom, but it didn't pan out. She described it without bitterness. If she regretted her high school experience, it didn't show. But then again, the world was newly open to her, and she had one foot out the door now. There was just the small matter of figuring out where she was going to go.

Don't ask about college, I instructed myself. *Don't ruin it.*

But Avery was the one who brought it up. As the meal wound down, she squared her shoulders and took a deep breath.

"I have something to tell you," she said, looking at me across the table. "You were right. Mom isn't going to pay for AUP."

Her voice was steady but her eyes were sad. I was impressed beyond speech when she continued, "I screwed up. I should have listened to you and Dad. I should have applied to more schools. I just . . . I really believed she would help me. She's the one who told me to go to Paris in the first place." Her eyes were wet.

After a beat of silence I managed to find my voice. "I'm so sorry, Ave," I said.

She gave a brave shrug. "I know it's my fault. And I have to deal with the consequences. I'll go to community college and I'll get a job and save money. Then maybe in two years I can transfer to a university." She had it all worked out, which made me think she'd known for a while.

"When did this happen?" I asked gently.

"A few weeks ago," she admitted. "I was getting ready to send in my acceptance to AUP and they needed a deposit. When I brought it up to Mom, she said, 'I'm not paying your tuition. Your father's got it covered.'" Her mouth was a bitter twist and I felt anger blooming in my chest.

"She'd told me I could get a loan," Avery went on. "But when I asked her to help me, she said, 'I'm not going to co-sign anything, Avery. That wouldn't be responsible. But I'll drive you to the bank.'"

I'll drive you to the bank?

"And she'd been buying herself a new wardrobe for Paris!" Avery burst out. "She bought a bunch of new dresses, and she was shopping for first-class flights. She was willing to spend ten thousand dollars for plane tickets, but nothing for my school."

My thoughts from the night before vanished. Jessica *was* the bad guy. I could have happily disemboweled her with my fork, I was so distraught by the look of utter heartbreak on Avery's face.

"She said I could go to community college and keep living with her, but she's not going to help me with that tuition either. She said, 'I'll let you live here rent-free. That'll be my contribution.' So I guess I've got to get a job this summer." She fiddled with the salt shaker. "I know it's my fault and I'm not complaining, but the thought of spending two more years in Vacaville . . ." She threw me an anguished look. "I *hate* it there."

"You do?" I was genuinely surprised. The girls had always claimed to prefer Vacaville.

"There's nothing to do there and the people are just . . ." She sighed. "I never made many friends there. And the thought of being stuck in that town for another two years . . . especially now . . . " She palmed a tear off her face and stared down at the table.

"Well, hang on a minute," I said. "That's not the only option."

She raised her head and looked at me. "It's not?"

"Of course not. You could take a semester off, get a job, and apply to more schools for spring admission. Or you could live with us and go to community college in Oakland."

"I could live with you guys?"

"Absolutely you could."

She looked humbled. "I wasn't sure if I'd be welcome."

My heart contracted with pain. I hoped to God I'd never done anything to make her feel that way. "This is your home, Avery. Always, always, always. Okay?"

A little glimmer of hope appeared in her eyes. "Thank you," she said softly.

"You're welcome. And don't worry, these are just temporary solutions. I know you don't want to live at home, and we'll do everything we can to help you get back on track." A thought occurred to me. "Did you ever hear back from Concordia?" Concordia was the one Canadian university that Avery had applied to.

She shook her head. "No, nothing."

"Nothing? Not even a rejection letter?"

"Uh-uh."

"Well, you should call them tomorrow and check with their admissions office, just in case. What do you think the chances are that you got in?"

She tipped her head, embarrassed. "Not so good."

Yeah, that's what I thought. In addition to tanking her application, she'd submitted it hours past the deadline. I wasn't even sure they'd reviewed it. But I was trying to lift her up, not bring her down. "Call them anyway," I suggested. "Just to see."

I paid the check and we walked home, talking again of casual things. Avery seemed like a weight had been lifted from her, and as we arrived at the house she said, "Thanks again for breakfast, Marie. And for . . . everything."

Around nine o'clock that night, after James had dropped the girls in Vacaville and returned home, he got a jubilant text from Avery.

I GOT INTO CONCORDIA!!!!!!!!!!!!!!!!

"Oh!" I gasped. "She got in? That's wonderful!" James and I slapped each other high fives and danced around the kitchen. "She got into Concordia! She got into Concordia!"

His phone buzzed again.

They sent me an acceptance letter 6 weeks ago, but I didn't see it 'cause I never checked my email!

"Huh," James said. He paused in his dancing and looked at me. "Are we sure she's ready for college?"

55

PAYBACK'S A BITCH

When Avery asked if she could spend the summer with us, James cried. It was as if a Great Wrong had finally been righted.

"I can't believe it," he said to me.

"I can't believe Jessica's allowing it," I replied. Avery was still a minor and beholden to the court order. But her relationship with her mom had hit rocky ground. According to Annabelle, they were fighting all the time.

Fighting all the time. It was music to my ears.

I knew I was being petty. And in my heart, I wanted the girls to have good relationships with both their parents. I truly did.

But first, I wanted them to rebel against Jessica—and raise holy hell in her house.

Payback's a bitch.

Before we knew it, Avery had lined up a summer job in Oakland and transported most of her belongings to our house. The girl was motivated when she put her mind to it.

She didn't want to be in Vacaville for one moment longer than necessary. And suddenly, we were facing her high school graduation.

Shannon and Daniel wanted to come, but Avery was only allowed four tickets. I didn't understand this ticket business—back in my day, graduation was held on the athletic field and there was room for everybody. Four tickets weren't even enough for both sets of parents and Annabelle. I worried that we would somehow be left out, but Annabelle solved the problem by offering to work at the graduation. So James and I drove to Vacaville to watch his baby girl cross that stage.

There were nearly six hundred kids in Avery's graduating class. I understood the reason for the tickets when I saw the overflowing bleacher seats and the crowds spilling onto the lawn. A chain link fence separated the graduates from their families, giving the atmosphere something of a prison vibe.

James skimmed the event program. "Geez, this thing is going to be hours long."

"I told you we should've brought the Travel Scrabble." I glanced around. "I'd better find a restroom before this thing kicks off."

I wound my way through the sea of bodies and waited in line for the ladies' room. When I finally gained entry I almost wished I'd skipped it; I'd seen cleaner restrooms on day three of a Phish show. Flapping my wet hands to air-dry them, I stepped back out into the sun—where the first person I laid eyes on was Jessica.

She didn't look particularly well. Not ill precisely, but drawn. Tired. She was neatly dressed as always in a pressed white blouse and black slacks, with a single strand of pearls around her neck. But she had shadows beneath her eyes, and for the first time in our history, when her gaze met mine, her glance skittered away.

Perhaps it was wishful thinking on my part, but she looked like a woman whose kid was giving her hell. And knowing Avery's temper, I suspected that she was getting all nine circles of Dante's inferno.

I drew myself up to my full five-foot-ten and gave her a cool, appraising glance. "Hello Jessica." I waited for her trademark plastic smile.

But something had changed between us. Jessica didn't smile, didn't try to engage me in phony small talk. She didn't even meet my eye, and that's when I knew: the balance of power had shifted.

Somehow, despite years of machinations, it had all gone wrong in the end. Her kid was gay, Canada-bound, and choosing to spend the summer with her dad.

And her stepmom.

The smile that spread across my face took its sweet time. I let it grow and grow, until it filled the space between us, and Jessica couldn't help but sense it; her eyes were pulled to mine and I held her there, locked in my gaze. The seconds stretched on forever.

Then I winked, breaking the spell. Jessica flinched. She ducked her head and hurried away.

And I sauntered back to my seat.

* * *

Free from the constraints of her mother's house, and with a summer job and college on the horizon, Avery was in the flush of new independence. She was abundantly cheery and acutely aware of her narrow escape from an unhappy future. Suddenly, college in Montreal was the answer to her prayers—and James and I were the ones who'd made it happen.

Jessica ignored all our attempts to talk about financing. Max was the one who sent Avery a letter detailing their household's contribution. "Congratulations Avery," it began. "Your mom and I are so proud of you. We know your dad's got college covered, so here's what we're able to do . . ."

James was pissed. "'We know your dad's got college covered'? Like hell I do!" We were pursuing every grant and loan we could find.

I skimmed the letter. "They're going to buy Avery a smart phone—but not a data plan—and give her a small weekly stipend." I did the math in my head. "So that's about two grand against the twenty-six thousand she owes for her first year." *How very generous of them.*

James shook his head. "Not even that. I'm still paying full child support, even though Avery is living with us this summer." I made a face. There was no way to address that without going back to court. "That's three and a half months of payments that she gets for free. So she's contributing a grand total of about two hundred and fifty dollars."

Avery bit her lip. We were—perhaps unwisely—having this conversation in front of the kids, but we wanted them to know what was really going on. Annabelle was trying hard to ignore us, focusing on the TV. I nudged her. "Are you paying attention? 'Cause we're going to go through all this again in another two years." She didn't reply.

But the future beckoned too brightly for Avery to worry long about a little thing like money. She was irrepressibly happy, and when the Pride parade rolled around in June, it was like rainbows burst forth from her soul.

For the first time ever, she wanted to march in the parade. Raelin did, too, and brought along a bunch of friends from school, so we had a bevy of teenagers joining our Mercy contingent. The kids were beyond excited, decking themselves out in rainbow gear, sparkles and beads. The only one who didn't want to participate was Annabelle.

"I don't like parades," she said. That was all she said, but I suspected there was a little more to it.

James was understanding. "Look, I know this isn't really your thing, but it's your sister's first Pride. It's kind of a big deal. Won't you come and support her?"

"No." So we let her stay home alone.

Marching down Market Street, her true self finally on display, Avery was as joyful as I'd ever seen her. She wore a bisexual pride flag tied around her neck like a cape, and it streamed out behind her in pink, purple, and blue stripes. She also wore a teeny little half shirt, which raised James' eyebrows nearly off his forehead, but he opted not to say anything. I wondered once again what Avery might get up to when she reached freedom.

But her joy that day was contagious, and my heart was full, watching her. We followed the kids down the street, covertly snapping photos as they danced to the music, waved to the crowds, and sang to the sky.

* * *

Annabelle was cranky.

She was shuttling back and forth between houses by herself and bore the full weight of her mother's attention. Avery hadn't been back to Vacaville since her graduation.

It was the first time the girls had ever lived apart, and though they claimed it was no big deal, the shift in Annabelle's attitude suggested otherwise. I thought she must feel a little betrayed. Avery showed no signs of missing her mother and no desire to visit. She was cavalier whenever Annabelle headed back to Vacaville.

"See ya!" she'd say, the picture of indifference.

Annabelle turned her frustrations on James and me. "You shouldn't abandon your family," she informed us angrily.

All we could do was shrug. "You're talking to the wrong people, kiddo." I could certainly understand her feelings, but we weren't going to force Avery to return to her mom's. That was her decision to make.

Plus, we loved having Avery around. It was so much fun watching her gain her independence, going back and forth to work on BART, hearing about her job and the classes she was considering for her first semester. I'd never been so involved in Avery's life, and James hadn't known her so well in years. We were reveling in it.

And she cooked for us! And baked! My pants were tight as a result of all the brownies and cookies that Avery brought forth. She loved to play with recipes, and I got used to finding her in the kitchen when I came home from work. James and I would have a glass of wine and chat with her as she chopped and diced.

The only area in which Avery had not matured was housekeeping. She still left messes everywhere she went, and the kitchen in particular was a disaster zone.

"It's like she has a cleaning disability," James marveled, daubing his finger in a sticky puddle of something. "Do you think they'll teach her how to wipe down the countertops in college?"

The shambles of our kitchen was quietly killing me, but Avery and I were getting along so beautifully that it didn't seem worth it to fuss. I just wanted to enjoy the time we had left with her. I took James' hand and pulled him from the kitchen.

"It's okay, we just won't go in there anymore. And once she's gone, we'll burn down the house and start over."

* * *

Shannon and Daniel came down late in the summer to celebrate Avery's graduation. This time they stayed in a hotel.

"You do realize that I see more of these people than I do my own family, right?" I said to James. He just shrugged.

We met them in the city on a Saturday evening and they took us out to dinner. Over dessert, they presented Avery with a pair of diamond earrings—and an even bigger gift.

"We want to pay for your college tuition," Shannon said.

YES! YES! YES!!!

"We'll take it one year at a time," she continued, "and see how things go. But for your freshman year, we have it covered."

A wave of relief washed over me. Tuition was only about a third of the total cost—room and board were the real killers. But it would help tremendously, and with student loans and a first year grant, we could pull it off.

"Thank you," James said sincerely, while Avery goggled at her grandparents in disbelief. She'd thought they would only pay if she went to UBC.

"And we want to do the same for you," Shannon said to Annabelle. "When the time comes." But Annabelle's face was stony.

The girls spent the night at the hotel with their grandparents and we rejoined them the next afternoon. "The kids have been wonderful tour guides," Daniel said. "They took us around Fisherman's Wharf and South Beach—"

"North Beach," Avery supplied.

"—and we've just worn ourselves out walking."

"Well, do you want to join me for a little drive?" James asked. "I've got to bring the girls back to their mother's." Avery had finally consented to spend a few days in Vacaville—although I thought she was mainly going back to retrieve her passport and the new phone she'd been promised.

There was a brief moment of silence, which Daniel smoothed over. "Sure. You know I love to drive." Daniel was a long-haul trucker.

For a moment I thought Shannon might refuse and stay behind with me. *Go with them, go with them,* I willed silently. I wanted to catch a movie.

But she rallied. "I'll come, too, so I can get a little more time with you girls."

I went to make my goodbyes, but then she said, "And Marie, when we get back, Daniel and I would like to have dinner with you and James."

"Oh, great," I said. *Great.*

At a little restaurant a few hours later, the four of us sat around a table, pretending it wasn't weird. Flight schedules had precluded them from going home until the next day, and there'd been no point asking Jessica to shift Annabelle's schedule. I was curious if her parents had tried to see her.

"*Pfft*. No." Shannon waved the idea away. "We just stayed in the car."

"We didn't even tell her we were coming down this time," Daniel said. I knew that he'd tried harder to stay in touch with his daughter, but Jessica's reaction to Shannon's illness had hurt him deeply. For the first time he seemed . . . *finished* with her.

Then Shannon dropped the bomb. "We've cut Jessica out of our will," she said. "We want to spend that money on the girls instead. And we want to do it now, while it's helpful, instead of waiting until after we die."

"Oh my goodness," I murmured. James looked surprised.

"We know Jessica's caused a lot of hardship for you," Daniel told him. "And she's cost you a lot of money." I suspected they didn't know the half of it, but I could see James was touched. "You've been so good about keeping the girls in our lives and we want to help out as we can." He patted James' hand, laying on the table. "You've done a good job, son."

I was glad that James didn't flinch at being called "son", but instead thanked Daniel warmly.

"Don't tell the girls," Shannon requested. "We don't want to cause any conflict between them and their mother."

"Of course not," James said. Not that the girls would be brave enough to drop *that* bombshell on Jessica.

"Did they give her the photo album, do you know?" Shannon looked hopeful. My mind flashed back to our return from Vancouver. I recalled Avery spiriting the album into her bedroom.

"Don't tell Mom about this, okay?" she'd said to Annabelle. "I don't want her to throw it away."

I gave a little shake of my head and Shannon's face fell slightly. "I think the kids really wanted to keep it," I said. It was an awkward explanation, but I suppose it was true.

"Ah. It's just as well," Shannon cast around for a change of subject. "Annabelle seemed a little quiet this trip. Is she doing okay?"

Annabelle had been a little quiet all summer. She was going into self-protection mode, I thought, putting some distance between herself and her sister.

"Well, Annie doesn't like it when her worlds overlap," James said. She's never really been comfortable with the fact that I'm the one who keeps in touch with you guys. And since Avery's been living with us this summer, I think she feels some increased loyalty to her mother."

"Plus, she's about to be left behind," I said. "Her big sister's going off to college, and it's going to be just her, navigating between these two households that can't get along. I'm sure it's not easy."

I didn't add that Annabelle had been showing some worrying signs of regression. The other week I'd caught her slipping out of Mercy's Sunday service and hiding up on the fourth floor. When I asked what she was doing, she shrugged and said, "I don't want to listen to the sermon. This isn't a real church." I'd made her come back inside, but she refused to sit with Avery and Raelin in the front row, instead going up the balcony and sitting alone. That same afternoon Jo told me, ruefully, that there had been complaints about Annabelle from the other Mercy Kids teachers. If she didn't mend her attitude, she wouldn't be welcome back next year.

I didn't think Annabelle wanted to go back. "How many times do I have to tell you that I hate it here?" she'd said. Her vehemence shook me. I thought we'd left all that behind.

"Annabelle's had more of Jessica's influence," James was saying. "She was two years younger when the girls moved in with their mum, and she'll have another two years there on her own. Things might get a little bumpy when Avery leaves."

"She'll find her way," Shannon soothed. "She's a good kid. And she knows that you love her. That's all it takes."

That was a patently false statement from the woman whose own daughter had cut her dead, but it was kindly meant. And I didn't think that Annabelle would turn out like Jessica. She had too much of her dad in her—and hopefully, I thought, a little bit of me.

I looked around the table at Shannon, Daniel, and James, and thought about the complex web that connected us. In a normal world I never should have met these people. If Jessica had been kind, or even reasonable, she would have stayed in touch with her family and James would have dropped off the Olins' radar years ago.

Then again, if Jessica had been kind, or even reasonable, James wouldn't be the man he was today. He'd learned patience from Jessica, I realized. He'd chosen to be kind in the face of her unkindness, to soften against her hard edges, and to love his kids no matter what they put him through. In fact, it was those very things that I loved most about him.

With a little shock, I realized that we'd all been shaped by Jessica—for the good. Each of us had been forced to learn patience, tolerance, compassion—virtues forged in the heat of adversity. We'd had to work harder at love, to mend the holes in our hearts and keep trying, always trying. The choices we'd made in response to her behavior had turned us into better people than we'd been. The truth was, Jessica had forced us to grow.

It was a startling revelation, but more bitter than sweet. Underneath it all remained the big, gaping question: *why?* Why did it have to be this way?

"Do you ever wonder if Jessica is undiagnosed with something?" I ventured to say. The three of them looked at me. "I mean, it would be so much easier to understand her behavior if there was an underlying reason for it." *Like schizophrenia or narcissistic personality disorder,* I thought, but I didn't say that aloud. Instead I suggested, "Maybe she's bipolar?"

"Oh no," Shannon said, surprised. "She's just a bitch."

56

Just Don't Leave

Avery turned the key in the door of her new college dorm room.

"Wow. It's so big," I said, walking in behind her. The apartment-style quad had a living room, kitchenette, bathroom, and two bedrooms.

"It's so . . . empty." We were clearly the first to arrive, and Avery looked a tad panicky. "Dad, I don't have any stuff! I don't have a broom, or pots and pans, or . . . toilet paper!"

"Relax," he said. "We'll take you shopping after you unpack."

"Let's go now," Avery said. "I can unpack later."

The three of us had flown into Montreal the day before. School had already started for Annabelle, and though we'd offered to take her, too, she didn't want to come. She was a little rude about it, making Avery feel as though she couldn't be bothered, but I thought it was an act. I knew she was going to miss her sister terribly.

The girls spent the day together before we left, just the two of them. They took BART into the city and visited their favorite spots: the wave organ near Crissy Field and the ice cream shop where James used to take them as children. Avery took pictures on her new phone and showed them to us afterward. There were a dozen sweet selfies of the girls with their arms around each other, Avery with her new short haircut, and Annabelle standing half a head taller than her big sister. It had been a bit of a rocky summer, but in those photos they looked like best friends again. Like two girls who'd faced the world together.

Avery's goodbye with her mother had been cordial but brief. Jessica and Max took her out to dinner a few nights before we left. I thought they'd be out late, but she was home by eight-thirty. She stood by the car for a few minutes, joking with Max, and then he got out and hugged her. Through the car window Jessica looked pale and out of place, like the third wheel on somebody else's date.

There'd been no question of Jessica taking Avery to college. She hadn't offered and Avery hadn't asked.

"I'd much rather it be you guys," she told us, and in private, we couldn't help but gloat. We weren't always the nice guys.

Four stores and several hundred dollars later, we returned to Avery's dorm room, laden with the essentials. In the kitchen was a young woman with shoulder length blond hair unpacking boxes.

"Hi, I'm Gwen," she said, giving a little wave.

"I'm Avery." They smiled at each other nervously. "Oh, and this is my dad and stepmom."

"Hello," we chorused.

"My dad just left." Gwen nodded at the door. "He wanted to get back on the road. We drove up today from Toronto," she explained. "Where are you from?"

"San Francisco. Well, Vacaville. Oakland." Avery shook her head, trying to get her story straight. "California."

"Cool. I think Candace is American, too. She hasn't arrived yet, but we've been emailing." I looked at the name tags on the bedroom doors and saw that Gwen would be rooming with Candace and Avery would share with Megan. A peek into Avery's room showed that Megan had come and gone, leaving a pile of boxes and an open suitcase. Off shopping, I surmised.

"I brought tons of kitchen stuff," Gwen said. The countertop was overflowing. "My dad's moving in with his girlfriend, and he gave me all his pots and pans and things."

I saw Avery's eyes light up, either at the thought of a kindred spirit or the sight of a mini blender. "Cool! I love to cook, but I couldn't bring much here on the airplane. Oh, you've got cookie sheets?"

"I've got everything," said Gwen, unearthing a casserole dish. "I don't cook much, but I love to bake."

"Me too!"

"That's great," I said, smiling at the two of them. "You guys will be the most popular people on the floor."

Gwen shot me a look that clearly said, *Why are you still here?*

"Um, you guys can take off now," Avery nudged.

"I was just going to charge my phone for . . . Oh." I trailed off when I saw her face. "Okay. I guess we'll leave you to it."

594

"Maybe we can grab lunch tomorrow," James suggested as she herded us to the door.

"Uh, maybe. I'll text you."

"Okay, we'll see you—"

"See ya!" She gave a cheery wave and shut the door in our faces.

This wasn't as cold as it sounds. We were staying in Montreal for the week. Javier owned a condo that was between renters and he graciously let us stay there for free, so we turned it into a little vacation. The city was as wonderful as ever. We rented bikes and explored all the offbeat neighborhoods we hadn't had time for on previous visits.

"I thought Avery would want to hang out with us a little more," James admitted. She kept turning us down for dinner, texting things like, "Can't tonight, Frosh event." Or, "Sorry—wine and cheese party!"

"She's settling in. It's a good thing." I patted his arm in reassurance. "Don't worry, we'll see her again."

In fact, we saw her twenty minutes later near the campus bookstore, where I'd been searching in vain for a *Concordia Stepmom* t-shirt. "This is bullshit," I complained. "They've got *Concordia Mom, Concordia Dad,* and *Concordia Grandparent.* I want to talk to the manager."

"Hey look, it's Avery!" James' face lit up as he waved at his daughter across the street. She was walking with Gwen and another girl whom I guessed to be either Candace or Megan.

"Oh, hey guys." Avery didn't seem thrilled to see us. "We're just out exploring. This is Candace and you remember Gwen." Candace waved, but Gwen shot us another look: *You again.* "I'll catch up with you later, okay?"

As they walked away I heard Gwen mutter, "They just don't leave, do they?"

* * *

On our last night in the city we met up with Avery for dinner. We chose a restaurant in the old part of town, in a lively plaza with cobblestone streets. Avery was aglow. She radiated happiness and didn't try to hide it.

"I love it here," she said passionately. "I love my dorm; I love my roommates. I know it sounds crazy after just one week, but I already feel closer to them than I ever did to my friends in Vacaville. They're like . . . Penelope."

Avery's friendship with Penelope had persevered. If the two weren't as close as they'd once been, they still had a bond that wouldn't break. Like Avery, Penelope had grown out of her bratty tween years and into a lovely young woman. She was at college now in Massachusetts, just a few hours away, and the girls were talking about meeting up at Thanksgiving.

"That's wonderful, Ave," I said, smiling.

"I knew I'd love college, but I had no idea how *much* I'd love it here," she went on. "I feel like a whole new person."

Indeed, she *seemed* like a whole new person. Her short-cropped hair made her look dramatically different, a petite, wide-eyed pixie. She was an expert with the makeup now, sporting smokey eyes and a rosy gloss that played up her bee-stung lips. In her faux leather thrift store jacket, she seemed ready to take on the city. Or maybe the world.

"Thank you, Dad," she said suddenly. "Thank you for helping me get here." She gave him an impulsive hug, and when she let go, his eyes were wet.

"Oh, and I know you guys won't believe this, but I'm the cleanest one in my dorm. I have to nag the others to do

their dishes, and then I think: *Oh God, I sound like Marie!*"
She gave me an impish grin.

After dinner we roamed for a while, taking in the street art. We paused to watch a silent video being projected on an alley wall.

"'*Cité Mémoire,*'" James read from a sign, mangling the French. "'One of the largest outdoor video installations in the world, illustrating scenes from Montreal's history.'" As he spoke, the spectre of a robed woman swept down the side of a building and onto the cobblestones in front of us.

"Whoa," I said, taking a step back. I'd never seen anything quite like that before.

"This city is amazing," breathed Avery.

We finished the night with a light show at Notre-Dame Basilica. It was much more impressive than I'd expected: an indoor fireworks spectacle with a booming orchestral score. I watched Avery as she followed the chase of lights up and down the domed cathedral walls. She looked so . . . *happy.* As the colors burst around her, it seemed like her life was bursting into color, too.

A fierce bolt of love surged through me, squeezing my heart. In that moment, I felt more like a parent than I ever had before.

We dropped Avery back at her dorm, where James said goodbye with a swift hug. I could tell he was trying to control his emotions, but I had no such restraint—I hugged and kissed her half a dozen times, a gift I'd never been permitted in the past.

"I love you," I told her. "I'm so proud of you."

"I love you guys, too," Avery said. "Uh, here." She dug into her purse and came up with two little envelopes, one of which she slipped to James, the other to me. "So we don't have to do the whole mushy goodbye." Plainly, I'd mushed too much already.

"Thanks," said James, his voice gruff. "Love you, Ave." He seemed to want to go before he lost his composure. He didn't like to cry in front of his kids.

"Oh—the suitcase! I almost forgot! I'll be right back." Avery made a lunge for the door. She'd borrowed Annabelle's suitcase to help move her things, and her sister would be wanting it back. We tried to follow her into the dorm, but Avery stopped us.

"I'll get it," she said. "It's kind of . . . not cool to invite your parents into the dorm after move-in day."

James and I exchanged a glance. *Well, pardon us.*

She was back a minute later, suitcase in tow. I hugged her again, unable to help myself. Then I gave her a moment with her dad.

James broke on the second goodbye. He pulled his daughter into a ferocious hug that lifted her off her feet and kissed the top of her head. "I love you Avery-girl," he said, tears dropping onto her hair.

"I love you so much, Dad," she replied, feet dangling off the ground.

Later that night, we lay on Javier's futon, staring out the window at the lane beyond. A mural of a slender woman in a backless dress decorated the brick wall. Garbage bags were piled at her feet. Even the trash-strewn alleyways of this city were beautiful.

"Do you think Avery's okay?" James asked, just as he did every night about that time.

"I think Avery's just fine." I kissed his ear. "And you will be, too."

He lay quietly against me, listening to the sounds from outside. People were walking home from the bars, talking in loud voices. A car horn honked. Suddenly, James stiffened.

"My letter!" He jumped up and rummaged in the pocket of his pants. "I almost forgot about it."

"Oh, me too!" I padded down the hall to the kitchen and pulled my letter out of my purse. Loosening the envelope, I spied Avery's distinctive, loopy handwriting. I carried it back to the bedroom where James was hunched over, reading.

My letter said:

> *Dear Marie,*
>
> *I know it seems strange to write this, not say it, but I want to get through it without getting mushy.*
>
> *Ever since we first met you, you've been kind and caring and supportive and accepting beyond belief. You've made such a wonderful impact on our lives and we're forever grateful for that. I know that we (Annabelle and I) don't express that enough. You're truly one of the most amazing people I've ever met, and one of the few people I can say will forever hold a very special place in my heart.*
>
> *Anyways, I'm not great at writing emotional letters, but I hope this was able to convey just how much I love you.*
>
> *I love you so, so, so much. And I'm going to miss you.*
>
> *Avery*

There was a lump in my throat. I sank against the pillows and James curled up beside me. We lay in silence.

After a while he said, "Was your letter nice?"

"Yes." I stroked his hair. "Was yours?"

"Yes." His voice was quiet. "It was the nicest."

And then I held him while he cried. But this time they were good tears—the kind you shed at the end of a long, hard journey, when you've made it safely home.

I wrapped my body around his, holding him tightly. For several minutes we just lay there, breathing quietly in tandem.

When he spoke, his voice was so soft I almost didn't hear it.

"Let's make a baby." He turned toward me, his heart laid bare between us. With exquisite tenderness, I kissed my husband's forehead, his swollen eyes, his cheeks, his lips. And as I'd promised to do, I loved him with extreme care.

And then I loved him with extreme care three more times.

ACKNOWLEDGEMENTS

I want to thank Amanda McKee, Emily Newhouse, Arin Hailey Reese, Kerry Baker, Timothy Lowe, and Angeli Fitch, whose edits and encouragement made this a better story. And Gina Zupo Moats, whose vibrant cover art made this story suddenly seem like a *book!*

Thank you to my beautiful stepdaughters. You cracked my heart open so more love could get in.

And thanks most of all to my very private husband, who almost certainly would have preferred that I write about anything else, but who supported me every step of the way. You are the best partner I could have hoped for.

Made in the USA
Middletown, DE
28 June 2021